W9-CBX-321

WHISKEY

STILL
WHISKY
STILL
No. 6

MICHAEL JACKSON

WHISKEY

WITH CONTRIBUTIONS FROM
DAVE BROOM • JEFFERSON CHASE • DALE DEGROFF
JÜRGEN DEIBEL • RICHARD JONES • MARTINE NOUET • STUART RAMSAY
WILLIE SIMPSON • IAN WISNIEWSKI

LONDON • NEW YORK • MUNICH
MELBOURNE • DELHI

Senior Editor Simon Tuite
Senior Art Editor Joanne Doran
Design Jo Grey, Cath Mackenzie, Sue Metcalfe-Megginson, Rachael Smith
Editorial Claire Folkard, Frank Ritter
DTP Designer Louise Waller
Production Controller Mandy Inness
Managing Editor Deirdre Headon
Managing Art Editor Marianne Markham

Photography Ian O'Leary and Steve Gorton
Maps and Illustrations Martin Sanders, Patrick Mulrey, and Simon Roulstone
Picture Research Sarah Hopper
Additional Research Owen D. L. Barstow, David Croll

First American Edition, 2005
Published in the United States by
DK Publishing, Inc., 375 Hudson Street,
New York, New York 10014

10 10 9 8 7 6 5

Penguin Group (USA), Inc., 375 Hudson Street, New York, New York 10014.
Penguin Group (Canada), 10 Alcorn Avenue, Toronto, Ontario, M4V 3B2 (a division of Pearson Penguin Canada, Inc.).
Penguin Books Ltd, 80 Strand, London WC2R 0RL, England.
Penguin Ireland, 25 St Stephen's Green, Dublin 2, Ireland (a division of Penguin Books Ltd).
Penguin Group (Australia), 250 Camberwell Road, Camberwell, Victoria 3124, Australia (a division of Pearson Australia Group Pty Ltd).
Penguin Books India Pvt Ltd, 11 Community Centre, Panchsheel Park, New Delhi – 110 017, India.
Penguin Group (NZ), Cnr Airborne and Rosedale Roads, Albany, Auckland, New Zealand (a division of Pearson New Zealand Ltd).
Penguin Books (South Africa) (Pty) Ltd, 24 Sturdee Avenue, Rosebank, Johannesburg 2196, South Africa.

A Cataloging-in-Publication record for this book is available from the Library of Congress.

ISBN 978-0-7894-9710-9

Color reproduced by Colourscan, Singapore
Printed and bound in China by Toppan

Discover more at
www.dk.com

CONTENTS

INTRODUCTION

No spirits have stimulated such curiosity or inspired such connoisseurship in recent years as have the whiskey family. This explosion of interest began as a distant revelation when Scottish whiskey rediscovered its origins in the glens. Single malts were only the beginning. New legends began to appear on the labels: Cask Strength, Single Barrel, Wood Finish, and Vintage.

Nor was Scotland the only source of such delights. Ireland, accustomed to the appreciation of its pubs, is experiencing a new interest in its whiskeys, especially the Pure Pot Still type. The days of unswerving loyalty to a favorite whiskey, or even to the distillates of a particular country, are fading fast. Distilleries that once bottled two or three expressions of their whiskey now offer 20 or 30. Macallan, at one stage, had more than 100 expressions. Scotland once had two or three specialist whiskey shops, and England not many more. Now, there are six or seven at London's airports alone.

AROMAS AND FLAVORS

The energy and creativity of today's best whiskey-makers and marketeers, and their eloquence in describing the aromas and flavors they find in their creations, would surprise, and perhaps shock, whiskey's hard-headed pioneers.

The word "whiskey" (spelled "whisky" in some countries) is of Celtic origin, thus enfranchising the Welsh to make their own contribution; in 2004, the first Welsh

YAMAZAKI: A JAPANESE CLASSIC

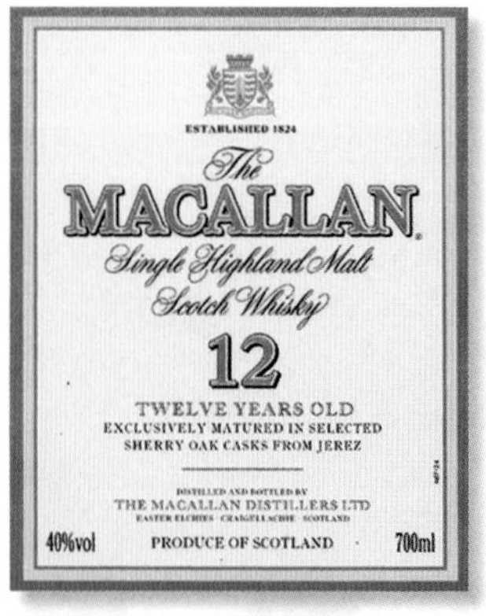

MACALLAN: SPANISH OAK CONTRIBUTES TO THE FLAVOR

whiskey emerged from the Black Mountains. The Bretons of France and the New Scots of Cape Breton, Canada, are also creating fresh dominions for whiskey.

In the United States, a nation given to the principle that big is beautiful, small-batch whiskeys have inspired a new hauteur in bourbon.

In Japan, decades of study and practice have presented the most captious critic with world-class single malts. Hakushu emerges as succulent as sushi; Yoichi as mouthwatering as wasabi; Karuizawa as tempting as tempura. Blends such as Hibiki are for the first time emphasizing Japanese oak.

Despite their family relationship, the various styles of whiskey indigenous to the British Isles and North America are each distinct in character, drawing on different materials and techniques. An American whiskey is not a failed attempt to make a Scotch, or vice versa. In recent years, this has been better understood.

GASTRONOMIC RECOGNITION

The new respect accorded to whiskey is evident in the birth of microdistilleries (not only in the Americas but also in Continental Europe), the popularity of tutored tastings, the blossoming of festivals—

THE INFLUENCE OF SHERRY
Michael Jackson tasting sherry at the El Agostado vineyard near Jerez, Spain.

such as Whisky Live—from London to Tokyo, and the arrival on the newsstands of publications such as *Malt Advocate* and *Whisky Magazine*.

The world's gastronomic capitals appreciated whiskey even when less sophisticated cities (sometimes in the regions of production) thought the drink old-fashioned.

The outstanding example is San Francisco, which has for decades consumed more whiskey per head than any other city in the United States, and takes the credit for popularizing Irish coffee back in the 1950s.

JAMESON: NOT JUST PUBS—WHISKEYS, TOO

THE NEW AMBASSADORS

In the 1990s, Fritz Maytag, already a wine-grower and beer-brewer, established the first US whiskey microdistillery, in San Francisco. He also became a rye revivalist, reaching out to a style from the opposite coast. In the same decade, Rhiannon Walsh established a whiskey festival in San Francisco.

WILD TURKEY: BIG AND BEAUTIFUL

There are also annual celebrations in the regions of production: in Bardstown, Kentucky, and in Scotland at the Islay and Speyside festivals. These include distillery tours, whiskey dinners, concerts, and ceilidhs.

To savor a whiskey, then to hear how it was created, is instructive and enjoyable. To talk afterward with the distiller or blender is even better. To drink socially with the distillery workers in their local pubs is a pleasure that lingers like the finish of a robust bourbon or a fine malt.

KITTLING RIDGE: NEW FROM CANADA

PEOPLE OF PASSION

Dusk can be more than a good time for a drink. It can be perfect: like the place, the guest, the host, and the drink itself. The woman in my life had an important birthday. She had chosen the Rainbow Room, behind which the sky was being painted with strips of gold as each floor of each office switched on its lights. Dale DeGroff was making Manhattans. "Fitzgerald?" he inquired. Surely not a bourbon in a Manhattan? No, he was about to load a CD: Ella's serenade to New York. "You once wrote that a particular whiskey was as sweet and enveloping as a solo by Ella Fitzgerald," he reminded me. Dale is profoundly well-versed in the literature of drink. His essay on whiskey cocktails is a valuable contribution to the genre. If you prefer your whiskey notes scored to rock themes, Dave Broom is your man. He is my tasting partner at *Whisky Magazine*. Our enthusiasm for Japanese whiskey has led us to have frequent drams under the baleful gaze of a stag called Mr. Yoshida at our favorite bar in Kyoto. Dave's robust writing reveals his passion for his native Scotland. Another Scot, Stuart Ramsay, remains untamed despite his living in Oregon. When he was expected to be amazed by a restaurant where you could choose your own lobster, Stuart explained that Scotland had something similar: look outside and

CONTRIBUTORS
A new generation of writers has been inspired by whiskey in the past decade. Each has his or her own perspective. Their own particular passion, too...

DAVE BROOM
Born in Glasgow, Dave is a contributing editor to Whisky Magazine, *a regular columnist on many international titles, has written ten books, and won three Glenfiddich Awards for his writing. He is a respected taster, and in demand as a teacher and lecturer.*

JEFFERSON CHASE
Jefferson Chase is a former professor of German literature and is currently a writer, journalist, and translator living in Berlin. (He has translated Thomas Mann's Death in Venice.*) His work has been published in some leading newspapers in Germany and the United States.*

JÜRGEN DEIBEL
Now an international consultant on distilled drinks, Jürgen trained as a chemist. Based in Hanover, Germany, he runs his own tasting and training seminars on distilled spirits. He writes on vodka for Mixology *magazine, and on other spirits for a number of magazines.*

DALE DEGROFF
America's foremost mixologist, Dale developed his talent tending bar for over 20 years at great establishments, most notably New York's famous Rainbow Room. He writes columns for several magazines in the US and the UK, and has recently published The Craft of the Cocktail.

select your own sheep. Those that graze on the shores of Islay are accustomed to Martine Nouet's early morning walks. At Ardbeg, she persuades me that the seaweed smells of saffron. I have ideas for my own tasting glass, and Jürgen Deibel helps me to realize them. He is a scientist who writes. Ian Wisniewski is a writer with a nose for the science (and art) of whiskey-making. We meet at a Polish restaurant in London, and the borscht they serve is a reminder of the first time aromas and flavors ever shocked me—when, as a small boy, I tasted this hot, purple, sweet-and-sour soup made by my Lithuanian grandmother, in Leeds, Yorkshire.

When in my 40s I wrote my *World Guide to Whisky* (published in 1987), the popular view was that whiskey was a doomed drink. I refused to accept this, being as obstinate as only a Yorkshireman can be. We, for example, insist that a rugby team fields only 13 men. Richard Jones, a Lancashireman living in Yorkshire, agrees. So does Willie Simpson, a New Zealander living in Australia. With such unyielding writers, the literature of whiskey is in safe hands. Writers are notoriously fond of drink, especially whiskey. Does it help, or hinder? Jeff Chase's fine essay serves as my answer.

Michael Jackson

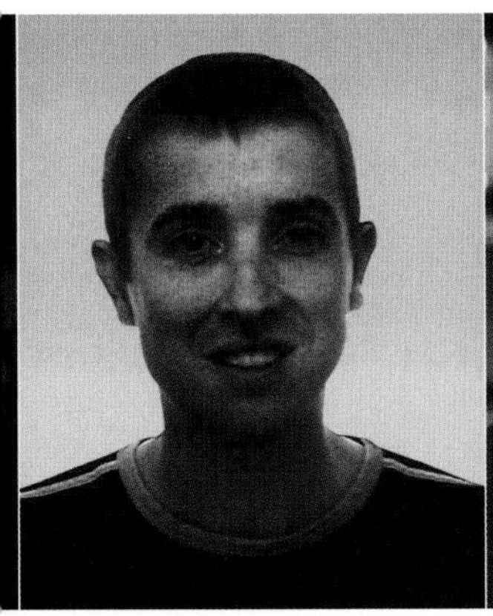

RICHARD JONES
Richard first developed a passion for whiskey while selling it from behind the counter at a chain liquor store. He now writes regularly for a range of wine and spirit publications, as well as producing tasting notes, back labels, and text for whiskey-related websites.

MARTINE NOUET
Martine is the only journalist in France who writes exclusively about food and spirits. She is a regular contributor to Whisky Magazine *and the editorial consultant for the French edition. She has also written a book on malt whiskey,* Les Routes du Malt.

STUART RAMSAY
Stuart was born in the Highlands of Scotland. Writer, editor, and public speaker, he is a leading expert on spirits, cocktails, and craft beer. He is the current contributing editor for Santé *magazine. He writes for many other publications, including* Cigar Aficionado.

WILLIE SIMPSON
Born in New Zealand, Willie Simpson is a writer on beer and spirits who now lives in northwest Tasmania. He is a regular contributor to the Sydney Morning Herald, The Age, *and* The Bulletin *magazine. He is the author of* Amber & Black: Premium Beers in Australia.

IAN WISNIEWSKI
Ian Wisniewski is a freelance food, drink, and travel writer, broadcaster, and consultant, specializing in spirits. His ten books include Classic Malt Whisky *and* Classic Vodka. *He contributes to various drinks publications, including* Decanter *magazine.*

UNDERSTANDING WHISKEY

CHEWY BEER

This painted limestone is evidence of the early production of drinks from grain. The person on the right is drinking beer through a straw. Such straws are shown in clay tablets from the Sumerian civilization. The actual straws can be seen in the Museum of Anthropology and Archaeology at the University of Pennsylvania. Their function was to dip below the head of the beer, which would have been dense with grain and wild yeast and not especially appetizing.

THE FAMILY OF WHISKEYS

MICHAEL JACKSON

The word "whiskey" is of Celtic origin. It indicates the spirit drinks native to Scotland and Ireland, and their offspring elsewhere in the world. Whiskey is produced from various cereal grains, almost always including a proportion of malted barley. It is distilled in such a way as to retain some of the aromas and flavors of the grain, and it develops a further complexity during a period of maturation in oak.

Only if distillation and at least three years of maturation take place in Scotland may it be labeled as Scotch, Scots, or Scottish whiskey. Malt whiskey is made only from malted grain, in Scotland always barley, in a pot still. A single malt is a whiskey that comes from just one distillery. If the whiskey is bottled from a single cask, that will be indicated on the label. More often, a bottling will be made from a variety of distillation runs and cask types.

MALT WHISKEY IS MADE ONLY FROM MALTED GRAIN

Wheat, corn, or unmalted barley are column-distilled to make grain whiskey. This contributes volume and lightness of body and flavor to blended Scotch whiskey.

Pure pot-still is the most distinctive style of Irish whiskey. The use of a significant proportion of unmalted barley is the defining difference. Other features of Irish whiskeys include the use of unpeated malt; a preference for blending grains in the mash tun; and triple distillation.

WHISKEY OR WINE?
When Glenmorangie took some whiskey from the usual bourbon barrels and gave it a few months' extra maturation in port pipes, a new category of Scotch whiskey was born: the wood finish. Examples have ranged from claret to Sauternes. While purists ask whether this is whiskey or wine, enthusiasts have nothing but praise for these additional flavors.

In Canada, distillers predominantly blend finished whiskeys in the Scottish manner. While in Scotland malt whiskey provides the big flavors, in Canada rye whiskey (in much smaller proportions) fulfills that function. Additions such as fruit "wines" are allowed.

The grains, rather than the whiskeys, are blended in the production of the American classics. If the term "straight" is used, the defining grain comprises over 51 percent of the grist. The original whiskey of the United States was straight rye, produced in Maryland and Pennsylvania. Today's principal style is Kentucky bourbon, made from corn, with smaller proportions of rye or wheat and barley malt. The term "small batch bourbon" is not precisely defined. The pioneer of this category, Booker Noe, based his selections on a particular floor in the warehouse. Tennessee whiskey has much the same ingredients but is leached through sugar maple charcoal before it is matured. It is also labeled sour mash, referring to the use of lactic residue to ensure continuity. This process is not unique to Tennessee; all American classics are made in this way. They do not taste sour; their dominant characteristic is a vanilla sweetness imparted by the use of new oak in maturation.

THE BARLEY HARVEST
Whether barley is being cut by the Moray Firth in Scotland; in Cork, Ireland; in Alberta, Canada; or in North Dakota, harvesting is a time of evocative sights and smells.

HIGHLIGHT

THE BEAUTY OF BLENDS

The son of a blender, Richard Paterson was born into this rare art, which he has practiced all his working life, mainly for Whyte and Mackay. Among the personalities in the industry, he is perhaps the most extroverted and committed spokesman for the qualities and merits of blended Scotch whiskey.

HUNTING LODGE
Today's hunters take home venison carpaccio and malt whiskey. The Highlands were just as fashionable when Landseer painted this hideaway in the 1820s.

THE FAMILY OF DISTILLED DRINKS

MICHAEL JACKSON

The making of drinks by fermentation predates civilization, but it is far less clear when distillation followed. When did we learn how to do it? In nature, fermentation takes place spontaneously, thanks to wild yeasts in the atmosphere. Some birds and animals routinely eat rotting fruit and appear to enjoy becoming drunk. Foraging humans had the same experiences, and learned from nature how to make wine.

"VODKA" IS A DIMINUTIVE OF THE SLAVIC WORD FOR WATER

Grain-based drinks have a different history. Cereals in the form of wild grasses were too hard, dry, and spiny to eat, yet when soaked by flood waters they became crunchy and edible when dried by the sun. The grain had to be made soluble by soaking, just as grain has to be malted for beer and whiskey-making today. Sumerian pictograms show grain being used to produce a beer that was probably similar to traditional brews still made in Africa. The Sumerians are shown drinking beer through straws, as do habitués of African traditional beer shops. In their milky, turbid appearance, fruity esteriness, and lactic note, African traditional beers can resemble the contents of a fermenting vessel in a whiskey distillery.

POTEEN
The word derives not from the potato, Ireland's best-loved vegetable, but from the pot still. Poteen is usually made from grain and sugar.

German monks surviving on thick, heavy beer during Lent referred to it as "liquid bread," and that survives as a colloquialism today. "Bread" and "brewed" have the same etymological origins. In brewing and distilling, the addition of yeast is known by the odd term "pitching." This is related to *pizza* and *pita*, from the world of flat breads. A brewer or distiller trying to achieve a proper aeration of his wort would appreciate the pizza-maker's efforts in throwing and juggling his dough.

ORIGINS OF DISTILLATION

In hot sun, a departing tide can leave salt on the shore. Was that another of nature's prompts? Aristotle mentions Phoenician mariners distilling seawater to remove the salt. The word "distillation," like "alcohol," has Arabic roots. The Moors may have brought the technique across the Straits of Gibraltar, with distilled drinks beginning to emerge in Europe in the early Renaissance.

The use of distillation in alchemy and medieval medicine perhaps gave rise to the phrase *aqua vitae*, or "water of life," as a term for spirit drinks. "Vodka" is a diminutive of the Slavic word for water ("of life" being understood). *Aquavit* or *akvavit* provide a northern outpost of the term in Scandinavia. *Eau-de-vie* may be the most widely used name of this type in the French-speaking world.

WHY CALL THEM "SPIRITS"?

Distillation involves the heating of liquids to create steam, which can be wraithlike in appearance. In the German language, the suffix *-geist*, which shares its etymology with the English word "ghost," appears in the names of some spirit drinks. But another group of terms, including the Spanish *aguardiente* and English word "brandy," refer to the use of fire to vaporize the liquid. In Dutch, brandy was *brandewijn*, or "burnt wine."

Romantic though these names were, they told the customer nothing of the origin of each "spirit." Few specified what the raw material was: grapes in the brandies of Spain, Gascony, and Cognac; pears and apples in the calvados of Normandy; and soft fruits in the "white alcohols" of Alsace.

Where fruits gave way to grain, the Low Countries added flavorings, including juniper (in French, *genièvre*, giving rise to the Dutch *jenever* and, in England, "gin"). Northern Germany has its own variation on gin, as well as plain corn schnapps, while the Scandinavians use wintry herbs, such as dill and caraway, to flavor their *aquavit*.

TO FOLLOW FIDDICH
By the river Fiddich stands the castle of Balvenie, with the distillery that makes this aristocratic after-dinner dram.

SCOTTISH SPIRIT *Kentucky owes much of its whiskey-making to hardy early Scottish settlers and their pot stills.*

WORLD SPIRITS

Which are the most complex of Europe's spirits? Whiskey-lovers would argue for Scotch and Irish over brandies such as Cognac and Armagnac. Neighboring England makes no whiskey: its national spirit is gin, whether London or Plymouth.

VODKA
Most vodkas are made from rye or wheat. The occasional potato vodka upholds popular legend.

BRANDY
Loosely, any fruit—typically grapes. Specific varieties, soils, and methods for Cognac and Armagnac.

GIN
Distilled from grain but aromatized with juniper. Other gin "botanicals" include citrus peel, roots, and spices.

RUM
Sugar cane, molasses, or other residues of refinement. Pungent or fragrant. Caribbean, Latin lands, even Nepal.

ALLOWED IN BOSTON
Enjoyment in progress at a bar in Boston. This city inspired the TV series Cheers, *a parable of praise to social drinking. Yet it is also known for its history as a puritan settlement. "Banned in Boston" is a phrase that resounds in American sociology. The desire for instant gratification and the heritage of the Pilgrim Fathers can make for ambivalent attitudes toward alcohol.*

THE ENJOYMENT OF WHISKEY

MICHAEL JACKSON

Whiskey illustrates perfectly our coyness about alcoholic drinks. We seem unsure why we enjoy them, or whether we should. Most of all, we seem reluctant to concede that we might like the taste, as well as the overall experience.

WHISKEY IS ARGUABLY THE MOST COMPLEX DRINK

Whiskeys can be refreshing, but their multilayered aromas and flavors mean that they are not the obvious choice. Equally, they are intoxicating, but they do not slip down unnoticed, like the most tame of designer vodkas. This applies to any adult drink—the taste has to be acquired—but whiskey is arguably the most complex.

A CHAMELEON DRINK

For this reason, whiskeys are sometimes thought too challenging for the young—or, even more patronizingly, for women. If there were only one style of whiskey, would it somehow be male and middle-aged? Possibly, but there are scores of styles, from Islay to Tennessee. In fact, single malts and small-batch bourbons are gaining sales among young drinkers of both sexes in mature markets like the US, the UK, and Japan, where the growing trend is to drink less but taste more. Those qualities that make these drinks allegedly difficult—their complexity and individuality—are what interest this new audience.

A malt lover might be skeptical about Cardhu with Coke, a combination popular in Spain, the country that, perhaps surprisingly, consumes the most whiskey, but a not-too-smoky blend such as Teacher's or The Famous Grouse makes a tasty refresher with dry ginger ale.

It could be argued that all alcoholic drinks are sociable, but some more than others. The lightly smooth Canadian whiskeys slip down easily, with just a touch of spicy dryness to call for another. Do the Irish need smooth, oily whiskeys to lubricate their eloquence? No; but they will have one anyway.

Maker's Mark has a wheaty creaminess, spiked with mint in juleps at the Kentucky

HIGH SOCIETY
The tasting panel at the Scotch Malt Whisky Society chooses treats for its members. The avoidance of chill filtration is part of the society's raison d'être.

Derby. The most horse-happy distilling country, Ireland, has a whiskey named after a horse—Tyrconnell. Both are ideal for filling up your hip flask.

Whiskeys can have aromas reminiscent of salt, pepper, mustard, vanilla, ginger, and cinnamon. For whiskey's place at the dinner table, or in the kitchen, see Martine Nouet's suggestions on pages 274–7.

People of a nervous disposition miss much. If they drink, they tend to reject spirits as being too strong for comfort. However, most spirits are presented in small servings, with ice and/or water, with the result that their strengths are much the same as those of other drinks. Only serious enthusiasts are likely to engage with the greater potencies of cask-strength whiskeys. In a well-rounded whiskey, the alcohol is warming, rather than burning. As the warmth gradually suffuses the stomach, especially after a meal, the feeling of contentment is a gentle embrace.

Kentucky Straight Bourbon Whiskey has a creamy sweetness of aroma and palate. Such bourbons are delicious with sweet treats.

In older bourbons, the creaminess almost starts to caramelize. Add a splash to Café Brûlot—the flamed coffee of New Orleans—for a wonderful partnership. In Scotland, sherry casks can impart raisin, prune, and apricot flavors that also suit coffee.

Once half-forgotten and now the focus of passion, Islay malts from Scotland's most famous whiskey island can be intensely smoky. Enjoy them with a book at bedtime or a good cigar.

HIGHLIGHT

SUKHINDER'S STASH

In London, Sukhinder Singh started collecting miniatures. Now he has 2,500 bottles in his private collection, and is a whiskey merchant. Conservative Sikhs do not drink, but alcohol is not banned. Moderation is counseled. Sukhinder is an experienced taster, and has a very extensive knowledge of whiskeys, especially single malts.

MURPHY'S LAW

In County Cork, there is both a stout and a whiskey called Murphy's. In Kerry, this pub offers these pleasures to the visitor.

WHISKEY IN LITERATURE

JEFFERSON CHASE

ROBERT BURNS
The eldest son of a poor tenant farmer, Burns was born in Alloway, Scotland, in 1759. He worked as an exciseman to support himself while writing verses celebrating all aspects of Scottish culture, including whiskey. More than 400 of Burns' songs, including "Auld Lang Syne," are still in existence. Some 10,000 people turned up to attend his funeral when he died at the age of 37.

Several professions have reputations for devotion to drink yet seek to be discreet about it, but writers are in the business of telling stories. They drink and tell. In the English-speaking world, their tipple tends to be whiskey. Scotland's national poet, Robert Burns, is also the laureate of its liquor. Burns pronounced that whiskey and freedom go together. He even chose to personify whiskey as the blood of John Barleycorn. Both the quality and quantity of his work would seem to confound the popular notion that alcohol impedes the creative process.

> "OH WHISKY! SOUL O' PLAYS AND PRANKS! ACCEPT A BARDIE'S GRATEFUL THANKS!"
>
> *Robert Burns*

Following Burns, Sir Walter Scott echoed his sentiments in works such as *The Antiquary* and *Rob Roy*. These novels, in turn, inspired the names of a blended Scotch and a whiskey cocktail, respectively.

During the 19th century, Scottish traditions of distilling and writing about the aftereffects of imbibing whiskey spread around the globe, initially to England and Ireland, and later to the United States and Canada. Novelist Walker Percy—a 20th-century descendant of the so-called Scotch-Irish immigrants to the American South—wrote of whiskey's unique ability to summon up past places and times; he described a shot of bourbon as a "little explosion of Kentucky USA sunshine in the cavity of the nasopharynx and the hot bosky bite of Tennessee summertime."

INTRUDER IN THE DUST
A NOVEL BY
WILLIAM FAULKNER

WILLIAM FAULKNER
With his 1929 novel The Sound and the Fury, *Faulkner established himself as one of the most innovative American authors, and in 1950, shortly after the publication of* Intruder in the Dust, *he was awarded the Nobel Prize for Literature. He died in 1961, at the age of 64, after battling alcoholism for years.*

THE ART OF CONTEMPLATION

Writing is a solitary, contemplative enterprise, and whiskey is a spirit to be mulled over, analyzed, and savored. Authors who wrote on whiskey—in both senses of the word "on"—includes the *crème de la crème* of modern literature: Wilde, Fitzgerald, Faulkner, Eliot, Shaw, Hemingway, Bellow, and Joyce. Joyce's *Finnegan's Wake* is about a workman who falls from a ladder and dies, only to be brought back to life at his funeral when whiskey is splashed over his corpse.

SIR WALTER SCOTT
Born in 1771, Scott had a passion for the history of his native Scotland. It was this passion, borne out in novels such as Rob Roy, *that brought him renown. He died in 1832.*

A WRITER'S RUIN?

While whiskey revives the spirit, it has also helped to send many an author to an early grave. Probably the most famous casualty of excess was the Welsh poet Dylan Thomas, who expired after consuming 18 measures of whiskey at New York's White Horse Tavern. Faulkner was also hospitalized with alcohol poisoning after overindulging on George Dickel to celebrate the completion of his novel *Absalom, Absalom!*

Becoming intoxicated is, however, a time-honored method of seeing the world in a different light. To quote Ernest Hemingway: "When you work hard all day with your head and know you must work again the next day, what else can change your ideas and make them run on a different plane like whiskey?" And in Gore Vidal's view, "Teaching has ruined more American novelists than drink."

A KEY CHARACTER

Literary treatments of whiskey run the gamut from the tragic to the comic. Whiskey is as omnipresent as the smoking revolver in the classic hard-boiled American crime fiction of Raymond Chandler, Dashiell Hammett, and Jim Thompson. Just as often, whiskey has been played for laughs. It was an essential ingredient in the wit of Dorothy Parker, and it recurs throughout the tales of Americans John Cheever and John Updike, Canadian Mordecai Richler, Britons Evelyn Waugh and Kingsley Amis, and underappreciated Irishman William Trevor. All of these novelists knew well that the parting shot is an art best learned over a drink or two.

JAMES JOYCE
Born in 1882, the son of a failed distiller in Dublin, Joyce emigrated early to the European continent, where in 1922 he wrote what many consider to be the greatest novel of the 20th century. Ulysses *is both a modern retelling of the ancient epic and a day in the life of bibulous Dublin, written in the impressionistic style later known as stream-of-consciousness. Joyce died in Switzerland in 1941.*

DYLAN THOMAS
Although highly regarded, Thomas' work never brought him much money, and he was initially better known as a hard drinker than as a poet. He died in New York in 1953.

GENERALLY MILD
Scotland's mild maritime climate nevertheless has fluctuations that affect the character of the barley each year, while temperature and humidity levels also influence the way the spirit matures in the aging warehouses.

THE INFLUENCE OF CLIMATE

IAN WISNIEWSKI

REGIONAL WEATHER DIFFERENCES ARE ALL SUBTLY REFLECTED IN THE WHISKEY PRODUCED WITHIN EACH AREA.

Attempting to understand why whiskeys taste as they do inevitably focuses on the more tangible factors such as ingredients, production methods, and barrel aging. But every whiskey is also a manifestation of the area in which it is made, reflecting the climate that enables a particular grain to grow there, and the weather continues to be an influence throughout the distilling and aging processes.

DETERMINING FACTORS

Alcoholic drinks are predominantly produced from either different types of grain or varieties of grapes. The ingredients used were, of course, entirely determined by the climate and what was either available or could be cultivated locally. The origins of alcoholic drinks were also due to the influence of climate. A sugary liquid would naturally ferment in warmer weather in conjunction with airborne yeasts to yield an alcoholic liquid.

Spirits are produced from a variety of grains, and the exact type of grain grown, and when it is harvested, depends entirely on the local climate. Rye, for example, is a staple of some vodka-producing countries; in whiskey terms, it prefers the cooler temperatures and moderate rain provided by US states such as North Dakota, Wisconsin, and Minnesota, as well as by the Canadian prairies.

Corn grows well in Iowa, although most of Iowa's corn output is consumed as food rather than drink, and also in Kentucky, Indiana, Illinois, and Ohio, where high rainfall means the corn can be harvested early, rather than waiting until August, which is the usual month. This is a great advantage, since corn needs to have matured before the local temperature becomes too hot.

Scotland's mild, maritime climate, with long hours of daylight in summer, is ideal for growing barley, especially on the east coast. However, too much sun and too little rain can dry out lighter soils, and cause the grain to ripen prematurely. High rainfall right before harvest time is also not desirable, since it can mean the loss of entire fields of ripening crops. Global warming has brought the barley harvest forward in recent years, with a general move from September to August, and even July. In the Scottish borders, the most southerly region, the harvest can precede northerly regions like the Black Isle by a couple of weeks. Localized microclimates can also produce earlier or later harvests in other regions of Scotland.

GLOBAL WARMING HAS BROUGHT SCOTLAND'S BARLEY HARVEST FORWARD

VINTAGE VARIATIONS

Annual weather patterns will create differences from one year's harvest to another, with higher levels of sunshine increasing the rate of photosynthesis. This raises the level of starch in the barley seeds, and results in a correspondingly higher yield of alcohol.

However, barley harvests do not reflect the weather patterns of each year to the same extent that grapes do. Rather than annual differences in the barley, the character of vintage malts deriving from a particular year is governed more by how the malt has been matured, the type of cask used, and the type of aging warehouse.

SEASONAL WATER

Water quality and character are also at the mercy of the climate, and this has a direct effect on several stages of the production process *(see p. 30)*. Seasonal

HOT AND COLD
This uninsulated metal-clad US warehouse responds more actively to prevailing weather conditions than a stone building would, and this can accelerate the aging process.

changes in water temperature will also affect the steeping process: the colder the water is, the longer the grains take to absorb it, and so the maltster will need to steep the grains for a longer period than normal to ensure that they take up enough water.

Weather will also have an influence on the end of the distillation process if the distillery uses worm tubs, as some do in Scotland. Water flowing through the tub cools the pipe, which in turn condenses the vapors passing through it. For much of the year the water is cold enough, at perhaps 33°F (1°C), and without too many temperature fluctuations, to produce a consistent spirit. However, during the summer the water temperature may rise as high as 70°F (20°C), particularly if the source is something like a shallow stream. Consequently, in order to maintain consistency in the character of the spirit, the distiller must allow this warmer water more time to cool and condense the vapors, and the distillation rate is slowed down.

EVAPORATION

Another, more direct, influence of temperature is the rate at which it causes evaporation from the cask during the aging process. Evaporation happens in a number of ways and with a variety of effects, not all of them easy to quantify, but this is certainly how some undesirable elements of immature spirit pass out of the cask during the early stages of maturation.

In Scotland, the average evaporation rate from a whiskey cask is around 2 percent per year of the volume, in a combination of water and alcohol, which results in a decline in the alcoholic strength of the spirit. Conversely, in the more continental climate of a region like Kentucky, with greater contrasts, the annual evaporation rate can be around 3–5 percent, and barrels on the hotter middle and upper floors of warehouses lose more water than alcohol, with the result that the alcohol becomes more concentrated and the whiskey increases in alcoholic strength during aging.

A consequence of these changes in alcoholic strength is that there will be a difference in the levels of alcohol-soluble and water-soluble compounds being extracted from the wood of the cask; the stronger the spirit, the more alcohol-soluble compounds are extracted.

A final consideration is that higher alcoholic strengths may also slow down oxidative reactions—changes in the spirit as a result of exposure to oxygen in the air. These reactions encourage the development of, for example, floral and fruit notes. Humidity in the air, on the other hand, is believed to encourage oxidation.

ENJOYING THE COLD
Some of Scotland's distilleries work with the weather by using external worm tubs—coiled copper pipes in a tank of cold water on the outside of the walls of the distillery—in which to condense the vapors coming off the still.

LAND OF CONTRASTS
The plains of Alberta provide perfect conditions for barley-growing, while to the west of the province the Rockies begin. This picture shows Medicine Lake, in Jasper National Park.

UNYIELDING ROCK

The granite rocks on Islay ensure that the water used at the Laphroaig distillery is soft and low in minerals.

GEOLOGY

RICHARD JONES

THE CHARACTER AND FLAVOR OF WHISKEY BEGINS IN THE GROUND.

The varied geology of Scotland is the key to the range of distinctive flavors found in its famous whiskeys. The mountain granite of the Grampians, the sandstone stacks of Sutherland, and the volcanic Cuillins of Skye all contribute their unique flavors. In Ireland, it is the basalt of Bushmills that is key to the flavor of the whiskey made there, and in Louisville and Lexington, Kentucky, it is the limestone.

WATER: THE VITAL INGREDIENT

The softer the rock, the more minerals within it are dissolved in the water running through it. In addition, the minerals contained by each rock type vary, so waters rising through different rock types taste different. Spring water is essential in the malting and distilling of whiskey, and it imparts its own flavor to the whiskey it helps to create.

Distillers in central Speyside talk proudly of their granite: this hard, igneous rock gives few of its minerals to the water rising through it. The water is consequently soft and pure. At Glenfiddich, the soft water from the Robbie Dhu spring is used for both mashing and bottling. Ben Rinnes and Aberlour are also excellent soft-water whiskeys. Water running through soft sedimentary rock is prized by brewers of pale ales for imparting a firm, crisp dryness. The hard water emerging from sandstone at Tain in the Northern Highlands has 10 times the mineral content of soft water, imparting a distinctive character to the Glenmorangie whiskey made with it.

A distillery can be established only where there is a plentiful supply of natural bright, clean water. The water must also flow freely throughout the year; if the water dries up, the distillery is forced to halt production until the supply returns.

SCOTLAND

One of the many reasons for the diversity of character in Scotland's whiskeys is the country's unusually varied, and often dramatic, geology.

The country owes its present geology to a number of major seismic events. Five hundred million years ago, Scotland was, together with Greenland and North America, part of a giant landmass named Laurentia. Around 410 million years ago, Laurentia and another landmass, Baltica, converged with a third landmass, Avalonia, driving a series of widely disparate geological terranes (areas dominated by one particular type of rock) together. The scars of this seismic event are still visible on the modern face of the country; the most southerly fault, the Iapetus Suture, broadly follows the border with England. Each fault neatly divides the country into distinct geological zones.

> SCOTLAND'S VARIED GEOLOGY GIVES RISE TO THE DIVERSITY OF ITS WHISKEYS

Nearly 350 million years later, an enormous tear developed on the western side of Scotland and a vast series of volcanoes formed along the fault. More seismic upheavals began to drive the North American landmass westward, helping to create the Atlantic Ocean. The remains of the volcanoes along the fault can now be seen as the black gabbro rock of the Cuillin mountains of Skye and Ben More on Mull. The eruptions of lava from these volcanoes created the basalt plateaus that form much of the remainder of these two islands (and many others).

After this, Scotland was subjected to a spell of geological fine-tuning. Prolonged periods of hot, humid conditions, followed by freezing conditions, including the ice age, conspired to carve out the geological features seen today. Lochs and lochans were formed, rivers cut into ancient stones—carrying vast amounts of sediment as they flowed eastward into the North Sea—and corries were fashioned out of bare rock.

THE ISLE OF SKYE
The spectacular Cuillin Mountains of Skye are the remains of ancient volcanoes. The water that rises up through them helps to create the delicate flavor of Talisker.

FEEDING GLENGOYNE
Soft Highland spring water flows down from largely sandstone rock on its way to Glengoyne distillery. From there it flows into Loch Lomond.

MINERAL WATER

When rainwater falls to the ground, it is naturally mildly acidic (from carbon dioxide in the atmosphere) and free from minerals. Its character is shaped by the rocks it encounters on its journey to the distillery.

GRANITE
Hard, igneous rock formed at high pressure and temperature. It imparts few minerals to the water.

SANDSTONE
Sedimentary rock made up of small grains of quartz. Partly responsible for the hard water of Glenmorangie.

THE GIANT'S CAUSEWAY
These tightly packed, upright basalt columns in Ireland were formed by volcanic activity, although their amazing geometric shapes almost make them look human-made.

SPEYSIDE

Although Speyside is widely associated with granite, it is not the only rock to be found there. Many distilleries outside the central Speyside area, based around the towns of Dufftown, Rothes, and Craigellachie, draw their water from springs that are dominated by either quartzites or old red sandstone. Examples of the former include Cardhu and Knockando, and of the latter, the fresh, fragrant charms of Inchgower.

IRELAND

Just a couple of miles away from the stately basalt columns of the Giant's Causeway off the shores of County Antrim in Northern Ireland sits the Bushmills distillery. Its slightly hard water rises through basalt, before flowing over clay agricultural land on its way to the dam at St. Columb's Rill. Midleton distillery, home of Irish whiskeys such as Jameson, Powers, and Paddy, takes its water from a single source—the Dungourney River. This small river rises from old red sandstone springs to the northeast and, despite crossing carboniferous limestone on its way to the distillery, remains soft in character.

NORTH AMERICA

Moving across to Kentucky on the other side of the Atlantic, the geology of the world-famous bluegrass region is no less important. The underlying geology of this area is dominated by limestone, created from the remains of marine organisms that lived in a shallow tropical sea covering the area around 450 million years ago. Over millions of years, this soluble limestone has been dissolved gradually by rainwater to create karst—a complex terrain dominated by caves, underground sinkholes, depressions, fissures, and streams.

KARST—THE PERFECT LANDSCAPE FOR BOURBON

For the bourbon industry, the benefits of this type of geology are twofold: first, the caves act as an aquifer—storing large reserves of water to ensure a steady supply whatever the weather—and second, the fissures and porous rock filters the water to yield a clean, iron-free product ready for mashing. Kentucky water is also rich in calcium, which not only strengthens the bones of its famous racehorses, but also helps to promote the growth of yeast during fermentation, encouraging the breakdown of sugars to alcohol.

JAPAN

In Japan, the Yamazaki distillery takes its spring water from the nearby Tennouzan Hill. The water rises through gravel and clay—the remains of an ancient lake—and is consequently relatively hard. In contrast, the water at the Hakushu distillery is—like Speyside's—relatively soft, having risen through the granite of the nearby Mount Kaikomagatake.

HAKUSHU, JAPAN
Soft, slightly sweet spring water flows down from the granite-based Mount Kaikomagatake to the Hakushu distillery in Japan.

COOLEY, IRELAND
Cooley distillery takes its spring water from Sliabh nag Cloc (the Mountain of Stones) in the Cooley mountains near Dundalk.

CAPE BRETON, CANADA
The Mary Ann Falls in Cape Breton, Canada, supply pure spring water that flows to the country's only single malt whiskey distillery, Glenora.

KENTUCKY

An aerial view over gently rolling Kentucky bluegrass landscape, perfect for racehorses and bourbon whiskey.

HIGHLIGHT

LIMESTONE CAVES

In the karst landscape of Kentucky, water can percolate directly through the porous limestone rocks, or filter down through a fracture, fissure, or sinkhole. Once the water reaches a layer of impermeable rock, it will usually flow along the rock as an underground stream until it comes to rest in a cave. Unless the cave is open, as here, or the buildup of pressure in the water forces it out through another fracture in the rock, a borehole will need to be sunk to tap into it.

HIGHLIGHT

ON THE ROCKS

Whether whiskey is served on its own, diluted with still spring water, or on the rocks is a matter of personal preference. Adding water changes the alcoholic strength, and just as the strength determines the range of flavors a whiskey shows, diluting can make whiskey taste slightly, or significantly, different.

WATER

IAN WISNIEWSKI

AN ABUNDANT AND CONSISTENT SUPPLY OF WATER IS ESSENTIAL FOR A DISTILLERY TO PRODUCE WHISKEY.

An essential element in producing whiskey, water can directly influence the flavor of a whiskey, depending on its characteristics. It is also the catalyst that encourages flavor development at various stages of the production process.

Water is used in such high volumes to produce whiskey that a good water supply always determines the location of a distillery. The largest volume of water is used in the condensers. Passing cold water through the condensers cools and condenses the spirit vapors, leading to a rise in water temperature. As a result, in Scotland, for example, strict guidelines govern the temperature and flow rate at which the water is returned to the watercourse.

THE MAIN CONSIDERATION IS WHETHER THE LOCAL WATER IS SOFT OR HARD

The main consideration for a distillery is whether the local water is soft or hard. The harder the water, the higher the level of dissolved mineral salts (calcium, magnesium, iron, and zinc). Most water in Scotland is soft. In Kentucky, where the water filters through limestone, the water is hard, with a high level of calcium, magnesium, and phosphate, but not iron. This combination of minerals facilitates the action of the enzymes during mashing, and can make that process more efficient.

The first opportunity for water to influence the character of the whiskey is when the grain is steeped in water to start the germination process. The next stage is when the malted barley is mashed. The water used in these two stages is referred to as "process water." In Scotland, process water may have a certain level of peatiness, having flowed through peat bogs on its way to the distillery. If flowing through peat constitutes an influence, as is traditionally believed, it is likely to be a minor one, and even harder to quantify if the malt is peated (*see p. 40*).

The calcium level of the water influences the rate of fermentation and the flavors formed during fermentation. Soft water has a low calcium content, which allows the yeast used for fermentation to get a vigorous start. The yeast

STEEPING
This is the first stage in which water can play an influential role: there is a traditional belief that peaty water adds phenolic characteristics to the barley.

MASHING
During mashing—as here at the Ardbeg distillery in Scotland, which is served by water from the loch nearby—it is the temperature of the water, rather than any inherent characteristics, that is the crucial factor: the water temperature and enzymes cause the starches within the barley to convert into fermentable sugars.

COOLING
Water temperature is also a crucial factor when condensing the spirit vapors in a worm tub, and the distillation rate is seasonally adjusted.

competes with naturally occurring bacteria for sugar, and a stronger start enables the yeast to compete more successfully.

Hard water is considered essential for the production of bourbon in Kentucky. It is used in conjunction with an individual strain of yeast, which also influences flavor formation.

DISTILLATION AND MATURATION

While the focus of distillation is on the spirit character, water is also an important factor. A complex interaction takes place between water and alcohol in the stills. During distillation, the alcoholic strength rises and peaks, then begins to decline, which means that the proportion of alcohol to water changes within the stills. This, in turn, influences the flavors formed in the spirit, which correspondingly change during distillation.

Water is also important as a component of the spirit, which is typically collected at around 70 vol. in Scotland, and around 60 to 65 vol. in Kentucky. This means that about 30 to 40 percent of the final spirit is water.

The alcoholic strength of the spirit is usually reduced for aging by diluting with water (known as "reduction water") to a standard strength of 63.5 vol. in Scotland, and around 55 to 60 vol. in Kentucky. This is typically considered the optimum strength for the subsequent rate of maturity. Some distillers believe that filling casks with spirit at a higher strength entails longer aging.

The water content in the spirit influences which flavor compounds are extracted from the oak cask. A higher filling strength will extract more alcohol-soluble compounds from the cask, while a lower filling strength will extract more water-soluble compounds.

BOTTLING WITH WATER

Using distilled water (effectively neutral water) when reducing the strength of mature spirit for bottling is standard practice throughout the industry. Using neutral water promotes the character created during distillation and maturation by not adding anything to it. If untreated water is used, there is also always a risk that the calcium present in the water will precipitate white crystals, creating an unattractive haze in the bottle.

ON ITS WAY TO WHISKEY

Water from this mountain stream at Hakushu in Japan eventually finds its way into the distillery's whiskey. It will be used for steeping, mashing, and cooling.

HEATHERS

Heather flourishes throughout the British Isles. Although many varieties are to be found in Scotland, only three are indigenous. Practical as well as decorative, heather was used for thatching, and woven into ropes, baskets, and brooms.

ERICA CINEREA
Also known as bell heather, this variety has pink or red flowers that enliven moors in June and July.

CALLUNA VULGARIS
This heather, known as Scotch heather or ling, produces brightly colored flowers in late summer.

ERICA TETRALIX
Flowering in July, this variety has pink flowers, and distinctive foliage throughout the rest of the year.

HEATHER

IAN WISNIEWSKI

FLORAL AROMAS IN THE BOUQUETS OF SCOTTISH MALT WHISKEYS PROVIDE AN AROMATIC JOURNEY BACK TO THE WHISKEY'S ORIGINS.

One of the traditional emblems of Scotland, heather scents the air around many distilleries and whiskey warehouses, and, in turn, heather aromas emanate from certain malt whiskeys.

Heather, together with various other floral aromas, including ferns, roses, passion fruit, daffodils, tulips, geraniums, jasmine, and eucalyptus, is characteristic of Highland and Speyside malts. The Glenlivet 12-year-old is a prime example, conveying the fresh, green, early summer aroma of heather, together with the richer, spicier notes of heather in full bloom.

HEATHER AROMAS ARE CHARACTERISTIC OF HIGHLAND AND SPEYSIDE MALTS

Heather can be seen throughout Great Britain, Europe, North Africa, and North America. Three types of heather are indigenous to Scotland. These varieties show a vibrant palette of colors when in flower, while attractive foliage provides a range of shades during the rest of the year.

Calluna vulgaris, also known as ling or Scotch heather, typically flowers in Scotland from mid-August to mid-September, showing a range of mauve, lavender, purple, and pink colorways, with white flowers a much rarer sight. Bell heather (*Erica cinerea*) displays pink and pale- to deep-red flowers, while *Erica tetralix* tends to have shell-pink flowers, with both varieties flowering in June and July.

A TASTE OF HEATHER

So how do heather notes develop in malt whiskey? The traditional theory (although difficult to quantify) is that water flowing over heather moors picks up floral characteristics along its way to the distillery, and exerts an influence during steeping or mashing. However, using peat that includes heather, certain types of yeast, a particular distillation method, and oak aging may all impart heather characteristics to whiskey.

PEAT

Peat is composed of various forms of vegetation, including heather, that have taken millennia to decompose. Peating (*see p. 40*) endows barley with a range of phenolic compounds that reflect the ingredients of the peat. Peated malts such as Highland Park show heather notes, and there is plenty of heather in the Orkney peat used at the distillery. A traditional Scottish practice, until the 1960s, was to place bunches of fresh heather on the peat when it was smoking in the kiln, which would have contributed some heathery smoke. Whether this actually influenced the final flavor is open to speculation. Meanwhile, there is also heather character in Speyside malts, which are either unpeated or very lightly peated.

FERMENTATION

Heather character in whiskey could equally be a result of the fermentation process. As the fermentation converts sugars into alcohol, it creates aromas and flavors—including floral notes—over and above the cereal character of the malt. A gradual, medium-length fermentation is considered to give the finest result, with shorter or longer fermentations creating different characteristics. The heather note may be derived from a combination

of the type of yeast used and the length of fermentation. There are many strains of distillers' yeast and brewers' yeast to choose from, each with their own effect on the character of the whiskey.

DISTILLATION

Some of the floral notes that show in the new make spirit of some distilleries can be caused by reflux during distillation. This happens when richer, heavier flavors, which have a higher boiling point, condense from vapor back into liquid before they can leave the still, and are redistilled over again. The reflux at Glenlivet, for example, creates additional floral notes in the whiskey, while also concentrating those created during fermentation. Taller, slimmer stills encourage a greater degree of reflux, because the temperature becomes relatively cool farther up the still, while lighter, fruitier flavors continue their journey to the condenser.

OAK AGING

Existing floral characteristics evolve during maturation, owing to the influence of oxidation, which can create a wide range of additional notes. Oxidation is a natural consequence of the porous oak cask inhaling and exhaling air. The resulting interaction between the spirit and air can create floral notes as part of a broader range of reactions that also develops fruitiness.

HIGHLAND MALTS
Floral aromas—including heather, geranium, jasmine, and rose—are associated with Highland malts, such as Glen Grant from Speyside.

The cask itself may be a source of floral flavors. Floral notes show more clearly in malts matured in bourbon rather than sherry casks, which contribute a richer, sweeter influence that is more inclined to "mask" floral character. A third-fill bourbon barrel has the mildest influence, thereby maximizing floral, heather notes created by oxidation.

NATURAL HABITAT
When in flower, heather's vibrant colors bring the Scottish countryside alive—particularly in the Highlands. Many other heather varieties can also be seen in Scotland's botanical gardens.

Sea Breeze and Seaweed

Ian Wisniewski

DISTINCTIVE MARINE AROMAS ARE A DEFINITIVE FEATURE OF CERTAIN SCOTTISH MALT WHISKEYS.

The evocative aromas of seaweed, iodine, and brine are released by some island and coastal malts. These marine characteristics transport the drinker to the source of the malt—a distillery situated adjacent to the sea, swept by sea breezes to the accompaniment of pounding waves.

Marine aromas tend to be a feature of peated malts, and, since they are considered the most challenging style, these malts have generated a cult following that transcends any age or gender issues. Marine, peaty features generally appear with a certain gusto, so sampling such a malt whiskey tends to be a "love it or leave it" moment for the drinker.

MALTS WITH A MARINE BOUQUET ARE CONSIDERED AMONG THE MOST CHALLENGING WHISKEY STYLE

SEA BREEZE

Confirming exactly how marine characteristics are created and evolve in malts is something of a quest for distillers and devotees. In the absence of definitive research, all the theories are based on experience and logic. The traditional explanation is that casks breathe in the sea breeze that permeates the aging warehouse. A typical, minimum aging period of 10 to 12 years certainly allows plenty of time for this to influence the spirit as it matures within the cask.

There is certainly no shortage of sea air along Scotland's abundant coastline. However, sea spray and iodine (which is present in seawater) can travel within a sea breeze only in the form of fine droplets of seawater, and the extent to which these elements may be inhaled by casks, or how influential they may be, is uncertain. The same uncertainty applies to the influence of seaweed aromas, which are volatile, "gaseous" compounds, carried by the sea air into the aging warehouse.

SEAWEED SPECIES

There are several hundred species of seaweed found throughout Scottish waters. Divided into green, brown, and red varieties, none of these species is unique to Scotland, and all can be found, for example, along the Norwegian and Icelandic coasts. Red seaweed predominantly occupies deeper water than green seaweed, which generally inhabits the shallowest water and rock pools. Brown seaweed is usually found at the top of the shoreline, and even out of water completely. This color-coded indicator is very convenient, but in fact, red seaweed can also be a feature of rock pools, and brown seaweed can cope equally with depths of up to 130 ft (40 m).

Regional differences include the "free-living" seaweed of west coast lochs, where the tides are so gentle that there is no need for any attachment to rocks, since there is no danger of being swept away. Technically known as "egg rack," this variety of brown seaweed is also nicknamed "crofter's wig" after its distinctive appearance.

Another important regional factor is water clarity. This affects how much sunlight penetrates below the surface of the water. Water clarity is far greater on the west coast of Scotland, as a result of which kelp can thrive up to 115 ft (35 m) below the surface, compared to 32 ft (10 m) on the east coast.

A ubiquitous type of brown seaweed, kelp can grow wherever there are rocks underwater for it to cling to. Each variety of kelp prefers slightly different conditions; for example, sugar kelp appears in sheltered areas, such as lochs. Kelp's association with iodine, which was traditionally extracted from it, brings us back to iodine as a classic aroma of island and coastal malts.

SEAWEED IN PEAT

Some whiskey aficionados believe that certain malts gain their marine character during the peating process. The composition of peat changes throughout Scotland. Closer to the coast, as well as on the islands, peat includes decayed seaweed. This may contribute iodine, salty, and other marine characteristics to the new make spirit.

While the debate continues, so does the divisive nature of malts featuring a marine bouquet. For fans, it is a form of aromatherapy; for others, it acts as a warning.

HIGHLIGHT

AN ULTIMATE EXAMPLE

Renowned as one of the most heavily peated malts, Laphroaig releases pungent aromas that include embers and bonfires on the beach, with marine and medicinal notes such as carbolic soap and briny sea breeze. The use of Islay peat, which contains seaweed, and maturing casks in warehouses that are located right by the edge of the sea, also influence the spirit.

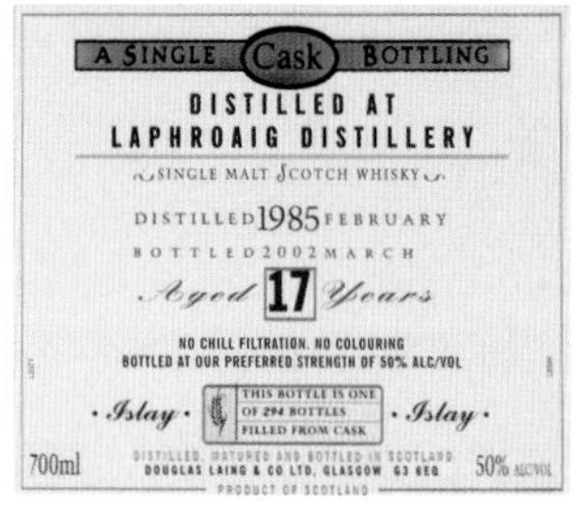

COASTAL AGING

All the Islay distilleries, including Lagavulin, are situated by the sea, which means the sea breeze doesn't have far to travel to enter the aging warehouses.

SEAWEED

Scotland's shoreline is increased in extent by a vast number of lochs, some of which provide a natural habitat for seaweed. Seaweed families vary in color, depending on where they are found growing.

RED SEAWEED
This type of seaweed is found in the deepest water, but also appears in rock pools.

GREEN SEAWEED
Warmer shallow water and rock pools are the usual places to find green seaweed.

BROWN SEAWEED
Typically found at the top of the shoreline, and even out of water, brown seaweed is the most visible type.

SEASHORE LOCATION
The extent to which a coastal location may influence the development of a whiskey during maturation is still being researched, and is hotly debated by distillers and devotees.

EGYPTIAN HARVEST
The ancient Egyptians were one of the earliest civilizations to cultivate barley, with the process of sowing and harvesting recorded for posterity in hieroglyphics.

BARLEY

IAN WISNIEWSKI

ONE OF THE EARLIEST GRAINS TO BE CULTIVATED, BARLEY HAS BEEN WIDELY USED TO MAKE ALCOHOLIC AND NONALCOHOLIC DRINKS.

Although barley has established itself as the foundation of the Scotch whiskey industry, this grain originated in Ethiopia. One of the first cereals cultivated by early civilizations, such as the Sumerians of Mesopotamia, barley was also a staple element of the ancient Egyptian diet, mentioned in hieroglyphics as early as 5000 BC. In ancient Greece, athletes believed additional servings of barley boosted strength and consequently their chances of being crowned an Olympic champion.

PRINCIPAL SCOTTISH GRAIN

Barley was, historically, the principal grain cultivated in Scotland until around the 16th century, when oats became more popular. As a staple ingredient in Scottish cooking, barley appears at the table today in various guises. Barley flour is used to make bannocks, a type of bread prepared from dough using buttermilk, and cooked on a girdle (a type of iron griddle placed on a stove or fire). The most popular type of barley is pearl barley, which is barley with the husk removed and the grain polished. This is used to make favorites such as Scotch broth, also known as barley broth, which combines pearl barley with mutton and assorted vegetables. Cock-a-leekie soup teams barley with chicken and leeks, while another specialty is black pudding: pig's blood thickened with barley and other ingredients.

BARLEY DRINKS

Barley water is such a long-standing favorite that even the Greek physician Hippocrates wrote about it during the fourth century BC.

Fermented barley formed the basis for one of the earliest alcoholic drinks, from which beer evolved during the early Middle Ages. Malted barley today contributes a range of sweet, malty flavors to beer, as well as to Scotch and Irish malts, and blended whiskeys. Other styles of whiskey, such as bourbon, also include a proportion of malted barley in the mashbill, in conjunction with their key grains.

MALTING BARLEY

Although barley was originally a human food crop, only a fraction of the world's barley harvest continues to serve this purpose. Feeding animals, as well as producing whiskey and beer, now accounts for the great majority of barley consumption. Cattle are often fed the residue barley left from mashing (when producing malt whiskey) in the form of "draff." Barley is grown in temperate regions around the world, principally the US, Canada, and Europe.

BARLEY'S HIGH LEVEL OF STARCH IS THE BASIS FOR MAKING ALCOHOL

Barley's importance to the distilling (and brewing) industry derives from its high level of starch, which is the basis for producing alcohol. Malted barley is also a natural source of the enzymes that are essential for converting starches into fermentable sugars during mashing.

Two principal barley varieties are considered the best for malting: two-row and six-row. This refers to the arrangement of seeds within the ear, or head. Two-row barley has a single row of seeds on each side, while six-row barley contains three rows of seeds on each side.

In Scotland, the main types of barley used to produce malt whiskey are two-row, technically *Hordeum vulgare*. Irish whiskey is also produced from two-row barley, while two-row and six-row barley are cultivated in the US.

BARLEY VARIETIES

A range of barley varieties has traditionally been cultivated in different parts of Scotland, one type of barley being suited to the growing conditions in one area but not necessarily to another.

In northern Scotland and the islands, such as Shetland, the traditional barley is bere, a wild barley that was one of the original varieties used to distill malt whiskey. Bere's sturdy straw helps it to withstand windy conditions on the islands, and to make the most of short summers. However, bere has a lower spirit yield compared to more recently developed strains.

The development of new barley varieties dates from the late 19th and early 20th centuries, when named cultivars began to emerge. This search for new barley was motivated by two factors: farmers wanted a higher yield of grain per acre, and distillers wanted a higher yield of alcohol per ton.

Up until the 1960s, only an insignificant amount of malting barley was cultivated in Scotland, partly because of the harsh climate. East Anglia, in England, was the primary source of malted barley for Scottish distilleries up to that time. Currently, the main customer for East Anglian malting barley is probably the brewing industry.

WAVING FIELD OF GRAIN

Various styles of American whiskey, including bourbon, use malted barley as part of their recipe of grains. This barley field is in Washington, one of the principal states that cultivate barley, along with North Dakota, Idaho, and Minnesota.

BLAIR ATHOL WELCOME

In addition to being decorative, the barley motifs that embellish the distillery's entrance gates serve as a reminder of the ingredient from which malt whiskey is distilled.

HIGHLIGHT

BRUICHLADDICH DISTILLERY

Located on the Scottish island of Islay, Bruichladdich is one of the most creative and pioneering distilleries in the malt whiskey industry. A comprehensive approach includes distilling spirit from barley that has been peated to various levels, enabling the distillery to offer peating levels that span from very mellow through to mild and up to a maximum of peaty smoke. Bruichladdich is also among the small number of pioneers distilling organic barley.

BEST BARLEY
The east coast of Scotland, which includes the Black Isle, offers the best combination of climate and soil for cultivating barley, making this a prime source of some of the finest grain.

HARVEST TIME
The date of the harvest is influenced by two principal factors: the climate, and whether the barley variety is early- or late-maturing. Global warming has had an influence, too.

NEW BARLEY VARIETIES

Everything changed with the development of one particular variety of barley, Golden Promise, which became available in 1968. Its strong straw and early maturity meant it could thrive in the adverse Scottish climate. As a result, there was an industry-wide uptake of Golden Promise in Scotland, and by the 1970s it accounted for over 90 percent of malting barley cultivated in Scotland.

Golden Promise continued to enjoy a monopoly until the mid-1980s, when it was superseded by newly developed strains that could outperform it in the field and in the distillery. New barley varieties continue to be developed specifically for cultivation in Scotland. Appearing on the market on a regular basis, they automatically render most of the previous generation obsolete.

SUPERLATIVE STATUS

Some of the world's finest barley is cultivated in Ireland, around Cork and Athy in County Kildare. The main source in the US is North Dakota, followed by Idaho, Minnesota, and Washington. However, Scotland enjoys a superlative status, able to produce the world's highest-yielding barley. This is mainly cultivated on Scotland's east coast, where lighter, sandier soils, and more moderate wind and rain, provide the best conditions for growing barley. This area includes the Borders, Lothian, Fife, Ross-shire, Perthshire, Angus, Morayshire, east Aberdeenshire, and the Black Isle.

However, to meet the demand from distillers, additional barley is imported from England, particularly from Norfolk and Northumberland. British malted barley is also exported to other countries, especially Japan.

CULTIVATING BARLEY

Spring barley is the standard choice of distillers, sown in March to early April, with seeds beginning to form once the barley flowers in late June. Photosynthesis produces sugar in the green tissue of the plant, which moves to the developing seeds and is transformed into starch.

The exact timing of the harvest, usually at some point between July and September, depends on the local climate, and whether the barley is early- or late-maturing. Early-maturing varieties are considered the safer option by farmers, since this entails less risk from the weather. Golden Promise can be harvested as early as July, whereas Optic cannot be harvested until August.

GOLDEN PROMISE
With so many new barley varieties, Golden Promise has virtually become an antique variety, but it continues to be used by Macallan.

TRIAL CROPS

Developed in the 1990s, Optic has been the leading variety of barley in Scotland this century, claiming around 50 to 60 percent of the market. How long this supremacy continues remains to be seen, as new varieties with a mission to outperform Optic are continually being developed.

Planted in trial plots next to established strains, which act as a control, a new barley must show significant benefits to be recommended by the London-based Institute of Brewing (which also oversees the distilling industry).

The desired improvements include greater disease resistance; physical resilience; and shorter, sturdier straw, which helps barley withstand adverse weather conditions. However, every variety has some drawbacks, particularly as fungal diseases evolve and sooner or later reach a form in which they can infect initially resistant varieties.

As new options appear on the market, some distilleries may update their choice of barley. Change can require certain adjustments, since different varieties may process differently. Seed sizes, for example, vary significantly, so the rollers of the mill may need readjustment when milling the barley prior to mashing. If the milling specification is not consistent, the rest of the process can be affected.

DISTILLERY LOYALTY

Some distilleries prefer to use more traditional barley varieties. There is an unusual degree of continuity at distilleries such as Macallan and Glengoyne, where Golden Promise (effectively a veteran, having been introduced so long ago) is used in conjunction with another type.

Macallan and Benromach have also distilled separate parcels of spirit entirely from Golden Promise barley, with a consensus being that using this particular variety of barley endows the spirit with greater body and complexity.

SINGLE ESTATES

Beyond varietal issues, some distilleries have been producing and laying down separate parcels of spirit using barley with a specific "single estate" provenance. Balvenie and Glenmorangie both use barley from particular estate farms—Balvenie from the Balvenie Mains estate, and Glenmorangie from the Cadboll estate.

Inevitably, any bottlings of this type will be limited editions, which only serves to make them all the more desirable. Once they are released, the interesting thing will be comparing them to the regular bottlings.

ECO-FRIENDLY MALTS

Several distilleries, including Bruichladdich and Benromach, are inaugurating a new eco-era, using spirit distilled from organic barley. While in one sense an innovation, this is, of course, also a return to tradition, since all malts were originally distilled from organic barley.

SEVERAL DISTILLERIES ARE INAUGURATING A NEW ECO-ERA, USING SPIRIT DISTILLED FROM ORGANIC BARLEY

Organic grain typically has a longer growing cycle than nonorganic, increasing production costs and therefore the retail price. Costs are also increased at the distillery. Before starting a separate distillation run from organic grain, all the equipment must be thoroughly cleaned, to prevent any possible influence on the spirit from any lingering elements from the previous nonorganic production run.

The initial concern of distillers is to know how organic grain behaves during the production process. Benromach distilled their first parcel of organic spirit in the year 2000, using Chalice barley, while Bruichladdich distilled the first organic Islay malt in December 2003, also using Chalice. Does organic spirit mature in a different way from nonorganic? No one knows the answer yet, so we will just have to wait. With luck, we will receive progress reports as the spirit develops.

TYPES OF BARLEY

There are two principal types of barley considered to be the most suitable for malting, referred to as two-row and six-row. This numerical reference indicates the number of rows of seeds, either two or six, arranged on either side of the ear of the barley.

TWO-ROW BARLEY
This is the usual type cultivated in Europe, though it is also used by American distillers.

SIX-ROW BARLEY
Six-row barley is mainly cultivated in the US, with Chicago and Milwaukee being malting centers.

BERE
One of the original barley varieties, bere was traditionally cultivated in northern Scotland.

PEAT IN THE DRINK
Ardbeg's products, and those of its neighbor, Lagavulin, are acknowledged to be among some of the world's most heavily peated malt whiskeys.

PEAT

RICHARD JONES

ONCE USED AS FUEL TO FIRE THE STILLS, PEAT IS RESPONSIBLE FOR SOME OF THE MOST INTENSE FLAVORS IN WHISKEY.

One of the most distinctive and assertive aromas and flavors to be found in Scotch whiskey is that of peat. Overall, Scotch whiskeys became far less peaty in the last decades of the 20th century as alternative fuel sources were developed, but the new millennium has seen some distilleries revert to tradition—or even exceed their past glories.

> TO SENSE PEAT IN WHISKEY IS TO SMELL AND TASTE THE SOIL OF SCOTLAND

A TASTE FOR PEAT

The return of peat is a reflection of connoisseur interest. The earthy, sooty, tarlike, smoky aromas and flavors of peat—often intensely dry—can be as addictive to connoisseurs as they are challenging to the novice or casual drinker. To sense peat in whiskey is to smell and taste the soil of Scotland, almost to take a bite out of the earth. Nowhere else is the word *terroir* more appropriate. The Lowlands are the least peaty part of Scotland, although they are notable for their raised peat bogs; the Highlands have peaty moorlands, and lunar-looking blanket bogs of the Flow Country to the north; while the islands can be the peatiest of all, especially Orkney and Islay.

A KEY INGREDIENT

Water flows over peat on the way to a maltings, where it may impart some of these typical flavors during the process of steeping the grain. A much more important influence, however, is the use of peat as a fuel in the kiln where the grain is dried. Here, techniques vary, and the duration and intensity of the process influence flavor; many of the key constituents that flavor the whiskey, including phenol, cresols, and guiacol, are not found in the peat itself, but rather are produced as the peat burns. If the same source of peaty water

DIGGING OUT THE PEAT
Gathering peat by hand—as opposed to using machinery, which is the norm in commercial peat harvesting—is a physically demanding task.

AIR DRYING
Peat must lose some of its excess moisture before it can be used. These cut slabs of peat are left out in the open, and will need four weeks or more to dry sufficiently.

FUELING THE KILN
Peat is shoveled into the kiln, and as it burns the smoke will be channeled up to the malted barley on the floor above, to dry it and lend some of its flavor.

is used in the distillery, the peat compounds may exert a further small influence. Even a peaty, earthy warehouse floor may play a minor role. Certainly, direct contact with peat smoke is not necessary to produce a peat influence: on Islay, common in entirely unpeated whiskeys. This can in part be attributed to naturally occurring phenols in the husk of the barley, but the peaty water on the island and smoky atmosphere at the maltings play a decisive role.

WHAT IS PEAT?

Peat is an accumulation of partially carbonized plant material, usually found in waterlogged areas; over millions of years, if subjected to heat and pressure, peat would eventually become coal. Peatlands and bogland areas cover between 5 percent and 8 percent of the world's landmass, with 90 percent found in the temperate and cold climates of the Northern Hemisphere. In Scotland, peatlands account for nearly 4,000 square miles (more than 1 million hectares), or 12 percent of the total surface area.

Blanket bogs, a name earned by their tendency to lie over broad areas of landscape regardless of topography, are the most important source of peat for the whiskey industry, and for Scottish peat supplies in general. As well as dominating the environment of Caithness and Sutherland, in the far north of Scotland, where the largest blanket bog in Europe can be found, they also feature heavily on

SOIL AND WATER
Typical blanket bog terrain. This is in Altnaharra, Sutherland, in the far north of Scotland, in what is known as the Flow Country. Sphagnum moss, in particular, thrives in waterlogged conditions such as this.

HIGHLIGHT

CUTTING TOOLS

Over the centuries, many tools have been developed to help with the peat harvest. Traditional tools include the flaughter spade, rutter, and tusker. The flaughter is used to remove the top, grassy layer, and the rutter to make cuts in the peat bank. The tusker is used to dig and remove the peat with a twist.

PEAT PLANTS

The species of plant and vegetation in the peat helps determine the influence it has on a whiskey. Although moss and heather are two of the most common constituents of peat, many other plants add to its character.

PURPLE MOORGRASS
An upright grass with a purple flower, in the past it has been used as thatching material for roofs.

BOG MYRTLE
Typically found in the Western Highlands, this plant has highly aromatic leaves and catkins.

BEARBERRY
A small shrub with evergreen leaves, it is still used in herbal medicine for its antiseptic qualities.

SCOTS PINE
A conifer widespread in Scotland around 6,000 years ago, it is now mainly confined to the Highlands.

far north of Scotland, where the largest blanket bog in Europe can be found, they also feature heavily on the islands of Islay, Orkney, and Lewis.

FORMATION OF BLANKET BOG

Blanket bogs first began to form around 5,000 to 7,000 years ago. Heavy rains leached minerals such as iron from the soil. These minerals accumulated below the soil, forming an impenetrable, watertight layer. Continued rainfall caused the land to waterlog, which encouraged the growth of certain species of plants. The organisms responsible for the decomposition of organic matter were unable to survive the inhospitable conditions, so, as the bog plants died, they remained intact, building up in layers over the years.

PEAT CUTTING

Peat can either be cut by machine or dug with a spade. Peat-cutting machines are pulled by tractor, and cut the peat to the required depth using a circular or chain saw. Different models of machine extract the peat in different ways, either compressing it in a chamber, squeezing it out like toothpaste, or milling it into a dry powder. Cutting peat by hand is the traditional method of extraction. First, the fibrous, mossy top layer is removed and set to one side. Next, a peat cutter or spade is used to determine the depth of the cut and to divide the peat into pieces around 24 x 6 in (60 x 15 cm). Finally, the peat is removed from the bed, using a tool known as a tusker. Before the peat can be handled, it must first be allowed to dry; machine-harvested peat normally requires around one month, whereas hand-cut peat needs a couple of weeks longer. During the cutting season, from April to September, peat cutters work long, back-breaking hours to maximize their yield.

Whether harvested by hand or machine, the peat that finds its way to the malting kiln is a direct reflection of the environment that created it. The landscape, climate, and topography of the terrain will have had a profound effect on the plants, trees, and living organisms that lived and died at that specific location over thousands of years. Once this material turns into peat, environmental factors continue to exert their influence: the level of moisture, acidity of the soil, and temperature in the ground all shape the character and consistency of the peat.

PEAT COMPOSITION

In Scotland, in keeping with many other parts of the world, peat composition is dominated by sphagnum moss. This remarkable plant is perfectly adapted to the waterlogged conditions of the bogland, intertwining with other plants to support the spongelike properties of its body. To the west of Scotland, thanks to higher rainfall, sphagnum is joined by bog myrtle, with its sweet, citruslike aromas, and purple moorgrass; moving inland, there tends to be more Scots pine, heather, and bearberry.

Coastal peat displays salty, seaside flavors in keeping with the maritime environment that shaped it; it also contains more sand, making it looser in texture. The suggestion that Islay peats contain seaweed is slightly more contentious, however. For example, Castlehill moss, the peat source for Port Ellen maltings, has spent its entire life too far inland to have accumulated anything more than token quantities of sea plants.

The peats on Orkney are much younger than those from Islay (around 1,800 years), and, as a result, the island's deepest peat bogs are a maximum of 10–13 feet (3–4 m) deep. Highland Park takes its peat from selected banks on Hobbister Hill, carefully combining cuttings

SPHAGNUM MOSS
By far the most important constituent of peat, the 300 species of sphagnum are ideally suited to life in the inhospitable conditions of a bog.

taken at three different levels to generate the desired distillery character. The top layer, known as the fogg, is removed from just below the surface and is particularly rich in heather and its rootlets. The next layer, called the yarphie, is darker and more compact, producing less smoke and more heat. The deepest layer, the moss, bears a passing resemblance to coal, and may contain the remains of ancient trees.

PEAT AROUND THE WORLD

Although peat is found outside Scotland, it is rarely employed in local whiskey production. Ireland, rich in peat bogs, abandoned the use of peat around the time that whiskey production moved from the country to the cities, since peat was an inefficient fuel. In Japan, peated malt is sometimes used in whiskeys, although the majority is imported from maltings in Scotland that have used Scottish peat.

THE PEAT BOGS OF ISLAY

NO OTHER WHISKEY REGION is more associated with peat than Islay, and it has plentiful supplies of its own to draw on. Although the whiskeys from some of the distilleries on the island hardly show any trace of peat, others have become international bywords for peatiness.

BUNNAHABHAIN
The amount of peat used at the distillery has varied over the years, but its whiskey is generally considered to be one of the lighter styles produced on the island.

◆ Bunnahabhain
Caol Ila ◆
ISLAY
◆ Bruichladdich
◆ Bowmore
GARTBRECK BOG
DUICH BOG
CASTLEHILL BOG
GLEN MACHRIE BOG
Ardbeg ◆
◆ Lagavulin
Laphroaig ◆

Key
◆ working distilleries

LAPHROAIG
In addition to using its own peat in its own maltings, Laphroaig is influenced by the peat dug from Castlehill bog, which supplies the maltings at Port Ellen.

BRUICHLADDICH
Peat used to play a minor role in the whiskeys of this distillery, but now its Octomore is one of the peatiest available.

CUT TO ORDER
Cutters are here at work at Glen Machrie, in the south of the island, harvesting peat in the traditional way for the distillery at Laphroaig, one of the Islay whiskey producers still operating its own floor maltings.

ARDBEG
The distinctive pagoda roof of Ardbeg's maltings. The whiskey produced here is one of the island's triumvirate of highly peated whiskeys.

BARLEY

Although barley is grown around the world, Scotland is the world's biggest producer. The east coast of the country provides the ideal combination of soil and climate in which to grow it.

MALTING

IAN WISNIEWSKI

INITIATING GERMINATION, AND THEN HALTING IT AT THE RIGHT MOMENT, IS THE SECRET TO SUCCESSFUL MALTING.

As the first step in the production process, it is vital that malting is carried out correctly; any shortcomings cannot be made up for later. Malted barley accounts for approximately two-thirds of the cost of producing new make spirit, so there is no margin of error.

The starch content of barley is initially locked within the center of the grain by cell walls lined with protein. Malting breaks down these cell walls during three stages: steeping, germination, and kilning.

MALTING RELEASES THE STARCH CONTENT OF THE BARLEY

STEEPING

The first stage of malting is to soak the barley grains with water in steeps (large vessels) to start germination. Two or three separate batches of water are added, with oxygen pumped into the steeps for a few hours between each batch of water (referred to as "air rests" and "wet time"). Oxygen raises the grain's energy levels, increasing the rate at which the water is absorbed.

Whether steeping water can contribute any flavors—if it has run through peat bogs, for example—is difficult to quantify. This is certainly a traditional theory, but since distilleries do not vary their water source, it is impossible to compare the result of using nonpeaty water.

GERMINATION

Germination is considered to begin once the grain leaves the steep, which typically lasts from 24 to 36 hours. Growth hormones released by the grain also trigger the creation and release of enzymes that begin breaking down the cell walls and protein layers, in order to access the starch. This serves as a food source, enabling the grain to develop roots and an acrospire (shoot).

The enzymes, collectively termed "diastase," include alpha-amylase and beta-amylase (the latter is already present in barley). These enzymes are essential for the subsequent conversion of starch into fermentable sugars during the subsequent process of mashing.

From the steeps, the grains are spread across malting floors, ready for turning. Malting floors are traditionally made from stone, and, more recently, concrete. A thoroughly minimalist venue, the malting floors building resembles a deserted village hall, in which windows are the only feature.

TURNING THE BARLEY

In order to encourage consistent germination rates, the barley needs to be "turned" (aerated) using a malt shiel (shovel), plow, or rototiller. This helps control and distribute the heat produced as a natural consequence of germination.

A "plow," effectively a large rake, gently aerates the surface by creating shallow grooves. For a greater degree of aeration, and to bring underlying barley to the surface, a maltman digs

HIGHLIGHT

TOOLS OF THE TRADE

Floor malting is the most traditional method of malting the barley. This entirely hands-on process also requires the use of traditional tools, including a malt shiel (shovel). This is used to turn the malt on the malting floor as it germinates. Turning the malt aerates it, which helps to dissipate the heat produced, and ensures a more consistent rate of germination.

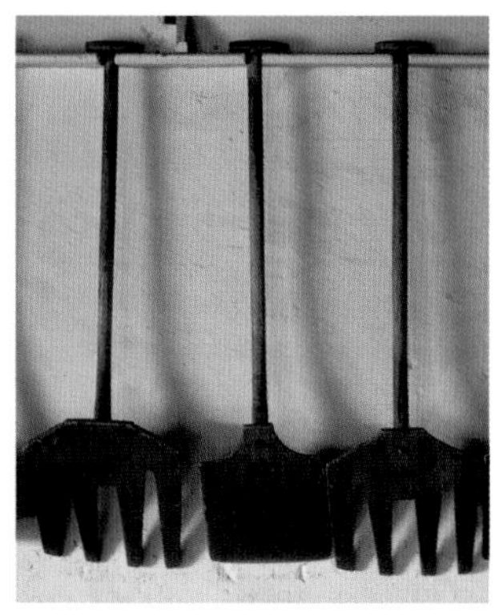

BARLEY FIELD AT BALBLAIR

Malt whiskey is distilled from spring barley, which is sown from early March to early April, and harvested between July and September. Some varieties mature more quickly than others.

into the grains using a malt shiel, and casts them over his shoulder to settle on another part of the floor. A rototiller equipped with paddles has a similar aerating effect.

KILNING

Germination takes from five to nine days, depending on the temperature—germination is quicker in warmer weather and slower in cooler weather. At a peak stage of development, when the cell walls are broken down, and the rootlets reach about three-quarters of the grain's length, growth is arrested by kilning. Any further growth would be counterproductive, since the embryo would start using up the starch, and a lower starch level means a reduced yield of alcohol.

Known at this stage as green malt, the grain is spread across a perforated floor at a uniform depth, to be dried by heat rising from the kiln beneath.

PEATING THE MALT

If the malt is being peated, an important consideration is that smoke is only absorbed by the grain, essentially the husk, while retaining surface moisture. This means that heat created by the kiln must remain mild enough to achieve the required peating level before the grains relinquish this surface moisture. Peating levels are measured as parts per million (ppm) phenol. A lightly peated malt is around 2 to 10 ppm, up to a peak of 50 to 60 ppm for a heavily peated style.

Kilning develops the malt's cereal, starchy flavor into a range of malty, cookie notes with a certain sweetness (heat brings out sugars within the grain). Peating adds a range of phenolic compounds beyond peaty, smoky notes, including tar, embers, bonfire, carbolic soap, and a marine character.

MALTING FLOOR
Continually monitoring the temperature of the barley during germination is vital, since it is influenced not only by seasonal changes but also by fluctuations in the daily temperature. A thermometer, planted directly into the barley as here, provides an accurate reading.

RAKING

Raking the malting floor creates shallow grooves that gently aerate the barley and allow the heat to dissipate.

MALTING CAPACITY

Malting floors can still be found at a number of distilleries, but most now have other functions—some are visitor centers. In fact, of Scotland's 90 distilleries, only five operate malting floors on-site: Balvenie and Highland Park in the Highlands; Bowmore and Laphroaig on Islay; and Springbank in Campbeltown. Visiting floor maltings is memorable, since only the maltmen have changed over the years.

The distilleries of Balvenie, Bowmore, Highland Park, and Laphroaig malt a percentage of their barley requirement on-site, with commercial maltsters delivering the rest. At Springbank, the capacity of the malting floors determines how much spirit is distilled. As a result, Springbank is the only distillery to malt all the barley for each individual whiskey at the distillery. This includes whiskeys with different peating levels; Hazelburn is unpeated, Springbank is lightly peated, and Longrow is heavily peated, using local peat. Springbank's malting floors also supply the neighboring Glengyle distillery, reopened in 2004 by the Mitchell family, who own Springbank.

ONLY FIVE SCOTTISH DISTILLERIES STILL OPERATE FLOOR MALTINGS

THE PRICE OF TRADITION

Malting barley using floor maltings is more expensive than buying from a commercial maltster. Manual rather than mechanized, floor-malting relies on experience and judgment. Floor maltings take longer, perhaps up to 12 days, compared to around seven days at a commercial maltings, and the spirit yield can be marginally lower.

Floor maltings require a significant amount of space, not just for the actual floors and steeps, but also for storage space for the barley and peat. In addition, several experienced staff are necessary, with Balvenie and Springbank distilleries, for example, employing four and six dedicated maltmen, respectively.

Since floor maltings are directly influenced by the ambient temperature, and Scotland's weather can vary greatly, the maltmen need to monitor conditions continuously and adapt the malting schedule accordingly, and then work around them.

Similarly, the steeping schedule depends on water temperatures, which can vary significantly throughout the year. Around 58–62°F (14–15°C) is considered ideal, and because colder water during the winter would slow the process down, it is heated to the required temperature. However, cooling warmer water in summer is not possible, which can mean adjusting the schedule of "wet time" and "air rests" to ensure that the resulting barley is of consistent quality.

STEEPING THE BARLEY

The malting process starts off by adding barley to large vessels known as steeps, containing water. The steeps here are at Highland Park, on Orkney. Growth is triggered as the barley gradually absorbs the water; the barley is then ready to begin germination.

COVERING THE FLOOR

Once the grain has absorbed sufficient water, the residual water is drained off from the steeps and the barley is then taken to the malting floor in wheelbarrows. The malting floor is carefully covered with the barley to an even depth. Here, two maltmen lay out the barley at Bowmore distillery on Islay.

ADJUSTING THE FLOOR

Checking the temperature of the barley laid out on the malting floor entails checking the thermometer that rises from among the grains. Scooping up handfuls of barley for a closer inspection, and walking on the floor to check the degree of sponginess underfoot, are other methods that experienced maltmen use to monitor the progress of the germination process.

The frequency with which the malt needs to be turned in order to dissipate heat generated by germination, and to separate grains to prevent them from sticking together, is entirely dependent on the ambient temperature. During the summer, the floor may require turning a couple of times during each shift. In winter, an entire shift may pass without anyone needing to intervene. A similar working pattern can occur within a 24-hour cycle if the daytime temperature is warm, but the night-time temperature low.

Whether the malt needs to be turned gently, or more vigorously, also depends on the ambient temperature, and determines which type of tool is used. A plow, which a maltman drags behind him, provides the gentlest aeration by raking the surface. A malt shiel and rototiller aerate the floor more vigorously, by disturbing the bed to a greater depth and bringing barley from the base to the surface. Using a malt shiel and plow is heavy work, and some maltmen wear weightlifters' belts to cope with the physical demands of the work.

Opening doors or windows is another way to control temperature and improve air flow, but again, this is a shift-by-shift decision. Even during the summer, unwelcome cold breezes may rise up suddenly, with airborne dust also being a concern.

CONSISTENT KILNING

Maintaining consistent kilning conditions is crucial, as different levels of heat and smoke can impart a varied range of phenols to the malt. Kilning is an acquired skill, the objective being to generate smoke, not flames. Again, climatic influences, such as a strong wind, can create problems by fanning flames in the kiln. Since phenolic compounds can be destroyed by flames, high winds are a significant concern.

The moisture level of peat varies considerably, so the kilnsman continually monitors the condition of the peat he is using during the kilning. He will add wet peat—either peat that retains its natural moisture or peat that has been dampened—to produce more smoke, or, alternatively, add dry peat to generate heat.

SILENT FLOORS

While commercial maltings operate year-round for maximum efficiency, floor maltings typically take a summer break, since higher temperatures present a risk that mold will develop, rendering the malt unusable. Having silent malting floors may be a necessity, but it obviously reduces profitability.

HIGHLIGHT

BARLEY INTO MALT

One of the first visible signs that germination has begun is the appearance of rootlets extending from the grains of barley. Within each grain, the embryo starts to break down the wall surrounding the starch, which provides energy for further growth. Kilning halts the growth within the grains, which would otherwise continue to consume the starch and so reduce the eventual yield of alcohol for the distiller.

TURNING THE MALT

Turning the barley as it germinates is a skilled job. The floor (this one is at Laphroaig, on Islay) requires careful monitoring to decide whether, when, and how the turning should be done at any given time.

PEAT AT THE READY

This kiln at Bowmore is fired by burning fuel such as coke. If the malt is to be peated, then peat is also added to the kiln. Burning peat creates smoke, which rises from the kiln and is absorbed by the barley.

THE HEART OF THE KILN

The right temperature has to be maintained over a lengthy period. Opening and closing the kiln doors to alter the air flow, and therefore the ratio of heat to smoke, is one of the few ways of controlling the fire.

HIGHLIGHT

PAGODA ROOFS

A typical and distinctive feature of distilleries across Scotland and Japan, the traditional pagoda roof above the kiln is visually arresting, but more importantly, it helps to maximize the flow of air through the kiln, making kilning a more efficient process.

MALT KILN ROOFS

Many Scottish distilleries are renowned for their attractive architecture. Strathisla is a prime example, its pagoda roof being one of its most distinctive features. Rising above the malt kiln of a number of other Scottish distilleries, pagoda roofs add an oriental flourish, tapering into an elegant finial. More importantly, pagoda roofs play a vital role during the kilning process.

The pagoda concept was developed in 1889 by Charles Chree Doig, an architect and civil engineer based in Elgin. He was commissioned to improve air flow in the kilns at Dailuaine distillery, to make the drying process more efficient. While aesthetics are easier to appreciate than technicalities, the improved air flow of what was to become known as the Doig Ventilator was created by the relationship of the height to the width of the pagoda roof. In addition, positioning the roof higher than usual above the louvers, which were also reduced in number, helped to improve the air flow.

THE PAGODA ROOF PLAYS AN IMPORTANT ROLE DURING KILNING

When Dailuaine declared Doig's vented roof a success, other distilleries wanted to follow suit, and a new architectural genre was established. Doig was commissioned by virtually every distillery in Speyside and beyond, and his distinctive roofs began to appear on kilns throughout Scotland. Doig became known as the premier distillery architect, and ultimately his work featured at almost 100 distilleries.

DESIGNER DISTILLERIES

Doig also designed entire distilleries, including Benromach in 1898. Numerous commissions to redesign interior layouts resulted in more streamlined layouts in many distilleries. Doig's designs included pot stills, although the extent to which the shapes and dimensions were of his own devising, or in collaboration with coppersmiths, is uncertain. He was also an expert on water sources, and patented a system of treating distillery waste products. Dailuaine's pagodas were destroyed by a fire in 1917, and it was three years before the distillery was able to reopen. Other examples of

HAKUSHU DISTILLERY
Japanese distilleries also employ the pagoda roofs designed by architect Charles Chree Doig, copying the well-established traditional Scottish design, although ironically the pseudo-temple style sits very comfortably in the Japanese landscape.

Doig pagodas have also disappeared, either as a result of distilleries closing or because they became victims of a modernization process. However, Knockando, Cardhu, Laphroaig, and Lagavulin are some of the distilleries that still retain Doig's original pagoda roofs.

A VERSATILE ARCHITECT

Born in 1855 into a farming family, at Linthrathen in Angus, Doig trained as an architect and surveyor at an architectural practice in Meigle, Fife, where he married Margaret Isabella Dick in 1881. The following year, Doig moved to Elgin, having been appointed assistant to a land surveyor, Mr. H.M.S. Mackay, who was based in the Union Bank buildings on High Street. Doig's abundant talent was clear to everyone, and within a few years he had become a partner in the business, renamed Mackay and Doig.

Although Doig received many commissions from malt whiskey distilleries, and his social circle included a number of distillers, designing distilleries was only one aspect of his career. Doig undertook over 1,000 other commissions, including shops, hotels, banks, village halls, schools, farm buildings, and residential country houses. Surviving examples of his work include the Elgin Auction Mart, an auction house completed in 1901, and the Meal Mill, also in Elgin, built as a maltings and retaining its original pagoda roofs.

Doig died in 1918, at age 63, after a day spent on a shooting party on the moors of Dallas, several miles outside Elgin, and he was buried in Elgin Cemetery. One of his three sons, also named Charles Doig, whom he had trained as an architect, continued the family practice.

ORIGINAL DESIGNS

An amazing collection of over 2000 of Doig's designs, together with three notebooks, has been compiled by the heritage department of Elgin Library. The designs are highly detailed pen-and-ink drawings, some of which are annotated, and include Doig's design for Dailuaine's pagoda roof. Many designs appear in duplicate: one version on thick paper, serving as the working design, and the other a master copy on linen, which was the usual practice in the 19th century.

LAPHROAIG DISTILLERY
Renowned for producing an intensely peaty, smoky malt whiskey, Laphroaig is also one of the most traditional distilleries and continues to undertake malting and peating on-site.

FLAVORS

Additional characteristics develop in the barley during kilning and peating, with numerous island and coastal malts exhibiting a range of peaty and marine aromas.

EMBERS
Hints of glowing embers and driftwood bonfires show in the nose of many island malts.

THE SEA
Coastal malts have years in which to breathe in sea air, with briny notes evident in the mature spirit.

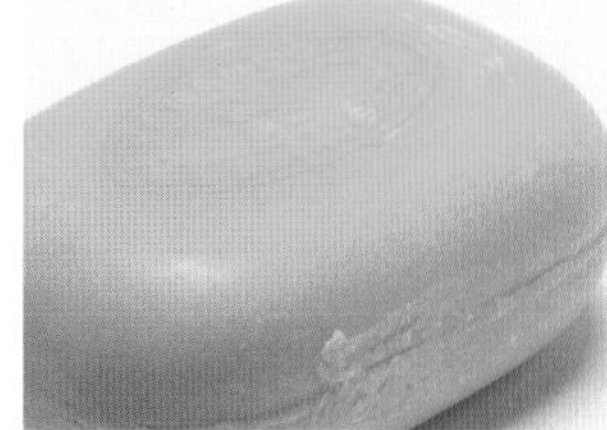

CARBOLIC SOAP
Among the more pungent aromas found in peated malts are medicinal ones, such as tar or carbolic soap.

SEAWEED
Seaweed lends its characteristic aroma to sea air, and is sometimes a component of coastal peat.

HIGHLIGHT

GERMINATION

The first stage of malting is hydrating the barley to begin growth and so instigate the process of germination. The use of a computerized and temperature-controlled regimen ensures that the barley germinates according to a strict timetable.

Commercial Malting

Ian Wisniewski

THE MAJORITY OF MALTED BARLEY IS PRODUCED BY SPECIALLY BUILT MALTINGS, RATHER THAN AT A DISTILLERY.

Commercial maltings were established during the early 20th century in the US, Canada, and much of Europe. Milwaukee and Chicago are key American hubs, with the cities of Cork and Athy prime maltster's territory in Ireland. However, Scottish maltsters did not really feature as a significant element of the industry until the 1970s. This was due to a combination of factors.

High rainfall meant that Scottish barley was typically harvested with a moisture level of around 20 percent. A lack of investment in drying facilities meant Scottish farmers were usually unable to reduce the moisture levels in the harvested barley by a sufficient amount. However, once commercial maltsters began investing in dryers and were able to eliminate the problem, Scottish barley was found to be eminently suitable for malting.

ESTABLISHING COMMERCIAL MALTINGS USING LOCAL BARLEY MADE SENSE

PROMISING DEVELOPMENT

An important breakthrough was the development of Golden Promise, a new barley variety launched in 1968. Up until then, barley was imported from England. Since most distilleries operated malting floors, there was no incentive to develop commercial maltings in Scotland. However, once Golden Promise became widely cultivated in Scotland, increasing the local supply, establishing commercial maltings that utilized local barley made economic sense.

Many distilleries increased production levels during the 1970s, adding more mash tuns, washbacks, and pot stills, and building more warehouses in which to age the whiskeys. However, devoting extra space to malting floors, with additional storage space for grain, was not a financially viable option. As a result, commercial maltsters gained more business. Using the latest technology and fewer staff, they could produce larger batches of malt to a more consistent specification and at a more competitive price.

PLACING AN ORDER

Most distilleries are supplied by independent commercial maltsters. Purchasing agreements with grain merchants or local farmers specify grain size and nitrogen and moisture levels, all calculated to maximize the spirit yield. Purchasing more than

MODERN MALTING AT GLEN ORD

This is one of four in-house maltings operated by Diageo, together with Port Ellen, Roseisle, and Burghead, which supply all 27 of the company's distilleries with malted barley.

SALADIN BOX

These automated troughs can process larger amounts of barley than drum maltings. Air is blown through a perforated floor below the grains at the right temperature to initiate germination, and the barley is turned by large, computer-controlled screws.

one barley variety is a safeguard against potential problems with the harvest, and offers choice to distilleries. Maltsters assess the grain's germination ability, and check for any mold or weevils.

Maltsters undertake steeping, germination, kilning, and peating, according to requirements agreed with each distillery. Data accompanying each malt delivery includes the PSY (predictable spirit yield). Calculated by maltsters, this figure is compared to the actual spirit yield at the distillery to confirm that the malt is performing.

Individual barley varieties are steeped separately, since different grain sizes take up water at different rates. Conical steeps have taken over from the traditional flat-bottomed style because they require less water and are easier to clean.

GERMINATING THE BARLEY

Germination takes place in saladin boxes or drum maltings, both of which can provide the same standard of barley in the same amount of time. Made of concrete, saladin boxes were originally rectangular, although, since the 1970s, most new boxes have been circular, with a central hole, allowing far larger batches to be processed. Air blown through a perforated floor controls the rate of germination, and the heat generated by germination is sucked away. The grain is aerated by a computerized turner. Suction pipes then convey the grain to the kiln.

Enjoying a peak of popularity during the 1960s, drum maltings have temperature-controlled air blown through perforated floors into the grain, while fans expel heat through vents. Rotating the drums automatically turns the grain, ensuring consistent growth in the barley.

KILNING AND PEATING

While kilning is computerized, it is still monitored by kilnsmen. Burning fuel to produce direct heat has largely been replaced by a method known as indirect heating. Air is heated by being conducted through pipes that are in turn heated by water from a boiler.

PORT ELLEN MALTINGS
Built in 1972, Port Ellen maltings on Islay supplies each of the island's seven distilleries with a proportion of their malt requirements.

DRUM MALTINGS
Temperature-controlled and ventilated, these large cylindrical drums are computer-operated and provide the ideal conditions for germinating the barley.

FROM THE HEARTLAND
Grown on a vast scale in the US since the 19th century, wheat has its most important role in the production of bread, but it also plays a part in the distillation of whiskey.

SELECTING THE GRAIN

IAN WISNIEWSKI

EACH WHISKEY IS A REFLECTION OF THE FLAVORS IMPARTED TO IT BY THE GRAINS FROM WHICH IT IS DISTILLED.

Wheat, rye, barley, and corn each contribute different flavor characteristics to whiskey. When combined in multigrain recipes—when producing bourbon, for example—they interact and create a group dynamic.

WHEAT

One of the earliest grains to be cultivated in Europe, wheat became popular in the United States during the 19th century. Kentucky, Ohio, Indiana, Kansas, and Nebraska are the main wheat producers.

Most distillers use winter wheat, planted in the fall and harvested late in the following summer, because it gives the desired ratio of high starch and low protein levels (compared to spring wheat, which is planted in the spring and harvested the following fall). In Scotland, wheat has largely replaced corn in the distilling of grain whiskey. While some grain whiskey is bottled as grain whiskey, the majority is combined in varying proportions with malt whiskey to produce blended Scotch.

Wheat lends smoothness, mellowness, and sweetness to whiskey, providing a rounder, more honeyed taste, and it can also reduce some of the more assertive character provided by corn. This explains why wheated bourbons have a reputation for being sweeter than nonwheated bourbons.

RYE'S CHIEF CONTRIBUTION TO FLAVOR IS A SPICINESS, EVEN PEPPERINESS

RYE

In Europe, rye was first dismissed as a weed in the wheat crop, although it later became popular in Germany, Poland, Russia, and Scandinavia. Vodka was distilled from rye in Poland and Russia.

Rye was originally cultivated in the US by the first German settlers, who brought with them a rye-distilling tradition. Rye was able to thrive in impoverished soils in which other grains could not become established.

Rye's chief contribution to flavor is a spiciness, even pepperiness, as well as fruit, softness, full body, and dryness to the palate. There is also a lingering warmth in the finish.

BARLEY

One of the earliest grains cultivated in Scotland and Ireland, barley was taken to the US by pioneer settlers. When surplus barley was distilled into whiskey, the American whiskey tradition was born.

Barley and rye thrive in Dakota, Wisconsin, and Minnesota, as well as across the border in the Canadian prairies. Malted barley is the most expensive ingredient in making whiskey.

WHAT'S IN THE SILO?

Wheat, rye, and barley were all cultivated in Europe before being introduced into the US by pioneers from Europe. The settlers distilled surplus grain into alcohol, and so founded the US whiskey industry. Corn is the only indigenous grain used to produce American whiskey.

WHEAT
Although only a few bourbons use wheat, it can play a major role in the flavor profile. Wheat adds sweetness and mellowness to the palate.

RYE
This flavorsome and versatile grain is used in bourbons, as well as in American straight rye whiskey. It is also a flavor component of Canadian whiskey.

CORN
The principal grain in bourbon, corn makes the greatest contribution in terms of yield of alcohol and flavor. Some distillers produce corn whiskey.

BARLEY
Barley is the only grain used when producing Scottish malt whiskey. Many other styles of whiskey contain a proportion of malted barley.

GRAIN TOWER
Large amounts of grain are continually required at every distillery, making it essential to incorporate enough suitable storage in the layout of a distillery site—as here at Girvan.

GRAIN ELEVATOR
The striking and individual design of this Jack Daniel's grain elevator also reflects in architectural form the location and heritage of the distillery.

It can contribute depth and softness to whiskey, manifested as a cookie-like sweetness, with a malted, creamy, cereal note, and even a hint of cocoa. However, some distillers add malted barley primarily for its enzyme content, in amounts that may not be sufficient to influence the flavor.

The milling process produces three grades of malt: husks, grits (medium-ground), and flour (finely ground). Around 20 percent husks is usually considered the optimum amount for mashing. Their fibrous composition helps water drain through the mash tun, and is also important in helping achieve a good conversion rate of starch into sugars, which, in turn, determines the final alcohol level.

CORN

It was the American Indians who showed early settlers how to cultivate the native corn. Current regulations stipulate that bourbon producers must use corn, which contains a high level of starch as well as protein. Most of the industry's supply comes from Kentucky, Illinois, and Indiana.

Bourbon is distilled from between 51 and around 70 to 80 percent corn, with rye, wheat, and malted barley accounting for the balance. The range of grains creates a broad spectrum of flavors, since each grain contributes something different. The proportions of each grain used in a multigrain mashbill is therefore crucial in determining the eventual flavor of the whiskey.

Corn gives the highest yield of alcohol per ton and, by providing most of the starch in the mashbill, is also the key flavor contributor to bourbon. This includes a subtle sweetness and spiciness, and earthy and husk characters. Higher percentages of corn can restrict the range of flavors and, at worst, give a heavy, grainy greasiness. However, corn's influence diminishes the longer bourbon matures in the cask, and the wheat character becomes more prominent.

Other styles of American whiskey also use a combination of grains. Straight rye whiskey contains a minimum of 51 percent rye, while straight corn whiskey includes at least 80 percent corn, with the balance provided by malted barley and other grains.

Canadian whiskey is based on corn, in conjunction with rye and malted barley. Spirit distilled from individual grains may be blended prior to filling the casks for maturation. Another practice is to blend mature spirit that has been distilled from separate grains.

FLAVORS

Various factors contribute to the taste of a whiskey: the choice of grain; the choice of yeast and distillation regimen; the choice of casks; and the length of time it is aged.

SPICES
Corn can contribute a range of spicy flavors, which develop further during the aging process.

HONEY
Wheat brings a sweet, honeyed taste to bourbon, balancing more pronounced flavors from other grains.

DRIED FRUIT
Rye is prized as a source of dried-fruit flavors, which add to the range and complexity of a bourbon.

COOKIES
Malty cookie flavors stem from malted barley, taking you straight back to the original ingredient.

THE GRIST MILL

A four-roller mill grinds the malted barley to grist in preparation for the next step in the process—mashing. The mill seen here is at Glenturret distillery.

MASHING AND COOKING

JÜRGEN DEIBEL

UNLOCKING THE NATURAL SUGARS IN THE GRAIN IS THE KEY TO SUCCESSFUL FERMENTATION.

Mashing is the process that extracts soluble sugars from the malted grain. Malted barley is the grain of choice in Scotland for producing malt whiskey, and it is present to a greater or lesser degree in almost all of the world's whiskeys because of its enzyme content. The enzymes convert the starch to sugar, first when malted, and then when mixed ("mashed") with water.

PREPARING THE MALTED GRAIN

Malt grains are crushed in a mill to open them up and make sugar extraction possible. The crushed grain is then known as grist. This is mixed with warm water and fed into a mashing vessel—a tun—and the conversion to sugar takes place of its own accord. The typical mash tun is a circular metal vessel containing stirrers on a revolving arm that mix the grist and water. In a modern lauter, or semi-lauter (taking its name from a German technique used in beer-brewing) mash tun, rotating knives or blades churn the mash. The mash tun has a slotted base, which is opened to drain off the liquid (wort) while retaining the grain residue.

THE MASH PROCESS

Depending on the malt and equipment used, some distillers in Scotland operate a three-water mashing system, while others opt for four-water mashing.

THE COPPER COVER OF A MASH TUN

A central post rotates the rakes inside the tun. The hatch on the right opens to allow the mashman to check progress.

TRADITIONAL RAKES
Once the grist and hot water have been added to the mash tun, the rakes turn the mixture to help extract the sugars.

A BREAK WITH TRADITION
Not all mash tuns have copper covers. This example, in gleaming stainless steel, is at the modern Yamazaki distillery in northern Japan.

A STIRRING SIGHT
The more recently designed mash tuns, like this one at Caol Ila on Islay, are more efficient and much easier to control.

The first water usually comes in at a temperature of 147°F (64°C), is mixed with the grist, and then allowed to rest. The weight of water used in this first mashing is about four times the weight of grist, although grist-to-water ratios vary between distilleries.

After about 30 minutes, the water is drained off and reserved, and the grist left behind is treated with a second, hotter infusion of water, this time at around 158–167°F (70–75°C). About half the original quantity of water is used, but no further grist is added. The wort is allowed to rest again, while more sugar dissolves out. The second water is then drained, combined with the first water, and collected in a worts receiver.

The grains left in the mash tun still contain a small amount of sugar residue. This is too valuable to waste, and a third water—the same quantity as was used for the first—is added. This third water is almost at boiling point. However, because the sugar content is much lower than when the first two waters were added, the resulting liquid is not transferred to the worts receiver, but cooled to the temperature of the first water, and used to start off the next mash cycle.

The water collected in the worts receiver is cooled and transferred to the washbacks for fermentation. The grains left in the mash tun are removed, and sold to either dairy farmers or industrial plants to be converted into cattle feed.

UNMALTED GRAINS NEED TO BE COOKED THOROUGHLY BEFORE MASHING

COOKING GRAIN

A different process is used in the production of most grain whiskeys, and in all the classic North American styles. Unmalted grains, especially corn, need to be cooked thoroughly before mashing. This cooking breaks down the cellulose walls of the grain, so that the starch is able to absorb water. The starch gelatinizes, which enables the enzymes present in the grain to convert the starch to sugar.

In some distilleries, the corn mash is fed into cooking vessels in a continuous process. In others, a vessel similar to a domestic pressure cooker is used. An alternative method is to use an open tub, in which the peak temperature will be lower. Grain can be cooked by heating the vessel itself, or by introducing live steam. Some distillers believe that a quick, steam-scalding method is less likely to overcook or scorch the grain. This method, however, is slightly less efficient in extracting fermentable sugars, but has the advantage that it avoids extracting some of the undesirable flavor compounds.

Once the corn is cooked, rye may be added as a seasoning, lending a slight dark-bread flavor. Rye is most often used to season various classic American whiskeys. Finally, a small amount of barley malt is always added, for its enzyme action. The temperature of the mash is reduced with each addition, and each cereal has its own preferred mashing temperature.

HIGHLIGHT

UNDER PRESSURE

As barley starts to germinate, starch is converted into soluble sugars with the help of naturally occurring enzymes. However, cereals such as corn have to be cooked prior to mashing, since their sugars are not as easy to extract. For this, a combination of a high temperature and pressure cooking helps speed the process along. Their sugar content, which derives from starch, is made accessible by cooking the grains in large industrial pressure cookers, like the one shown here at the Woodford Reserve distillery in the US.

BREWER'S YEAST

One of the strains of Saccharomyces cerevisiae, *brewer's yeast is believed to produce a flavorful aroma in whiskey after fermentation and distillation.*

YEAST AND FERMENTATION

JÜRGEN DEIBEL

WHISKEY DISTILLERS NOWADAYS SELECT THEIR STRAIN OF YEAST, AWARE OF THE EFFECT IT WILL HAVE ON FLAVOR.

The fermentation process in whiskey-making is similar to that for many other alcoholic drinks. Alcohol is converted from sugar with the help of yeast, resulting in strengths varying from 7.5 to 10 percent. The role of yeast goes beyond alcohol conversion, however. It is now widely believed that the choice of yeast strain makes a significant contribution to the aromas, flavors, and complexity of whiskey, just as it does in all other alcoholic drinks.

Until recently, most whiskey distillers dismissed this notion. Their argument was that any aromas or flavors created by the yeast in fermentation would be lost during distillation. However, that would be true only if they were distilling to the point of neutral alcohol.

YEAST IS THE ONLY ORGANISM ALLOWED IN WHISKEY-MAKING

YEAST STRAINS

Emil Christian Hansen (1842–1909), a Danish fermentation physiologist who worked at the laboratories of the Carlsberg brewery in Copenhagen, made the breakthrough discovery that yeasts were composed of different kinds of fungi, and that specific cultures could be created.

Although malt and other cereals do contain natural wild yeasts, high-performance cultured yeast is added to initiate the fermentation process. Adding cultured yeast is known as "pitching the wort." Strains now tend to be selected to provide the particular composition and flavor characteristics desired in the distillate: especially affected is the ester content.

Specialist yeast suppliers are able to match the amount of flavor and alcohol produced by certain strains. In most American distilleries, yeasts are precultivated on site in vessels called dona tubs and added to the washtubs 24 hours later.

FERMENTATION VESSELS

In small-scale production, fermenters (or washbacks) are closed vessels, traditionally made of wood (Oregon pine or larch). The capacity can vary from

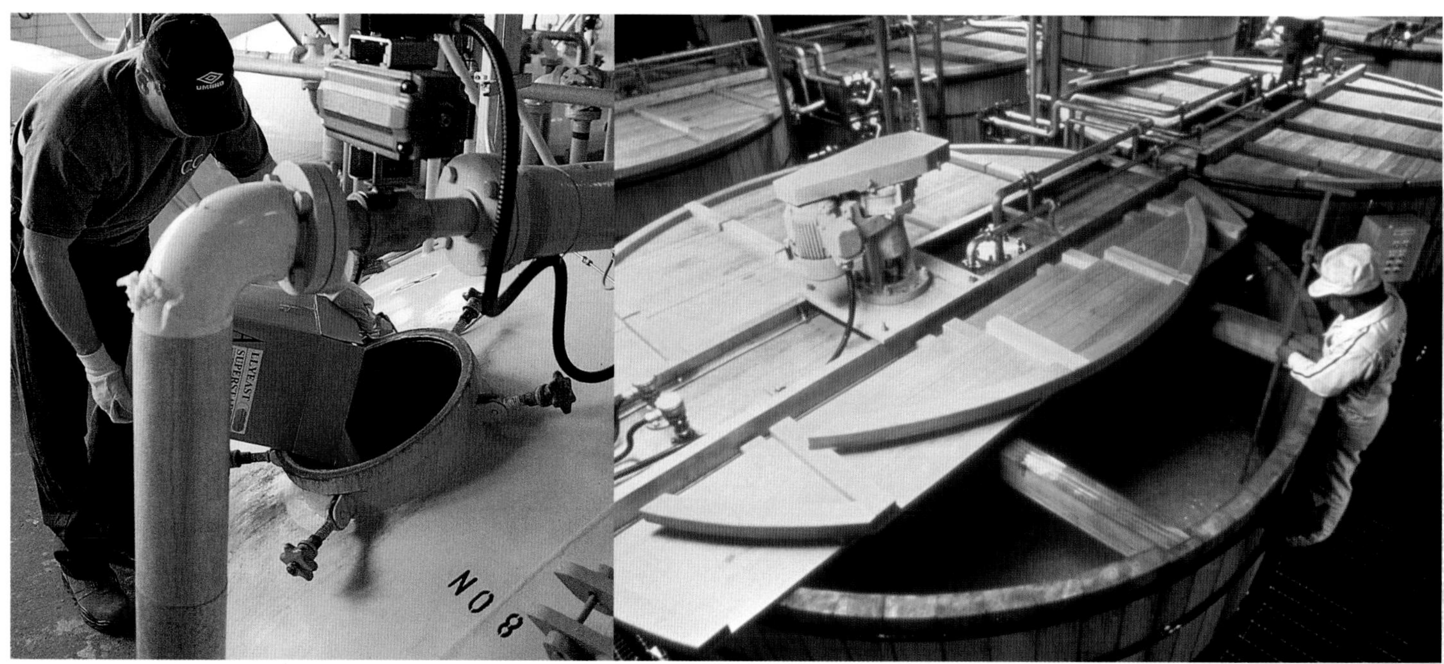

PITCHING THE WORT

Yeast is added to a fermentation vessel. Closed vessels like this one help guard against microbiological spoilage during fermentation.

JAPANESE WOODEN WASHBACKS

In small-scale production, wooden fermentation vessels are still widely used, and are often made of pine or larch. Here, the brewer at Yamazaki controls the ongoing fermentation process.

PREPARING THE YEAST
Many American distilleries cultivate their own yeast strains. Some use one yeast; others feel that they require several. This freshly prepared liquid yeast solution will be added to the mash.

5,300 to 26,000 gallons (20,000 to 100,000 liters). Large-scale production generally uses stainless-steel fermenters. Large fermenters can have a capacity of up to 66,000 gallons (250,000 liters), and are used mainly in grain whiskey production.

A typical washback in Scotland or Ireland will run for about 40 to 50 hours; when set over the weekend, the time may extend to 100 hours. If the fermentation period is too short, the aroma and alcohol are not fully produced; if the fermentation period is too long, there is a danger of bacterial growth (mainly *Lactobacillus*), which would reduce the amount of alcohol generated, and could harm the final flavor. Lactobacilli produce acids that, in turn, produce lactic and acetic acids. It is, of course, of paramount importance that all vessels used in the mashing and fermentation processes are kept clean and free from bacteria.

CONGENERS

In addition to producing alcohol, fermentation and mashing form other substances. These are referred to as secondary constituents, or congeners, in spirit or whiskey. While the quantities are small, they have a marked effect on the taste, character, and quality of the spirit. Congeners fall into four categories: acids, aldehydes, esters, and higher alcohols, and all play an important role in the character of the spirit produced. An excessive amount of aldehydes would lend an unpleasant smell to the spirit, and would also spoil the flavor. Generally speaking, higher alcohols and acids provide what is termed "body" in the spirit, while some esters tend to be aromatic, sometimes lending, for example, floral notes to a whiskey.

HIGHLIGHT

SOUR MASH

Perfected by Dr. Crow in 1823, sour mash is used in many North American distilleries to produce straight American whiskey. The unfiltered, fermented distiller's beer is distilled, and some of the residue from the still, called stillage or backset, is passed back to the fermenter. The exact amount varies from one distillery to another. The backset is used to keep the mash at a particular level of acidity or "sourness" to maintain spirit quality.

OPEN TO THE AIR
These wooden washbacks are at the Woodford Reserve distillery in Kentucky. The fermentation is already well under way; carbon dioxide produced by the process is vented to the atmosphere.

MAKING BEER
The first references to alcohol are from ancient Egypt. This terra-cotta statue—made in about 2400 BC—shows a young Egyptian servant preparing fermented barley for beer-making.

POT STILLS

JÜRGEN DEIBEL

ONCE JUST SMALL CLAY POTS, POT STILLS ARE NOW GLEAMING COPPER CONSTRUCTIONS, ALMOST SCULPTURAL INSTALLATIONS.

Distillation is the boiling of the fermented wort, known in Scotland and Ireland as "wash" and in the United States as "distiller's beer." Distilling works by applying heat to this mixture. Alcohol will boil at a lower temperature than water (173.2°F/78.4°C) and is driven off as vapor, leaving the water behind. The alcohol vapors are collected and cooled, which converts them back into liquid form as spirit.

Distillation is an ancient art, practiced by the Egyptians perhaps as early as 3000 BC. However, they made alcohol not to drink, but to use in perfumes and medicines. The pot used was usually made of clay, and guided the rising vapors to an air-cooled chamber at the end of the vessel.

> THE POT STILL IS THE TRADITIONAL METHOD OF DISTILLING MALT WHISKEY

THE POT STILL

In the production of malt whiskeys, the distiller's beer is distilled twice or, sometimes, three times. Of the methods currently in use, the pot still is the most traditional. The basic design of the pot still, probably first developed by the Dutch in the late 16th century, has changed little over the centuries. It is a circular pot or kettle made of copper, which is heated from below. Copper is ideal because it is a good conductor of heat and can be easily shaped; it also reacts chemically with the spirit, removing unwanted sulfur compounds. A pot still consists of three distinct parts: the pot (where the fermented wort is heated); the swan neck and the lyne arm, or lye pipe (along which the evaporated alcohol travels); and the condenser—either a worm tub or a shell-and-tube construction (where the alcohol vapor cools and condenses back into a liquid). Variations in the sizes and shapes of the component parts of a still affect the final flavor of the spirit in different ways. When a still reaches the end of its working life and has to be replaced, every effort is made to replicate the construction of the old one.

LABOR-INTENSIVE

Pot-still distillation is a fairly inefficient process, involving several steps that must be carried out under the watchful eye of the stillman. First, the still is filled with the fermented wort; it is then heated up, and the usable alcohol separated from the undesirable alcohol. After the separation, the pot is allowed to cool down before it is cleaned and any residues inside the still removed.

In the early days of large-scale distilling, direct firing with coal and, later, gas was used to heat the stills from underneath. Today, this system is found in only a few distilleries in Scotland (for example, Glenfiddich, Glenfarclas, and Glendronach). Instead, most distilleries use steam. Steam was introduced as early as 1885 at the Scapa distillery on Orkney, but came into widespread use only during the

HEATING COILS
Steam flows through coils at the bottom of the still, thereby guaranteeing an even distribution of heat.

HEATING POTS
Another way of heating distiller's beer is to use steam pots, as at this Suntory-owned distillery in Japan. The advantage of this method is that the pots provide a greater surface area.

WIDE-BODIED STILLS
These impressive stills are at Glenkinchie, one of the few remaining Scottish Lowland distilleries. The large size of the stills and the width of the necks are all part of the reason for the quality of this distillery's whiskey.

№ 1
LOW WINES
STILL
CONTENTS
20.998
LITRES
№ 1
WASH STILL
CONTENTS
30.963
LITRES

Sight Glass

A sight glass and security valve are placed three-quarters of the way up the neck of a pot still at Glen Grant distillery. This small window enables the stillman to monitor the distilling process.

A TYPICAL POT STILL

The heart of every distillery is the pot still. Made of copper, the shape and size will be unique to each distillery. After boiling in the pot, vapors travel up the neck and along the lyne pipe to a condenser. Nowadays, steam is used for heating. In Scotland, double distillation is carried out in most distilleries in a set of two stills, consisting of one wash and one spirit—or low wine—still. The latter are usually smaller in size. Irish whiskey is triple distilled in three stills.

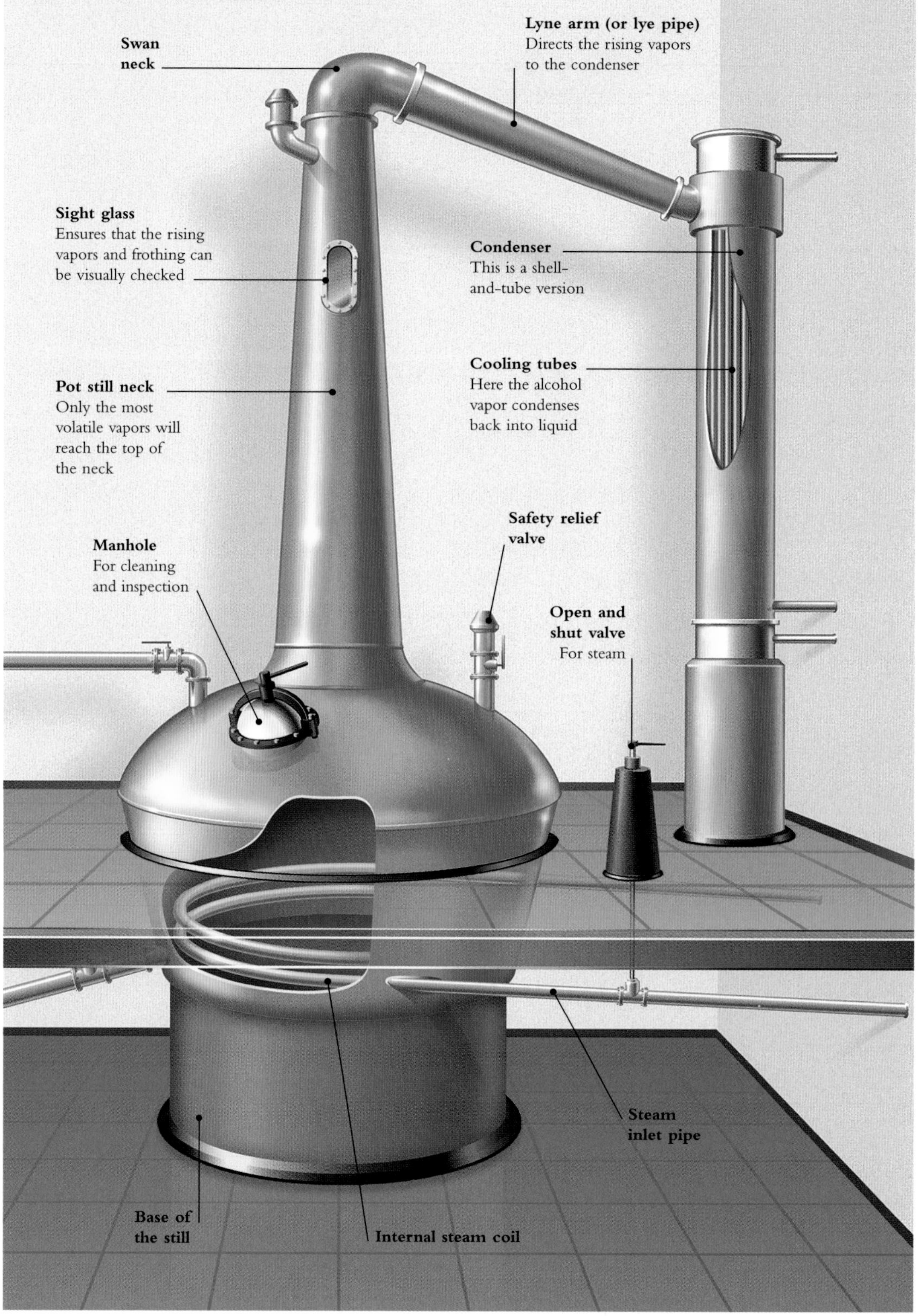

Swan neck

Lyne arm (or lye pipe)
Directs the rising vapors to the condenser

Sight glass
Ensures that the rising vapors and frothing can be visually checked

Condenser
This is a shell-and-tube version

Cooling tubes
Here the alcohol vapor condenses back into liquid

Pot still neck
Only the most volatile vapors will reach the top of the neck

Safety relief valve

Manhole
For cleaning and inspection

Open and shut valve
For steam

Steam inlet pipe

Base of the still

Internal steam coil

Manhole Cover

Although this inspection hatch is on a pot still at the Woodford Reserve distillery in the US, it was made by skilled coppersmiths in Scotland, where many of the classic stills were designed.

1960s. Steam-filled coils, or a small circular radiator, sit in the base of the pot still, heating it. The advantage of such devices is that they ensure a much more even distribution of heat.

DOUBLE DISTILLATION

Today, malt whiskey is produced by the double distillation method, for which two stills are required. The first distillation is carried out in the wash still and the second in the spirit (or low wines) still. The wash still is used to separate alcohol from water and the spirit still is used to separate out the drinkable alcohol from the unwanted alcohol with its undesirable flavors. The wash still produces a distillate called low wines, and the spirit still produces a distillate comprising foreshots (unwanted flavors and methanol), spirits (which later become whiskey), and feints (impure spirits). The whole process takes several hours, and its timing is determined by the mashing and fermenting cycles in the distillery.

The size of a pot still varies according to its intended use: if it is the first still—the wash still—it will almost always be bigger than the low wines or spirits still.

THE WASH STILL

The wash still is filled with preheated fermented wort until the pot is almost three-quarters full. As it is heated further, vapors are driven off from the liquid and rise up the neck of the still. The wort tends to froth at this stage. As soon as the froth reaches the upper part of the neck, the heat is turned down, the frothing virtually stops, and only vapors enter the lyne arm. The vapors now move slowly toward the condenser, where they are cooled and converted back into liquid form.

The low wines generated by the wash still are collected in a receiver (the low wines, or low wines and feints, receiver), and then passed through the spirit safe, made of glass and either brass or copper. The spirit safe is the control point for the distilling operation. Here, samples of the running distillate can be drawn off remotely and tested for strength by means of a hydrometer located inside the safe.

THE SPIRIT STILL

After the first distillation, the alcohol content of the liquid has risen from around 7.5–9.0 vol. to 21–28 vol. The second distillation separates out the undrinkable alcohol—the foreshots and feints. Foreshots contain residue of the previous still run and also the more volatile and toxic methanol. The stillman usually knows to separate the foreshots early (after between 5 and 45 minutes). Their presence is detected by adding water. If the liquid turns cloudy, foreshots are coming off the still; if the liquid remains clear, they have passed.

The drinkable spirit is then run slowly through the spirit safe to the spirit receiver. This clear liquid, with an average alcoholic strength of 70 vol., is then transferred from the spirit receiver to the cask for maturation. Sometimes referred to as "the heart of the distillation," the usable spirit can represent less than 20 percent of the complete still run, and is usually no more than 20 or 30 percent of it.

THE STILLMAN'S CRAFT

Now the heat is turned up again and the feints are run through. They contain fusel oils, which would give the spirit undesirable leather or tobacco flavors if left in. Together with the foreshots, they are collected in a separate receiver and redistilled in the next spirit run.

None of these liquids—foreshots, spirit, and feints—can be accessed directly by the stillman as they flow through the spirit-safe, so he must judge the right moment to separate them, based to a large extent on his knowledge and experience. Even

HIGHLIGHT

PURIFIER

Some distilleries like to install purifiers as an attachment to the lyne arm (this one is at Glen Grant, in Scotland). Their function is to allow only the most volatile of the alcohol vapors to pass, and to trap and recycle the other vapor compounds. The less volatile compounds condense into liquid form, and are led back into the pot still via a small pipe to be redistilled. Purifiers have the effect of lightening the style of the distillery's whiskey.

SHELL-AND-TUBE CONDENSER
This modern heat-exchange system cools and condenses the spirit vapors as they are given off by the still. Water flows through pipes inside the vertical casing, and cools the vapors in the surrounding area of the shell.

TRADITIONAL WORM TUB
A coil of copper pipe (the worm) is immersed in a wooden tub filled with cold water, usually outside the distillery. The vapor is cooled as it works its way along the tube.

SPIRIT PIPES
The spirits that flow through the pipes can be identified by labeling, as here at the Lagavulin distillery on Islay, or by color-coding.

though computerization has come to the whiskey industry, as it has almost everywhere else, the decision as to which part of the run will finally become whiskey is mainly dependent on the skill of the stillman.

THE REFLUX

When vapors rising up from the pot to the neck condense back into liquid before they get the chance to escape down the lyne arm, they drain back into the pot and are heated all over again. This process is known as the "reflux." As the liquid runs back, it strips out the less volatile elements of the ascending vapors and allows only the more volatile and lighter aroma compounds to pass through to the condenser. The longer or wider the neck above the still, the greater likelihood there is of this happening.

A slow rate of distillation is essential to initiate the reflux. The same effect can be achieved by using a wider neck, or a boil ball (a bulge shape) between the pot and the neck of the still, or a lantern-shape neck, tapering at the very top.

THE PURIFIER

In some Scottish distilleries (for example, Ardbeg, and Glen Grant—*see p. 61*) there is also a water-cooled purifier box in the lyne arm. Vapors rising up the neck and into this box are guided through a set of baffles. This slows down the vapor stream and cools it, with the result that only the most volatile and purest compounds reach the condensers. The liquid trapped by the purifier box is drained back via a small pipe and redistilled.

COOLING SYSTEMS

There are two main systems commonly used to cool and condense the alcohol vapors that come off the still. One uses worm tubs (so called because of the spiral shape of the coil immersed in a tub of cold water), and the other uses modern shell-and-tube condensers (a bundle of tubes arranged in a vertical casing). Both are made of copper.

Worm tubs are said to produce a heavier spirit, although this also depends on the distilling regimen and other factors, such as purifiers and heating methods. Shell-and-tube condensers cool vapors down more rapidly and expose them to a greater surface area of copper. This tends to produce a lighter and more fragrant spirit.

LOMOND STILLS

The Lomond still was developed in Scotland in 1955 by Alistair Cunningham, in collaboration with Arthur Warren. Cunningham was a chemical engineer working for Hiram Walker, the Canadian company that at the time owned a large number of Scottish distilleries, and Warren was the company's draftsman. Cunningham's brief was to find a way to increase the variety in the company's whiskeys. His solution was a cylindrical still with a water jacket mounted vertically above it. Within the still neck

SPIRIT RECEIVER
The clear, drinkable spirit, from the second distillation, is collected in this wooden container. Sealed by Customs and Excise, it holds what is later to become whiskey.

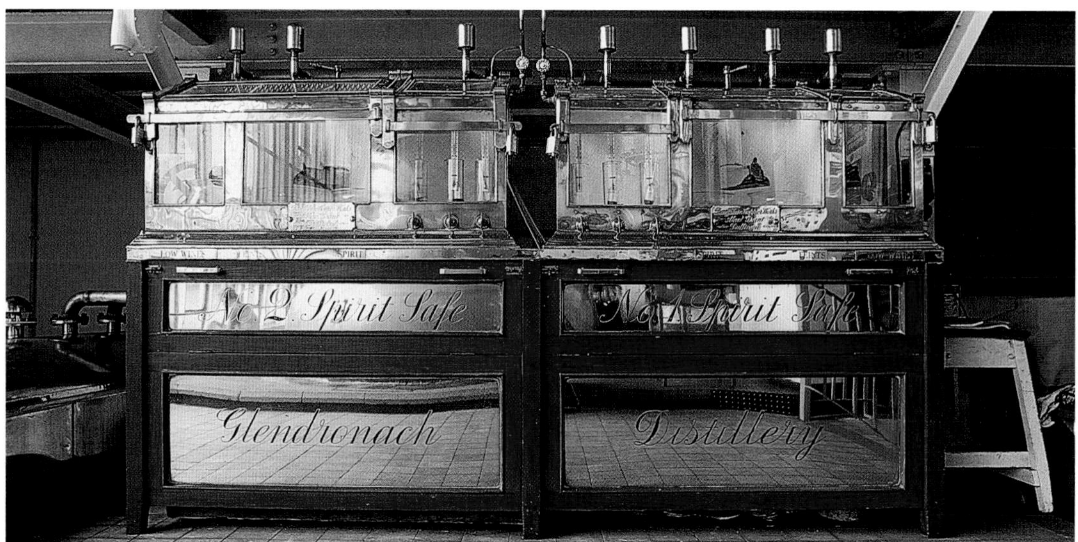

PADLOCKED SPIRIT SAFE
None of the liquids can be accessed directly by the stillman. During the second distillation, he is able remotely to separate the drinkable spirit from the foreshots and feints. He adds water to a sample of the spirit as it flows through the safe. If the spirit turns cloudy, it still contains foreshots or feints. However, not all of these elements are necessarily undesirable, and some stillmen will retain a small proportion of these in order to add interest and character to the end product.

SHAPELY NECKS

Pot stills are designed in a number of ways, depending on the style of whiskey required. Consequently, they look different at every distillery, and even similar ones will have slight variations. Generally, pot stills with long, tall necks produce lighter and more fragrant spirits, while those with short, wide necks produce oilier and heavier spirits. To slow down the distillation process, and prevent the froth from boiling over into the condenser, several refinements have been developed; these include the wide neck, the lantern neck, and the boiling ball, illustrated below.

WIDE NECK
The wide neck on this still at Lochnagar rises from the shoulders of the pot. It reduces the speed of the rising vapors, as well as cooling the distiller's beer to prevent the froth from boiling over.

LANTERN NECK
The lantern stills at the Jura distillery are very large, but their small necks restrict the vapors before they enter the wider space above: here they cool and slow down, and only the most volatile rise to the top.

BOIL, OR BOILING, BALL
This ball neck at Old Pulteney has the same effect as a lantern still. The ball stops liquid from boiling over, and any froth is broken down. Once again, only the most volatile vapors reach the neck.

were three rectifying plates that could be adjusted horizontally and vertically, and water-cooled or left to dry to vary the degree of reflux. The angle of the lyne arm could also be changed to allow for even greater control of the reflux. It resembled the Coffey still (*see p. 64*), developed for distilling Irish grain whiskey. However, the plates often became clogged with residue, and the still fell out of favor in Scotland.

TRIPLE DISTILLATION

Adding a third distillation stage delivers an end product that is generally higher in alcohol (around 80 vol.) than at the end of a double distillation. Only a few distilleries in Scotland use this technique. However, in Ireland, triple distillation is the most common method of making whiskey, and there is one US distillery (Labrot & Graham's Woodford Reserve distillery) that uses it. Triple distillation extends the flavor spectrum and gives a lighter, more fragrant, fruity, floral, and spicy character to the whiskey.

THE STILLMAN
The stillman at Bruichladdich distillery closes the manhole of a pot still. When opened after distillation, the manhole enables the stillman to inspect and clean the pot.

HIGHLIGHT

AENEAS COFFEY

Born in Dublin in 1780, Aeneas Coffey worked for many years as an exciseman in Ireland. After the Distilling Act of 1779, resentment against the Excise grew as unpopular taxes were introduced. The inspectors also met with strong resistance from the illegal still owners who faced severe penalties. Having endured many violent clashes, Coffey eventually decided to resign and became a distiller himself: he developed the first continuous still at his Dock distillery in Dublin. Coffey's super-efficient invention was patented in 1830, and was eventually used for making spirits worldwide.

COLUMN STILLS

JÜRGEN DEIBEL

COLUMN STILLS ARE FASTER, MORE VERSATILE, AND LESS DISCRIMINATING ABOUT THEIR DIET THAN POT STILLS.

For years, a way was sought to improve on the time-consuming and labor-intensive methods of pot-still distillation. By 1830, a more efficient continuous distillation process, also known as patent or column distillation, was developed, principally by Robert Stein and Aeneas Coffey to distill grain. This still is sometimes referred to as the Coffey still. With this method, it became possible to run a still continuously, producing a spirit that was high in alcohol and light in style.

The core ingredient for continuous distillation is a grain mash. Imported corn was used for many years, but since the early 1980s, Scotland and Ireland have tended to use wheat. In the US, bourbon has a mashbill, or recipe, mainly composed of corn, while rye is the principal grain in rye whiskey.

THEY CAN MAKE FLAVOR-PACKED BOURBON, GRAIN WHISKEY... OR NEUTRAL VODKA

MULTIPLE STILLS

The number of column stills used in a distillation depends on the degree of purification (technically known as rectification) required. Anything from one or two stills to as many as five can be grouped together and run continuously. As with the pot still, the aim is to drive off the unwanted, unpleasant flavors, while concentrating the desirable ones. The tall, columnar stills are made of stainless steel with copper plates inside. These plates, or trays, are perforated, like sieves, allowing liquid to trickle back down against the rising vapors. Each plate can be thought of as a mini-distillation stage, allowing the more volatile compounds to pass, while holding back the heavier compounds, so that at the top of the column, only the most volatile compounds escape into the second distillation.

Hot steam enters at the bottom of the first column still and flows up against the fermented mash coming in at the top. An exchange of compounds takes place, and the heavy compounds run out at the bottom of the still, while the volatile compounds leave the top of the still in the form of vapor.

In the second distillation in a multiple-column setting, as practiced in Ireland and Scotland, the vapors are cooled as they rise up the column from plate to plate. At a given height in the second still, drinkable alcohol vapors (ethanol) revert to liquid. This is drawn off at that point for further processing.

ECLECTIC DISTILLERY
Ireland's small independent Cooley distillery, situated near Riverstown, uses a combination of pot and column stills to produce its whiskey. In the past, the columns had been used to make vodka.

MULTISTORY STILLS IN KENTUCKY
Column stills can be several floors high. Here, a segment passes between floors at the family-owned Heaven Hill distillery in Kentucky, which is known for its fine bourbon.

PRODUCT
BEER STILL NO.2
SERIAL NO. 422

A Close-Up View

A detail of the column still at Four Roses distillery. This well-maintained distillery, which is located on the banks of the Salt River, is arguably the most beautiful in Kentucky.

THUMPERS AND DOUBLERS

In an American distillery, the first column is called the beer still, and the second distillation is usually carried out in a thumper or doubler, which is usually pot-still shaped. A doubler acts like a pot still: the liquefied vapors drawn from the beer still are redistilled to create the final product. The alcoholic content rises slightly in a doubler, to 65–69 vol., and the resulting spirit is called doublings, or high wines.

A thumper differs from a doubler in that it has hot water in the bottom, through which vapors from the beer still pass for further purification. When these vapors come in contact with the hot water, there is often a thumping sound, hence the name. Today, thumpers are used in only two US distilleries: Early Times and Bernheim.

EFFICIENT AND VERSATILE

A column still is highly efficient, and can be used to provide new make for flavor-packed bourbon, grain whiskey, vodka, and neutral alcohol. The alcohol level achieved from this form of distillation can be as high as 94.8 vol. for grain whiskey. The end result of this highly efficient process is a product that is very different from the whiskey produced by a pot still.

However, although it may sound easier to run a continuous distillation, getting the balance right between the steam, the fermented distiller's beer, and the resulting alcohol is a precise business, relying as ever on the skill of the stillman.

AN INFLUENTIAL INVENTION

Continuous distillation stimulated two important developments: the use of cereals other than malted barley in the making of whiskey; and the blending of the milder-flavored grain whiskeys produced by column stills with the more complex-flavored malt whiskeys from pot stills.

The main sites at which grain whiskey is produced in Scotland are Cameronbridge, Girvan, Invergordon, North British, Port Dundas, Dumbarton, and Strathclyde.

The Doubler

This is the second distillation unit at the Buffalo Trace distillery in Kentucky, which produces doublings, or high wines. Although it is not nearly as attractive as a pot still, it is similar in its workings.

Two Types of Still

The distillery at Loch Lomond offers a clear comparison of a traditional pot still (background) and a rarely seen Lomond-type still in the foreground. Scapa distillery on Orkney also runs a Lomond-type still.

Inspection Hatches

The inspection hatches, seen here on the column still at the Cooley distillery in Ireland, can be opened so that the copper plates can be easily adjusted. Each perforated tray allows the more volatile compounds to rise.

A TYPICAL COLUMN STILL

THE FERMENTED distiller's beer comes in at the top of the rectifier (right), where it is warmed by the heat of the rising vapor. Once heated, it enters the top of the analyzer. As it descends, the steam extracts the alcohol and aromas and takes them to the bottom of the rectifier. It starts to rise, and gradually cools. When it is almost at the top, the desired quality and grade of alcohol is extracted for further processing.

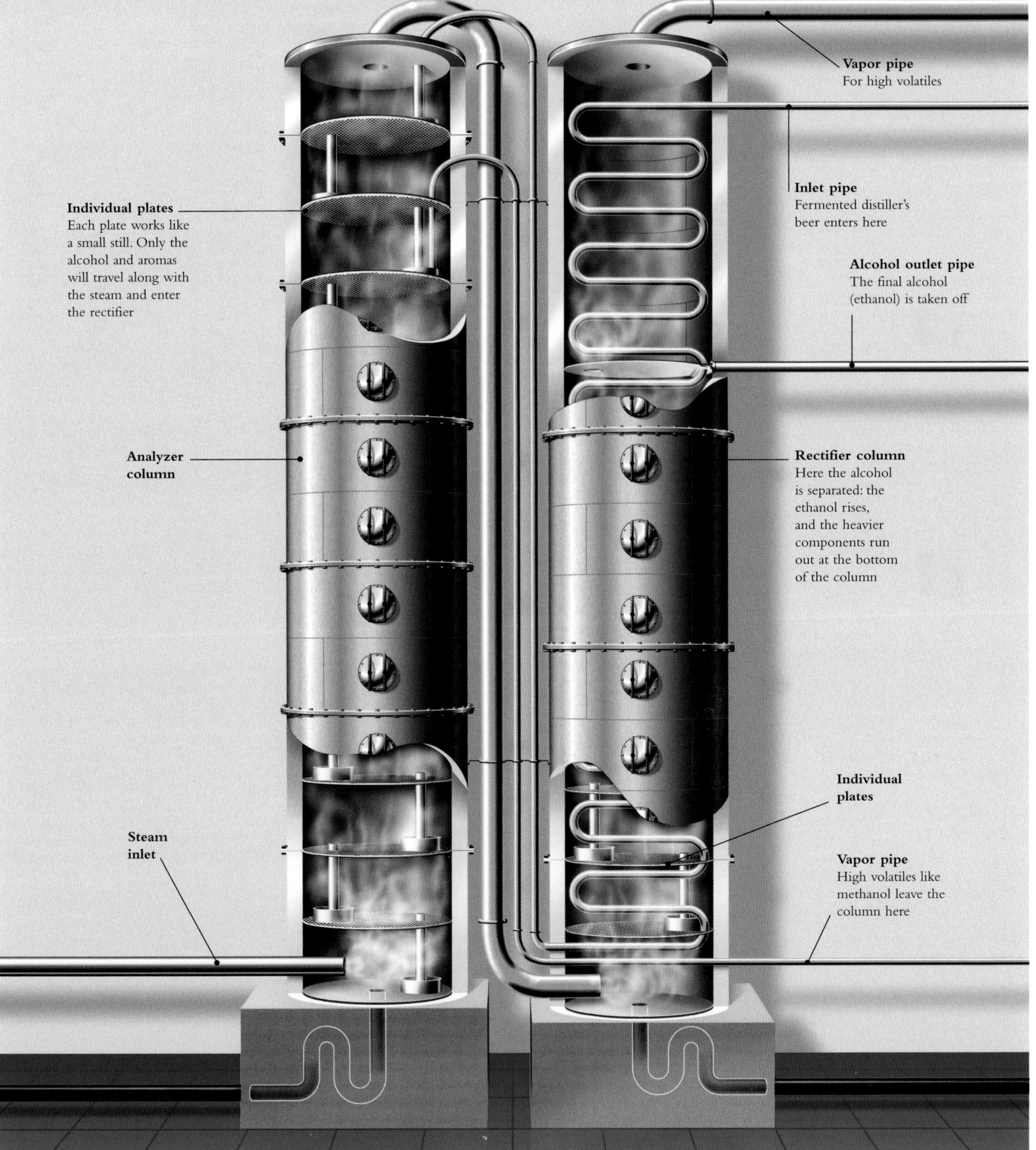

The Influence of Wood: European Oak

Michael Jackson

GREAT WINEMAKERS OF FRANCE FAVOR LIMOUSIN OAK BARRELS. WHISKEY DISTILLERS LOOK FARTHER SOUTH, TO SPAIN.

How long did it take for the aromas and flavors in your whiskey to develop? The age on the label, whether 8 years or 18, tells only part of the story; it has spent time in an oak cask.

During those years, flavors of the wood itself were being taken up, along with reminders of its previous contents; and reactions were taking place between vanillin from the oak and traces of copper from the stills. The results were also influenced by the variety of oak from which that vessel was constructed. The age of the tree—ideally about 100 years—is yet another consideration. It took the industry almost as long to appreciate this.

Now, Scottish distillers are spotted far from home, sometimes in Europe, sometimes in the United States, hunting not for barley but for wood for their casks.

THE AGE ON THE LABEL TELLS ONLY PART OF THE STORY

A nimble nose might be able to deconstruct a great single malt by pinpointing the region where the barley was harvested; the valley whence the water flowed; and the slope where the oak was felled.

BIRTH OF A TRADITION

The British sherry trade with Spain is centuries old. In the cask, sherry was landed at the ports of Bristol (England) and Leith (Scotland) and bottled there by merchants. The empty casks were purchased by Scottish distillers and transported to the north. Some of the most delicious whiskeys tasted even more wonderful after they had matured in a sherry butt.

When Macallan decided, in the late 1960s, to offer their whiskey as a single malt, their warehouses contained butts from a great diversity of sherry styles, all being used to mature whiskey for inclusion in various blends. They had to decide what style of sherry cask they wanted for their single malt, and to lay down sufficient stock to ensure an adequate volume of consistent product in 10 or 12 years.

From Tree to Cask

The oak trees are cut down only when they are mature. At that point, they are typically 20–25 feet (6–7.5 m) tall and about 3 feet (1 m) in diameter. The tree trunks are sawn into manageable lengths, ready for trucking to a sawmill in Lugo, in the Spanish province of Cantabria.

On Its Way to a Barrel

A wedge is cut into the tree until the trunk is almost severed. The coup de grâce *is administered with a power saw—or sometimes just a kick. The lumberjacks work in teams of two.*

Assembly Line

The logs are cut into quarters, like huge lengthwise wedges of cheese. They are then sliced into planks, from which the staves are cut.

HIGHLIGHT

COMPARING STAVES

The reddish Spanish *Quercus robur* (stave below right) is more knotted, producing somewhat twisty staves. The whiter American oak, *Quercus alba,* (stave below left) yields straighter staves, is finer-grained, and is slower to mature the whiskey. Higher tannin levels in the Spanish oak contribute to the flavor and fragrance of Macallan, lending nutty, apple, apricot, and nutmeg qualities. American oak produces vanilla, creamy, coconut, banana notes.

After extensive tasting, Macallan favored butts that had contained dry oloroso sherry for a maturation period of approximately two years. Dry oloroso sherry seemed to impart raisin, apricot, and Seville orange flavors.

THE CASK SHORTAGE

The second half of the 20th century sherry presented distillers with two new problems: sales of sherry in Great Britain had diminished, and Spanish trade unions lobbied successfully for the bottling of Spanish wines to be carried out locally.

One solution, albeit expensive, was pursued by several distillers, most famously Macallan. They began to have casks made in Spain, and lent them to sherry bodegas for a couple of years' seasoning with sherry.

The problem was solved for a decade or so, until the sherry bodegas turned against their own oak, concerned by the continuing fall in the sales of sherry. Their response was to modernize sherry by making the drink lighter in body. To achieve this, they began in the 1980s to discard European oak in favor of the less assertive American version. Soon after this, however, Macallan came to a surprising conclusion: that the sherry was less influential than the wood.

Macallan decided to travel farther back down the supply chain, and now went to the wood-yards and the forest. "We may eventually have to go back to the acorn," said David Robertson, the distillery manager at that time. "We need to understand the whole relationship: whiskey, sherry, and oak."

There are many varieties of oak; the one Macallan has been using, *Quercus robur*, comes from Cantabria, in the northwest of Spain. Most of Spain's *Quercus robur* grows in this region, and, although the area also supplies timber for construction and furniture, much of the output is for the Scotch whiskey industry.

> "WE MAY HAVE TO GO BACK TO THE ACORN"

Inland from the town of Santander, the roads climb around rocky outcrops and boulder-strewn mounds that form valleys big enough to accommodate a narrow belt of steep woodland. These woods are typically about 250 acres (a couple of hundred hectares) each. The land soon rises into a small mountain range called the Picos d'Europa, snow-capped in winter. Almost, but not quite, reminiscent of the Scottish destination of the barrels to be made from the oaks in the foothills.

HOOP DREAMS
Metal hoops are used to hold the staves in place during the assembling of the casks, and to secure the finished product. No screws, nails, or glues… no metallic flavors in the spirit. The cask is a designer's dream.

THE COOPER
Even with precision machinery, the cooper is a craftsman who has to use traditional skills to create 21st-century versions of one of the oldest forms of container. He must plane the staves so that they fit without leaking; form the correct, elegant, shape; and ensure that casks have the appropriate capacity.

A NATURAL BEAUTY
Sometimes the ends of casks are painted as a form of color-coding, but most are not. Unpainted oak can breathe, which lets its contents interact with the surrounding air—and it has the beauty of natural wood. A touch of sanding—being carried out here—heightens that quality, making the barrel attractive to look at as well as easier to handle. A whole warehouse full of sherry butts looks even better.

Hot Drink?

Sudden bursts of roaring flame, dragon-worthy hisses of scalding steam, and screams as shrill as steel... a cooperage can seem the work of Dante. Fire is used to bend the oak. Surely that also led to the ritual of deliberate charring (as practiced by Bourbon distillers to help the spirit penetrate the oak).

Hole in the Corner

After all the effort that has been expended to keep the spirit in the cask, arrangements must also be made for its eventual escape later on. This corner of the cooperage is quieter, almost discreet, but there is still the whirr of the drill.

STRAIGHT STAND

The distillery buyer requiring white oak to be made into barrels for bourbon, and later for whiskey, looks primarily for straight-growing stands on well-drained slopes. The wood from such trees has the optimum density for aging spirit over a long period.

THE INFLUENCE OF WOOD: AMERICAN OAK

MICHAEL JACKSON

OLOROSO WITH A TOUCH OF THE OZARKS... MONTELIMAR OR MISSOURI?

Terms like "heavily sherried" or "bourbon-aged" are not about to vanish just yet, but the emphasis is shifting away from what the cask originally contained and toward the wood from which it was constructed. Increasingly, that wood is from the United States.

Sherry will maintain a presence for two reasons. First, its devotees still believe that the wine itself is influential in imparting flavors, whatever Macallan's research may suggest. Second, sherry casks arriving in Scotland and being newly filled with spirit have a job for at least a decade, if not 12, 15, or 18 years, perhaps even longer. When the first fill is decanted, there will be a second.

Some blenders and distillery managers feel that sherry casks are something of a blunt instrument on the first fill. They take the view that the sherry influence is so strong as to be hard to deploy with subtlety. Second-fill casks are greatly favored for their balance and restraint. By the third fill, the cask should still be in good shape structurally and well worth using, but it will no longer be earmarked as a sherry cask. As to what is, or is not, a sherry cask, practices vary.

Former sherry casks made from American oak are a new element in the mix. In 2004/05, Macallan launched a new range of half a dozen single malts matured in American oak. This selection is called Macallan Fine Oak. Skeptics were ready to dub it "Macallan Lite," but were confounded when they tasted the whiskeys. The complexity and individuality of Macallan malt whiskey came singing through, but still enriched to a surprising degree by the oak. The vanilla, cream, and coconut expected from American oak seemed to conspire in a nougatlike luxury; a taste that

MANAGED TIMBER

In the Ozark Mountains, timber lots are small and privately owned. Cutting is managed to leave space for seeding and new growth. Some of the foresters have worked in the forests all their lives.

BOTANIST AND DISTILLER

With a degree in forestry and specialized wood technology, Bob Russell gives distiller Bill Lumsden a guided tour of a Missouri white oak log. The marks on the sawn end show how it will be cut into quarters at the sawmill, then made into planks.

RAW MATERIAL

Stacks of logs by the roadside are a common sight in and around Altenburg, Missouri. The logs are brought out of the woods by a tractor typically equipped with a bulldozer blade to push the logs, and a powerful winch to haul them. The stacks of logs are collected by tractor-trailers with heavy lifting gear.

evoked Montélimar more than Missouri. Asked whether these American oak casks had previously contained sherry or bourbon, Macallan indicated that both types were used.

BOURBON BARRELS

When sherry butts first fell into short supply, bourbon barrels were an obvious alternative. Over the years, many bourbon and Scotch whiskey distilleries have had links of ownership or distribution. Classic styles of American whiskey are required to be matured in new oak, and this typically lasts for little more than four years. After their distillery debuts with bourbon, the still-young barrels are ready for a new life. The powerful, fruity, nutty, flavors of sherry cannot be matched by bourbon, but its own vanilla spiciness works especially well with some delicate Scotches.

Over the years, some Scottish distilleries, especially those that concentrate on providing fillings for blenders, have accrued a miscellany of casks, largely determined by their clients. If they wish to bottle a small quantity of single malt, they will look at their available stock, select the best casks of a suitable age, and seek to make a well-balanced blend. The ratio of sherry to bourbon, or Spanish to American, will be, within reason, whatever emerges.

UNMASKED GLENMORANGIE

Distillers that actively promote their whiskey as bottled single malt are more inclined to have developed a policy on wood with a view to showcasing their stock and ensuring continuity. In the course of all this barrel-rolling, bourbon wood has cast off any suggestion of being second-best. It will never be as flamboyant as sherry wood, but it is now the mainstream. Bourbon barrels are recognized for their ability gently to round out a malt without masking its house character.

BOURBON WOOD HAS CAST OFF ANY SUGGESTION OF BEING SECOND-BEST

Decades ago, Glenmorangie committed itself to a regimen of aging its principal product for 10 years in former bourbon barrels. Its wood policy is a mirror image of Macallan's. In the styles of their whiskeys, Macallan and Glenmorangie are polar opposites: one using the industry's shortest,

PERFECT CURVES

The word "stave" is etymologically related to "staff," meaning a pole or stick (as in a bishop's staff). At a glance, a stave looks nothing more than a small plank. Given a closer look, it has a sophisticated geometry, with each of its surfaces cut to a curve or bevel. There are typically 32 staves in a barrel, and a further 15 pieces to form the ends.

HEAVY HAULAGE

Tractor-trailers like this one first serve to carry logs from roadside to sawmill. There, the logs are sawn into planks and dried, usually in a kiln. If air-drying is preferred, they are simply left stacked in the woodyard. This process of seasoning can take months or even years. Glenmorangie likes its air-dried oak to be seasoned for between two and four years. Air-drying drives off unwanted sappy moisture without closing the pores of the wood. The truck shown here has been loaded at the sawmill with over 12,000 planks.

HIGH-TECH SAWMILL

The planing of planks into staves can be carried out with great precision at this sawmill, which opened in Clifton, Tennessee, in 2001. The plant is equipped with highly efficient new saws, vital in a business where every extra fraction of an inch of wood utilized is a bonus.

MEN AND MACHINES
Compared with cooperages in Spain, those in the United States are slightly more mechanized, but this is a matter of degree. Even in Japan, coopering remains a very labor-intensive industry. To some, cooperage machines look like instruments of torture.

fattest stills to make a big, rich whiskey, aged in Spanish oak sherry butts; the other using the industry's tallest, thinnest stills to make a light, delicate whiskey aged in bourbon barrels. These opposite approaches are equally successful, making Macallan and Glenmorangie two of the world's top-selling malt whiskeys. Given that success, they have to guarantee large volumes of suitable casks.

THE OAK HUNTERS

While Macallan is preoccupied with *Quercus robur* and finds it in the Picos d'Europa, Glenmorangie wants *Quercus alba*, and seeks it in the Ozarks. Both distilleries have enjoyed a degree of autonomy while being subsumed into larger groups. Both have invested in talented whiskey-makers and sent them to the forest to supervise the cutting of the wood. While the man from Macallan drives across Northern Spain to say "yes" in Santander or Lugo, his counterpart at Glenmorangie flies to his destination via Louisville, Kentucky.

WORKING THE WOOD
Operators at the Dixie Cooperage take a great pride in the speed, efficiency, and skill with which they coax the wood into barrels. The number of processes seems infinite, like passes and runs in a football game.

Aboard a small Beechcraft, Glenmorangie's Dr. Bill Lumsden flies onward from Louisville to Cape Girardeau, about 100 miles (160 km) southeast of St. Louis, Missouri. Another 35 miles (55 km) of highway, and he is into hill country. Lumsden is traveling with botanist Bob Russell, who notes along the way cherry trees, walnuts, and red oak, but only really engages with his surroundings when he begins to see white oaks.

The roll of the countryside in this part of the Ozarks means that the soil drains well; otherwise, the roots would absorb unwanted minerals. "This is perfect soil: silt-loam on top of limestone," says Russell. It is February, and there is a patina of snow, lit by a relaxed sun. "There are proper seasons here," comments Russell. The Ozarks are rich in woodland, and he knows the hills from Arkansas to Iowa. In parts where the weather is too warm, the growth is too quick and the wood becomes too densely textured. In some places, woodpeckers are a problem. Where it is too cold, the trees have difficulty budding.

The oaks are looking healthy, standing tall in thickets between dairy farms as the road enters Altenburg, which still describes itself on its sign by the German word Stadt. This town, settled by Lutherans from Saxony, has what Lumsden seeks. For a decade he has been exploring the Ozarks for oaks that will deliver a truly rich aroma.

ARTISAN CASK

The trees selected in Missouri for Glenmorangie go to a sawmill in Tennessee. They are air-dried (no kilning), and made into barrels at the Dixie Cooperage, Louisville, Kentucky. They have a heavy toast but only a light char. After being used to mature one vintage of Jack Daniel's, they are sent to Glenmorangie. The original plan was to phase these "designer casks" into the company's considerable maturing stock, but Lumsden was so pleased with early results that he released a bottling, under the designation Artisan Cask, in 2004/05. The name reflects the hands-on nature of the wood selection. The whiskey was creamy in aroma, flavor, and texture. Reminiscent of trifle scattered with chocolate chips, it has the balancing, spicy dryness of cinnamon-dusted coffee.

COMPLETING THE BARRELS
The clamor in the cooperage becomes more metallic as the final stages are reached. It takes 45–60 minutes to assemble a barrel, but they chase each other through the cooperage at the rate of more than 250 units per shift.

HIGHLIGHT

THREE DEGREES OF CHAR

Bourbon barrels are toasted or charred on the inside to enable the whiskey to permeate the wood. Charring gives the spirit access to positive properties and flavors in the wood. American cooperages typically offer three degrees of char: light, medium, and alligator. The latter, heaviest char leaves the wood burned in a pattern of squares reminiscent of an alligator's skin.

READY FOR FILLING

Brand-new white oak casks at the end of the production line wait for the journey to the bourbon distillery, where they will impart sought-after flavors to the spirit.

MATURATION: THE WAREHOUSE

IAN WISNIEWSKI

A BARREL'S POSITION AS IT AGES IN A WAREHOUSE INFLUENCES THE FLAVOR AND STRENGTH OF THE SPIRIT IT NURTURES.

RACKED WAREHOUSES

The racked warehouse is the most widely used type of whiskey-aging warehouse in the industry. Typically built on a vast scale, accommodating thousands of casks, racked warehouses can be seen at many distilleries in Ireland (the one shown here is at Midleton), Scotland, Kentucky, Canada, and Japan.

Up to 70 percent of the flavor and character of a whiskey is formed during the aging process. Throughout this vital maturation period, every cask of whiskey is confined to what is known as an aging warehouse. This provides a silent, somewhat minimalist, environment, with a twilight air about it since windows are usually absent. The air inside these warehouses becomes saturated with whiskey fumes, creating a highly aromatic atmosphere. In Scotland, the minimum legal aging period before the spirit can be bottled as Scotch whiskey is three years, and in Kentucky it is two years. However, most whiskeys are aged for far longer than the legal minimum.

THE WAREHOUSE PROVIDES A SILENT, TWILIGHT, MINIMALIST ENVIRONMENT

A QUESTION OF MATURITY

A complex series of reactions between the spirit and the oak starts to take place as soon as the cask is filled. However, the stage at which the master distiller decides a whiskey has reached maturity and is ready for bottling varies enormously: some whiskeys are at their best earlier than others. In addition, many distilleries bottle the same whiskey at progressive stages of maturity in order to provide a variety of choices to suit different tastes. The way in which whiskey reaches maturity is influenced by the type of warehouse, its location, and the climate. Different warehouses at the same distillery, and even different areas within the same warehouse, experience individual microclimates that exert varying influences.

Whiskey may be aged on site at the distillery, although there are vast warehouses in Scotland's central belt where whiskeys from a variety of distilleries are matured. Apart from the obvious economies of scale, the central belt also offers the temperate climate that is considered ideal for maturing whiskey.

TYPES OF WAREHOUSES

There are two principal types of aging warehouses used in Scotland, one known as "dunnage" and the other as "racked." The dunnage warehouse is the most traditional, but the racked warehouse is the most universal type, and is also used throughout the US, Canada, Japan, and Ireland.

A dunnage warehouse is a low-level, stone or brick building, with thick walls and a slate roof. This style of construction ensures the most stable temperature, with an earthen floor to encourage humidity. Casks are usually only stacked three high within this comparatively low building, so there is no significant temperature difference between the casks on the upper and lower levels. Consequently, dunnage warehouses encourage leisurely maturation, which is widely believed to give the finest results. The capacity of a dunnage warehouse can be limited to several hundred casks.

In contrast, a racked warehouse can handle up to 20,000 casks, using a multistory system of steel racks. A tin roof and thin walls mean that the temperature can vary throughout the year far more than in a dunnage warehouse. Temperature fluctuation at the upper levels is greater than at the floor level of the warehouse.

DUNNAGE WAREHOUSES

A particular feature of malt whiskey distilleries in Scotland, dunnage warehouses are the most traditional type of aging warehouse. Neighboring dunnage warehouses on the same site will often have different microclimates.

In Kentucky, there are two types of racked warehouses: iron-clad open rick, and brick-built. Open-rick warehouses, which can house barrels stacked up to 24 high, date from the 1870s. They are usually sited on exposed hilltops or open fields, in order to experience the full impact of seasonality. Tin roofs ensure that the full range of temperatures is experienced within the warehouse.

THE EFFECT OF TEMPERATURE

In any Scottish aging warehouse, casks lose about 2 percent in volume (water and alcohol) per year due to evaporation, which means a slowly declining alcoholic strength. In Kentucky, brick-built warehouses are more insulated than iron-clad ones, limiting the temperature fluctuation to perhaps only 42–46°F (6–8°C) and reducing the impact on maturation.

In the open-rick warehouses of Kentucky, however, the temperature can vary by as much as 11°C (20°F). Over 10 to 15 years, the barrels on the relatively cooler, lower stories will suffer a slight loss of alcoholic strength. On the middle stories, more water than alcohol evaporates, so the spirit may rise in alcoholic strength. On the upper stories, the strength can rise even higher than on the middle floors.

Temperature also influences the flavor of the whiskey. In higher temperatures, the spirit expands, enabling it to extract flavors from the oak at a faster rate; in cooler temperatures, it contracts and withdraws from the oak.

MANAGING TEMPERATURE

Traditionally, bourbon barrels were moved around the warehouse to ensure consistency of temperature. However, uniformity is generally achieved by blending whiskey from barrels that have been aged on different floors. The aging process can also be controlled by heating. A system known as "cycling," pioneered in 1874, uses dry heat (from steam-heated coils) to raise the temperature in the warehouses and accelerate the aging process.

The microclimate within a warehouse certainly impacts on the strength and flavor of the whiskey it houses. Ultimately, however, the whiskeys matured in different types of warehouse vary in terms of character, not quality.

WOODFORD, KENTUCKY

Racked warehouses are the standard choice for aging bourbon in Kentucky, and offer a multistory storage option up to 24 barrels high.

A Traditional Distillery

Jürgen Deibel

THE MAGIC OF WHISKEY-MAKING IS HIDDEN AWAY IN SCOTLAND'S DISTILLERIES, MOST OF WHICH ARE OPEN TO VISITORS.

All whiskey distilleries look different. Some are very old and quaint, others monsters of modern brutalism. The individual layout of each depends on the site chosen, the available space, and the buildings. Shown here is a traditional, old-fashioned layout for an imaginary Scottish whiskey distillery. All the units needed for whiskey production are illustrated: grist mill, mash tun, washback, pot stills, condensers, spirit safe, spirit receiver, and casking facilities. A local water source would be close by, and warehouses to mature the final spirit would also most likely be on site.

GRIST MILL

The first step to making whiskey in every Scottish distillery is to convert malted barley, today delivered mostly by commercial maltsters, into grist with the help of these four-roller mills.

MALTED BARLEY STORE

Tons of malted barley, either brought straight from the malt floor or delivered by commercial maltsters, are stored in large bins. This is where whiskey-making starts.

CONVEYER

In most distilleries conveyer belts carry the grist to the mash tun.

MASH TUN

Once poured into the mash tun, the grist is mixed with water. Small mash tuns are equipped with rakes that stir the mixture and help to extract the sugars.

Barley chute

Wash still

WASHBACK

The sugars in the fermented wort are converted into alcohol with the help of yeast. Washbacks are traditionally made of wood, but can be found nowadays in stainless steel as well.

Pot Still

Copper pot stills are the heart of every distillery. By using heat, the alcohol and aromas are separated from any unwanted compounds. The picture shows the inside of a pot still with a steam heating system.

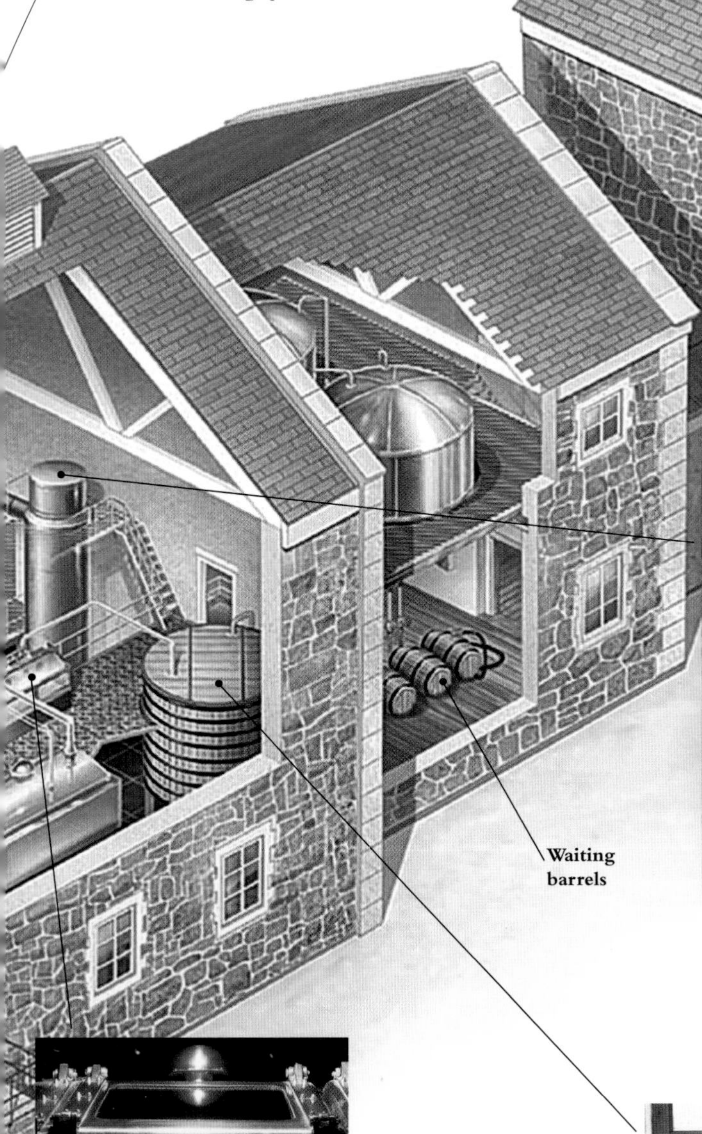

Barrels

The wooden casks in which whiskey matures are usually either Spanish sherry casks or are made up from American bourbon barrels. They are filled with new make spirit, which then has to be left to mature for a legal minimum of three years before it can be called whiskey.

Waiting barrels

Condenser

The spirit leaves the pot still in vapor form. Cooled by water, these large modern condensers (shell-and-tube type) reduce the temperature of the vapor so that it becomes liquid again.

HIGHLIGHT

WORM TUBS

Traditionally, worm tubs also act as condensers for cooling down the vapor from the pot stills. A copper coil, immersed in cold water, guides the vapor along it, cooling it down and turning it back into liquid again. Worm tubs and modern condensers of shell-and-tube types are used throughout the industry. Which of the two systems is better is often debated, but distilleries have used both types over the years.

Spirit Safe

This is where the separation of the new make from feints and foreshots is controlled. Padlocks ensure that Customs and Excise controls the spirit.

Spirit Receiver

All new make spirit is collected in the spirit receiver. Made of wood or steel, these units can hold tens of thousands of gallons of fresh distillate. After being diluted to cask strength, the new make is poured into casks for maturation.

SELECTING WHISKEYS
Before blending, whiskey samples are carefully checked for the desired characteristics, and sometimes a test sample of the combined whiskeys will be prepared by the master blender.

SHADES OF GOLD
The color a whiskey gains from its cask varies widely, depending on the type of cask used for maturation and the length of time the whiskey remains in the cask.

BLENDING AND VATTING

IAN WISNIEWSKI & JÜRGEN DEIBEL

WITH DISTILLERIES EXTENDING THE RANGE OF THEIR WHISKEYS, BLENDERS HAVE MORE DECISIONS TO MAKE THAN EVER BEFORE.

Blending is the term used to describe the mixing of whiskeys of different ages and characteristics. In Scotland, grain and malt whiskeys selected from different casks are blended to produce whiskey with a consistent flavor. Vatting is the name for the identical process when talking about malt whiskeys.

CASK SELECTION

A cask's individuality stems from the fact that the same batch of spirit aged for exactly the same period in neighboring barrels of the same type will not produce identical whiskeys. Differences in aroma, flavor, and color between casks can be subtle, but on the other hand they can also be spectacular, and it is part of the blender's art to smooth out these differences.

> DIFFERENCES BETWEEN CASKS CAN BE SUBTLE

Cask individuality is the result of a variety of influences. The capacity of a bourbon barrel, for example, can vary from 48 to 54 gallons (180 to 205 liters), which is a key factor in the ratio of oak to spirit. A cask's position within a warehouse—higher or lower—can also be influential, determining the degree of temperature differential throughout the year. Since most whiskeys are made continually available, cask individuality is removed by blending in order to ensure a consistent flavor from one year to the next.

BLENDING

A blended Scotch uses whiskeys from a wide range of distilleries, and typically comprises 20–50 grain and malt whiskeys of varying ages and different types of casks. As the availability of whiskeys fluctuates, the challenge for the blender is to find alternatives when required. Computerized records show what is available, although a missing malt may require more than just one other to replace it.

Standard Scotch blends may contain anything from five to over 70 percent malt whiskey. "Standard," "premium," and "deluxe" tags tend to denote the amount of malt whiskey in a blend, with progressively higher levels of malt whiskey in each category. Twelve- and 15-year-old blends typically contain around 40–60 percent malt. An age statement on a blend indicates the age of the youngest whiskey used. "Super-deluxe" whiskeys do not necessarily include a higher level of malts, since this, in itself, does not guarantee greater complexity. What matters is the caliber of the malts and the balance attained, although lighter blends tend to contain a higher percentage of grain whiskeys.

Generally, blends contain a mix of lighter-bodied and fuller-bodied whiskeys in varying proportions. Scotch grain whiskey, Irish grain whiskey, American light whiskey, and neutral grain spirit are regarded as light. Scotch malt whiskey, Irish pure pot-still whiskey, and many column-still whiskeys are distilled to a lower ethanol concentration, and are heavy-bodied whiskeys. In Ireland, Black Bush blended whiskey contains 80 percent malt whiskey, and only 20 percent light-bodied grain whiskey.

Ensuring consistency of color is essential in branded whiskeys. Although the use of caramel to adjust the color of blended whiskey, and some malts, is standard practice in Scotland, some blenders maintain color consistency using the natural range of hues from different casks.

VATTING

Vatted malts (blends of malt whiskeys from more than one distillery) are put together in the same way as blends, with interaction creating dimensions that are not apparent in the individual malts. A recipe may consist of just a few malts, or up to 30, some of which may need to be replaced when they become unavailable. And even single malts require vatting to maintain an established flavor profile, since recipes tend to draw on different fills of bourbon and sherry casks.

CONTROLLING QUALITY

The responsibility for virtually all quality control belongs to "noses," the experienced blenders who check the whiskeys. Samples are usually assessed on the basis of the aromas, and not generally tasted, hence the term "nosing." Many leading "noses" have 30–40 years' experience; most are men, but women are starting to appear in the profession. A recent study found that women are better at putting descriptions to tastes and aromas than men.

In a typical day, a few hundred samples, diluted with water to 20–25 percent vol., are nosed. A good memory is needed to accurately identify the different flavor characteristics, although past tasting notes and a library of samples provide backup. Gas chromatography can be used to analyze certain characteristics within a whiskey, such as phenolic compounds and esters, but technology can never replace, or even match, the ability of the human nose to distinguish nuances of flavor and aroma.

NEW "NOSES"

Nosing panels (comprising employees with proven nosing abilities) provide support for "the nose," as well as training opportunities for new recruits. Trainees are encouraged to develop their sense of smell by familiarizing themselves with aromatic items, such as herbs and spices, to widen and develop their own memory bank of scents. Nosing potential is evident within two years, although it takes around five years to learn the profiles of individual whiskeys. "Noses" need a total of about 10 years of training to acquire the necessary skills.

WHISKEY BLENDER
Richard Paterson is the master blender at Whyte and Mackay. His sampling room contains hundreds of whiskeys from distilleries all over Scotland, each of which he will bear in mind while making his selections. His objective is to recreate his company's branded blends, as identically as possible, time after time.

HIGHLIGHT

TASTING AT THE DISTILLERY

If you are fortunate enough to be able to taste the whiskeys at a distillery, you may also get the chance to discuss them with the master distiller and master blender. You can talk over cask selection and the different recipes used for the distillery's range of expressions, and see each stage of the production process at first hand.

HIGHLIGHT

A CLASSIC BLEND

One of the longest-established and most successful blended Scotch whiskeys, Bell's dates from the first half of the 19th century, although the name was not registered until 1895. The range includes a five-year-old vatted malt, an eight-year-old, and a 12-year-old. The age statement refers to the youngest malt or grain whiskey used in the blend.

THE BLENDING PROCESS

Most whiskey-producing countries have strict regulations and traditions for building their blended whiskeys. Several steps are involved in the process of producing bottles of blended whiskey:

1. Casks of the whiskeys selected by the master blender are delivered from the distillery warehouse to the blending plant, where they are opened and poured into a stainless-steel trough.

2. Transferred to a huge blending vat, the whiskeys are mixed thoroughly. Mechanical agitators or compressed air generally carry out this task.

3. Demineralized water is added to reduce the blend to bottling strength.

4. Blenders add spirit caramel to adjust the color. Spirit caramel tastes bitter, but the tiny quantity used does not affect the final whiskey flavor.

5. A blender may choose to mature (marry) the blend further in casks. This may take up to two years, as in Chivas Royal Salute. The casks do not normally add further character to the blend.

TRANSFERRED TO A HUGE BLENDING VAT, THE WHISKEYS ARE MIXED THOROUGHLY

CANADA AND THE US

In Canada, distillates may be mixed prior to maturation (so-called preblending). In the US, the components of a blend tend to be produced at only a limited number of distilleries. Exchanging casks, or purchasing casks for blending, is not common practice. Instead, different cereals, fermentation conditions, distillation parameters, and varying warehousing and cask conditions are applied. For American blends, heavier-bodied spirits include bourbon, rye, wheat, malt, rye-malt, and corn whiskeys. The light-bodied components are usually grain whiskeys or neutral grain spirit. In the US, distillers are allowed to add up to 2.5 percent of "blenders"—wines or sherries that bring more character to the blend.

IRELAND

Irish blends are made from a wide variety of individual components, ranging from pure pot-still whiskey to malt-and-grain whiskey. The quality is determined by the selection of the cereals to create the mash, the distillation process, the final cask selection, and maturation in the warehouse.

JAPAN

Japanese blenders face the same problems as their counterparts in the US or Ireland. Only a limited number of distilleries are available to choose from, and, again, flavors are controlled by varying the production factors. Japanese blends frequently include imported malt whiskey from Scotland as a way of increasing the range of whiskeys offered.

SAMPLING BARRELS
Maturing whiskey is sampled (here at Bruichladdich, on Islay) using a long pipe called a valinch.

TOPPING OFF
Early in the maturing stages, barrels are checked to ensure that each is completely filled with spirit (here at the Woodford Reserve distillery, Kentucky).

BOTTLING THE BLEND
Master blenders rarely actually taste the blend until the final stages before bottling. Samples of new-make spirit, mature whiskey straight from the cask, and vatted recipes are generally nosed rather than tasted.

MAKING THE BLEND
The contents of individual casks of whiskey, selected from a number of different sources, are emptied out and combined in large vats. There are currently eight distilleries in Scotland producing grain whiskey for blends. The malt whiskey comes from around 100 distilleries, including some silent ones from which stock is still available.

SAMPLING THE BLEND
When all the component whiskeys of a blend are brought together ("married") and filtered, the blender may taste a sample of the finished whiskey.

THE NOSE KNOWS

Writers on whiskey, like distillery managers and blenders, nose first, then taste. The person who monitors quality is sometimes known as "the nose."

HOW TO NOSE AND TASTE

MICHAEL JACKSON

WHICH AROMAS AND FLAVORS CAN YOU FIND? THIS IS A GAME ANYONE CAN PLAY, AND THERE ARE NO WRONG ANSWERS.

Whether we are aware of it or not, the enjoyment of whiskey, as with any drink, engages all our senses: hearing, touch, sight, smell, and taste. You hear the whiskey being poured, and you feel the texture of the whiskey as you sip it. Every sense contributes to the pleasure, with smell and taste being the most revealing.

EVERY SENSE CONTRIBUTES TO THE PLEASURE

The social drink in the pub or bar is not the moment to deconstruct a dram, but to nose a whiskey at home can pay dividends. Learning to recognize aromas and flavors, and to judge body, palate, and finish, is fun. The knowledge and experience gained also heighten the enjoyment, and can perhaps be shared with others in a tasting evening arranged for friends.

For whiskey-drinking, the traditional, cut-glass tumbler or old-fashioned glass have their merits, but also some crucial failings. The bevels in cut glass illuminate the color of the whiskey, but they also distort it. More important, the tumbler shape does a poor job of delivering aroma.

The ideal tasting glass has no decoration on the bowl, so that the color of the whiskey can be appreciated to the full. It should have an inward curve, or a slightly pinched waist above the bowl, to hold in the aroma, and then a slight flare to direct the bouquet to the nose. A lid, to retain the aroma between sniffs and swallows, is useful. Tulip-shaped glasses have been developed by whiskey critics, distilleries, and glassware manufacturers for sale to the enthusiast. Professional tasters use a glass resembling a sherry copita.

WATER WITH WHISKEY

It is conceivable that the early romantic heroes of Scottish history drank their whiskey straight, but contrary to myth, today's Highlanders do not. For social drinking in Scotland, "half-and-half" is a popular choice. In the American South, "bourbon and branch water" is enjoyed as much for its alliteration as any other merit. The "branch" simply means a creek. In Japan, a mizuwari is a tall tumbler or Collins glass, packed with cracked ice, over which the whiskey is poured, making a very diluted drink for social drinking.

Some zealots resist dilution on principle. Others feel that the texture of the bigger, richer, sherryish malts is spoiled by water. The problem is that neat whiskey can numb the palate. This can be countered by drinking a glass of water after a whiskey. Adding a small drop of water to a whiskey disturbs the molecular composition of the whiskey, and can open out the aromas and flavors. Equally, ice with whiskey makes a refreshing drink but can freeze the tongue, limiting appreciation.

BRANDY SNIFTER

The simple lid shown here retains the aroma until "the nose" is ready. It is known as a watch glass. Some tasters prefer a more elaborate, fitted lid.

ORGANIZING A TASTING

It is a good idea to warn guests in advance that smoking is forbidden, and also to ask them not to wear strong perfumes. Aim to provide between six and a dozen whiskeys. Try to arrange them in ascending order of intensity, with the lightest first.

Provide appropriate glasses, and also bottled still water, small pitchers, and water glasses. Water is needed not only to open out the flavors, but also to cleanse the palate between tastings. Plain crackers or bread can also be used, although some tasters find that these leave a floury aftertaste.

You will need pencils and paper for taking notes, and for convenience you could produce tasting sheets with headings (*see below*) already in place. Remember: there are no wrong answers, and no description can be too strange. Individuals have varying sensitivities to flavors, and each person will find different ways to describe them.

COLOR

Hold the glass against a sheet of white paper or a white wall and look at the color. Pale, golden colors suggest that the whiskey was matured in former bourbon casks. Darker colors suggest sherry wood and nuttier, apricot-like flavors.

NOSE

Smell or "nose" the whiskey. Some professionals like to get their nose into the glass; others retreat slightly. You may experience the sweetness of malt, the smokiness of a peat fire, or the salt and seaweed resulting from maturation somewhere by the sea. Professional distillers sometimes work only with their nose, without actually tasting the whiskey.

PALATE

Taste the whiskey straight to gain an impression of the body. Is it big, rich, creamy, firm, smooth, soft, gentle? Add water gradually to see how the aromas and flavors develop with dilution. Between sips, cleanse your palate with water. Whiskey writers tend to work slowly, in order to build up a description. Blenders work more quickly, and often dilute heavily from the start to minimize the effect of the alcohol. They are usually monitoring familiar malts, and are checking for consistency.

FINISH

Consider the aftertaste. Do the maltiness and smokiness linger? A great whiskey, with a complex finish, leaves the drinker in reflective mood—a moment to think before writing your tasting note.

TYPICAL AROMAS AND FLAVORS

Some of the aromas and flavors generally found in whiskeys derive from the raw materials, others from the various stages of production, but opinions differ on their origins. All whiskeys are complex, but some are especially good examples of a certain characteristic.

FLAVOR PRODUCER		RESULTING FLAVOR
	GRAIN Cereal grains are members of the grass family, and different grains have their own accents. Barley can taste nutty; rye can be spicy or minty; wheat can be crisp; and corn can lend a creaminess.	• Hard grains • Grassiness • Grassy sweetness • Lemon grass • Bison grass
	ROCK & WATER The rock from which water rises is another contributor. In Kentucky, limestone makes for firm-bodied whiskeys, while the softness of some Speyside malts is attributed to granite.	• Soft, clean • Iron, passion fruit • Chalky • Firm-bodied • Scorched earth
	PEAT Flavors of peat may be absorbed by water flowing over moors and bogs, or picked up in damp warehouses. Primarily they derive from the use of peat fires to dry the malt.	• Smoky • Fragrant • Tarlike • Reminiscent of burned grass
	FLOWERS & HEATHER The flowery or honeyed characters of some whiskeys are often attributed to the heathery hillsides over which the water flows. A floral note may also be created during fermentation.	• Violets • Heather • Honey • Ferns
	FERMENTATION A drink classed as whiskey cannot contain fruits or spices, but natural reactions in fermentation or maturation can result in flavors that mimic those of certain fruits.	• Strawberries • Oranges/citrus fruits • Pears • Apples
	OAK New oak or first-fill ex-bourbon barrels impart vanilla and coconut flavors. Sherry butts give "dark fruit" character. Musty smells mean that either the cask or the whiskey has been kept too long.	• Apples • Raisins • Apricots • Vanilla • Coconuts
	WIND & SEA The wind deposits vaporized sea water on the boggy shores of Islay, Orkney, and parts of the Scottish mainland. Either this water or the atmosphere of the warehouse can impart flavors.	• Sea salt • Brine • Sand • Seaweed

THE WHISKEY COUNTRIES

SCOTLAND

The astonishing diversity of single malts has aroused a new passion, from Islay to the Spey

MINIATURE SCOTLAND
A collection of miniature whiskey bottles shows some of the range and diversity of the country's national drink.

THE STORY OF SCOTCH

DAVE BROOM

Scotch whiskey springs from an epic landscape, a place where you can read the rocky poetry of Earth's birth. This is an ancient land, unimaginably old. The Lewisian gneisses that make up the Outer Hebrides and the Rhinns of Islay are some of the oldest rocks on Earth, formed around 300 million years ago. Scotland came into being through a slow metamorphosis, a drift around the globe, the slow grind of plate tectonics. It is an age-old place of collision and eruption; of granite, ancient sandstones, lava, and basalt. It has been etched by ice, ground out by retreating glaciers that left behind glens, lochs, and fjords, and a tattered west coast. It is a place of fertility, of rich, thick loams where barley grows, and of decomposition—a land masked by dark and acidic peat mosses. Scotland is also the homeland of a unique and proud people.

A PLACE WHERE YOU CAN READ THE ROCKY POETRY OF THE EARTH'S BIRTH

EARLY STORIES

Legend has it that the Scots derive their name from Scota, the Egyptian wife of the Spanish Celtic King Milesius, who planned an invasion of an island, now known as Ireland, in around 1699 BC. The king died before departure, but Scota and her sons still made the trip. The island was named Scotia, and its people the Scoti. Then, in about AD 500, the Scoti established the kingdom of Dalriada (today's Argyll) and

AN IDEAL SITUATION
A remote mill by a fast-flowing burn with fields on either side—the perfect spot for a small farm distiller to perfect his or her craft.

SCOTLAND'S DISTILLERIES

ALMOST EVERY REGION in Scotland is home to a distillery: from the islands off its west coast to the Lowlands and Borders, and from the tip of Kintyre to the central Highlands, the northeastern strip, and even Orkney.

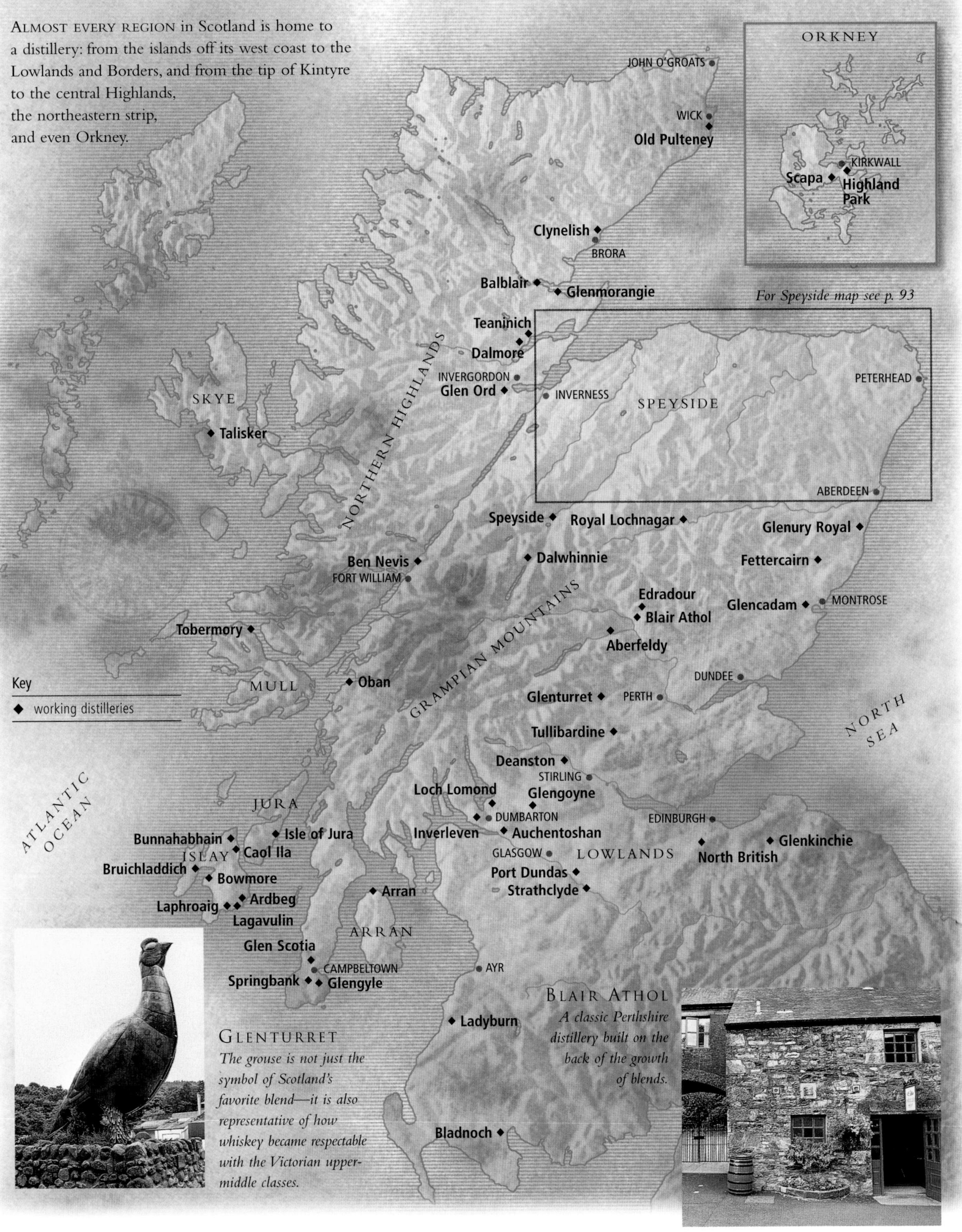

GLENTURRET *The grouse is not just the symbol of Scotland's favorite blend—it is also representative of how whiskey became respectable with the Victorian upper-middle classes.*

BLAIR ATHOL *A classic Perthshire distillery built on the back of the growth of blends.*

RECHARRING BARRELS
A greater understanding of wood chemistry and advances in technology have paid dividends in terms of quality for distillers in recent years.

eventually gave their name to the whole of this northern part of Britain.

The Scoti were far from the only invaders to displace the Picts, Scotland's original inhabitants. Vikings, Welsh, Romans, and Normans, and in recent years Italian, Indian, Bangladeshi, and even English immigrants, have all played a part in the creation of the country and its people.

Around the world, Scotland and Scotch go hand in hand, but not in Scotland itself. The Scots prefer to describe their national drink simply as "whiskey," conceivably on the basis that there is no serious rival in any other country. Certainly, no other nation is as readily associated with whiskey as Scotland. Nowhere else is it quite such an integral part of the culture and economy. Nor does any other country have as many whiskey distilleries, or such a complex and noble product.

THE ORIGIN OF DISTILLATION

Distillation arrived relatively late in Scotland. The year 1494 saw the first record of a distillation taking place in the country, although it is probable that the science was practiced for many years before that. Sadly, the date of the first distillation is unknown, and the the identity of the first distiller equally mysterious. Most scholars, however, agree that the art of distillation arrived in Scotland from Ireland, either with the monks of the Celtic Church or, as appears more likely, with members of the MacVey (Beaton) family, who were physicians to both the court of Ulster and Scotland. They had translated Latin medical texts that contained information on distillation into Gaelic—texts that had previously been translated from originals in Arabic.

IN SPEYSIDE, peat, water, a ready supply of barley, and generations of experience have come together to provide the greatest concentration of malt whiskey distilleries in Scotland—and the world. Flowing from south to north, the river Spey and tributaries like the Livet and the Dullan provide the axis of this diverse and productive region.

RIVER LIVET
Fed by high rainfalls and winter snows, it is the fast-flowing Livet on whose banks the modern whiskey industry was born.

SPEYSIDE'S DISTILLERIES

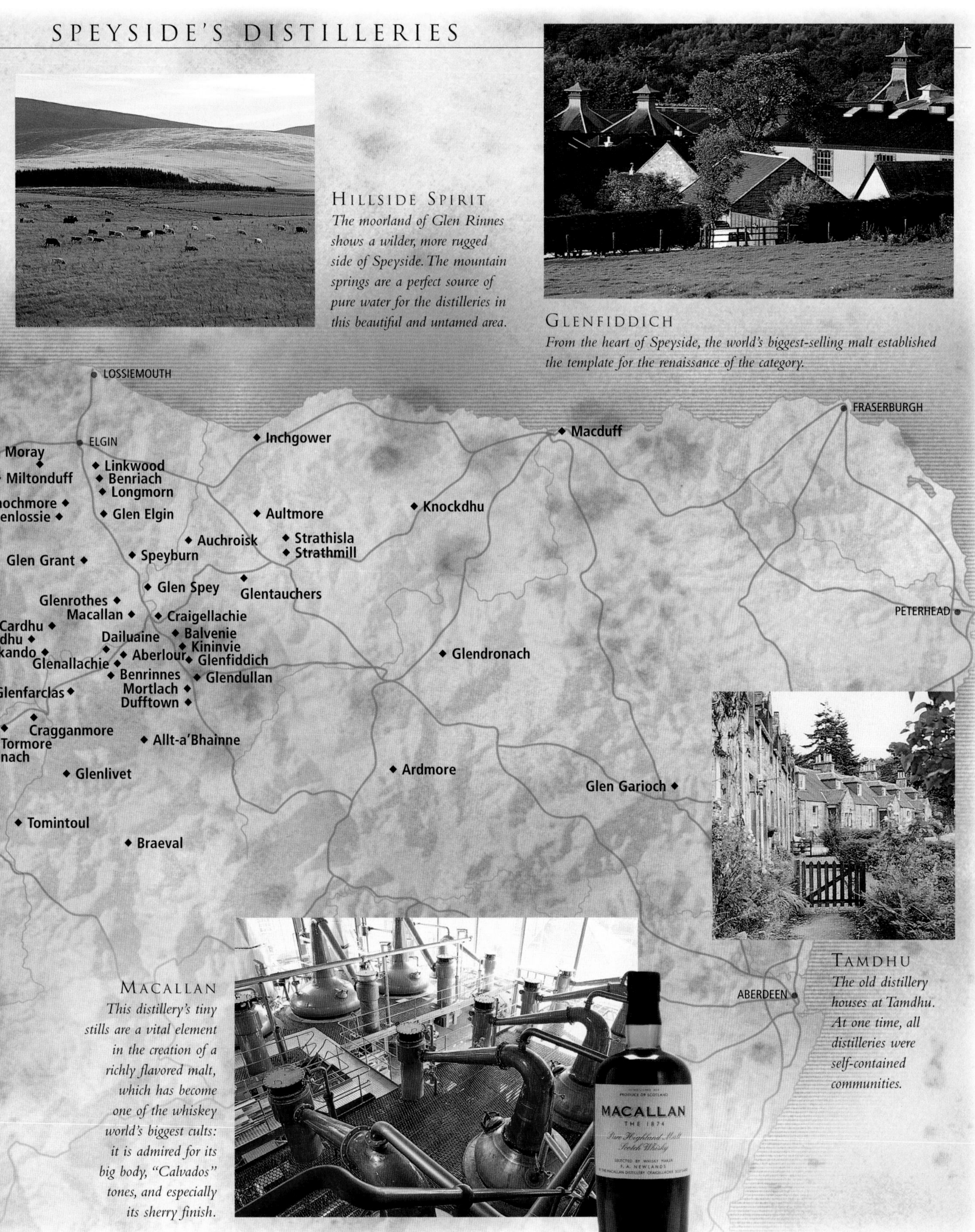

HILLSIDE SPIRIT
The moorland of Glen Rinnes shows a wilder, more rugged side of Speyside. The mountain springs are a perfect source of pure water for the distilleries in this beautiful and untamed area.

GLENFIDDICH
From the heart of Speyside, the world's biggest-selling malt established the template for the renaissance of the category.

TAMDHU
The old distillery houses at Tamdhu. At one time, all distilleries were self-contained communities.

MACALLAN
This distillery's tiny stills are a vital element in the creation of a richly flavored malt, which has become one of the whiskey world's biggest cults: it is admired for its big body, "Calvados" tones, and especially its sherry finish.

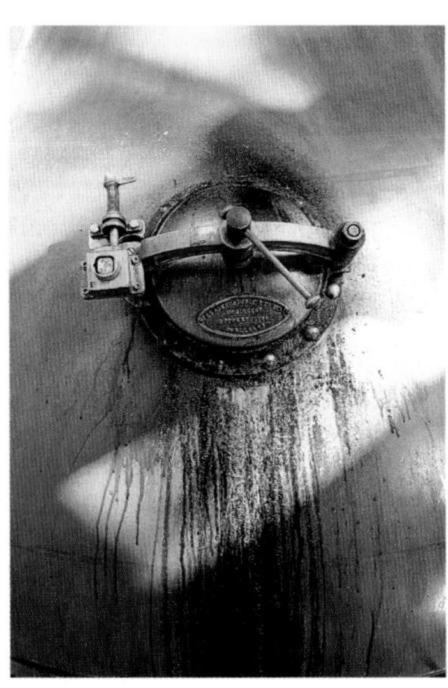

COPPER ALCHEMY
Copper is one of the magical elements in the creation of a whiskey's flavor.

HOLED FISHING BOAT: ISLAY
This scene is a reminder that for many Scottish communities, the sea or the land provided the only means of subsistence, so extra income from illegally distilled whiskey was often vital.

The early Scottish distillers were doctors—and in Scotland, as elsewhere, spirits were initially for medicinal use. In 1505, the Guild of Surgeon Barbers was given a monopoly of manufacture, although there were soon prosecutions for the abuse of this privilege. In all countries, the early distillers produced spirits that were too raw to drink, and most had flavorings added—honey to sweeten them, herbs and spices to give added flavor and efficacy. The first "whiskeys" more closely resembled liqueurs.

Nor were all of these spirits exclusively barley-based; any cereal crop was an option. Oats and wheat were available as well, but since barley was widespread, it became the favorite choice. Distillers were both agents of subtle transformation and men of total practicality, using whatever grew around them as the basis for their magic.

WHAT IS WHISKEY?

When the Scottish Parliament first taxed drinks in 1644, it referred in English to "strong water," in Latin to *aqua vitae*, and in Gaelic to *uisge beatha* or *usquebaugh*, all terms that mean "water of life." It is widely thought that "whiskey" came about as a corruption of *uisge*. Whatever its origins, the word finally achieved formal recognition in 1755 with its entry in the dictionary of Dr. Samuel Johnson, a man not widely remembered for his fond thoughts of the Scots. By this time, spirits were familiar in two distinct forms, flavored and unflavored, the latter being known as "plain." Though casks would have been used to store the drink, it is only in relatively recent times that the influence of the wood in maturation has been appreciated.

Whiskey remained a local spirit for centuries. In the Highlands, a type of malt whiskey would have been made in small stills for use by the local communities, although some substantial distilleries were established by the 18th century. The Lowlands, meanwhile, had begun to produce larger volumes of whiskey, mostly for export to England, where it was redistilled with botanicals into gin.

LEGALIZATION

The late 18th and early 19th centuries saw a series of attempts to bring distilling under some sort of fiscal control. Instead, it drove whiskey-making underground. Farmers saw whiskey-making as their right, and it was often their sole means of paying the rent. At the same time, Lowland distillers had upped

WOODEN ALCHEMY
Whiskey is only aged in secondhand casks, made either from American white oak—typically used to mature bourbon—or European oak—previously used to mature sherry.

JUST OFF THE STILL
A close and careful monitoring of the colorless new make spirit is a vital element in quality control.

production to such levels that quality had dropped drastically, increasing demand for the illicit stuff made in the Highlands. The smuggling era lasted until 1823, when the use of smaller stills was legalized and the modern Scotch whiskey industry was born.

It took the invention of the patent or continuous still to change a national specialty into a global spirit. By the 1850s, merchants began to blend the lighter grain whiskeys with the bolder malts to create a drink with broader appeal. Blended Scotch was then given a boost in the 1870s, when phylloxera devastated the French vineyards, precipitating a global shortage of brandy. Whiskey stepped into the gap, and the rest is history.

THE WHISKEY REGIONS

Scotland has historically been divided into four whiskey-making regions: the Lowlands, Campbeltown, Islay, and the Highlands and Islands. While the diversity of single malts is one of Scotland's greatest joys, it is accepted that there can be similarities between those made in each of the four regions.

Several studies of single malt whiskey have attempted to group or divide the Highlands and Islands into more manageable subregions, without having arrived at a formal categorization. This book seeks to make the exploration of whiskey easier by grouping distilleries geographically. If the exploration is to be carried out by car, it is helpful to know which distilleries are neighbors. If the exploration is by glass, an understanding of geographical origin helps to make sense of the whiskeys being tasted.

This distillery tour also looks at each island and every important valley as a district. Grouping the single malts in this way highlights how, in some instances, whiskeys from a specific region, district, island, or glen can share a similar character.

DISTILLERIES

In most cases, a single malt whiskey simply has the same name as the distillery that produced it. In a few instances, the identity is lost to a minor brand name designed by some heather-brained importer or distributor, and the consumer is left to guess the source of the whiskey. Today, there are almost 120 malt distilleries, although more than a dozen are closed and a similar number have not

MOUNTAIN MALT
Dalwhinnie's distillery is situated at the meeting of ancient drovers' trails, and is the highest and coldest in Scotland.

BEST SELECTION
Specialist whiskey shops have sprung up across the country: this one is in Dufftown.

UNIQUE COOLING
The copper pot still at Fettercairn has a water cooler around its neck—the old technology and ancient understanding is still relevant today.

produced for some years. In early 2005, there were 84 in full production.

Long after a distillery has ceased production, it may hold stocks of whiskey aging in the barrel; these will gradually find their way into the bottle and onto the market. Just as actors talk about a theater being "dark," whiskey people say that a distillery is "silent," whether for a short season or forever. Many a long-silent distillery survives in spirit, so to speak, its presence haunting bars and liquor stores in faraway places.

What we know today as Scotch whiskey is the result of a fusing of enterprise, capital, and native knowledge in the 19th century, with a healthy dose of good fortune. If Prohibition had not happened, would American or Irish whiskey have taken over the world instead? Scotch whiskey's story is one of geology, climate, chance, art, capital, and the distiller's skill. For Scotch is all about people, from the mystery man who was the first distiller—be he Irish monk, medicine man, or "wizard" at the court of the Holy Roman Empire—to the men and women who distill, blend, bottle, and sell it today. This journey is their story.

Glenkinchie

THE SCOTTISH LOWLANDS AND BORDER AREAS HAVE TRADITIONALLY PRODUCED GENTLER-TASTING WHISKEYS. OF THE HANDFUL OF DISTILLERIES WORKING IN THESE AREAS IN THE 19TH CENTURY, ONLY GLENKINCHIE SURVIVES.

The dividing line between England and Scotland today is the river Tweed. The border itself runs down the center of the river until it makes a little northward turn at the coast, neatly grabbing the seaside town of Berwick-upon-Tweed in England. The Scots see Berwick as theirs; after all, its soccer team, Berwick Rangers, plays in "their" league. The town—whose name means "a farm growing bere" (barley)—is home to the largest family-owned maltsters in the UK, a firm that will happily use barley from both sides the Tweed. Why not? As long as the malted barley exits Berwick heading north, the whiskey it will make can be deemed to be Scottish.

You do not have to dig deep to find further whiskey connections in the Borders. The journey through Northumberland may have taken you past Flodden Field. Here died James IV, the perfect Renaissance prince—alchemist, philosopher, and warrior—whose commissioning of Friar John Cor to make aqua vitae in 1494 led to the first recorded distillation in Scotland. Sadly, not even the largest draft of the good friar's medicine helped him on that slaughter ground.

These Border lands were home to the novelist and poet Sir Walter Scott, the man who, depending on your viewpoint, either popularized Scotland or created a wealth of Scottish clichés. The truth, as ever, lies somewhere in between. Many may bridle at it, but Scott's works helped to make popular what was considered a barbaric country—and thereby gave whiskey a new credibility.

DISTILLERY DETAILS

GLENKINCHIE FOUNDED: 1837. OWNER: Diageo. METHOD: Pot stills. CAPACITY: 449,000 gallons.

THE FIRST SCOTTISH DISTILLER?

In the 13th century, Scott's ancestor, Michael Scot(t), a philosopher at the court of the Holy Roman Empire, was known throughout Europe as a wizard or alchemist. A translator of Arabic texts, he knew the secret of distillation. He even appears in Canto XX of Dante's *Inferno*. It is believed he spent his last years back in Scotland, before being buried in Melrose Abbey. Could he have been the first Scottish distiller? The hills and moorlands of the Borders are home to many ballads and tales—some of them based on fact.

Crossing the Lammermuir Hills, heading toward the coast, brings you into a strange mix of former coal-mining towns, Victorian seaside resorts, and rich arable farmland. With grain and coal in such plentiful supply, no wonder the Lowland farmers turned to whiskey-making. As you close in on Edinburgh, you pass Ormiston, home

THE RED-BRICK WAREHOUSES *of Glenkinchie hold one of whiskey-making's underappreciated gems.*

to the father of modern Scottish agriculture, John Cockburn. It was Cockburn's "improving" approach to farming (large farms, mixed crops, use of modern technology, improved transportation) that here in 1735 prompted the building of a model village complete with farm, brewery, and distillery.

GLENKINCHIE

In 1825, 2 miles (3 km) away from Ormiston, the Rate brothers began operations at their Milton distillery. It stands on land that once belonged to the de Quincey family, whose name, transmuted into "Kinchie," had been given to a nearby stream. In 1837, the Rates gave their distillery the name Glen Kinchie, and ran it as a typical small and self-sufficient operation, similar to the other 115 licensed Lowland distilleries of the time. Today, it is one of only three, and is by far the largest.

These are fertile lands. The 19th-century writer William Cobbett talks of "such corn fields as never were surely seen before in any country on earth," and as such they do not fit Walter Scott's stereotypical so-called proper whiskey-making country: all heather-girt hillsides and rocky crags. Whiskey is made in the north, in the rugged Highlands, not here in rich farmland.

Yet from the late 18th century onward, these coalfields and farms helped to feed the growing demands of the Lowland distiller. Larger units with huge stills were built, producing ever-larger volumes of whiskey—to be consumed in Scotland or exported to England for rectification into gin.

ALTHOUGH GLENKINCHIE *looks more like a mill than a distillery, it is a classic Lowland site.*

A UNIQUE STYLE

In time, a Lowland whiskey style evolved. Larger stills (Glenkinchie has the largest in the whiskey industry: each one has a 8,500-gallon/32,000-liter capacity) tend to produce a lighter spirit, and the Lowland distiller would also have used a mix of different cereals, adding wheat and oats to the barley and so altering the flavor profile. Plentiful supplies of coal meant that peat was little used. A Lowland style, still seen today, had begun to emerge.

It is a surprise to discover that, even in the boom of the 1880s, there were few malt distilleries south of Edinburgh. Glenkinchie, hidden from sight in its gentle valley, was an exception. What you see today is the result of expansion that occurred in the 1890s; Glenkinchie was one of the few distilleries to produce throughout World War II.

"Edinburgh's malt" is a classic example of the Lowland style. Light, floral, and sweet, it is a dram of delicacy. Marketing it as an "introductory" malt has done it no favors—these days, lightness is less valued than heaviness, peat is considered essential, and finesse is overlooked for power.

Take the trouble to seek out this solid, red-brick Victorian distillery, with its bowling green. Look at those classic, big-bellied, Lowland stills, see how the owner has retained traditional worm tubs to give the spirit a bit more weight on the palate, and enjoy this classic, floral Lowland malt.

TASTING NOTES

GLENKINCHIE HAS the largest pot stills in Scotland, which contribute to the whiskey's light, floral character. Taste it and see how the fresh fruits, grass, and summer flowers mingle with a tickle of peat. Give it a chance before dinner and see how "light" need not mean bland.

GLENKINCHIE
10-YEAR-OLD
40 VOL.

Color Light gold.

10-YEAR-OLD GLENKINCHIE

Nose Very fresh and slightly floral. Meadowlike. Lemon peel.
Body Gentle and smooth.
Palate Remarkably spicy. Ginger and cinnamon on top of silky malt.
Finish Light oak. Delicate.

GLENKINCHIE DISTILLER'S EDITION
1989
43 VOL.

All of Diageo's Classic Malts come with a finished option. Glenkinchie's has spent its second period of maturation in amontillado casks.

Color Gold.
Nose Sweet, soft, and inviting. Hot fruit scones, honey, orange, barley sugar, a hint of struck match.
Body Gentle and silky. Midweight.
Palate Balance struck between sweet, cooked fruits and dry nuttiness. Light malt notes.
Finish Clean and soft.

DISTILLER'S EDITION GLENKINCHIE

The Lowlands: Closed Distilleries

MOST OF THE OLD MALT WHISKEY DISTILLERIES OF THE SCOTTISH LOWLANDS ARE NOW SILENT. ONLY THE GRAIN DISTILLERIES SURVIVE—RESPONSIBLE FOR THE GLOBAL MARKET IN BLENDED SCOTCH.

You might assume that the bars and retailers in a whiskey region would promote their local specialties. Speyside and Islay do, yet, in the Lowlands, the whiskey-lover has to search hard to find locally produced drams. The reason is that the majority of the region's malt distilleries are silent, victims of the "whiskey loch" of the 1980s, created when supply exceeded demand. Some great whiskey pubs exist in Glasgow (The Lismore and Pot Still) and Edinburgh (The Canny Man's and the Scotch Malt Whisky Society Rooms), and are well worth visiting for a tasting session.

DISTILLERY DETAILS

ROSEBANK FOUNDED: 1790s.
OWNER: Diageo. CLOSED: 1993.

ST. MAGDALENE FOUNDED: 1765.
OWNER: DCL. CLOSED: 1985.

LITTLEMILL FOUNDED: 1772.
OWNER: Loch Lomond Distillery Co. Ltd.
CLOSED: 1993.

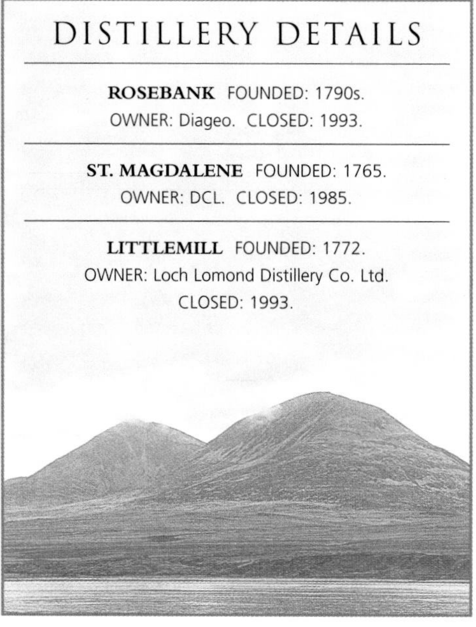

ROSEBANK

It is in places such as these that the seeker of those elusive Lowlanders will have the most success. The whiskey they are most likely to be looking for is the finest of all—Rosebank. It originates from a distillery in Falkirk, on the banks of a canal that linked the Firth of Forth with the River Clyde.

This is a malt that charms you—fragrant and with hints of white fruits and cut flowers. It is an example of triple distillation being used to produce a light, delicate whiskey that is both subtle and complex. Its appealing character, however, could not prevent it from falling silent in 1993.

When Diageo put together its six-strong Classic Malts range, it had to choose between Glenkinchie and Rosebank for the Lowland representative. Most people in the firm would have chosen Rosebank, but in marketing, image is all; Rosebank sat next to a disused canal and bridged a busy main road, while Glenkinchie lay in pretty farmland, with more tourist appeal.

Why, though, close Rosebank down? Even if it was insufficiently pretty to be a frontline distillery, the quality of its spirit was such that it deserved to be in the portfolio. Today, the canal is open and industrial heritage is celebrated, but Rosebank remains closed.

ST. MAGDALENE

The same goes for St. Magdalene, from nearby Linlithgow. Built on the site of a convent, the distillery started in 1765 and was dismantled in 1985. Some of the buildings have been converted into apartments. As with Rosebank, you can find bottlings (sometimes under the name Linlithgow) either from an independent bottler or as part of Diageo's Rare Malts collection. All show a whiskey with a direct character and (often slightly burnt) grassy notes.

LITTLEMILL

The final member of the silent Lowland club is Littlemill. It sits on the banks of the Clyde a few miles outside Glasgow, close to where the Forth and Clyde Canal joins the river. Although it can lay claim to being one of Scotland's oldest distilleries—established in 1772—it seems unlikely that it will ever produce its slightly oily whiskey again. These days, the title of Glasgow's Malt is borne by its near neighbor, Auchentoshan *(see page 104)*.

INDUSTRIAL DISTILLING

The central Lowland belt was the heartland of Scotland's industry. Today, the steelworks have closed, the mines are gone, and the shipyards are no more. Instead, there are call centers, dockside developments, and heritage parks. Whiskey distilleries have also suffered.

This was the land of the industrial distiller, typified by families such as the Steins and the Haigs. These firms concentrated on producing grain whiskey and, in the Haigs' case, developed their own blends. Although malt distilleries are rare in the Lowlands today, the bulk of Scotland's whiskey, namely grain whiskey, responsible for the global market in blended Scotch, continues to be distilled here.

But even grain distilleries have suffered. Cambus, Caledonian, and Moffat are gone. The grandest of all, red-brick Dumbarton, has been demolished. It was one of a select club of grain plants that contained malt distilleries, housing Inverleven and Lomond *(see p. 106)*. Moffat produced Glen Flagler and Killyloch, and Caledonian produced Kinclaith. The occasional bottling of each still appears.

ST. MAGDALENE *was dismantled in the 1980s after over 100 years of production, although some of its bottlings can still be found lurking in bars.*

ROSEBANK *was deemed insufficiently attractive to be maintained as a working distillery. Ironically, the area now pulls in many visitors with other attractions.*

The Lowlands: Girvan and Bladnoch

IN THE BEAUTIFUL COUNTRYSIDE OF SOUTHERNMOST SCOTLAND CAN BE FOUND TWO EXTREMELY DIFFERENT DISTILLERIES: ONE GRAIN, AND ONE MALT.

The Clyde coast is fringed with golf courses, the firth studded with islands: the Cumbraes, Bute, Arran, and the strange granite cap of Ailsa Craig. The coast itself is a playground for city-dwellers, somewhere to play golf or just wander on the sandy beaches. Inland is fertile farmland. While many farmers working the Highlands became full-time, legal whiskey-makers in the 19th century, here in the Lowlands there was less incentive to go down that path. Good money could be made from rearing cattle, providing Glasgow with its food.

This is Robbie Burns country. Scotland's national poet was born to farming stock, and his poems confirm that he and his Ayrshire friends were not unfamiliar with whiskey. What were they drinking? Moonshine, most likely, smuggled in from Arran or made on their own farms. There is no evidence that Alexander Walker, the tenant of Todriggs Farm, ever distilled, but his son John founded one of the great whiskey dynasties when he invested in an "Italian grocer's" business in the nearby town of Kilmarnock. By 1850,

DISTILLERY DETAILS

GIRVAN FOUNDED: 1963.
OWNER: William Grant & Sons. METHOD: Column stills.
CAPACITY: 726,000 gallons.

BLADNOCH FOUNDED: 1846.
OWNER: Raymond Armstrong. METHOD: Pot stills.
CAPACITY: 26,000 gallons.

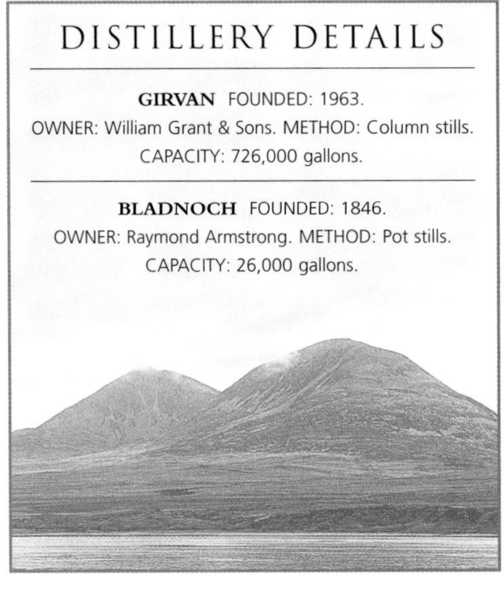

John's son, named Alexander after his grandfather, had begun to blend whiskeys and sell his Johnnie Walker's Old Highland Whisky to the world. "Whisky and freedom gang thegither," wrote Burns. "Whisky and commerce do the same," one of the hard-headed Walkers may have added.

Girvan *may be lacking in the looks department and not have the romance of the older distilleries, but it is without doubt Scotland's most high-tech plant.*

GIRVAN

It is a short distance from Burns' birthplace in Alloway to the Clyde coast's only distillery. The firm of William Grant (best known for its Glenfiddich single malt) chose the quiet seaside town of Girvan as the site of its grain distillery in 1963. Three years later it constructed a short-lived malt distillery called Ladyburn within the plant. Although this disappeared in 1975, every so often a bottling will appear. Girvan, however, is still very much in operation, and claims to be Scotland's most high-tech whiskey-making distillery. Its sweet, soft product can be found under the guise of Black Barrel, although those with deeper pockets should seek out the superb 1963 single grain that was released recently.

BLADNOCH

The journey southwest through Ayrshire and toward the Solway Firth takes the whiskey traveler into a region with few actual distilleries. In the 1880s, while the rest of the country was enjoying a whiskey boom, the southern counties of Scotland had only four malt distilleries. Annandale, in the town of Annan, reverted to being a farm in the 1920s, although it looks as if it could open up again at some stage in the near future. The two sites in Langholm, Glen Tarras and Langholm, are long gone, leaving only tantalizing references to the "Birch Whisky" made at the latter and the former's "rich and flavorsome" make. Only Galloway's Bladnoch is still working. Galloway is a district of woodland, hills, and small fishing villages; in many ways it resembles the northern counties of Ireland. Bladnoch, Scotland's most southerly distillery, lies about a mile (2 km) outside Wigtown.

You may think that if a great distillery like Rosebank (*see p. 100*) was unable to survive, then there would be little hope for a remote distillery, but Bladnoch has held on. Founded after the liberalizing of excise laws in 1817 and enlarged in 1878, it has had a rocky history, with four different owners between 1930 and the mid-1980s, at which point it became part of the Bell's stable. It was made part of that company's malt whiskey range alongside Inchgower, Blair Athol, and Dufftown, but Bladnoch was shut

Bladnoch distillery, *deemed surplus to requirements by its previous owners, now produces a moderate amount of excellent malt every year.*

in 1993, another victim of the whiskey loch. However, the story does have a happy ending. In 1994, Raymond Armstrong, from Ulster, Northern Ireland, bought the site with the intention of converting the buildings into vacation homes. Then he tasted the floral, well-balanced whiskey (there is none prettier) and realized that reopening the distillery would be a good commercial opportunity.

Although the volume Armstrong can make each year is restricted due to a clause in the purchasing agreement, Bladnoch is flourishing. More than just a distillery with a working still, the site also houses a museum and is home to Scotland's first whiskey school, where malt-lovers can learn the craft of distilling. It deserves to succeed.

TASTING NOTES

A CANDIDATE for Scotland's most remote distillery—and certainly its most southerly. Happily, the exceptionally light and flowery malts of Bladnoch were saved at the brink of extinction.

BLADNOCH
23-YEAR-OLD
(DISTILLED 1977)
RARE MALTS
53.6 VOL.

Color Gold.
Nose Delicate and summery. Aromatic: lemon, icing sugar, almond cake, vanilla, red fruit, and basil leaf.
Body Light to medium.
Palate Floral with a sweetly attractive start but good texture mid-palate.
Finish Strawberries, then dry and malty. Delicate yet complex.

BLADNOCH 23-YEAR-OLD

BLADNOCH
1989, 13-YEAR-OLD, CADENHEAD, 54.9 VOL.

Color Straw.
Nose Crisp and delicate with lifted summery aromas. Grass, straw, lemon zest, almond, creamed coconut.
Body Light and floaty.
Palate Sweet. Flowery mid-palate with white currant, violet, then fresh lemon and grass. Summer fruits.
Finish Fragrant but zesty.

BLADNOCH
1991, GORDON & MACPHAIL 54.8 VOL.

Color Light gold.
Nose Mouthwatering and fragrant. Lily, freesia, then apple, including blossom.
Body Delicate.
Palate Vibrant with good feel and fresh, natural ripeness. Orchard fruit, hard candy, gentle oak. Good balance and complexity.
Finish Lightly dry.

PRETTY BLADNOCH *not only produces an excellent floral malt, it also offers the chance for anyone to learn the craft of distillation in its unique whiskey school.*

Auchentoshan

ONCE, GLASGOW WAS ENCIRCLED BY AROUND TWENTY MALT WHISKEY PRODUCERS. TODAY, ONLY ONE OF THESE LOWLAND DISTILLERIES REMAINS.

The third operating Lowland malt distillery lies on the north bank of the Clyde, on the road to Dumbarton. Upstream is Glasgow, which has recently transformed itself into a modern European city. Only a short distance to the north are the Highlands. Given this setting on the cusp of the rural and the urban, it seems appropriate that there should be a distillery here. Whiskey, after all, came into its own during the 19th century due to a melding of Highland tradition and Lowland capital, although that was not enough to save the many distilleries that once produced here.

DISTILLERY DETAILS

AUCHENTOSHAN FOUNDED: 1823.
OWNER: Morrison Bowmore Distillers Ltd..
METHOD: Pot stills. CAPACITY: 423,000 gallons.

AUCHENTOSHAN

As you go west out of Glasgow toward Loch Lomond and all points north and west, you will catch a glimpse of a modest-looking, white-painted building wedged between the river and the highway. Spirits may have been been made in this corner of the field (or *Auchentoshan* in Gaelic) from the 17th century, when a monastery occupied this spot. It is highly likely that whiskey was distilled here from the turn of the 19th century.

Auchentoshan went legal in 1823. It passed through a number of hands during the 20th century, most of them belonging to brewers, before being bought by Eadie Cairns, an entrepreneurial publican, in 1969. It became part of the Morrison Bowmore stable in 1984. Many of its workforce are expatriate Ileachs (natives of Islay).

This was the first distillery encountered by many visitors to the west of Scotland, but few could stop here. It was not until 2004 that the doors were finally opened to the general public—the curse of the Lowlands strikes once more. Perhaps now that visiting is allowed, more Glaswegians will take a trip to the banks of the Clyde and explore the distillery that makes one of the malts that can claim to be the city's own. It is all part of Morrison Bowmore's plan to build "Auchie" into an important brand within its portfolio.

The place has been somewhat overlooked by its own city. It has its own particular quirks. The washbacks, for example, are on the outside of the building, though its real claim to fame is the still house. Auchentoshan is the last of the Lowlanders to triple distill, and it uses its own technique, which involves having higher than normal strength charges for the intermediate (or low wines) and spirit stills.

TRIPLE DISTILLATION

The wash still is run as normal. Low-strength "tails" from the intermediate still are then mixed with the low wines to form its next charge. Although this has little effect on the alcoholic strength of the liquid, it does have

TASTING NOTES

THE LAST OF the Clydesiders and also the last triple-distilled Lowland malt, Auchentoshan offers more than just a fine example of Lowland subtlety; it is an opportunity to taste the culmination of decades of whiskey evolution, in sight of Glasgow.

AUCHENTOSHAN
10-YEAR-OLD, 40 VOL.

Color Gold.
Nose Light, crunchy, very malty. Whole-wheat bread, bran flakes, then an intense orange zestiness.

AUCHENTOSHAN THREE WOOD

Body Light.
Palate Clean, pretty, and citric, with a crisp, cereal maltiness creeping in toward the finish.
Finish Short, nutty.

AUCHENTOSHAN SELECTED CASK VATTING
18-YEAR-OLD, 58.8 VOL.

Color Full gold to bronze.
Nose Linseed, saddlery.
Body Smooth, layered, soft.
Palate Linseed, fresh leather, perfumy.
Finish Clean, lemony, scenty.

AUCHENTOSHAN THREE WOOD
NO AGE STATEMENT, 43 VOL.

Color Umbrous.
Nose Malt alongside dried fruit and nut, then burned toffee, red fruits, and a pronounced pruney, sherried quality.
Body Rich and soft.
Palate Very sherried, with a certain soft, sweet fruitiness in the center, and a dry maltiness underneath.
Finish Dry, charred fruit (raisins in rich fruitcake).

a significant impact on flavor. The mix is then distilled in the intermediate still and once again the resulting distillate is split into two. The high-strength "heads" are collected as part of the charge for the spirit still, while the "tails" are diverted back as part of the intermediate still's next run.

The heads are then mixed with the "feints" collected from the previous run of the spirit still, although, as we will see, this term is a bit of a misnomer. When this mix has been distilled in the spirit still, only a minuscule cut (average strength 80 vol.) is collected. After this head is separated, the rest of the run is classed as feints. This means that the strength of the spirit still's charge is twice as high as in a "normal" (double or two-still) distillation. Once again, this has a direct and significant impact on flavor.

Triple distillation is often thought of as the classic Lowland method of making whiskey, but not every Lowland distillery produces its spirit in this fashion. Indeed, when Alfred Barnard visited Auchentoshan in the 1880s, there were only two pots. However, triple distillation remains a technique that can produce the lightly flavored whiskeys now synonymous with the Lowlands.

THE LOWLAND STYLE

In the past, Lowland whiskeys were made from a mix of cereals—wheat and oats as well as barley—for the simple reason that there was a wider choice of grains available in this part of the country. The fact that the Lowlands have always had a relatively large population resulted in the use of big stills, and for many years the distillers undertook to supply large volumes of spirit to English gin distillers. All of these factors impacted on the Lowland whiskey style, specifically in the creation of its lighter character. In time, these more delicately flavored whiskeys became what the local populace demanded. There is always more to a regional style than simply the impact of the immediate environment.

On account of the high-strength spirit that is collected from the distillery's spirit still, Auchentoshan belongs firmly in this Lowland camp of light and fresh whiskeys. Taste it as a youngster and you will find it resolutely dry and malty, with a light burst of lemon. The grassiness that links all the Lowlanders together is there, but there is precious little of the floweriness that appears in its rivals. On first tasting one of these young versions, you would not think it to be a whiskey likely to bloom in later life, but it is.

Auchentoshan has remarkable staying power. The hard cereal casing is cast off as it matures, the grass seems to sweeten, and a light, citric-accented fruitiness is revealed. That is not to say that Auchentoshan does not have any guts. It has a hidden steeliness that prevents even its oldest expressions from being overwhelmed by oak. Charming yet tough? Attractive yet deep? Of course. It is Glaswegian, after all.

AUCHENTOSHAN *continues to produce whiskey by the triple-distillation method, rarely used in distilleries today. The technique results in a crisp, fruity malt.*

The Western Highlands

ALTHOUGH POSSESSING SOME OF SCOTLAND'S MOST SPECTACULAR SCENERY, THE WESTERN HIGHLANDS HAVE A LOW DISTILLERY COUNT. THOSE THAT HAVE SURVIVED THE CENTURIES OFFER A WIDE SPREAD OF STYLES AND FLAVORS.

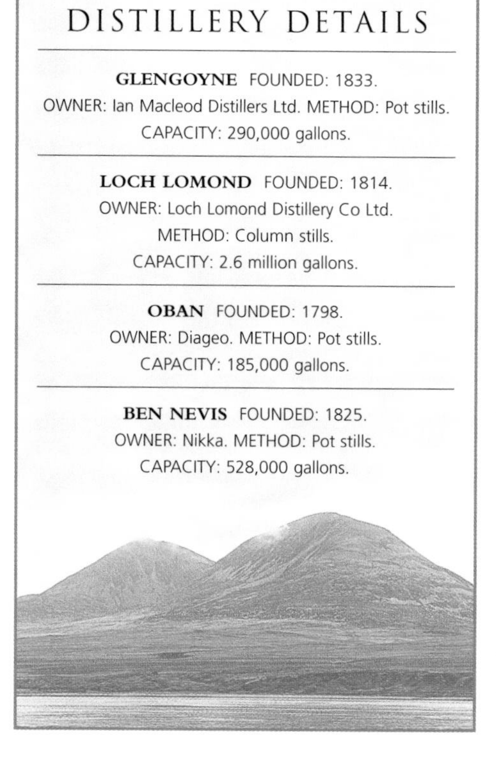

DISTILLERY DETAILS

GLENGOYNE FOUNDED: 1833.
OWNER: Ian Macleod Distillers Ltd. METHOD: Pot stills.
CAPACITY: 290,000 gallons.

LOCH LOMOND FOUNDED: 1814.
OWNER: Loch Lomond Distillery Co Ltd.
METHOD: Column stills.
CAPACITY: 2.6 million gallons.

OBAN FOUNDED: 1798.
OWNER: Diageo. METHOD: Pot stills.
CAPACITY: 185,000 gallons.

BEN NEVIS FOUNDED: 1825.
OWNER: Nikka. METHOD: Pot stills.
CAPACITY: 528,000 gallons.

Scotland is divided by a pair of diagonal geological faults that split the country into three areas. One of these long diagonals marks the border between the Lowlands and the Highlands. It slashes across the country from the west to the east, passing close to the northwestern suburbs of Glasgow. It may be quintessentially urban, yet Glasgow is on the edge of the Highlands. A half-hour drive north and you can be walking in the Campsie Fells. From the air, these low-lying hills appear like a dun-colored exclamation mark, with the strange knoll of Dumgoyne as its full stop.

GLENGOYNE

At the foot of that knoll is the second malt distillery that can claim to be Glasgow's own, Glengoyne. Geographically, though, it is in the Highlands. In the 18th and 19th centuries that Highland line offered a way to restrict the market for Highland whiskey, legislation that drove distillation underground. The Campsie Fells offered ideal hideaways where the moonshiners could distill.

Today, Glengoyne betrays its origins as a farm distillery; it produces a malt that has made great play out of being unpeated, and the absence of smoke allows its juicy, sweet character to show. From 1876, Glengoyne was owned by traditional Glasgow blending house Lang Bros., which experimented with aging in Scottish oak, and released a series of fine one-off bottlings. Glengoyne has now been bought by Ian Macleod and is a perfect fit for this small, enterprising distiller-bottler.

LOCH LOMOND

A few miles to the west of Glengoyne, on the shores of the loch, lies Alexandria, the home of the Loch Lomond distillery, where a greater range of whiskeys (many of them peated) are being made. With pots, Lomond stills, and a column setup, this is a mini-whiskey industry in one building. Inchmurrin, Old Rosdhu, and Croftengea are the most commonly seen malts—but most of the fillings are destined for anonymous supermarket labels.

The whiskey trail now heads up the western shore of Loch Lomond, before moving into the long glacial valleys that cut deep into the heart of Argyll—and the low distillery count is purely due to this geography. The fabric of the land here has been rent by glaciers and flooded by the sea, making west–east communications difficult, and isolating many distilleries from the blending centers of Glasgow and Perth.

OBAN

Past the isles of Scarba and Luing, along the Crinan canal, lies the port of Oban. The canal route to the blending centers enabled Oban's distillery to thrive, where others did not. A rail link built in 1880 ensured its success.

The distillery was established in 1798 by the Stevenson brothers. They built houses and ships, and sold slate and kelp; a classic example of how whiskey-

The Ben Nevis *distillery may be owned by the Japanese company Nikka, but the whiskey—and the livestock—are thoroughly Scottish.*

Ben Nevis distillery *has recently focused more attention on the quality of wood used in its barrels. This has undoubtedly improved the malt.*

making changed from a small-scale farm industry to one run by men of capital. Oban manages to be both a West Highland malt and a coastal one, having a marked marine tingle to it even though virtually all the spirit is matured inland. Worm tubs fill out its belly, giving extra weight to the mid-palate.

BEN NEVIS

The west coast's second distillery, Ben Nevis, sits in the shadow of Great Britain's tallest mountain at Fort William, and the water to make their whiskey is drawn from the the Mill Burn, which starts as snow-melt. In 1825, the owner, "Long John" MacDonald, used the rail and ferry links to send his malt to the central belt, and at one stage employed 230 people. The distillery had fallen on hard times when it was bought by Japanese giant Nikka in 1989, under whose stewardship it is now finally realizing its potential. It is a big dram that copes well with European oak.

TASTING NOTES

UNPEATED, lightly peated; coastal, hillside, and lochside; worm tubs, Lomond stills, and condensers: all Scotland is here.

GLENGOYNE

Owing to its location at the foot of the Campsie Fells, this farmhouse-style distillery can be considered the first of the Highland malts.

GLENGOYNE
10-YEAR-OLD, 40 VOL.

Color Gold.
Nose Fresh grass, butter churn, sweet maltiness. Delicate cooked fruit notes.
Body Light/medium.
Palate Soft and creamy. Hint of malt, stewed apple, vanilla.
Finish Sweet and clean.

GLENGOYNE 10-YEAR-OLD

GLENGOYNE
17-YEAR-OLD, 43 VOL.
Color Rich gold.
Nose Full. Raisin, vanilla, cigar box/spruce. Juicy malt.
Body Medium. Soft.
Palate Good rich depth. Old apple, fragrant oak. Some sweet dried fruits.
Finish Long, drying.

LOCH LOMOND

A huge number of styles of whiskey are produced at this distillery, mostly for third parties. There are, however, some occasional distillery bottlings.

INCHMURRIN
29-YEAR-OLD, CADENHEAD
54.4 VOL.
Inchmurrin is one of the small islands that lies at the south of Loch Lomond close to the distillery.

Color Full gold.
Nose Marshmallow, apple sponge, then hot tarmac . Hints of dry bracken, green fern.
Body Medium.
Palate Assertive. Hazelnut, semidried fruit, hawthorn, green note, fern.
Finish Peppery. Oak

INCHMURRIN
1973, GORDON & MACPHAIL
40 VOL.
Color Light gold.
Nose Yeasty, flour sacks, lemon. Leather saddles. Lead piping.
Body Light. Firm.
Palate Lean and unformed, some green fruits. Quite rigid.
Finish Tight, short.

OBAN

OBAN
14-YEAR-OLD, 43 VOL.

Color Bright gold.
Nose Aromatic and lightly spicy. Crystallized ginger, hint of peat. Good depth and some complexity.
Body Assertive, tingling.
Palate Starts sweet and light but smooth, complex, spicy depth. Lightly aromatic. Hint of smoke.
Finish Dry, slightly marine-like.

OBAN 14 YEAR OLD

OBAN
1980, DISTILLER'S EDITION
43 VOL.
Finished in Montilla fino casks.

Color Light amber.
Nose Rounded and fat. Into semidried fruits (apricot), ginger in syrup. Hint of marine character.
Body Medium-bodied. Ripe.
Palate Unctuous with hidden depth. Quite sweet and concentrated. Good balance between freshness and sweet and warm spices.
Finish Long. Sweet. Tingling.

BEN NEVIS

BEN NEVIS
10-YEAR-OLD, 46 VOL.

Color Amber.
Nose Vanilla, orange peel, bitter chocolate. Touch of mossy peat smoke. Aromatic and slightly waxy.
Body Big, rich.
Palate Rounded with dried fruit/nut and chocolate. Vanilla. Powerful.
Finish Ripe. Burnt sugar.

BEN NEVIS 10-YEAR-OLD

BEN NEVIS
26-YEAR-OLD (DISTILLED 1975)
53.9 VOL.

Color Gold drifting to amber.
Nose Fresh and pleasingly light. Privet, cut grass. Lime blossom.
Body Crisp. Medium.
Palate Cooked/dried fruits. Some sweetness. Malted milk.
Finish Medium length. Drying.

Arran

THE ISLAND OF ARRAN HAS A LONG HISTORY OF WHISKEY-MAKING (MOST OF IT ILLICIT), BUT IT WAS ONLY AT THE END OF THE 20TH CENTURY THAT IT FINALLY GOT ITS FIRST TRUE DISTILLERY.

Arran is the most accessible of the western isles, embraced on the east by the Clyde coast and on the west by the peninsula of Kintyre. A quick ferry trip either from Ardrossan on the Clyde coast to Brodick, or from Claonaig in Kintyre to Lochranza, brings you to an island that typifies Scotland's ability to compress all of its natural attributes into as small a space as possible. The walking enthusiast can head into the granite crags in the north; the more sedate can drift around the attractive villages on the coast or the gentle glens of the fertile southern end.

Up until the 18th century, every island made whiskey. It helped lubricate social gatherings as well as maximizing the income from poor-yielding bere barley. When the exporting of Highland whiskey was banned, distilling simply went underground. Arran led the way in this. The island was sufficiently remote for policing to be ineffective, while it was easy to transport the illicit hooch to the mainland. Even though there were three legal distilleries operating in 1793 and Arran was exporting barley, the moonshiners continued—often using either "sour beer" smuggled in from Ireland, or molasses. What is perhaps more perplexing is why, of all the islands, Arran only recently became a whiskey producer once again.

DISTILLERY DETAILS

ARRAN FOUNDED: 1995. OWNER: The Arran Malt Whisky Co. METHOD: Pot stills. CAPACITY: 198,000 gallons.

Kilmory in the south of the island was the most (in)famous center for illicit distillation. As J. A. Balfour and W. M. Mackenzie remark in *The Book of Arran* (published 1910): "there were few, if any, in the parish who at some period of their lives were not engaged in some department of smuggling... it was considered rather an honourable occupation."

LOCHRANZA

Legal distilling won the day briefly; but the Lagg distillery only ran until 1837. This could have been due to the land clearances of the 1820s and '30s, problems with transport and distribution, or simply that the whiskey didn't make the grade. Whatever the reason, Arran fell silent as a whiskey island and remained so until 1995, when Harold Currie, the former managing director of Campbell Distillers, decided to take the bold step of building a distillery in the north, at Lochranza.

To help raise the necessary capital for his new business he hit upon the idea of issuing $750 bonds to the public which would entitle them to five cases of whiskey produced by the distillery in 2001. The gamble paid off. It did so because Harold Currie was a whiskey

The Arran distillery's *location at Lochranza is spectacular—looking out to sea and backed by mountains, the setting could not be more apt.*

A NATURAL SUPPLY OF *plentiful cold water, like this river near Lochranza, is essential in whiskey-making.*

man. He understood that this is a long-term business, and also that ultimately a distillery lives or dies by the quality of its spirit.

A NEW DISTILLERY

The Lochranza distillery is custom-built, a member of the new wave of distillery design which can also be seen at Cape Breton (*see p. 206*), Benromach (*see p. 144*) and Glengyle (*see p. 113*). All are small distilleries, in which the equipment is contained in one room and on the same level. Not only easy to operate, such distilleries are easy for the public to understand. After all, not every visitor to a distillery is a graduate of malt.

Every distiller has to wait at least three years before he can even sell his spirit as Scotch, which makes the first three years very difficult financially. Most sites survive because they provide fillings for blends, but none of the blending houses needed Arran. That meant taking the single malt route, which meant waiting a lot longer than three years before building a new brand. The income required to offset this has come from the tourists, lured by the visitor center and the spectacular setting of Lochranza, a beautiful natural harbor with a stunning, mountainous backdrop.

From the beginning, Arran has shown that it is a well-made spirit. Its tiny stills produce a light, very clean and malty spirit, but as it has matured a previously hidden fruitiness has begun to emerge. The sole complaint is that so far the distillery has resisted calls to make a batch of peated malt every year—something that would be in keeping with the island's whiskey-making heritage, and appeal to a new generation of malt lovers who like a bit of smoke in their drams.

TASTING NOTES

AN ISLAND IT may be, but Arran's malt is in the sweet, light "Highland" style.

ARRAN SINGLE MALT

43 VOL.

ARRAN SINGLE MALT

Color Straw with lemon highlights.
Nose Floral and soft with some malty dryness to balance.
Body Light to medium.
Palate Vanilla and mixed flowers. Young but not at all harsh.
Finish Malty.

ARRAN, NON-CHILL-FILTERED

46 VOL.

Color Pale gold.
Nose Fresh, young, and lively. Green grapes, sour apple, crisp malt.
Body Light to medium-bodied.
Palate Softer than the nose suggests but full of the taut firmness of youth.
Finish Clean, malty.

ARRAN

8-YEAR-OLD, DOUGLAS LAING, 46 VOL.

Color Gold.
Nose Light and soft. Lemon and orange peel. Creamy cookie. Resinous European oak.
Body Medium. Gentle.
Palate Youthful. Cooked fruit, mushroom, orange. Good intensity and feel.
Finish Dried fruits. Raspberry.

ARRAN, CALVADOS FINISH

Arran, too, is branching out into finishing.

Color Bright gold.
Nose Intense and spicy: cinnamon, green grass, apple pie. With water, green banana, toasted oak.
Body Light to medium.
Palate Appley and intense. Sweet and spicy. Grassy. Good balance.
Finish Apples.

Campbeltown

ONCE SCOTLAND'S PREMIER DISTILLING TOWN, CAMPBELTOWN BECAME AN ISOLATED WHISKEY OUTPOST. HOWEVER, DESPITE THE DECLINE IN DISTILLERIES, IT IS NOW HOME TO ONE OF THE CULT MALTS OF THE WHISKEY WORLD.

Were we to look for the cradle of distillation in Scotland, we would look not to Michael Scot's Melrose, nor to Fife where Friar John Cor was (probably) domiciled, nor even to Islay, but to the peninsula of Kintyre. It was here where the MacVey/Beth family (Beaton in English) first arrived in Scotland in 1300. Physicians to the court of Ulster, they were part of the entourage of Agnes O'Cathan when she married Angus Og, then Lord of Kintyre. Versed in the teachings of Arab scholars, it is highly likely they understood the art of distillation. The shift from medicinal alcohol to social drink came much later, but when it did, Kintyre was a major producer—and its center was Campbeltown.

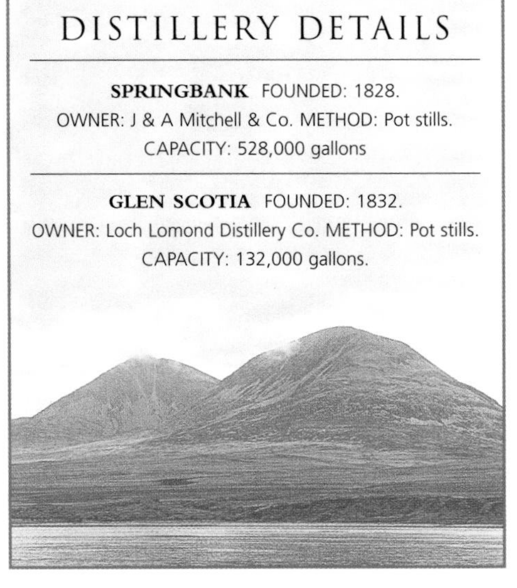

DISTILLERY DETAILS

SPRINGBANK FOUNDED: 1828.
OWNER: J & A Mitchell & Co. METHOD: Pot stills.
CAPACITY: 528,000 gallons

GLEN SCOTIA FOUNDED: 1832.
OWNER: Loch Lomond Distillery Co. METHOD: Pot stills.
CAPACITY: 132,000 gallons.

SCOTLAND'S WHISKEY CAPITAL

Thanks to the Crinan canal, Kintyre can be considered an island—and many of its residents like to think of it as such. Drooping down toward Ireland, its west coast looks out to Jura, Islay, Gigha, and the Antrim coast; its eastern seaboard looks across to Arran and Ayrshire. Kintyre was strategically important, a stepping stone to the west, and in the days of sail, Campbeltown was a major trading hub with links not just to Scotland and England, but to North America, too.

Yet in these car-centered days, it is considered remote, and its time as Scotland's whiskey capital is but the dimmest of memories. You can get to Campbeltown by plane from Glasgow to the deserted air force base at Machrihanish, but most visitors have to endure what former resident Paul McCartney called "the long and winding road."

Cupped around a natural harbor at the southeastern tip of Kintyre, Campbeltown was established in the early 17th century by the Dukes of Argyll on the site of the older settlement of Kilkerran, as part of a policy to improve the agriculture of Kintyre. It attracted many farmers from central Scotland, including, at the end of the century, a family called Mitchell, who would become the leading distillers in the area.

Where there were farms, there was always whiskey, and by 1794 there were 22 legal distilleries in Campbeltown—and 292 seizures of illicit ones. Whiskey was in the blood, and

An improved wood *policy at Springbank distillery has paid off.*

Springbank's *three stills are used to produce three different malts: Springbank, Longrow, and Hazelburn.*

LWS
No 2
CONTENTS
12274 LTRS

when the laws were changed in 1824, Campbeltown's boom period began. By 1887, Campbeltown's 21 distilleries were producing 2.4 million gallons (9 million liters) a year, enough to allow the town's whiskey barons to build the grand houses that still stand on the north shore of the loch. By 1891 it the town was thought to have the highest per capita income in the UK, and barley was being imported from the Baltic to keep the stills running. Today, however, there are only three distilleries, one of which opened recently.

The demise of Campbeltown, a town that once supported 20 distilleries, has long intrigued whiskey scholars. It seems that there were several factors. The traditional Campbeltown style—heavy, oily, and powerful—started to fall out of favor with blenders, who turned increasingly to the lighter whiskeys from Speyside. In addition, local coal supplies were exhausted, driving up fuel costs at the same time as the world recession reduced demand. Then the effects of Prohibition hit. Although Campbeltown had long-established trading links with North America, many distillers did not have the alliances with the Canadian middlemen who helped build the reputation of many blends. Those who did sell direct were forced to reduce prices further. Their answer was to run the stills fast and make as much low-cost spirit as possible. As a result, Campbeltown began making bad whiskey and collapsed.

SPRINGBANK

One distillery refused to die: Springbank, founded by John and William Mitchell in 1828 and still run by the same family today. Ironically, it survived because its whiskey was lighter than that of its neighbors. Today, it is the only self-sufficient malt distillery in Scotland, and one that is a glimpse into the past—and into a future. It malts all its own barley, uses local peat, distills the spirit two and a half times (i.e., some of the final new make has been distilled three times, some twice), ages, and bottles on site. Once thought of as wildly idiosyncratic and old-fashioned by most of the industry, now many small malt brands are following its lead, while even the largest distillers have started bottling their top-end malts at higher strength, non-chill-filtered and with no caramel addition.

Medium-peated with touches of sweet citrus fruits, allied to a briny note and a lightly oily texture, Springbank offers all of Scotland's malt styles in one package and

TASTING NOTES

CAMPBELTOWN'S full-flavored malts are complex, often briny, and normally show the influence of peat, perfect for people not afraid of character.

SPRINGBANK 10-YEAR-OLD

SPRINGBANK

SPRINGBANK
10-YEAR-OLD
46 VOL.

Color Gold.
Nose Light brine, spice, rounded malt, pear. Elegant for a youngster.
Body Rich and oily. Mouth-coating.
Palate Fantastic mix of dry and sweet, canned pear, citrus. Suggestion of smoke.
Finish Melon.

SPRINGBANK
15-YEAR-OLD
46 VOL.

Color Light amber.
Nose Sophisticated. Dundee cake, vanilla, new leather, pipe tobacco, dried apricot, peat, tea.
Body Full and rich. Mouth-coating.
Palate European oak is there, but not dominating. Sweet tobacco, nut, smoke in the background. Complex.
Finish Soot, malt. Brine.

SPRINGBANK FRANK McHARDY ANNIVERSARY, 1975
46 VOL.

Color Rich gold.
Nose Nutty, spicy oak, mandarin/curaçao, macadamia, herbs, light smoke. Oaky.
Body Creamy and soft.
Palate Coconut, pine, citrus, coffee. Spices to the finish.
Finish Nutty, sooty.

LONGROW
The heavily peated, double-distilled malt from Springbank.

10-YEAR-OLD (1992), 46 VOL.

LONGROW 10-YEAR-OLD

Color Light gold.
Nose Sweet, full yet slightly floral. Has medicinal, earthy notes as well. Good balance.
Body Robust, succulent.
Palate Peaches and soft fruit under the peat. Good nutty depth.
Finish Dry, peaty.

GLEN SCOTIA

GLEN SCOTIA
Campbeltown's forgotten distillery has only run intermittently in recent years—stylistically, it is a classic old-style Campbeltown malt.

14-YEAR-OLD
40 VOL.

Color Old gold.
Nose Rounded and perfumed. Acacia, ripe melon. Becomes oily with notes of waxed pine.
Body Oily.
Palate Moist coconut, soft and round. Some smoke.
Finish Cream, little brine.

really hits its stride in its mid-teens. Just to keep things interesting, two other whiskeys are made here: the rich, heavily peated, double-distilled Longrow, and the fragrant, triple-distilled, unpeated Hazelburn.

THE REBIRTH OF GLENGYLE

Wandering around Campbeltown is an exercise in distillery archaeology. Tantalizing glimpses of old sites remain—a cracked and faded painted sign, the shape of the windows on an apartment building, the incongruous sight of a supermarket with a pagoda roof. The fragility of the whiskey industry is evident, and for all the thick red sandstone walls that remain, there are infinitely more that have gone.

In 2004, however, something remarkable happened. A distillery that had been silent for almost 80 years reopened. The shell of Glengyle, established in 1872 by William Mitchell (co-founder with brother John of Springbank) was to become Scotland's newest distillery. Arran (*see p. 108*) may quibble over this, but since the building was derelict, Glengyle can be considered a new distillery. Along with the opening of a wind turbine manufacturing plant and the possibility of a ferry link being reestablished with Ireland, the new distillery is another indication that Campbeltown is coming back to life. Glengyle's exterior has been repointed, while the interior has been designed by Frank McHardy, who manages both this and Springbank distillery. When it finally appears, the malt will not carry the name of the distillery, but is to be called Kilkerran, as the owner of Campbeltown's other distillery owns the Glengyle brand.

EAGLESOME'S EXTERIOR. *This shop is one of the few traditional "Italian warehousemen" left in Scotland.*

GLEN SCOTIA

That other distillery is Glen Scotia, which is now owned by the Loch Lomond Distillery Company. It is a distillery with a checkered past—it is allegedly haunted by the ghost of former owner Duncan MacCallum, who drowned himself in the loch in 1930. Although it is now working once more, bottlings have been extremely variable.

EAGLESOME

For a truly satisfying range of bottlings, take a visit to Eaglesome. The traditional grocer carries everything from the Springbank range (plus its excellent Campbeltown Loch blend) and also the extensive range from independent bottler Cadenhead. Like Springbank and Glengyle, both shop and bottler are owned by John Mitchell's great-great-nephew. There's one whiskey baron left.

EAGLESOME'S INTERIOR. *The fine array of whiskeys available here is guaranteed to delight any malt-lover who visits this shop, which is situated in the heart of whiskey country.*

Islay: The South

GAELIC SCHOLARS HAVE LONG DEBATED WHAT ISLAY MEANS; MANY BELIEVE THAT THE NAME SIMPLY MEANS "THE ISLAND." MOST WHISKEY-LOVERS WOULD HEARTILY CONCUR. FOR THEM, IT IS "THE" ISLAND.

Islay does not seduce you like other islands. Instead, it invades and takes possession of you. Its constant wind carries a mix of sweet, salt-laden air, the whiff of the sea, the coconut aroma of hot gorse, a hint of peat smoke and bog myrtle, and the smell of a just-spent fire on the beach. All the notes you pick up in its malts are there, floating in the Atlantic wind.

As an island, Islay may not be as immediately spectacular as Skye or Rum, or as eerily lonely as Jura, but as you explore you can see how it compresses its secrets into tight parcels: dune-fringed beaches, remote hills, cliffs, caves, peat bogs, standing stones, lost parliaments, abandoned townships, and Celtic memories. It is a tapestry of geographical and historical treasures through which whiskey runs like a golden thread.

DISTILLERY DETAILS

ARDBEG FOUNDED: 1815.
OWNER: Glenmorangie PLC. METHOD: Pot stills.
CAPACITY: 291,000 gallons.

LAGAVULIN FOUNDED: 1816.
OWNER: Diageo. METHOD: Pot stills.
CAPACITY: 449,000 gallons.

LAPHROAIG FOUNDED: 1826.
OWNER: Allied Distillers Ltd. METHOD: Pot stills.
CAPACITY: 634,000 gallons.

The best way to approach the whiskey island is not via the ferry terminal or the airport but by boat from Ireland, sailing like the 6th-century monks did, gliding through the Ardmore islets, which string out like an exposed reef guarding the southern shore, past rocks and sandy bays where seals bask and lazily view you slipping by.

It may have been those monks who brought distilling with them on their short crossing from Ireland, which lies only 17 miles (28 km) away—closer than the Scottish mainland—to Kildalton. So the starting point should rightly be Kildalton, next to the last perfectly preserved Celtic High Cross with its patterns of intricate carvings, biblical imagery, and hints of a not-quite-forgotten paganism.

ARDBEG

Close by the site of the long-abandoned Tallant distillery, and a little farther south, lies Ardbeg. Founded in 1815 by a family of tenant farmers named MacDougall, by 1853 Ardbeg was the biggest producer on Islay and the center of a 200-strong community.

THE RESURRECTED ARDBEG *distillery is guarded by the reef of the Ardmore Islands—its whitewashed buildings add to the dramatic coastal landscape.*

Despite its high reputation, Ardbeg has had its share of troubles in recent times. It was noted as being the most overtly peaty of the Kildalton trio—the result of its kiln not having any extractor fans. Today's single malt enthusiasts, with their love of peat, adore Ardbeg's peaty flavor, but until recently, Ardbeg, like virtually every distillery, existed to provide fillings for blends.

When the slump of the 1980s hit, Ardbeg was one of two peaty Islay distilleries owned by Allied Distillers and was, quite simply, surplus to requirements. In 1982 it closed, and though it was run intermittently in the early 1990s, often making unpeated "Kildalton" malt, it soon fell into disrepair. In 1997, however, an unlikely savior appeared in the form of Glenmorangie, the producer of one of the lightest, non-peaty Highland malts. Ardbeg's rapid resurrection from moldering shell to hot single malt is one of the most heartening stories in the whiskey industry. Its stills are working again, the warehouses are being filled, and its café (which occupies the old kiln building) offers the only good food in this part of the island.

Today, Ardbeg buzzes with energy, as if the buildings themselves are eager to get on with things, as if to prove themselves after years of neglect. The whiskey is still heavily peated, but there is a subtlety lying beneath the smoke: hints of lime, cereal, lanolin, and a slight marine hit.

ARDBEG'S *character begins to be formed in its wooden washbacks.*

LAGAVULIN

If Ardbeg has a village feel, then its near neighbor, Lagavulin, is a fortress. Tall, severe, and white, it guards the seashore opposite the ruins of Dunyvaig (pronounced "Dun-oo-vague") castle, the fortress of the Lords of the Isles, a place that those of a romantic disposition see as the possible setting for James IV's first taste of distilled spirits in 1493.

Lagavulin was built in 1816 when the 10 illicit bothies located in the immediate vicinity joined forces and went legal. In time, the distillery passed into the hands of the irascible Sir Peter Mackie, of White Horse fame, who built its reputation for quality. It is now part of the Diageo stable.

It is a magical location. On a clear day from the pier you can see the coast of Ireland to the south, and the Mull of Kintyre to the east. There are fishing boats bobbing in the bay, divers seeking out Islay's juiciest scallops, and a bell on the clifftop seems poised to sound the alarm if invaders are spotted. The white-painted distillery rises like a castle wall behind you. There are few more evocative locations in the world of whiskey.

The interior has been renovated in such a fashion that you would not be surprised to see the ghost of Sir Peter walking toward you down the corridor. A tour of any distillery is also a tour of different aromas—the cereal sweetness of the mash tun, the prickle of carbon dioxide and bready yeast in the tun room—but Lagavulin's still-house has an aroma that seems to have a greater intensity and sweet peatiness than most. This is where Islay's most complex malt is formed.

The stills, fat-bottomed and sensuous as the curves of a Renoir nude, seem almost too plain to make such a dram, yet their shape and the slow-paced distillation allows the spirit vapor to caress the copper for a long time. Copper removes heavy elements from alcohol, and it is this extended contact between vapor and metal that helps to give Lagavulin its singular character.

But what if Lagavulin were made in the same way, but with unpeated malt? You would taste a light, fragrant, multifaceted spirit, and it is this complex delicacy that is its hidden secret. Any peated malt needs to have a balancing sweet element within it—there is nothing more one-dimensional than a dram that is simply smoky. Ardbeg has this element, as does its neighbor, Lagavulin.

Aged in refill casks, Lagavulin is a malt that the world has now fallen in love with, something that was completely unforeseen when Diageo chose it as the Islay component of its Classic Malts range. The thinking in the early 1990s was that newcomers to malt whiskey would start with a light, Lowland malt—such as Glenkinchie (*see p. 98*)—and slowly graduate through the Highlands, to Speyside, where most would eventually stay. A few hardy souls would understand Talisker (*see p. 126*), but even fewer would appreciate the smoky complexities of Islay. It was a perfectly logical analysis—but nonetheless a wrong one.

Today, hardly anyone drinks light Lowland malts—everyone wants the distinctive taste of peat. This unexpected demand would not have been a problem were Lagavulin not a brand that was bottled at 16 years of age. Sixteen years ago the distillery was only working two days a week. The single malt has therefore been on allocation for some years (normal service is planned for 2006). To show that the stock is coming back into line, a cask strength bottling at 12 years old has been released.

LAGAVULIN *as seen from Dunyvaig Castle, the ancient seat of the Lord of the Isles. Its smoky single malt is making a slow return.*

LAPHROAIG'S *stills, with their nipped-in waists and onionlike shape, are vital to the smoky malt's character. They are smaller than most of their neighbors.*

LAPHROAIG

Little more than a mile south of Lagavulin, between a pine wood and the sea, lie the farm buildings that comprise Laphroaig. On one side of the road you may spot flags where the Friends of Laphroaig have staked out the square foot of peat bog that they "own." Established in 1826 and now owned by Allied Distillers, the main building contains a working malt barn. Inside, the kiln piles on the peat to the same phenol level as its neighbors (and Caol Ila).

That said, there is more to these malts than smoke. Technically, they are peated to the same level, but all are distinct individuals. A lot comes down to the stills—Laphroaig's are small with nipped-in waists. In addition, the cut here is made later than at most distilleries, thereby maximizing the tarry phenols that can be captured at the end of the run. All Laphroaig is then aged exclusively in American oak barrels. The result is the most maritime of Islay's malts: medicinal, with touches of iodine, kippers, engine rooms, and

TASTING NOTES

THE KILDALTON MALTS, from the coastal distilleries, are the peatiest on Islay: intense, marine, and complex.

ARDBEG

ARDBEG 10-YEAR-OLD

46 VOL.

Color Pale straw
Nose Lime leaf, sooty, intense
Body Light to medium. Intense.
Palate Needs water to ignite the smoke. Kipper.
Finish Sooty.

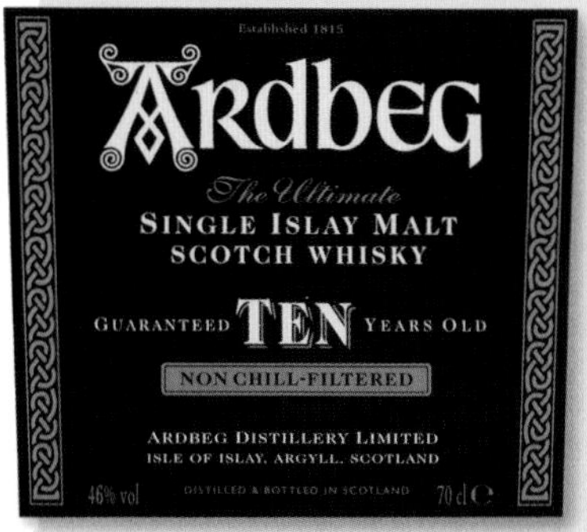

ARDBEG 10-YEAR-OLD

ARDBEG UIGEADAIL

54.2 VOL.

Color Light gold.
Nose Sweet yet pungently smoky: lime and peat, cocoa, salted herring. Beach barbecue. Raisin.
Body Light, firm.
Palate Rich, concentrated, and powerful. The wood gives a subtle frame. Sooty with tarry notes.
Finish The lime returns. Oatcake.

LAGAVULIN

LAGAVULIN 12-YEAR-OLD

57.8 VOL.

Color Light straw.
Nose Pungent and complex. Smoked eel, coal tar, applewood-smoked cheese, burlap, bitumen, smoked tea, rock pools.
Body Medium. Ripe feel.
Palate Intensely peaty and mouth-filling. Rounded with big kick of flavor: marine character, fragrant smoke (peat/cigar), and a dusting of black pepper.
Finish Smoke.

LAGAVULIN 16-YEAR-OLD

43 VOL.

Color Dark amber/bronze.
Nose Rich, aromatic, and complex, with gunsmoke/fireworks, trawler ropes, stewed prunes, and sticky toffee pudding. Cigar smoke, lapsang souchong.
Body Full.
Palate Highly complex. Dried seaweed, perfumed smoke.
Finish Very long. Smoke, stewed tea.

LAGAVULIN 16-YEAR-OLD

LAPHROAIG

LAPHROAIG 10-YEAR-OLD

40 VOL.

Color Pale gold.
Nose Intense, marine. Tar, engine oil. A firm, crunchy cereal note and some light vanilla.
Body Medium.
Palate Slightly austere. Malty start, then lemon, and finally a huge blast of tarry smoke.
Finish Long, drying. Smoke.

LAPHROAIG 17-YEAR-OLD SINGLE CASK BOTTLING

55.2 VOL.

Color Bright gold.
Nose Smoke and cream. Coal tar soap, deck oil, dried seaweed; sugared almond, vanilla.
Body Soft and silky.
Palate Sweet. Fruit candy, pecan, cream, then peaty, ointment, iodine.
Finish Medicinal, dry.

smoke, but softened by the sweetness of the oak.

So jealous was Lagavulin's owner, Sir Peter Mackie, of his neighbor's malt barn that he built an exact replica at his distillery. However, despite his best efforts and those of his descendants, Malt Mill was never able to recreate Laphroaig's character. Science may lead us to believe that location is not important where distillation is concerned, but somehow the spirit of a place undoubtedly has a part to play in a malt's personality.

PORT ELLEN

From here, the road winds south through serrated rocks, which pierce the turf like compound fractures, to Islay's second town, Port Ellen. Behind the town rears the Mull of Oa, one of the main centers for illicit distilling on the island in the 18th century. Though these distillers set a crude template for Islay's malt, they would have used any crop that came to hand—oats as well as bere barley—and, as the 18th-century traveler Thomas Pennant observed, they would have made it palatable with thyme, mint, anise, and other herbs. In many ways those proto-whiskeys would have been more akin to today's whiskey liqueurs than the refined single malts that have become so desirable.

Port Ellen played an important role in the development of Islay's whiskey industry. Its distillery was established in the late 1820s, but it only became a force when the business was taken over by John Ramsay. This most remarkable man—politician, pioneering agriculturalist, benign landlord, innovator, and distiller—established the ferry service between Glasgow and the island, built up direct transatlantic whiskey sales, and even built what are now the oldest duty-free warehouses in Scotland.

Ramsay's distillery, however, is no more. It became part of Distillers Company Ltd. in 1925, but was closed from the 1930s until the boom of the 1960s, at which time the company constructed a malting plant next door in order to supply Port Ellen, Lagavulin, and Caol Ila. The slump in the 1980s meant all three were not viable, and although the maltings still supply malt to every distillery on Islay, as well as to Mull, Jura, and the Japanese distilleries, Port Ellen distillery closed for good and was demolished. Thankfully, there are still stocks of its austere, oily, smoke-accented malt available, so look for it and catch it while you still can.

ISLAY: LOCH INDAAL

AFTER THE EXTREME PEAT OF THE KIDALTON TRIO, ISLAY'S NEXT TWO DISTILLERIES, BOWMORE AND BRUICHLADDICH, OFFER A GENTLER ASPECT TO THE ISLAND'S WHISKEY CHARACTER.

The landscape changes dramatically as you leave Port Ellen and head north. Here are Islay's flatlands. On both sides of the arrow-straight road is peat bog—at times the asphalt seems to be floating on top of it, causing your car to buck and bounce as you drive along. Bog cotton fluffs in the wind, which carries the sound of skylarks to your ears, and on your left you can see the fringes of the low dunes that border the Big Strand—8 miles (13 km) of golden beach.

Pause and stand on the peat. Here is one of the secrets of Islay's identity. There are no trees, and therefore no source of firewood, which meant that the early whiskey-makers would have had nothing but peat to dry their malted barley—so they made a peaty whiskey. Look at how the iridescent blue oil forms on the surface of the pools, the same oils that perfume the smoke that inveigles its way into the drying malt.

DISTILLERY DETAILS

BOWMORE FOUNDED: 1779.
OWNER: Morrison Bowmore Distillers Ltd.
METHOD: Pot stills. CAPACITY: 528,000 gallons.

BRUICHLADDICH FOUNDED: 1881.
OWNER: The Bruichladdich Distillery Co. Ltd.
METHOD: Pot stills.
CAPACITY: 370,000 gallons.

BOWMORE

Back on the road, you rise up a small hill, and in front of you sits a white-painted round church, built like this so that the devil would have no corners to hide in. No doubt many of the ministers who preached here felt that the devil had taken up residence in the large building sitting at the bottom of the wide street that leads to the harbor. We have arrived in Islay's capital, Bowmore, and the building in question is the town's distillery. The flagpole often has a Japanese as well as a Scottish flag flying—in 1994 the distillery was bought by Suntory. But Bowmore remains Scottish at heart, still producing fine malts in the heart of Islay.

Bowmore, whose outer walls form part of the town's sea defenses, has successfully lasted the test of time and remains long after so many other distilleries have gone. Here, as at Laphroaig, you can see the whole whiskey-making process, from malting to distilling, done on site. Its malt barns provide up to 30 percent of its needs. It is hard work, turning the floors by hand, making sure the golden carpet of grains germinates evenly, an almost-forgotten craft, which still ties Bowmore to its earliest incarnation. Not so long ago, all whiskey was made like this. Medium-peated, with delicious accents of orange, chocolate, dried lavender, and heathery smoke, Bowmore is the perfect dram to introduce a beginner to the delights of fine, peated malts.

BRUICHLADDICH

Past the warehouses, you come to a stony beach where pastel pebbles are interspersed with the odd piece of smoothed red brick, the remnants, perhaps, of the old Port Charlotte distillery chimney, which used to sit behind the white-painted houses across the wide, shallow loch. A little to the right of the house, you can just see a long white wall—the exterior of Bruichladdich.

Like Ardbeg, Bruichladdich has recently been brought back from the dead. It was one of the beachside stills built in the late 19th century to help satisfy the demand for peated malts from Glasgow blenders. By the time it closed in 1995, its style had changed and it was making a whiskey with only a hint of smoke. A silent distillery is a sad thing; the paint begins to flake, shingles fall off, dust settles on the stills, rust tightens its grip, and a chill pervades the site. It seemed unlikely that Bruichladdich would work again.

However, in 2000 a consortium of Islay landowners, an independent bottler/wine merchant, and Bowmore's former manager did the unexpected. The distillery was painted, the rust chipped away, the roofs fixed, the ancient mill overhauled, the stills heated up, and Bruichladdich's spirit began to flow again. The whole island turned out for its reopening. The new owners have reevaluated the stock and improved the malt by allying the fresh, softly fruity distillery character to the sweet vanilla tones of American oak. In addition, they have taken a leaf out of Springbank's (*see p. 112*) book and are making two other styles of spirit: medium-peated Port Charlotte and heavily peated Octomore.

WHITE-PAINTED *and sea-bordered, Bowmore is a classic Islay distillery. Across the sea inlet of Loch Indaal, the lighthouse at Bruichladdich faces it.*

TASTING NOTES

A GENTLER SIDE to Islay emerges with the fragrant and smoky medium-peated Bowmore, and the breezy freshness of Bruichladdich.

BOWMORE

BOWMORE 12-YEAR-OLD

BOWMORE
12-YEAR-OLD
40 VOL.

Color Light gold.
Nose Attractive, perfumed, and smoky. Light orange notes, hint of coffee, putty, plenty of malt.
Body Medium.
Palate Rounded, and soft, then it dries halfway as the peaty notes (burlap, smoke) take over, then comes parma violet, rose, and finally, melon.
Finish Nut and fragrant smoke. Buttered kippers.

BRUICHLADDICH

BRUICHLADDICH
10-YEAR-OLD
46 VOL.

Color Pale gold.
Nose Light and fresh. Floral, with crunchy green apple, verjuice, lemon, fresh malt.
Body Light to medium.
Palate Clean, zesty, and direct. Apples, cream, vanilla, light orange. Hint of spice. Very fresh.
Finish Breezy.

BRUICHLADDICH 10-YEAR-OLD

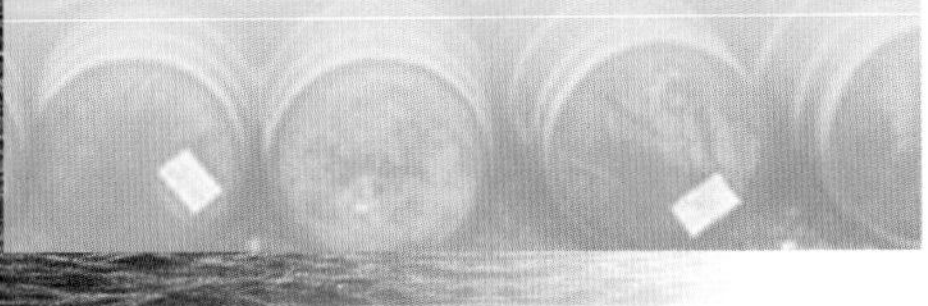

Islay: the Sound of Islay

THE WHISKEY ISLAND'S FINAL PAIR OF DISTILLERIES LIES ON ITS REMOTE EAST COAST. THOUGH LESS WELL KNOWN THAN SOME OF THEIR NEIGHBORS, THEY ARE ISLAY'S LARGEST DISTILLERIES—AND ITS TWO BEST-KEPT SECRETS.

The transformation of Islay from a peasant, subsistence economy to a model island was wrought by Daniel Campbell of Shawfield, politician, slave trader, and businessman. He bought the island with the compensation money he was awarded when a mob burned down his grand house in Glasgow in 1725, in protest at the malt tax for which Campbell had voted.

He introduced the cultivation of flax to the island and began to modernize Islay's agriculture (precipitating the inevitable emigration of many islanders). His grandson, Daniel the Younger, continued making improvements. He established two-row barley strains and other crops, and created a linen-weaving industry and a fishing fleet. Islay's population gradually increased again, leading to the building of a model town complete with distillery—Bowmore (*see p. 118*). Many more followed, and at any one time in the 19th century there were up to 21 distilleries operating on the island. Seven remain today.

DISTILLERY DETAILS

CAOL ILA FOUNDED: 1846.
OWNER: Diageo. METHOD: Pot stills.
CAPACITY: 951,000 gallons.

BUNNAHABHAIN FOUNDED: 1881.
OWNER: Burn Stewart Distillers Ltd. METHOD: Pot stills.
CAPACITY: 726,000 gallons.

Bunnahabhain's barrels *(left) lie in warehouses that overlook the beautiful Sound of Islay (below).*

These distilleries are: Ardbeg, Lagavulin, Laphroaig, Bowmore, Bruichladdich, Caol Ila, and Bunnahabhain.

THE ISLAY CIRCUIT

To complete the Islay circuit, head first into Port Charlotte, either for the legendary seafood lunch at its eponymous hotel or (for the bolder traveler) the music, beer, malt, and madness of the Lochindaal—Islay's finest bar. The road then takes you down the side of Loch Indaal to the island's southwesterly tip at Portnahaven, where the Atlantic rollers beat against the reef and cruelly smash the foundations of its lighthouse. Next, head up the west coast to the dunes of Kilchoman and Saligo, and gaze out across the gray-blue sea toward Newfoundland. There, listen as choughs jabber and wheel above and corncrakes cry in the grasses, sounding like two pebbles being scraped together.

Then loop inland to wooded Bridgend and head due east, pausing at Finlaggan, where the Lords of the Isles had their parliament. Wrested from the Norse kingdom and ambivalent toward Scottish rule, this loose and sometimes quarrelsome collection of clans controlled a quasi-autonomous state that at one stage encompassed Kintyre, Argyll, and the Hebridean islands, as well as Islay. It was they, many now feel, who first possessed the knowledge of distillation thanks to the appointment of the Beatons/MacBeaths as court physicians in the 14th century.

The horizon is now dominated by the three Paps of Jura, a view that, unsurprisingly, also distracts the visitor from Islay's last two distilleries, Caol Ila and Bunnahabhain. Although they are the biggest distilleries on the island, they are also the least well-known: hidden giants lurking at the end of steep paths that plunge toward the coastline.

CAOL ILA

Seemingly wedged into a niche carved from the sea cliff, Caol Ila was built in 1846 and became part of the DCL stable in 1927. It was rebuilt in the early 1970s and survived the slump thanks first to its size, second to its importance as a blending malt, and finally as a result of its ability to produce a quality unpeated "Highland" style as well as a more traditional, peaty Islay make.

This sleeping giant has now been (belatedly) awoken as a single malt by Diageo and is fast building a following for its distinctive yet appealing mix of smoky bacon, fish boxes, grass and, on occasion, wet coal.

This brass door *contrasts with the copper body of the spirit still at Caol Ila. Its upper plate proclaims the spirit still to be the work of R. G. Abercrombie in Alloa, a coppersmith and brassfounder.*

BUNNAHABHAIN

The Islay tour ends farther up the coast at the bulky, gray-stone distillery, Bunnahabhain. Built in 1881, this was one of the two distilleries that founded Highland Distillers. Sadly, like so many distilleries, its recent history has been blighted by intermittent production. The rusting wreck of a trawler, the *Wyre Majestic*, which lies just off its pier, seemed, until recently, to symbolize Bunnahabhain's fate. The distillery was loved by those who work there and by serious malt fans, and recently it was bought by CL Brands (best known for their angostura bitters). The future now looks considerably brighter, not just for the soft, sweet, gingery single malt but also for its blend, Black Bottle. Islay is once again "the" island.

TASTING NOTES

Islay's forgotten east coast is home to two large distilleries and two big but contrasting drams: the dry and distinctive smoky bacon of Caol Ila, and the rich, gingery Bunnahabhain. For lovers of smoky, marinelike malts, Caol Ila is unmissable.

BUNNAHABHAIN

BUNNAHABHAIN
12-YEAR-OLD, 43 VOL.

Color Rich amber.
Nose Ripe and soft. Thick honey, fruitcake, gingerbread. Some citrus peel notes behind, and light maltiness. Very appetizing.
Body Medium weight. Soft texture.
Palate Has good maturity.
Finish Long with sweet spices.

BUNNAHABHAIN 1968 AULD ACQUAINTANCE

BUNNAHABHAIN 1968 AULD ACQUAINTANCE
1969, 43.8 VOL.

Color Mahogany.
Nose Mature. English Christmas pudding. Moist, dark Jamaica ginger cake. Raisin, plum, walnut. A hint of smoke.
Body Rich, weighty.
Palate Huge, sweet. Has maturity but with soft cocoa, dried fruit.
Finish Sweet, then dusty.

CAOL ILA

CAOL ILA
12-YEAR-OLD, 43 VOL.

Color Pale straw. Green glints.
Nose Fruit, linseed oil, malt, green olive, and smoky bacon/smoked fish.
Body Medium weight. Good feel.
Palate A mix of juicy, sweet fruit, fish oils, and a dry smokiness. Some wet-grass notes.
Finish Dry. Smoke.

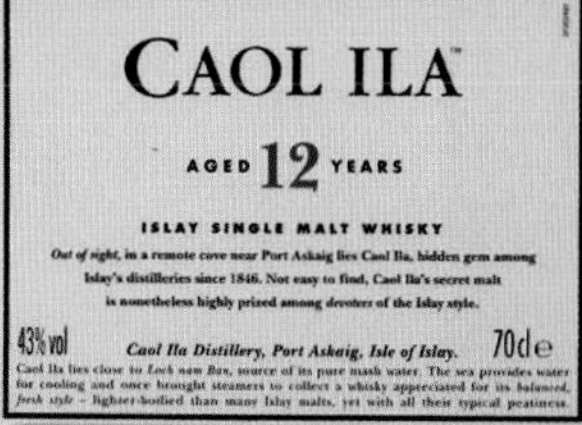

12-YEAR-OLD CAOL ILA

CAOL ILA
18-YEAR-OLD, 43 VOL.

Color Amber.
Nose Vanilla/banana, dried herbs, bluebell woods. Piers, fish boxes.
Body Medium to full.
Palate Sweet start and begins to dry on the mid-palate. Subtle and rounded with woody notes.
Finish Dry and crisp.

CAOL ILA, CASK STRENGTH,
NO AGE STATEMENT, 55 VOL.

Color Pale.
Nose The most marine: seashell, hot sand, bacon fat. Damp coal. Citrus, fennel, chamomile, silage.
Body Light but oily.
Palate The smokiest of the three. Citrus oil, anise. Oily texture.
Finish An eruption of smoke. Clove. Feisty.

JURA

ALTHOUGH JURA IS ISLAY'S NEXT-DOOR NEIGHBOR, ITS LANDSCAPE COULD NOT BE MORE DIFFERENT. WILD AND REMOTE, JURA HAS JUST ONE OF EVERYTHING—ONE ROAD, ONE TOWN, AND ONE DISTILLERY.

Jura is usually, if wrongly, seen in the context of Islay. The Sound of Islay (known locally as "Caol Ila") splits the two islands and marks the division: the soft from the hard, the green from the dun, the gentle from the stony. The fast-flowing tides of the sound can turn what is normally a three-minute ferry trip into an epic as the captain sets a course north for Colonsay, knowing how the tide will swing the landing craft into the safety of the landing strip at Feolin.

When you land on Jura, you know you are somewhere unusual. It has one village with one hotel/pub, and one distillery. Above you are the Paps, topped in scree, glinting in the sun. Cattle lumber along the road and deer bound across it. Over the widening sound, Islay's deserted eastern shore looks rich compared with the heather and tussocky grass that now surround you.

The drive to Jura's only settlement, Craighouse, underlines how lonely Jura appears. No houses can be seen until you dip into the village. Jura seems to typify the barrenness of much of the Hebrides; a deserted, depopulated landscape. However, you would be wrong to think that. Jura's limited population has been dictated by its rock. The silvery quartzite that is exposed on the Paps' tips is Jura's bedrock. The island's soil is thin; the sole areas suitable for farming are on its eastern coast. Even in pre-Clearance times, Jura could support a population of only 1,300. By the turn of the 20th century, it was 600. Today, it is fewer than 200. You have to be tough to live here.

JURA'S MASSIVE STILLS *were specially designed to produce a lightly peated style of malt whiskey.*

DISTILLERY DETAILS

JURA FOUNDED: 1810.
OWNER: Whyte and Mackay. METHOD: Pot stills.
CAPACITY: 660,000 gallons.

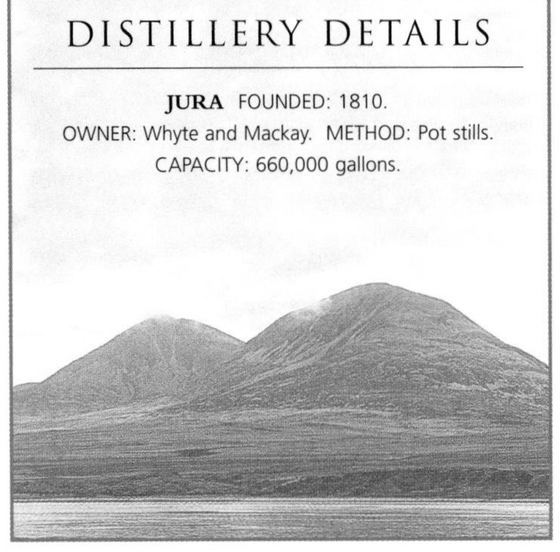

A SOURCE OF INCOME

Whiskey would have been part of the rhythm of Jura life for centuries before a permanent distillery was built. With the island on the main drover's route from Islay to the mainland, there is little doubt that cattlemen would have smuggled small kegs of the island's whiskey into Glasgow under the bellies of their black animals, giving the island's crofters a little supplementary income.

Prior to a legitimate distillery being built in Craighouse, whiskey-making allegedly took place in a cave on the site. The laird at the time, Archibald Campbell, saw that there was money to be made, and in 1810 the Small Isles distillery (named after the string of islets that guard Craighouse Bay) was built.

The distillery was not a great success, and a succession of owners failed to make it thrive. It was only when James Ferguson took out the lease in 1875 that the heavily peated Small Isles malt began to make money. Unfortunately, that did not last, either. Ferguson and his son fell out with the laird and stripped the plant of its equipment in 1910. In 1920 the roofs of the distillery were removed. Small Isles was no more.

Why, then, did Jura, of all places, reopen? It comes down to the rock again. By the start of the 1960s, Jura's population had fallen to 150. In an attempt to bring people to the island and boost its economy, two landowners—Robin Fletcher (who rented Barnhill to George Orwell) and Frank Riley Smith—decided that a new distillery would be the answer.

In 1963, they hired the famous distillery designer William Delme-Evans. He created a modern distillery intended to make a lightly peated Highland-style spirit, and installed huge stills to assist his vision. It worked; not only did it bring 100 people to Jura, but the business still thrives today.

How, though, did an expensive site like this survive when its one-time sister Bruichladdich closed? The answer is the stills. Jura has been primarily a blending malt, and those big stills produce a lot of spirit.

Somehow, by sticking to the virtually unpeated model, its owners (now Whyte and Mackay) seemed to loosen the whiskey's ties with its place of birth. It is a decent-enough dram, but not what you might expect from this peat-covered landscape.

However, things are changing. Now, every year, Whyte and Mackay makes a small amount of peated malt, and that smoke has given the malt a new depth, seen to its best in the new Superstition brand. It is almost as if a piece that had been mislaid has now been rediscovered—the new smoked malt completes the distillery's portfolio.

JURA'S DISTILLERY *buildings lie clustered around the rocky seashore, presenting a typical Scottish coastal distillery scene.*

TASTING NOTES

THE VERY SOFT water of Jura flows over the island's quartzite rock before it reaches a distillery designed to produce a light whiskey. The Superstition brand is the exception: heavier, smoky, and peaty.

ISLE OF JURA

10-YEAR-OLD, 40 VOL.

Color Amber.
Nose Nutty and malty. Parmesan. Turf and flour sacks. Rising dough.
Body Light to medium.
Palate Firm structure with a slightly hard mid-palate, sweet bracken around it. Fresh and clean.
Finish Squeeze of fruit juice, then malt.

ISLE OF JURA SUPERSTITION

NO AGE STATEMENT
45 VOL.

Color Amber.
Nose Malty and milky with cocoa, cherry, raisin. Very light, peat. Some complexity. Sweet hay (stables), heather.
Body Medium to full.
Palate Silky and juicy, semidried peach. Sweet underneath and smoke. Balanced.
Finish Dry, light smoke.

JURA SUPERSTITION

ISLE OF JURA

16-YEAR-OLD, 40 VOL.

Color Full gold.
Nose Heather blossom, muesli/malt bins, buttered scone. Freshly baked bread.
Body Medium.
Palate Very light raisin, good oak extract. Light toffee. Charming.
Finish Light, crème filling.

Mull

THOUGH LARGE AND WITH A HERITAGE OF WHISKEY-MAKING, TODAY THE ISLAND OF MULL HAS ONLY ONE DISTILLERY, SITUATED IN ONE OF THE PRETTIEST TOWNS TO BE FOUND IN THE HEBRIDES, TOBERMORY.

Looking north from Bunnahabhain's pier on a clear day, the low-lying island of Colonsay can be seen, framed between Jura's shore and the very top tip of Islay. Behind it floats a just-discernible indigo shape that you could think is a cloud or a strange shading of the sky. Rather, it is the upper slopes of Ben More ("the big hill"), which dominates the southern end of the island of Mull.

Car-free explorers can reach this part of Mull from the same pier. The *Lady Jayne* calls in every Monday night and, after an overnight stop on Colonsay, will ferry you onward to Uisken, a place name that makes one think immediately of whiskey. From there, it is a short hike to the big hill or to the Fionnphort ferry that travels between Mull and the holy island of Iona.

Tobermory, with its *with its brightly colored row of seafront houses, is a magnet for sailors, tourists, children, and whiskey-lovers.*

DISTILLERY DETAILS

TOBERMORY FOUNDED: 1823.
OWNER: Burn Stewart Distillers Ltd. METHOD: Pot stills.
CAPACITY: 238,000 gallons.

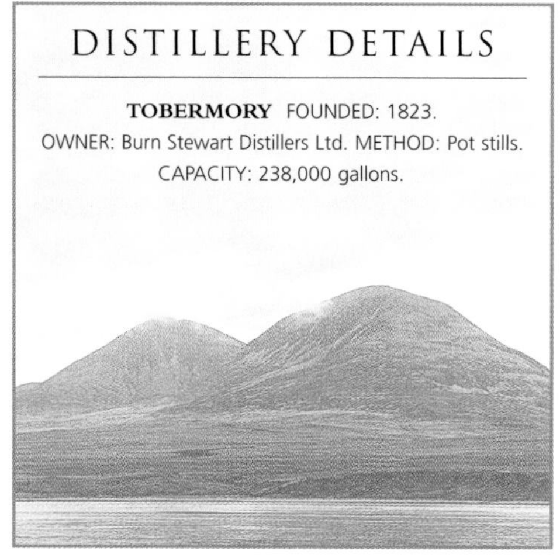

It is an environment within which you can easily succumb to romantic notions: Mendelssohn composed *Fingal's Cave* after a trip to the astonishing basalt columns of the nearby island of Staffa, also the subject of a painting by J. M. W. Turner. A whiskey romantic could also spin a plausible enough tale linking the siting of St. Columba's Abbey on Iona (the first such in Scotland) with the arrival of distilling, but sad to say, there is no evidence for this.

Although it is the second largest of the Inner Hebrides, Mull has a smaller population than Islay and most visitors are day-trippers, nipping across on the ferry from Oban, and heading straight for Iona. These days, though, there's an increase in the numbers taking the two-hour crossing from Oban to Tobermory, Mull's capital, which is located in the northeast of the island. It would be nice to think that this was due to the town's eponymous distillery being open once again, but it is more likely to be due to the fact that Tobermory is the setting for a popular children's television series.

The first great whiskey explorer, Alfred Barnard, mused over why Tobermory should "apparently be so neglected." He found an island that "is uneven and mountainous, but nevertheless the soil is deep and fertile ... (though with) a very boisterous coast." That

High-necked stills *at the Tobermory distillery produce particularly light, clean, and fragrant spirits.*

TASTING NOTES

Mull's sole distillery, situated by the harbor in the main village, makes its famous malt with, and without, the influence of peat.

TOBERMORY
10-YEAR-OLD, 40 VOL.

Color Gold.
Nose Assertive, malty, and crisp. Light fragrance behind.
Body Light. Soft texture.
Palate Nutty and spicy. Sweet oak.
Finish Soft and remarkably sweet.

TOBERMORY 10-YEAR-OLD

LEDAIG
7-YEAR-OLD, 43 VOL.

Color Full gold.
Nose Hot bitumen, smoked meat. With water, a creamy maltiness.
Body Medium. Soft.
Palate Soft and sweet. Ripe pear, malt, and understated smokiness. Good balance.
Finish Smoky, medium length.

rich land should have been supplying barley for a number of distilleries. Instead, even in the 1880s, malt was imported from the mainland. Mull had been depopulated, owing to the Clearances—the mass expulsion of people from the land from the late 18th century onward. The farmers of Mull had been forced to abandon the barley fields and had taken up smallholdings on that boisterous coastline. Why? Because of the seaweed. The farmers were trying to cash in on the increased demand from glass and soap manufacturers for kelp.

The Muileachs (as the inhabitants of Mull are known) were noted whiskey-makers and enthusiastic drinkers. When Martin Martin visited the island in 1695 he wrote, "... the natives are accustomed to take a large dose of *aqua vitae* as a corrective when the season is very moist." Before the Clearances, up to a quarter of the island's cereal crops was used for distillation.

TOBERMORY

Tobermory itself was built by the Stevensons, enterprising industrialists who were behind the transformation of Oban (*see p. 106*). In 1823, a kelp baron and shipping merchant, John Sinclair, opened Tobermory's distillery. Unfortunately, it was not a success, and it closed between 1837 and 1878.

A brief period in the DCL (Distillers Company Ltd.) stable ended in the 1930s, and once again the distillery lay silent, until a consortium decided to fire it up again in 1972. This too was a failure, lasting a mere three years. The brand name and stock were bought and the whiskey sold as a vatted malt—containing some make (whiskey) from the distillery plus other single malts. This confused matters, and although it did not quite cause the same hostile reaction as when Diageo tried the same tack with Cardhu (*see p. 155*), the resulting liquid did not do anything for Tobermory's reputation.

Thankfully, like Bladnoch, this is another distillery that simply refused to die and, in 1993, it became part of the Burn Stewart stable. Its new owner cleared out the cheese that was stored in the tun room and started the stills into life once more. These spirit stills are strange-looking creatures with a 90-degree bend in their uphill lyne arms (similar to Braeval), a design that helps to produce a light and slightly sweet spirit. Burn Stewart has, very sensibly, also restarted production of the peated variant, Ledaig (the original name of the town), using barley malted at Port Ellen. A cheeky little seven-year-old shows massive potential.

SKYE

DRAMATIC AND ROMANTIC, SKYE IS RICH IN TALES OF MAGIC AND BRAVERY, BUT THE TRUE ISLAND CLASSIC IS TALISKER, A WARM AND RUGGED SINGLE MALT DISTILLED BY THE SHORES OF LOCH HARPORT.

This is an uncompromising island. Skye's mountains rear abruptly from the sea, their black and red rocks looking hard and polished in the sun; its glens swoop deep into its heather-clad heart; its midges bite ferociously. It is an elemental place—of dead volcanoes, strong seas, and scudding clouds. To get a taster, the whiskey traveler should pause and stand at the bar of the Sligachan Hotel and listen to mountaineers' tales of that day's breathtaking exploits on the Cuillins.

We have a tendency to think of the Hebridean islands as being remote, whereas to the people living on them they are the center of the world. We see them from an urban perspective. Indeed, it was the shift from country to city that helped close so many remote distilleries in the early 19th century. The usage and production of whiskey changed from local to national, from a drink made for a community to a commodity for sale. Even today, the journey to this part of the world is a long one. When all supplies had to come by sea, it was a genuine outpost of commercial distilling, and it was this remoteness that caused the closure of the seven stills operating on the islands in 1823.

DISTILLERY DETAILS

TALISKER FOUNDED: 1831.
OWNER: Diageo. METHOD: Pot stills.
CAPACITY: 502,000 gallons.

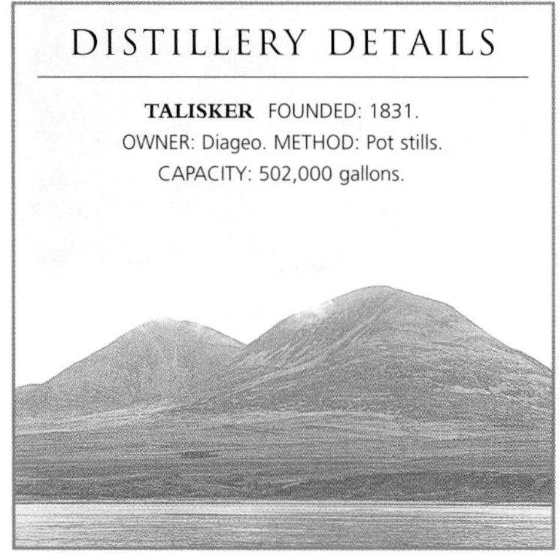

Tiree, the flat, sunlit island with its white sands and rich grasslands, is one victim. In Gaelic, Tioridh means "land of grain" and, as late as the mid-19th century, this granary of the Isles supported a population in excess of 4,000 and was a net exporter of whiskey. Those days are long gone; economics and politics put paid to that. Tiree, ultimately, was too remote to justifiably support a distillery.

The same could be said of most of the other Hebridean islands, with the notable exception of Islay. There is, however, one Skye distillery that has not just clung on, but carved a solid niche for itself.

TALISKER DISTILLERY

The road splits at the Sligachan. The left-hand fork heads northwest past the end of Loch Harport, on whose shores sits the white-painted huddle of buildings that make up Talisker distillery. It is a calm spot, the long,

LONG-EXTINCT VOLCANOES *now form the wild and craggy Storr, which provides a spectacular backdrop for the Talisker distillery.*

TASTING NOTES

ELEMENTAL, SMOKY, marine—Skye's characterful sole malt is a distillation of its place. Robert Louis Stevenson described it as the "king o' drinks" in 1880.

TALISKER

10-YEAR-OLD, 45.8 VOL.

Color Full gold.
Nose Dry, almond, heather, earth, lobster pot, licorice. Interplay between dry smokiness and sweet notes.
Body Medium.
Palate Ripe pear, smoke, light minty note. Heather blossom. Creamy oak.
Finish Peppery.

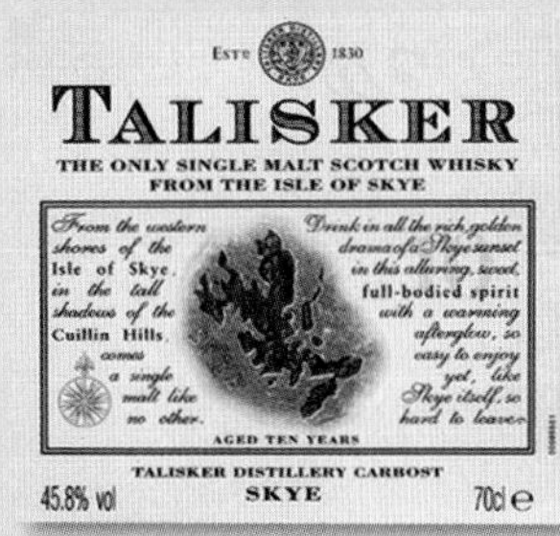

TALISKER TEN-YEAR-OLD

TALISKER

18-YEAR-OLD, 45.8 VOL.

Color Gold
Nose Complex, burning heather, sweet tobacco, old warehouse, spent bonfire. Underneath is almond paste/nougat butter cookies and a lightly herbal note. Plenty of smoke. Rich and complex.
Body Rich.
Palate A slow start, then pepper, a light smoked fish note, fruit syrup. Builds in stages to an explosive finish.
Finish Red peppercorn.

TALISKER

20-YEAR-OLD, 58 VOL.

Color Straw/light gold.
Nose Light smoke. Complex. Macadamia, wet rope, salt, burning moorland, sooty chimney, wet seaweed.
Body Rich.
Palate Delivers all its complexities here. Restrained oak, heather, sweet pearlike fruits, and dark smokiness.
Finish Iodine. Long. Sweet.

curved loch giving shelter from the often ferocious seas at its mouth. Turning to look behind, you see the cloud-ripping ridge of the Cuillins soaring dramatically into the sky. To say the location is awe-inspiringly spectacular does not do it justice.

The MacAskill brothers, Hugh and Archie, relocated here from Eigg in 1825 and acquired the "tack" of Talisker House (where Boswell and Dr. Johnson stayed during their peregrinations around the Highlands). The MacAskills were not good distillers, and Talisker distillery passed through various hands until, 50 years after its foundation, it found its saviors in A.G. Allan and his business partner, Roderick Kemp, who rebuilt it. Kemp left in 1892 to buy Macallan, at which point Allan then merged Talisker with his other distillery, Dailuaine, which was at that time the largest whiskey producer in the Highlands. In 1925, Dailuaine and Talisker distilleries joined DCL (which had held a stake in the firm since 1916). Ironically, like so many quality distilleries, Talisker had been saved by the blenders.

Today, you can buy "Isle of Skye" whiskey and a range of Gaelic whiskeys, including Poit Dubh and Te Bheag, from Skye-based retailer Praban na Linne. Talisker is the sole distillery on this, the largest of the Hebridean islands. However, Sir Iain Noble, who established Praban na Linne, is purportedly planning to run a small still in the south of Skye.

THE STILLMAN *at the Talisker distillery gets ready to boil up another charge.*

TALISKER WHISKEY

The reason Talisker has prospered despite its location is its quality. This is a top-grade dram used not only as a single but also as a blending malt. As if to reinforce this, the striding figure of Johnnie Walker once adorned its label. Unusually for an island malt, Talisker was triple-distilled until 1928, and even now it is set up to produce a highly individual malt.

There are five stills; two wash and three spirit. The lyne arm has a U-shaped kink in it, with a purifier pipe located at the base of the dip to maximize reflux. All the spirit is condensed in old-style worm tubs, a technique that helps to give richness to the distillate. Add in a fair amount of peat and you have the template for a highly complex malt and one that manages to speak of its place: a distillation of burning heather, peat smoke, seaweed, salt spray, and wet rope.

If Talisker can survive thanks to quality, and Arran can now hold its own with a brand new distillery (*see p. 108*), it makes you wonder whether it might not be time to rethink the viability of Tiree. Stranger things have happened in the world of malt whiskey.

Orkney

THE MOST NORTHERLY OUTPOST OF DISTILLING IN SCOTLAND, ORKNEY IS A REPOSITORY FOR MYRIADS OF CIVILIZATIONS AND HOME TO TWO OF SCOTLAND'S FINEST MALTS.

The visitor to Orkney is first greeted by the sight of flat, green discs sitting on a silvered ocean. From that moment begins the realization that Orkney is different. Like nowhere else in the Northern Hemisphere, the 70 islands that make up Orkney somehow blur the boundaries between past and present. It is a magical, otherworldly place, a northern, floating world. Orkney's history is alive. Everything exists in the now.

The islands have long had this strange effect on visitors. On first setting eyes on the archipelago, the Greek explorer Pytheas thought he had seen Ultima Thule, the edge of the world. Yet this is no uninhabited fringe of civilization—these islands have been occupied since 8000 BC. The house at Knap of Howar, on Papay, was built in 3600 BC; it is older even than the remarkable Skara Brae, a wonderfully intact Neolithic settlement that quietly shocks you with its perfectly preserved cupboards and beds.

This is a landscape of standing stones, brochs (towers), and chambered cairns, a place where each successive civilization has left its mark: the runic graffiti left by Vikings on the walls of Maes Howe, indecipherable Pictish carvings. All combine to give the place a strange power. Even Kirkwall's St. Magnus Cathedral, with its crude, heavy, red and gold sandstone pillars, has a greater gravitas than the refined elegance of its equivalents in England, such as Ely or Wells. Perhaps it is because, unlike anywhere else in the UK, when people leave their mark in Orkney, that mark stays, and becomes part of the landscape. Where else in the world would it seem perfectly normal for Italian prisoners of war to transform a Nissen hut into a classical chapel complete with a *trompe l'oeil* marble floor?

DISTILLERY DETAILS

HIGHLAND PARK FOUNDED: 1798.
OWNER: The Edrington Group. METHOD: Pot stills.
CAPACITY: 660,000 gallons.

SCAPA FOUNDED: 1885.
OWNER: Allied-Domecq. METHOD: Column stills.
CAPACITY: 264,000 gallons.

While constitutionally part of the UK, Orkney is defiantly not British; it is not even Scottish. Part of the Norse Western Empire for 700 years, Orkney was the perfect base from which to launch forays across the north and west coasts of Scotland, and down England's east coast. Strategically important, it became the power base for the western limits of the Norse holdings. The Hebridean islands (including Islay) remained loyal to Norway throughout the 13th century; Angus Mor, Lord of Islay, fought on the (losing) Viking side at the Battle of Largs in 1262, a defeat that resulted in the Hebrides being leased to Scotland for payment of an annual rent.

By the mid-1400s, Scotland had not paid the lease for decades and owed Norway's King Christian I a huge sum. In turn, Christian wanted closer ties to Scotland, and so married his daughter, Margaret, to King James III in 1465, promising as a dowry to write off the debt and pay 60,000 florins. Only 2,000 florins were paid, so he gave Orkney as a guarantee. The Danes then spent the next 300 years trying to redeem "their" islands, but to no avail. Orkney had become part of Scotland, or at least that is what the Scots thought. The Orcadians have never quite seen it that way.

The Orkney islands *possess a wealth of Neolithic sites, including the famous Skara Brae settlement.*

HIGHLAND PARK

Whiskey has played its part in this long and turbulent history, and in Highland Park the islands have one of the finest malts of all. The most northerly malt distillery in Scotland, Highland Park was founded in 1798 by Magnus Eunson, a man who managed to reconcile being a preacher by day and a smuggling moonshiner by night. This figure of the "whiskey priest," the man who can apparently square two seemingly opposed personalities and sets of values, runs throughout Celtic, and Norse, history.

TASTING NOTES

One of Scotland's most outstanding distilleries, Highland Park produces a range of excellent malts, all tinged with that unique Orcadian taste of heather.

HIGHLAND PARK
12-YEAR-OLD
40 VOL.

12-YEAR-OLD HIGHLAND PARK

Color Full gold moving to amber.
Nose Spiced honey. Sweet orange peel. Light peat. Walnut.
Body Medium.
Palate Slightly dry. Tablet, heather honey, dried herbs. Light malt.
Finish Long, quite dry. Heather.

HIGHLAND PARK
18-YEAR-OLD, 40 VOL.

Color Amber.
Nose Dried fruits (raisin, date), dried flowers, vanilla pod, chocolate, heather blossom, rose-water.
Body Ripe and rich.
Palate Full-flavored, unctuous. Honeyed, caramelized peach, heather.
Finish Long, sweet, then smoke.

HIGHLAND PARK
25-YEAR-OLD, 40 VOL.

Color Amber.
Nose Thick and sweet. Malt, bitter orange, apricot, overripe pear, barley sugar. Toasted almond, warm spices, fudge, beech nut.
Body Rich, full.
Palate Balance between caramelized fruit, fruit peels, honey, and heathery smoke. Mouth-filling. Fudge/chocolate. Chewy.
Finish Soft. Toffee. Smoke.

Highland Park *sits up high, overlooking the windswept town of Kirkwall. Many of the staff have whiskey in their blood—they are following in the footsteps of previous generations who devoted their working lives to whiskey-making.*

Around the turn of the 18th century, Kirkwall was a center for smuggling, and churches were often used as deposits for the stashed hooch. Local councillors were in the habit of laying on lavish banquets for visiting excisemen, purportedly to thank them, but in reality to learn their plans.

LEGALITY AND EXPANSION

Magnus Eunson's farm was situated on the "whiskey road" that ran from Kirkwall to Holm. The distillery's name came from his use of water from two springs that rose in the High Park (the highest field). Although he was finally arrested in 1813, Eunson was never prosecuted—however, his arresting officer, John Robertson, promptly bought the High Park estate, complete with distillery, and went into legal distillation.

The distillery was expanded and by the mid-19th century was providing fillings for a number of the top whiskey houses, such as Chivas, Gilbey, Haig, Ballantine, and Dewar, as well as selling a small percentage as a single malt. It became part of Highland Distiller's portfolio in 1936.

ORCADIAN MALT

In its earliest incarnation, Highland Park was made in a peculiarly Orcadian fashion. Bere barley (the archaic strain of barley widely used by early distillers) remained in use here for much longer than on the mainland. The distillery also had a heather house; here, bunches of dried heather blossom were stored in readiness to be thrown into the flames of the kiln, where it was thought the fragrant smoke would give the malt an extra, perfumed lift. These two factors gave the Orcadian malt a unique style and flavor.

The only concession to the old ways that visitors can see today lies in the distillery's strange Y-shaped maltings, which still provide 20 percent of the malt (and all the peated component). This is not a contemporary, specially built distillery, but one whose clutter of buildings have grown organically as demand (and fame) has grown. You duck between rooms, and enter them at strange angles. It is one of those distilleries that says clearly, "I am here to make whiskey. I'm not a tourist attraction."

A GREAT WHISKEY

Highland Park's water is hard, which is unusual but by no means unique in Scottish malt distilling, but that does not make any great difference to its make. The Orcadian peat may have an impact, however. Made up almost entirely of decomposed heather, this may just be the key to the whiskey's extremely evocative aroma.

All of the peated component of Highland Park is malted and kilned at the distillery; the rest is brought in from Highland Distiller's maltings at Tamdhu.

Both old and modern (there is computer control), Highland Park makes whiskey that manages to combine the best of all the other Scottish regions and meld them into a seamless, luxuriant whole. There is peat, there is honey, there is orange, a fudgelike sweetness, and a rich, raisined depth. Above all, there is balance. Highland Park's layers of flavor resemble the strata of civilizations that cover these islands. Like any great dram, it is a complex amalgam of ingredients, place, and people. Nowhere else could make it, but then nowhere else is quite like Orkney.

SCAPA

Such is Highland Park's standing (it is one of the few malts that all distillers agree is a class act), one tends to forget that Kirkwall actually has another distillery. Over the past eight years, visitors to Highland Park would have driven straight past the crumbling

A RUSTING BLOCKSHIP *from World War II continues to impede the entrance to Scapa Flow.*

buildings of its near neighbor, Scapa. Owner Allied-Domecq ran the distillery briefly every year to top off stocks, but it used staff from Highland Park to do so. When the electricity failed and the roof came off the mash house, it seemed certain that Scapa's death certificate was finally being written.

Miracles can happen in whiskey-making, though, and in 2004 Allied-Domecq announced a planned $4 million refit for Scapa. Even better, the company decided to start promoting the whiskey as a frontline malt. A distillery that in 1887 Alfred Barnard was able to call "the most complete little distillery in the Kingdom" is, over a hundred years later, on the way back.

Scapa houses one of the last Lomond stills remaining in operation, and it is this invaluable asset that gives the malt such a luscious, almost oily, juiciness. Scapa is a shamefully drinkable malt, one that can be taken neat, mixed, chilled, or even frozen. It is good to see it back.

No such luck for the last Orcadian distillery, Stromness, which closed in 1928. From Barnard's description, this sounded like one of the most intriguing plants in Scotland, consisting of little more than a illicit still that had received a license.

Whereas most distillers took the opportunity to install larger stills and expand their distilleries when they went legal, the owner of Stromness continued to use the small stills that had obviously served him well in his moonshining days. "Its body is shaped like a pumpkin and is surmounted by a similarly shaped chamber one-fourth the size to prevent the goods boiling over, through which the neck passes to the head of the still." This weird-sounding contraption was only making 8,500 gallons (32,000 liters) per annum in Barnard's day, at a time when Scapa and Highland Park were making a much more considerable 48,000 gallons (180,000 liters) and 36,000 gallons (135,000 liters), respectively, though size is not always a guarantor of ongoing success.

In a neat twist, the site of the old Stromness distillery became a housing development where the Orcadian laureate George Mackay Brown lived—another layer laid down on Orkney's history.

SCAPA DISTILLERY, *snuggled into its green glen next to the sea, produces the overlooked classic of Orkney.*

TASTING NOTES

SCAPA MALTS have been forced to take second place in the pantheon of Orcadian whiskey, yet their richness has gained them cult status among the cognoscenti.

SCAPA
12-YEAR-OLD,
40 VOL.

Color Old gold.
Nose Super-ripe fruits (apricot/peach), peach stone, honey, and a whisper of smoke. Plump.
Body Rich, soft, unctuous.
Palate Exotic, mouth-coating. Filled with tropical fruit: mango, guava, fruit salad. Long.
Finish Chewy. Coconut.

12-YEAR-OLD SCAPA

SCAPA
16-YEAR-OLD CHIEFTAIN'S CHOICE
Sherry finish

Color Deep amber/russet.
Nose Fat, sherried aromas: walnut/pecan, date, molasses toffee, leather with oily/honeyed notes.
Body Thick, sweet, and very juicy.
Palate Ripe and full with dry nuttiness around it. Robust.
Finish Soft. Dried fruits.

Old Pulteney

NORTHEASTERN SCOTLAND CONTAINS SOME OF THE COUNTRY'S MOST IDIOSYNCRATIC MALT WHISKEY DISTILLERIES, MANY OF WHICH ARE RELATIVELY UNKNOWN. OUR VOYAGE OF DISCOVERY STARTS WITH THE MOST ISOLATED OF ALL.

The town of Wick lies about 18 miles (30 km) south of John o' Groat's and is one of those places that people tend to pass. The few who stay in Wick find a sizable town, one that obviously attracted much money at some stage of its existence. It reminds you somehow of Campbeltown (*see pp. 110–13*), another once-grand place trying to find ways to recapture its past glories.

It was not always like this. In the first four decades of the 19th century, Wick was transformed from a fishing village to the moderate town we see today. For six weeks every summer, Wick became the herring capital of Europe and, by the 1840s, there were over 1000 herring boats operating out of its newly built harbor. Itinerant workers from across the Highlands and Islands descended on the town, fishing, gutting, curing, and packing the "silver darlings" for sale to markets from England to the Baltic.

A DEMAND FOR WHISKEY

These itinerant fish workers needed regular sustenance, mostly of the liquid, and alcoholic, variety. According to one local minister, the public houses of Wick were no less than "seminaries of Satan and Belial," and they served whiskey. Lots of it.

"It may seem incredible," the reverend continued, "but it has been ascertained that during the six weeks of a successful fishing, not less than 500 gallons [600 US gallons/2,275 liters] of whisky a day are consumed."

This ferocious thirst demanded a local distillery. Moonshiner James Henderson built his distillery in 1826, in Pulteneytown (named after herring baron Sir William Pulteney). According to contemporary reports, old-style Pulteney whiskey was a peaty monster—the lack of any other fuel meant that even the stills were peat-fired.

Old Pulteney *distillery may not be particularly pretty, but it certainly is effective, producing 265,000 gallons (one million liters) of excellent malt annually.*

DISTILLERY DETAILS

OLD PULTENEY FOUNDED: 1826.
OWNER: Inver House Distillers Ltd.
METHOD: Pot stills.
CAPACITY: 265,000 gallons.

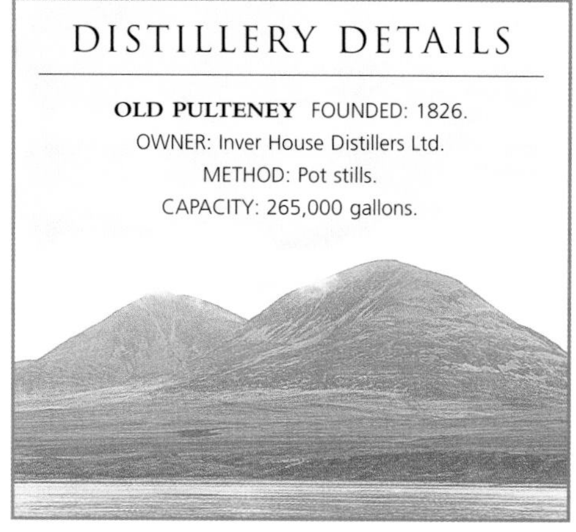

But boom leads to bust. The herring boats were requisitioned by the Admiralty in the World War I, and the fleet never returned. By the end of the 1920s, unemployment was rife and there were bread lines on the street. In a misguided attempt to solve the problems of drunkenness, in 1922 Wick was one of 57 Scottish towns to prohibit the sale of alcohol, a ban that stayed in force until 1939. In 1930, Pulteney's then owner, DCL, closed the distillery. It remained silent for 20 years before being bought by the owner of the Balblair distillery (*see p. 136*).

In 1959, both distilleries were sold to Hiram Walker (now Allied-Domecq). Finally, things began to look up for Pulteney. Its new owner rebuilt the distillery and upped production to supply fillings for then high-flying blends such as Ballantine's. Once again, though, the boom did not last and the drop in the blended market meant that distilleries, especially remote ones, were the first to be seen as being surplus to requirements.

Pulteney staggered on until 1997, when it was saved once more, this time by Inver House, which, sensibly, started to promote it as a single malt. The revelation was how good the spirit was. It has a slight marine note, an oily texture, and a bone-dry finish.

OLD PULTENEY

It seems strangely apposite that this virtually forgotten distillery from one of the lesser-known parts of Scotland should be hidden away in the backstreets. It is equally appropriate somehow that it should also be one of the most idiosyncratic distilleries of all. Peculiarly, its distilling equipment appears to be too big for the rooms in which it sits. Though you can barely walk around the

The barrel yard *at Old Pulteney tends to contain casks previously used to age bourbon. Visitors to the Wick distillery might expect Old Pulteney, which is nicknamed the "Manzanilla of the North" to be aged in sherry casks, but these are rarely, if ever, used.*

TASTING NOTES

As QUIRKY as the distillery itself, Old Pulteney whiskeys offer an array of surprising tastes and sensations.

OLD PULTENEY
12-YEAR-OLD,
40 VOL.

Color Gold.
Nose Oilskin, mink oil, coconut, milk chocolate, mango.
Body Rich, soft.
Palate Butterscotch, honeycomb, ripe nectarine, a light maritime tingle.
Finish Slippery. Long.

OLD PULTENEY

OLD PULTENEY
8-YEAR-OLD
GORDON & MACPHAIL
40 VOL.

Color Gold.
Nose Dusty warehouse. Hint of marine character and soft fruits.
Body Firm.
Palate Good oily feel, juicy fruit chewing gum. Touch of smoke, dry oak.
Finish Fresh and crisp.

mash tun, it is worth the squeeze, because the still-house contains two of the most peculiar-looking stills in the whiskey trade.

The wash still has an exaggerated boil bulb that sits like a goiter above the rounded base. It also has a flat top. The spirit still has a lyne arm that swoops and twists like an odd brass instrument before passing through the wall to coil around the inside of a worm tub.

This wonder has not only been saved, but is prospering. Maybe more people should have paid attention to author Neil M. Gunn, who wrote this about his local dram: "When I got of an age to understand Old Pulteney, I could admire its quality... recognizing in it some of the strong characteristics of the northern temperament."

Whiskey undoubtedly springs from its landscape, not solely in terms of *terroir* but also in the way in which its creators often impart something of their characteristic in it. It is, therefore, perhaps no surprise that the whiskeys of the northeast coast are among the most individual of all.

VISITORS ARE AMAZED *by the enormous spirit still at Old Pulteney, which looks as though it was made out of a monstrous instrument from a giant's brass band. Connoisseurs of distilling archaeology will find much else to intrigue them at this fishing port distillery.*

Northern Highlands: Clynelish

THE NORTHEAST'S INDIVIDUALITY IS REINFORCED AT THE SECOND OF ITS DISTILLERIES. BLENDERS HAVE LONG KEPT THE UNIQUE OILY AND WAXY-TEXTURED MALTS THAT ARE DISTILLED THERE FOR THEMSELVES.

DISTILLERY DETAILS

CLYNELISH FOUNDED: 1819.
OWNER: Diageo. METHOD: Pot stills.
CAPACITY: 898,000 gallons.

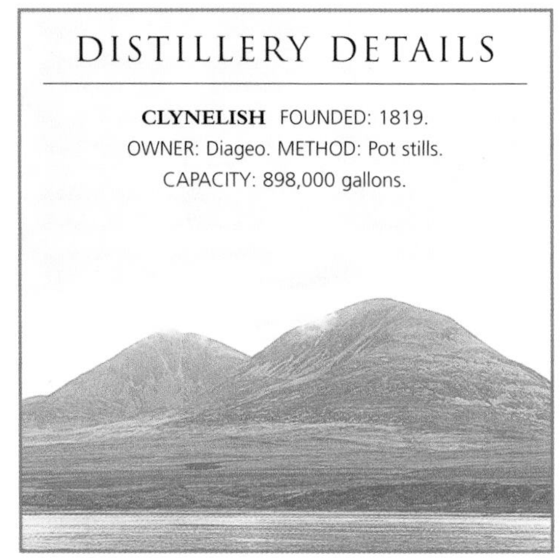

The complex landscape of the northeast begins to reveal itself fully once you leave the sandstone cliffs and farmlands around Wick. At first glance, these northern flow lands are just a relentless vista of peat bog, but it is teeming with life: a complex and unique biosystem of animals, birds, insects, and plants. This great brown, dun, and orange-colored watery desert is punctured by the great peaks of Morven and Scaraben to the south, and Ben Hope and Ben Loyal to the west.

Only in the broad fertile valleys (straths) that penetrate this landscape could human life survive. At the start of the 19th century, there were 15,000 people living in the straths that constituted the estates of the Duchess of Sutherland. By the middle of the century, the valleys were empty, and the people replaced by sheep. The Duchess, Duke, and their factors, Patrick Sellar and Francis Suther, had cleared the land ruthlessly, burning the tenants out of their homes. The people were forced to move to the coast, and the farmers were expected to become fishermen. Today, local people still talk of this period with bitterness.

In 1819, the Duke had another idea. He built a distillery in the coastal town of Brora, where there was plentiful water and coal. This would provide employment and also stop the tenants from making illegal hooch (and money). It was probably the only decent thing he ever did. The Clynelish distillery soon built a high reputation for itself, and in 1896 was rebuilt and enlarged into a classic Victorian plant, crowned with pagodas.

Clynelish became part of DCL in 1912, and four years later, John Walker & Sons bought an interest in it, mainly to safeguard supplies for their own blends. Although highly prized as a filling malt, Clynelish was available as a single malt, and was one of the malts mentioned by Charles Saintsbury in *Notes on a Cellar-Book* (1920).

NEW CLYNELISH

Visitors today cannot see inside the original distillery, but instead are shown the utilitarian-looking building that houses the new Clynelish. Built in 1967, this is a modernized replica of the original, with the same-shaped stills and producing the same style of whiskey:

The new Clynelish distillery *continues to use the original water supply from Clynemilton Burn to ensure that the quality of its single malt is unchanged.*

The old Brora distillery *is now silent, but its name lives on in special bottlings of its fine whiskey.*

unpeated, and filled with notes of pulpy fruits. The old distillery was mothballed when its neighbor was built, only to be revived two years later when its owner began to run short of heavily peated "island-style" malt for its blends, specifically Johnnie Walker. It was, confusingly, called Clynelish "B," but the name was soon changed to Brora. Sadly, it closed in 1983, the *annus horribilis* of malt distilling. Diageo has been the making the last remaining stock available as special bottlings (though at a premium price), in recognition of the sheer quality of this malt that reeks of peat, lanolin, wet canvas, and occasionally a hint of brine.

What sets Clynelish (and Brora) apart from all other malts is their distinctly oily and waxy texture: when Clynelish is young, it is reminiscent of gun oil, waxed jackets, and candle wax, developing into a rich, mouth-coating sexiness when mature. It gives a fantastic mouth feel to blends—mainly in the Walker stable, but other distillers use it as well—and is one reason why it has not been pushed as a major malt brand.

The secret of Clynelish's waxiness is a strange tale. In every distillery during the distilling year, a natural and harmless sludgy deposit is built up in the feints and foreshots receiver. During the silent season in every distillery except Clynelish, the tanks are cleaned and the sludge is removed. This is where the waxiness is found.

Today, Brora is best known for its whiskeys, its knitwear, and its golf course, but the past is never far away. On the road south to Golspie, your eyes are drawn upward to the monstrous monument erected by the Duchess of Sutherland for her late husband, who is still referred to in these parts as The Black Duke. Nearby, you can see the Gothic excesses of their palatial home—the appropriately named Dunrobin Castle.

TASTING NOTES

Beloved by blenders and malt enthusiasts, Clynelish and Brora are two of the most individualistic of all malts.

CLYNELISH
14-YEAR-OLD
46 VOL.

Color Bright gold.
Nose Complex. Candle wax/beeswax with touches of dried tropical and citric fruits, and honey. Exotic.
Body Honeyed, soft. Waxy.
Palate All about texture. Charcoal, honey, peach. Oak in balance. Light spices.
Finish Dry, light pepper, becomes gentle.

CLYNELISH 14-YEAR-OLD

BRORA
30-YEAR-OLD, 52.4 VOL.

Color Old gold/amber.
Nose Hugely complex. Heathery smoke, lanolin. Sweet oak, caramelized fruits, licorice, coffee, serrano ham, spent candle.
Palate A mouth-filling melange of sweet fruits, and a dry, smoky frame.
Finish Very long. Spices, oil, and fragrant smoke.

BRORA 30-YEAR-OLD

Balblair and Glenmorangie

THE FINISHING SCHOOL: HOW ONE OF GREAT BRITAIN'S BIGGEST-SELLING MALTS REINVENTED ITSELF—AND CREATED A NEW CATEGORY—AND A LOOK AT A LITTLE-KNOWN GEM.

Leaving Golspie, the whiskey trail continues on its southwesterly trajectory, through the cathedral town of Dornoch, across its eponymous firth, and into the village of Edderton. Here is one of the prettiest distilleries in Scotland, Balblair. Like its companions on this coast, it is little known by most whiskey-drinkers. This is ironic, since there has been a distillery in the "Parish of the Peats" since at least 1790, and some suggest that whiskey was being distilled on the old Ross farmstead half a century earlier.

BALBLAIR

The distillery you see today was built in 1872 to take advantage of the railroad. In 1997, after a period of virtual silence, Balblair was bought by Inver House. What was a relatively modest, expensive, antiquated distillery to its previous owner, the giant Allied-Domecq, was perfect for this smaller firm that has cleverly acquired a portfolio of characterful, traditional sites.

The change of ownership has also meant that Balblair is now beginning to appear as a single malt, and a very pleasant, soft, middle-of-the road dram it is. Balblair, however, will always have to play bridesmaid to its near neighbor, Glenmorangie, for many years Great Britain's No. 1 malt brand.

DISTILLERY DETAILS

BALBLAIR FOUNDED: 1790.
OWNER: Inver House Distillers Ltd.
METHOD: Pot stills.
CAPACITY: 343,000 gallons.

GLENMORANGIE FOUNDED: 1843.
OWNER: Glenmorangie PLC. METHOD: Pot stills.
CAPACITY: 1.1 million gallons.

GLENMORANGIE

Before arriving in Tain, the distillery's location, it is worth pausing in Tarlogie, where the springs that provide Glenmorangie's water percolate to the surface. This is another distillery that uses hard water, the downside of which is that it tends to fur up pipes, although the mineral composition may create minuscule differences during fermentation that could create different congeners.

Glenmorangie started life as a brewery, only switching to distilling in 1843. A chronic lack of money meant it was not until 1887 that it began to go full steam ahead—the phrase is used advisedly, as this was the first distillery to install steam coils in its stills. The stills themselves were interesting as well—they were taken from a London gin distillery.

One of the most overused terms in describing a still-house is cathedral-like, but Glenmorangie deserves it; the fragile-looking copper flutes soar to almost 17 feet (5 meters).

For most of the 20th century, the stills provided fillings for Glenmorangie's former parent company, Macdonald & Muir. In the 1970s, the firm switched emphasis to single malt, at that point still an infant category.

In 1977, the maltings were closed and converted into a still-house capable of holding four stills (two of them new). It proved a success and in 1990 the number of stills doubled again.

CREATING A CLASSIC

Glenmorangie's success comes down to its sheer drinkability, and that derives from a combination of the shape and size of the stills and the type of wood used to age the spirit. The height of the neck means there is a long contact time between the vapor and copper, which helps to produce a light, fragrant spirit.

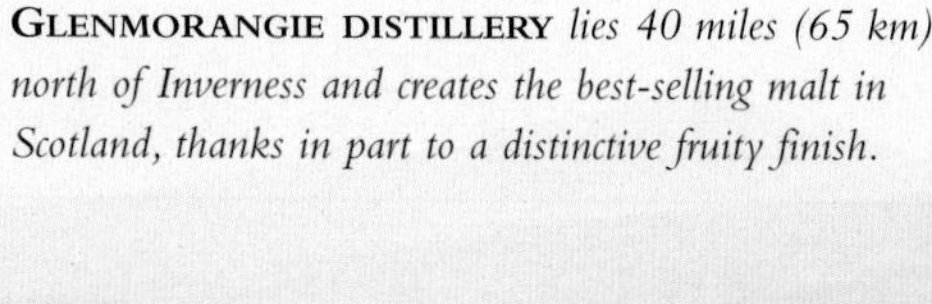

Glenmorangie distillery *lies 40 miles (65 km) north of Inverness and creates the best-selling malt in Scotland, thanks in part to a distinctive fruity finish.*

American white oak, with its notes of vanilla, coconut, and spice, is the most suited to show this character. Few firms have embarked on such an in-depth examination of wood, and today the firm not only specifies the type of oak, but designs its own casks, using air-dried wood grown on north-facing slopes. This results in a wood with less acidic notes and a wider pore structure (a result of slower growth), which allows for greater extract.

The problem with being a one-brand firm, as Glenmorangie was until its purchase of Ardbeg, is keeping consumers connected with the brand. Ever-older age statements is the traditional way, but Glenmorangie instead pioneered finishing. The malt is aged as normal in American oak and then decanted into barrels that have previously held another liquid. Glenmorangie chose port, madeira, and sherry, and all three finishes were a hit. Over the years Glenmorangie has released many others, and the best have shown how the correct cask can bring out new flavors in the whiskey and send it in new directions.

AT GLENMORANGIE, *creating barrels of Missouri oak is the first step in making highly sought-after whiskeys.*

TASTING NOTES

BALBLAIR AND Glenmorangie are as gentle as their surroundings, yet with a subtle complexity.

BALBLAIR

BALBLAIR
10-YEAR-OLD, 40 VOL.

Color Light gold.
Nose Malty: all-bran, then caramel apple sweetness. With water, dry oak, vanilla, and a light earthiness.
Body Light to medium-weight.
Palate Sits on the tongue with light oakiness on the sides. Toffee-soft with touches of buttered fruit loaf.
Finish Lightly dry and fruity.

BALBLAIR 10-YEAR-OLD

BALBLAIR
16-YEAR-OLD, 40 VOL.

Color Amber.
Nose Rounded and weighty: furniture polish, Brazil nuts. Spices, creamy butter, and dried fruits.
Body Firm.
Palate Soft, gentle, and rounded: butterscotch, hot cross buns, light, sweet spices.
Finish Spicy.

GLENMORANGIE

GLENMORANGIE
10-YEAR-OLD

Color Pale gold.
Nose Fresh, citric. Passion fruit, light malt, orange peel, ripe pear. Hint of vanilla.
Body Delicate. Light.
Palate Floral, nutmeg. Some malt. Good citric burst. Gentle.
Finish Short. Fresh.

GLENMORANGIE TRADITIONAL
NO AGE STATEMENT, 57.2 VOL.

Color Bright gold.

GLENMORANGIE 10-YEAR-OLD

Nose Very light and estery: citrus fruits, vanilla, wet grass/gorse, floral, subtle oak tones.
Palate Sweet and summery: lemon, orange, coconut, vanilla, dried apple, and light oakiness.
Finish Soft, oak, spices.

GLENMORANGIE SAUTERNES FINISH
(DISTILLED 1981, BOTTLED 2002) 46 VOL.

Color Old gold.
Nose Licorice. Brioche, caramelized pulp fruits/apple, cream, vanilla pod, honey, apple tart. Intense.
Body Heavy, rich, silky.
Palate Ripe and well rounded. Baked banana, orange. Thick baked fruits. Grippy wood.
Finish Richly wooded.

Dalmore

GRAIN PRODUCTION, OIL RIGS, WHISKEY FOR WOMEN, AND ODD-LOOKING STILLS; THE CENTRAL PART OF NORTHEAST SCOTLAND HAS A FASCINATING HISTORY. IT IS ALSO RESPONSIBLE FOR THE GROWTH OF WHISKEY-MAKING.

As well as three distilleries, Glenmorangie owns a manor house—Cadboll—located in the anvil-shaped flatlands that separate the Dornoch and Cromarty firths. These lush, arable pastures, mostly planted with barley, are the most visible reminder of the remarkable changes in agriculture that took place in this part of Easter Ross in the 18th century, changes that had a direct impact on whiskey production.

At the beginning of the 18th century, agriculture in Easter Ross was similar to that anywhere else in the Highlands: small townships of subsistence farmers, each with their own plot. Self-sufficiency was the aim, although the excellent fertility of the soil in this coastal part of the county meant that grain was also exported. Changes were afoot, however; the "improvements" that had brought greater efficiency to farming in England and the Lowlands of Scotland were perfectly suited to this part of the Highlands.

Large farmhouses were built, fields were walled in, and boggy land was drained. It was an enormous undertaking that made fortunes for the Lowland settlers. The original tenants either became farm laborers or emigrated to North America, tempted by the offer of free land. Interesting to think that some of these émigrés could have been among the first American whiskey-makers.

The strange-looking *stills at the Dalmore distillery add weight to the character of the malt.*

DISTILLERY DETAILS

DALMORE FOUNDED: 1839.
OWNER: Whyte and Mackay Ltd. METHOD: Pot stills.
CAPACITY: 845,000 gallons.

Dalmore's large *traditional distillery is run by a small band of stillmen, who originate from local families.*

This is a part of the country where major programs have often taken root. In 1961, a big grain distillery was built at Invergordon, part of a strategy bringing investment via major industry into the Highlands. For a short period, Invergordon grain was sold as a 10-year-old, the first whiskey aimed specifically at female drinkers. Like most grain distilleries, Invergordon also had a hidden malt distillery.

The Ben Wyvis distillery (named after the mountain that dominates the southern part of Easter Ross) ran intermittently from 1965 to 1976. Its plain, angular stills, which look like the Tin Man's hat in *The Wizard of Oz*, are now producing once more at Glengyle in Campbeltown, which was designed and is managed by Frank McHardy, who started his career of 40-plus years' distilling at Invergordon.

DALMORE

Whyte and Mackay has a monopoly on this stretch of the firth, since it also owns Dalmore. This eight-still plant was established in 1839 and was for many years owned by the Mackenzie family, which merged with Whyte and Mackay in 1960. Dalmore is another distillery where the past has, sensibly, been left alone. The wash still is flat-topped with a lyne arm sticking out of the body of the still, while the spirit stills sport copper cooling jackets.

It is clear that the distiller who designed these stills wanted to get the spirit to condense as quickly as possible; he wanted a heavy character, and that is what Dalmore makes. It is more than just heavy, however; it is sweet and rich with an aroma reminiscent of wild black fruits. Most spirit is matured in European casks.

Dalmore is now gaining in reputation. In 2004, a 62-year-old Dalmore (a vatting of 1868, 1878, 1926, and 1939) fetched $48,000 at auction. A more affordable dram with a sweet, voluptuous nature has been crafted to accompany a fine smoke: the Cigar Malt.

TASTING NOTES

Black currants and sweetness are the signature flavors of Dalmore.

THE DALMORE
12-YEAR-OLD, 40 VOL.
Color Ruby, amber.
Nose Sweet. Black currant jam. Rum and raisin.
Body Sweet and rich.
Palate Smooth and long. Super-ripe, basil, menthol. Dried fruits.
Finish Malt, balanced oak.

THE DALMORE
12-YEAR-OLD

THE DALMORE CIGAR MALT
40 VOL.

Color Umber.
Nose Big, sweet, and concentrated. Chocolate orange, cocoa, raisins, black fruits, and madeira-like.
Body Big, fat.
Palate Rum and raisin, boiling marmalade. Then chocolate, dried citrus peel, vanilla.
Finish Bitter chocolate.

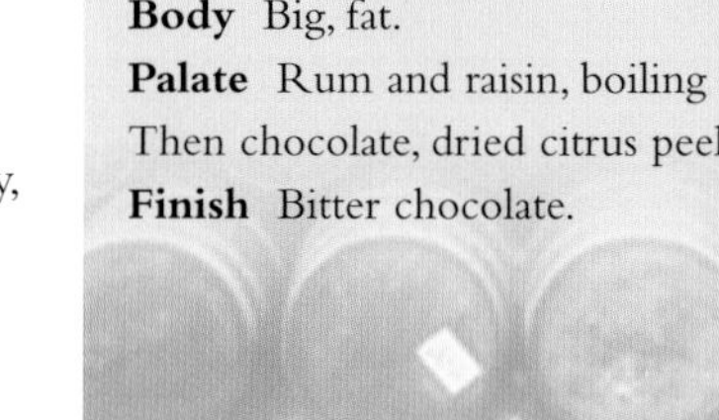

Black Isle

A TALE OF SMUGGLERS, WHIGS, COMPENSATION, PRIVILEGED DUTY-FREE STATUS, AND A LAMENT FROM SCOTLAND'S NATIONAL POET ALL COME TOGETHER ON THE DEEP-EARTHED PENINSULA OF THE BLACK ISLE.

Less than a mile inland from Dalmore lies Teaninich, the last of the northeast coast's distilleries, and its nearby neighbor, Ben Wyvis, which sits at the mouth of the Moray Firth.

DISTILLERY DETAILS

TEANINICH FOUNDED: 1817. OWNER: Diageo. METHOD: Pot stills. CAPACITY: 713,000 gallons.

GLEN ORD FOUNDED: 1838. OWNER: Diageo. METHOD: Pot stills. CAPACITY: 898,000 gallons.

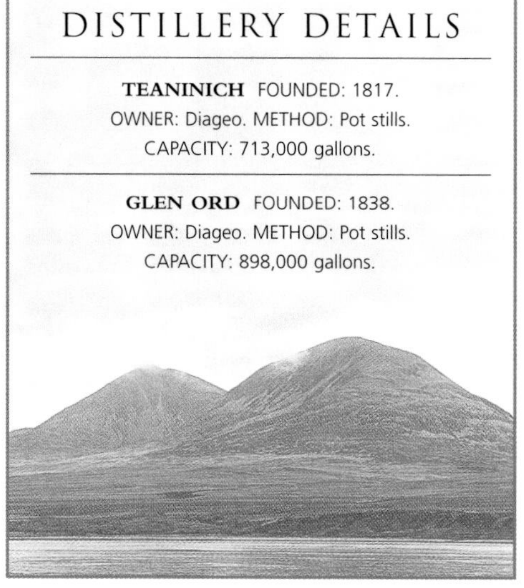

TEANINICH

Relatively obscure in single malt terms, Teaninich's produce is a major player in blending. Yet this distillery, first established by local landowner Captain Hugh Munro to supply his own needs, is another of the overlooked malts of this part of Scotland. Like its neighbors, it is fascinating for the malt enthusiast because it is so different. This is not a region that has embraced a general style and stuck to it. Neil Gunn's "strong northern characteristics" are once more to the fore. Each of the malts on the northeast coast is an individual.

Today, Teaninich is owned by Diageo and, like Linkwood, it is a distillery with two still-houses, although only one is currently in operation. The company runs distillation experiments here, the most recent success being the installation of a mash filter. Its make (fresh distillation) goes straight into blends and therefore rarely appears as a single malt, but when it does—particularly in Diageo's Rare Malts series—it shows real character. It is austere and grassy with a hint of smoke, bison grass, tea leaves, and citrus.

BEN WYVIS

The whiskey road now rounds the end of the firth and enters Dingwall. In the 19th century, Dingwall was home to the region's largest distillery, the original Ben Wyvis. Its size counted for little, however, and it closed in 1926. The other Ben Wyvis, the mountain that looms over the southern part of Easter Ross, is now behind the traveler. The landscape continues to soften as the road cuts across the deep-earthed, diamond-shaped peninsula of the Black Isle. It is a long way from the peat desert of the far northeast.

FERINTOSH

This rich, arable farmland was home to Scotland's first commercial distillery, Ferintosh. The original distillery was razed in 1689 by Jacobite supporters of the exiled James II (Old Pretender). It was owned by Duncan Forbes of Culloden who, as a Whig, was loyal to the newly imported Protestant monarch William of Orange. After the Uprising failed, Forbes' son, also named Duncan, was compensated with a payment equivalent to about $11 million in today's terms and granted the privilege of distilling whiskey made from grain grown on his own land duty-free.

This incredible arrangement lasted for nearly 100 years, netting the Forbes family yearly profits equating to about $3.8 million in today's currency. The estate grew to support three distilleries that supplied two-thirds of Scotland's legally produced whiskey. The

Glen Ord *is surrounded by fields that supply many distilleries with barley. The crops flourish in the dark, fertile earth that gives the Black Isle its name.*

Ord distillery *has a huge maltings that supplies many of the northern distilleries. It also produces a soft, turfy malt that is gradually gaining appreciation under the "Hidden Malts" banner of Diageo.*

duty-free status was retracted in 1786, prompting Robert Burns to pen:

Thee Ferintosh! O sadly lost!
Scotland lament frae coast to coast!
Now colic grips, an' barkin hoast
May kill us a';
For loyal Forbes' charter'd boast
Is ta'en awa'

Burns, that staunch republican, was always capable of switching allegiance if his muse demanded it. Though a certain Donald Murray revived the name in the late 1790s, Ferintosh was another of the licensed Highland distilleries that suffered as a result of confusing legislation that was imposed at the end of the 18th century to stop whiskey smuggling.

ORD

For such a barley-rich area, it is surprising that the Black Isle supports only one distillery, Ord. Built in 1837 just outside the town of Muir of Ord, it had to wait until the latter part of the century before it began to operate with any great consistency. A clue as to why can be found in Barnard, who claims that "even to this day [smugglers] carry out their illegal business," Old habits die hard. Ord was eventually bought in a joint venture between Dewar's and Walker before being absorbed into the huge DCL setup. Today, it is a dual-purpose site with a neat, modern distillery dwarfed by the huge maltings that dominate the entrance to the site. These maltings supply the needs of Diageo's northern distilleries as well as supplying the peated malt for Talisker.

In recent times, Ord was positioned as a "fighting brand" by Diageo, although it was a strategy that did not meet with huge success. Today, it has been relaunched as one of the company's "Hidden Malts." It is good to see the firm persevering because this is a gentle, turfy malt that deserves a wider audience. The recent and numerous name changes—Glen Ord, Muir of Ord, and Glenordie—have been confusing and cannot have helped its cause. But it seems, for now at least, that Ord is the order of the day.

TASTING NOTES

Think of grass in all its guises and you will get an idea of the character of these two distilleries. Renowned for supplying whiskey blends, they also produce some fine single malts.

TEANINICH

TEANINICH
10-YEAR-OLD
FLORA & FAUNA, 43 VOL.

Color Light gold.
Nose Intriguing, perfumed. Green tea, dry grasses, floral. In time, a birch-sap note along with sandalwood, lemon verbena.
Body Medium. Good feel.
Palate Almost sugary start, a solid mid-palate with a lovely oily feel. Slightly austere.
Finish Dry, soft, oily, addictive.

10-YEAR-OLD TEANINICH

TEANINICH
27-YEAR-OLD (DISTILLED 1972)
RARE MALTS, 64.2 VOL.

Color Very pale gold. Green glints.
Nose Intense, exotic, perfumed. Sandalwood, sweet hay, citrus peel, heather, pine sap, succulent malt, bergamot.
Body Mouth-filling.
Palate Earl Grey tea, pine honey, grass. Lean yet rich. Exotic spices.
Finish Peppery.

GLEN ORD

GLEN ORD
12-YEAR-OLD, 43 VOL.

Color Full gold.
Nose Dried grass with light oak and a mossiness/fresh-turned sod. With water, coconut pulp, orange, nougat.
Body Medium.
Palate Dry, crisp, and quite oaky. Some light honey, orange again alongside malt and light honey.
Finish Dry, short but appetizing.

ORD, CADENHEAD
19-YEAR-OLD, 63 VOL.

Color Gold.
Nose Fresh and clean. Green grass, lime, shortbread, and bourbon cookie. Grassier with water.
Body Medium. Clean but rigid.
Palate Sweet (honey, apple, orange), and then dries (malt, nuts).
Finish Dried apple. Short. Aperitif.

Closed Distilleries

INVERNESS WAS A MAJOR PRODUCER OF MALT AND THE HOME OF THREE DISTILLERIES, BUT TODAY THERE REMAINS ALMOST NO TRACE OF ITS GREAT WHISKEY-MAKING PAST.

The main city of the Scottish Highlands formerly boasted three distilleries, but a combination of factors forced their closure in the 1980s. Some bottlings are still available, but it is not known for how long, and as yet there are no plans to reintroduce whiskey-making into the city.

DISTILLERY DETAILS

GLEN ALBYN FOUNDED: 1846.
OWNER: DCL.
CLOSED: 1983.

MILLBURN FOUNDED: 1807.
OWNER: DCL.
CLOSED: 1985.

GLEN MHOR FOUNDED: 1896.
OWNER: DCL.
CLOSED: 1986.

INVERNESS

From Muir of Ord to Inverness is a short jump skimming around the end of the Beauly Firth, the last of the wide stretches of water that slice the northeast coastline. To the south is the Great Glen, the long diagonal fault line that divides the northern and southern Highlands. Its lochs—Ness, Oich, and Lochy—are joined together by the Caledonian canal that runs from the last of the three into Loch Linnhe at Fort William. Whiskey tourists wanting to discover the west coast will head off in this direction, keeping half an eye open for the monster that allegedly lurks in Loch Ness's depths, but those heading toward malt's golden heartland of Speyside will continue on into Inverness.

The capital of the Highlands is enjoying a mini-boom at the moment, with increased investment bringing new jobs to the region. Sadly, none of these are in whiskey. Amazingly for a town of this size and location, Inverness now has no distillery of its own. Prior to the 1745 rebellion, the city produced the bulk of Scotland's brewing malt, thanks to the proximity of the Black Isle and the Laich O'Moray. Yet the trade ultimately collapsed through a combination of greed—the maltsters decided they could make beer as well and sank money into large breweries, most of which failed—and what Alfred Barnard enigmatically calls "the revolution." Culloden is close by, and one can only speculate that there must have been a backlash against Highland beer.

The ruins of *Urquhart Castle, surrounded by fields, sit on the western shores of Loch Ness.*

GLEN ALBYN, MILLBURN, AND GLEN MHOR

In 1846, one of the failed breweries, Glen Albyn, was converted into a distillery by James Sutherland, the town's Lord Provost. It was predated by almost 40 years by Millburn, which struggled to succeed for many years until it was rebuilt in 1876, but then ultimately closed due to lack of space for expansion in the 1980s. In 1896, Glen Mhor was erected. Today, you will search in vain for traces of them all. Glen Albyn's site has become a retail park, Glen Mhor (where the novelist Neil Gunn once worked as an exciseman) has been demolished, while Millburn is now a steakhouse.

These three distilleries were owned by Distiller's Company Ltd. (DCL), and when the great purge came in the 1980s, the decision was made to shut them all. The reasoning was that not only were they surplus to requirements, but they just did not make an exceptional whiskey. In Glen Albyn's case that was probably true, but Glen Mhor had a sooty weight, and Millburn was a rich, honeyed, slow-maturing beauty; both were well worth seeking out.

Hindsight is a wonderful thing, and there is little doubt today that if the malt market had been more advanced and whiskey tourism more developed, at least one of the distilleries would have been saved. Instead, the capital of the Highlands, the place where most tourists visit, has no whiskey heritage to show; it is a lost opportunity.

Glen Albyn's *canalside warehouses still stand, the name clearly indicated on their side. They have remain unused for over 20 years since the closure of the distillery in the 1980s.*

THE FINDHORN

A REJUVENATED DISTILLERY, A NEW AGE COMMUNITY, A MUSEUM OF DISTILLATION, AND SCOTLAND'S LARGEST MALT PRODUCER—THE BANKS OF THE FINDHORN RIVER HAVE A MULTITUDE OF OFFERINGS.

Speyside is a complicated region with a high concentration of distilleries. The easiest way to make sense of its complex geography is to follow its rivers from sea to source and discover the whiskey heritage on and close to their banks.

ROYAL BRACKLA

Western Speyside starts with a Shakespearean connection. According to the Bard, Macbeth's elevation to Thane of Cawdor signaled the start of his bloody rise to power. The village of Cawdor today can not only boast his castle, but extends the regal connection to its local distillery, Royal Brackla.

Established in 1812 by Captain William Fraser, the distillery received its first royal warrant in 1835. Although the Royal household approved, one can imagine that the Captain was not popular with his Scottish compatriots during the early stages of his distilling career: memories of Culloden and the end of the Jacobite cause would still have been fresh in their minds. Today, Royal Brackla is part of the Bacardi stable.

BENROMACH

The Findhorn reaches the sea close to the site of the Findhorn Foundation: the non-doctrinal spiritual community established on the sand dunes in 1962 by Peter and Eileen Caddy and Dorothy Maclean. There is a whiskey connection here, as some of the unusual houses used by the residents have been made from disused washbacks.

Some of these may have come from Benromach in nearby Forres, a compact, white-painted distillery that was saved from dereliction in 1994. Another of the DCL distilleries that was mothballed in the early 1980s, Benromach's stills had been ripped out when Gordon & MacPhail (*see p. 146*) bought it. Benromach is a manifestation of all the experience built up by the company over more than a century of working in the whiskey industry. It may be an old building, but the interior is new: new mill, semi-lauter mash tun, and wood washbacks and stills. The washbacks and stills are different in size and shape from the previous ones, with fatter necks and a boil bulb on the spirit still. The only item remaining from Benromach's previous incarnation is the tall, red-brick chimney. It is not used anymore, but the company was asked to keep it in place because it is a useful marker for pilots arriving at nearby Kinloss air force base.

DISTILLERY DETAILS

BENROMACH FOUNDED: 1898.
OWNER: Gordon & MacPhail. METHOD: Pot stills.
CAPACITY: 53,000 gallons.

DALLAS DHU FOUNDED: 1899.
OWNER: DCL. METHOD: Pot stills.
CLOSED 1983.

TOMATIN FOUNDED: 1897.
OWNER: Takara Co. Ltd. METHOD: Pot stills.
CAPACITY: 1.8 million gallons.

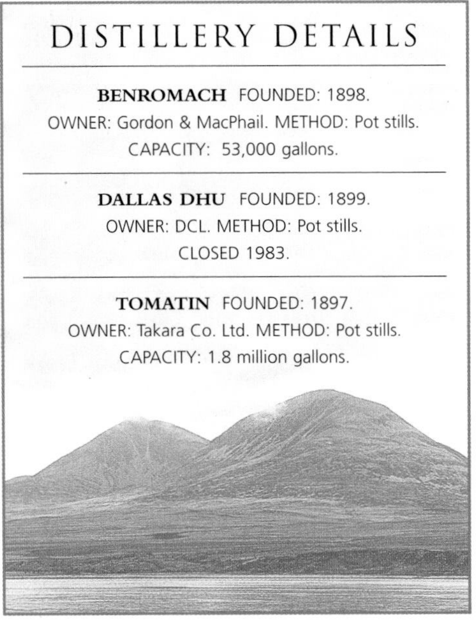

BENROMACH DISTILLERY *has been brought back from the dead by bottlers Gordon & MacPhail, and now produces a fine mix of old and new malt whiskeys, including an organic range.*

The distillery produces an interesting mix of old and new whiskeys. Most Speyside whiskeys have gradually dropped their peating levels in the past few decades and many are also noticeably lighter in style: the complex, almost oily character and the combination of floral notes, smoke, and silky palate have largely disappeared. Benromach aims to bring that back. Its owner is also experimenting. A low-peated malt and a heavily peated malt are being used for small batch releases, and various barley strains have been trialed. An organic whiskey (certified by the Soil Association) has also been made.

Benromach is just one of the new wave of small, independent distilleries that are beginning to appear. All are finding ways to assert their individuality—either by making a number of different styles, exploring finishes, or operating whiskey schools—and their efforts are adding enormously to the malt's diversity.

DALLAS DHU

Were that only the case with Forres' other distillery, Dallas Dhu, which has been turned into a museum. In many ways it was a museum piece anyway; it was powered by a watermill until 1971. Its silence is a real loss to the world of malt because the bottlings that have appeared since its demise have been excellent.

GLENBURGIE

The road going east from Forres to Elgin passes between Diageo's two enormous maltings at Burghead and Roseisle on the coast, and Allied-Domecq's Glenburgie

The charming Dallas Dhu *distillery has now become a museum of distillation.*

distillery. Like most of the company's output, very little of this light, appley whiskey is ever seen as a single malt. The vast majority of it is used in Ballantine's blends. In common with a number of Allied-Domecq's distilleries, Glenburgie also has a Lomond spirit still that allows the distillery to produce two rather different styles of malt; Glenburgie's lush, fruity, alter ego is called Glencraig.

TOMATIN

Following the Findhorn a further 40 miles (64 km) downstream, you reach Scotland's biggest malt whiskey distillery. The buildings come as something of a surprise in this high, isolated, moorland setting in the foothills of the Monadhliath Mountains, especially since its design is a triumph of modern industrial brutalism.

This is Tomatin—the Big "T," as its blend is appropriately dubbed. Founded in 1897, it was a standard, two-still operation until the 1950s when an expansion program was started to cope with the boom in blends. This continued throughout the next two decades, until the distillery had a total of 23 stills. To no one's great surprise, Tomatin went bust in 1985, but it was saved by Japanese firm Takara Co. Ltd., which does not operate it at full capacity. The malt is rich, round, and toffeelike.

Tomatin distillery *remains Scotland's biggest malt distillery. Home to 23 stills, only a handful of which are in operation, it produces a decent single malt.*

TASTING NOTES

From perfumed sweetness and light peat to chunky power, the Findhorn covers the spectrum.

BENROMACH

BENROMACH TRADITIONAL
40 VOL.

Color Pale gold.
Nose Floral (freesia, stock) with light vanilla, pine, cashew, clover honey, and a wisp of peat.
Body Medium. Soft texture.
Palate Soft, then butterscotch, spices, malt. Excellent breadth. Oak in balance.
Finish Light oak, orange peel.

TOMATIN

TOMATIN
12-YEAR-OLD,
40 VOL.

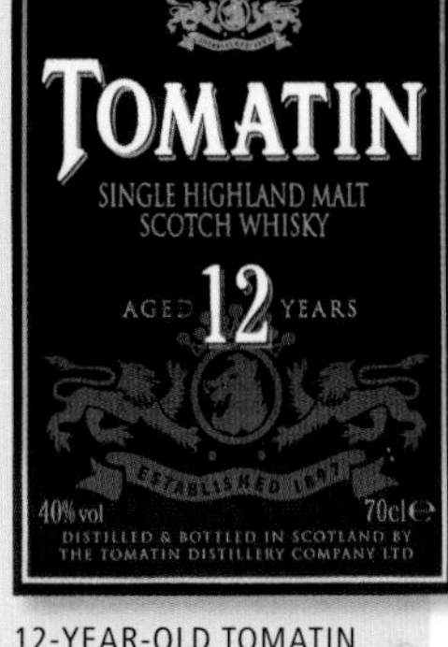

12-YEAR-OLD TOMATIN

Color Gold.
Nose Mix of nut, bracken, and an aroma that is like old slippers: rubber, inner tubes. A seed-like cereal note.
Body Medium. Sweet.
Palate More on the body than the nose: burnt toffee, sugary, nutty. The rubbery note reappears.
Finish Pink marshmallow.

The Lossie

THE TOWN OF ELGIN AND ITS ENVIRONS ALONG THE RIVER LOSSIE ARE HOME TO SOME OF THE WHISKEY INDUSTRY'S TOP DISTILLERIES—YET VERY FEW ARE KNOWN TO THE WIDER PUBLIC.

The coast road passes through some of the most fertile barley-producing land in Scotland, the Laich o' Moray ("Laich" means low country). This part of Speyside is drained by the Lossie, which meanders around the business capital of the region, Elgin, a small but quietly grand town.

GORDON & MACPHAIL

On Elgin's main street is a shop that, for 100 years, has been a Mecca for all whiskey (and food) lovers: Gordon & MacPhail. One half of the store is a high-class delicatessen, the other is dedicated to a stellar range of whiskeys, most of them bottled by the company itself.

The firm's warehouses are a treasure trove of malt. Unlike virtually all other independent bottlers, Gordon & MacPhail fills its barrels with new make, giving the company control from start to finish. Without its dedication, few would know of Mortlach, Aultmore, or Linkwood.

GLEN MORAY

The Lossie is a turbulent stream, prone to flooding, something that both Gordon & MacPhail and Glen Moray, the first of the Lossie distilleries, know only too well. Glen Moray lies below the level of the river, so it is often badly affected in winter.

DISTILLERY DETAILS

GLEN MORAY FOUNDED: 1897.
OWNER: Glenmorangie PLC. METHOD: Pot stills.
CAPACITY: 528,000 gallons.

MILTONDUFF FOUNDED: 1824.
OWNER: Allied Distillers Ltd. METHOD: Pot stills.
CAPACITY: 1.3 million gallons.

GLENLOSSIE FOUNDED: 1876.
OWNER: Diageo. METHOD: Pot stills.
CAPACITY: 291,000 gallons.

MANNOCHMORE FOUNDED: 1971.
OWNER: Diageo. METHOD: Pot stills.
CAPACITY: 343,000 gallons.

LINKWOOD FOUNDED: 1821.
OWNER: Diageo. METHOD: Pot stills.
CAPACITY: 608,000 gallons.

BENRIACH FOUNDED: 1898.
OWNER: BenRiach Distillery Co. METHOD: Pot stills.
CAPACITY: 687,000 gallons.

LONGMORN FOUNDED: 1894.
OWNER: Chivas Brothers. METHOD: Pot stills.
CAPACITY: 872,000 gallons.

GLEN ELGIN FOUNDED: 1898.
OWNER: Diageo. METHOD: Pot stills.
CAPACITY: 476,000 gallons.

Originally a brewery, Glen Moray's site seems larger than its four stills require—the legacy of the Saladin maltings that operated here for 11 years. Part of the Glenmorangie stable, Glen Moray has been repositioned recently as a low-priced, introductory malt, finished in white wine casks. Sadly, there are few malt aficionados who take this charming, slightly grassy malt as seriously as they should.

MILTONDUFF

On the back road to Dallas 6 miles (9 km) to the southwest lies Pluscarden Abbey. Founded in 1230, the abbey was abandoned during the Reformation and only renovated toward the end of the 20th century. In an enviable spirit of equanimity, the monks are happy that the springs that rise by the abbey are used by the neighboring Miltonduff distillery, which was built on the site of the original meal mill.

A major player in Ballantine's, Miltonduff has had low visibility as a single malt. Even more rare are examples of Mosstowie, its sister malt made in Lomond stills.

GLENLOSSIE/MANNOCHMORE

To the east are two Diageo distilleries on the same site: Glenlossie and Mannochmore. The former is the older of the pair, dating back to 1876, but extended to its current size in the 1960s. It produces a light, slightly oily style. Mannochmore was created in 1971 for fillings. It is best known for being the malt that was used to create the "black whiskey," Loch Dhu, which made a short, fateful foray on to the market in the 1990s. Ironically, Loch Dhu has now become a cult whiskey and bottles are highly prized.

LINKWOOD

The left bank of the Lossie plain is bisected by the road that links the town of Elgin with that of Rothes. Spread

GLENLOSSIE DISTILLERY *is one of the forgotten few, responsible for a soft and gentle, light, slightly spicy style of whiskey.*

out along this road is a clutch of some of Speyside's most underrated distilleries. Closest to Elgin is the tranquil Linkwood distillery with its meticulously kept gardens. This is another double site, with an old, pagoda-topped distillery facing its modern, box-shaped neighbor.

Linkwood's massive spirit stills produce one of Speyside's most fragrant malts, with its wonderful aromas of apple blossom, peach skin, and freshly mown grass. Linkwood is also one of the smokiest Speyside malts, in both its palate and its long finish, and is well known for its big, assertive, malty body.

BENRIACH AND LONGMORN

These are two more stills on the Rothes road. They were both owned by Chivas Brothers until 2004, when the former was bought by a group of investors called Intra Trading, headed by former Burn Stewart director, Billy Walker. Known for its sound, gentle dram, Benriach's new owners amazed everyone by uncovering stocks of a heavily peated variant. Longmorn is the hidden jewel in the Chivas Brothers portfolio. Its dumpy stills make a rich, deep, fruity, and complex malt that demands to be better known.

GLEN ELGIN

With six stills and worm tubs, Glen Elgin produces a highly prized malt, formerly exclusively used for blends, but it is now beginning to appear as a single. Softly fruity with good depth, it seems to sum up the shy, modest air that pervades the Lossie area.

TASTING NOTES

Capturing an aromatic world of flowers, soft fruits, and complexity, these fine, relatively unknown Speyside malts are well worth seeking out.

GLEN MORAY

GLEN MORAY
NO AGE STATEMENT, 40 VOL.
Mellowed in white wine barrels. Pleasant but a little bland.

Color Yellow gold.
Nose Light, malty with butter, honey, and a hint of damp earth.
Body Fresh and light.
Palate Well-balanced and on the soft, light side with a vanilla undertow and a hint of honey.
Finish Short.

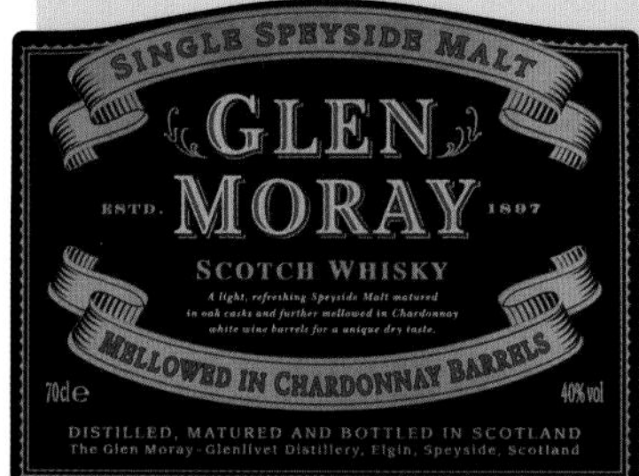

GLEN MORAY

MILTONDUFF

MILTONDUFF
15-YEAR-OLD, 46 VOL.

Color Gold.

15-YEAR-OLD MILTONDUFF

Nose Very soft fruits, toffee, pigskin. Jam cookies.
Body Velvety.
Palate Aromatic herbs: rosemary and thyme. Toffee. Soft and gentle. A demure dram.
Finish Almond and chocolate.

GLENLOSSIE

GLENLOSSIE
10-YEAR-OLD, 43 VOL.

Color Light gold.
Nose Clean and light. Red apple, sweet hay, vanilla, buttered popcorn, and rice cakes.
Body Soft and gentle. Medium.
Palate Sweet grass. Touch of spices. Slight oily note, but straight down the middle of the palate. Attractive.
Finish Light, quite short.

MANNOCHMORE

MANNOCHMORE
12-YEAR-OLD, 43 VOL.

Color Golden.
Nose Sweet, light, and perfumed. Dried flowers, lemon, soft fruits, hazelnut, and syrup.
Body Light to medium. Frothy and frivolous.
Palate Floral and attractive. A hit of lemon meringue pie and all very light, sweet, and fragrant.
Finish A little short.

LINKWOOD

LINKWOOD
12-YEAR-OLD, 43 VOL.

Color Straw.
Nose Perfumed: green apple, peach blossom, jasmine, muscat grapes, and just-mown grass.
Body Seems light but has hidden silky depths.
Palate Rounded yet delicate. Green apples, scintillating spiciness. Fills and perfumes the mouth.
Finish Soft. Apple again.

LONGMORN

LONGMORN
15-YEAR-OLD, 45 VOL.

Color Rich amber.
Nose Soft, generous. Baked fruits with caramel, sticky toffee pudding, a hint of damp chamois leather.
Body Substantial and well built.
Palate The soft fruits sitting within a firm structure and a lovely mint note.
Finish Nutty.

GLEN ELGIN

GLEN ELGIN
12-YEAR-OLD, 43 VOL.

Color Full gold.
Nose Generous and rich: stewed peach/apricot, honey, heather, moist raisin cake, some sulfur/burned matches.
Body Medium to full-bodied.
Palate Ripe, sweet fruits with honeyed concentration which becomes nuttier and a little smoky.
Finish Licorice and vanilla.

12-YEAR-OLD GLEN ELGIN

Rothes

A GALLANT MAJOR AND HIS GARDENS, A SECRET GLEN, A WHISKEY PIPELINE, AND ANOTHER HIDDEN SURPRISE: ROTHES IS A TAPESTRY OF WHISKEY TALES.

There is a slow and subtle shift in landscape as you travel toward Rothes and the Spey. The soft, expansive coastal plain recedes and hills slowly begin to exert a tighter grip. Just before Rothes, you can see the pagoda roof, gray walls, and the Highland slate roof of the Speyburn distillery, hidden in a small, deep glen. Like most of the five stills in Rothes, Speyburn prefers to keep itself out of the immediate public gaze.

SPEYBURN

Speyburn is a small site, another of the old-style distilleries purchased by Inver House in 1991. It is an ideal fit for the smaller company. Not only is the location idyllic, but the whiskey is as soft, sweet, and gentle as any in the region; a good buy.

GLEN GRANT

Most of the small towns of Speyside have over time acquired a collection of distilleries: Forres, Elgin, Keith, Dufftown, and Rothes are all whiskey towns, although few would imagine it when they drive through the last of these. The only distillery in plain sight is Glen Grant, and that was a deliberate move by James and John Grant when they built the distillery in 1840. Here is Victorian wealth in its finest, grandest expression. Clearly the Grants wanted people to know that they, one of the major families in the district, had joined the whiskey trade.

Rothes is home to *Forsyth's, Scotland's top still-maker, supplier to distilleries around the world.*

DISTILLERY DETAILS

SPEYBURN FOUNDED: 1897.
OWNER: Inver House Distillers Ltd.
METHOD: Pot stills.
CAPACITY: 462,000 gallons.

GLEN GRANT FOUNDED: 1840.
OWNER: Chivas Brothers. METHOD: Pot stills.
CAPACITY: 1.4 million gallons.

GLENROTHES FOUNDED: 1879.
OWNER: The Edrington Group. METHOD: Pot stills.
CAPACITY: 1.5 million gallons.

GLEN SPEY FOUNDED: 1885.
OWNER: Diageo. METHOD: Pot stills.
CAPACITY: 370,000 gallons.

Glen Grant was inherited by James Jr., also known as the Major. It was under his paternalistic gaze that it prospered. When he was not hunting in Africa, he devoted considerable time to building up the distillery into a substantial producer. He also created the remarkable gardens that are now as much of an attraction as the whiskey-making part of the site. Sadly, the atmosphere within the distillery has not been the same since the coal fires were removed.

The five-year-old whiskey is a huge seller in Italy, although it takes much longer for Glen Grant to get into its stride. Those strange stills with their helmetlike bases and purifiers produce a clean, dry, and lean malt. Unfortunately, many of the older expressions have been obliterated by spending too much time in sherry cask. Taste the right cask in its mid-teens and it sings.

Over the road is the mothballed Caperdonich. It has the same-shaped stills as Glen Grant, but the whiskey, which was once carried across the road in an overhead pipe, was different and not as good. Maybe the stillmen were too busy watching the action on the soccer field outside their window.

GLENROTHES/GLEN SPEY

Rothes does have another gem hidden away, somewhat gloomily situated next to the town graveyard. Glenrothes was the founding partner (with Bunnahabhain) of Highland Distillers (now Edrington), and although the company still owns it, the site is used mostly by Berry Brothers & Rudd as the home of its blend Cutty Sark. In recent years, Berry Brothers has released a series of vintage single malts that demonstrate why this is considered a malt-lover's malt. It has a light fragrance, good spiciness, and a rich depth.

Across the burn from the Glenrothes distillery stands Glen Spey. This Diageo-owned distillery started life as a mill. Its light, bone-dry, nutty malt is a classic example of the Justerini & Brooks style.

FORSYTH'S STILLS

The town's final whiskey connection is not on public display. Rothes is home to Forsyth's, arguably the world's most famous makers of traditional copper pot stills. Not only does the firm build and repair stills for its native Scotland's malt whiskey industry, but it also has contracts with firms around the world. You can see the familiar, fat, gleaming Forsyth stills in distilleries from Canada to Jamaica.

The Glenrothes distillery *is the home of the Cutty Sark blend, and also, more recently, of a series of excellent vintage single malts. These are so good that they are regarded as a malt-lover's malt.*

TASTING NOTES

Dry, clean, light, and soft typifies the whiskeys produced by these distilleries. A tasting of Glenrothes must not be missed.

SPEYBURN

SPEYBURN
10-YEAR-OLD, 40 VOL.
Color Light gold.
Nose Soft and malty. Heather, orange, spicy.
Body Medium. Soft feel.
Palate A light, dry, malty start before a spicy mid-palate. Good balance.
Finish Spicy and slightly dry.

GLEN GRANT

GLEN GRANT
10-YEAR-OLD
43 VOL.
Color Yellow/gold.
Nose Light and sweet. Touch of malt. Floral.
Body Light, soft.
Palate Clean, light fruit, and crisp maltiness.
Finish Dry. Short.

GLENROTHES

GLENROTHES
1989
43 VOL.
Color Rich amber.
Nose Sweet spices with toffee, banana, cream, dried pear, and fruitcake. Complex.
Body Medium to rich. Deep.
Palate Spiciness, giving a subtle lift to the rich fruits, light sherry, and ginger cake.
Finish Long and soft.

GLEN SPEY

GLEN SPEY
12-YEAR-OLD
43 VOL.
Color Light gold.
Nose Dry and slightly dusty; spice, coffee, bran, vanilla, and nut.
Body Medium.
Palate Estery and floral with sweet grass. Some maltiness.
Finish Short and nuttily dry.

12-YEAR-OLD GLEN SPEY

The Spey

SCOTLAND'S LONGEST RIVER HAS ALSO GIVEN ITS NAME TO ITS PREEMINENT WHISKEY REGION. ITS UPPER STRETCHES ENCOMPASS A TANGY COASTAL MALT, A MODERN STILL, AND THE FIRST GLIMMERINGS OF ITS HEART.

The Spey, Scotland's longest river, starts as a burn flowing out of Loch Spey, a tiny nodule of blue in the southern Monadhliath range, no more than a short steep climb from the Great Glen. It then forges northeast before meandering in its distillery-rich middle, until at Rothes it makes a final, fast, straight rush to the sea.

Around 60 miles (100 km) of its length are tracked by the Speyside Way, the long path that follows the route of the now abandoned Strathspey railroad, which helped to make the area whiskey's preeminent player. Speyside was forged by its native whiskey-makers. The distilleries appear so frequently that they are as much a part of the scenery as the trees that shade the fast-flowing river.

INCHGOWER

Buckie lies close to where the river Spey finally disgorges into the Moray Firth. A fishing town, it is home to a large number of oystercatchers. The piercing "kleep" of these birds is a soundtrack that accompanies much of the upper reaches of the Spey, and it is an oystercatcher that adorns the label of Inchgower, the malt from this coastal town. The distillery stands just outside Buckie in an area that was once noted for illicit distilling.

Inchgower is an intense dram with a jasminelike floral character, underpinned by a resolute saltiness that makes it a natural accompaniment to fish and seafood, and in particular, oysters. It is possible that this could be the result of being distilled relatively close to the sea, although not every coastal malt has this saline character. But it seems only right that one of the Spey's drams should remind the drinker that this river does not just vanish into countryside, but ultimately mingles with the sea itself.

DISTILLERY DETAILS

INCHGOWER FOUNDED: 1871.
OWNER: Diageo. METHOD: Pot stills.
CAPACITY: 580,000 gallons.

AUCHROISK FOUNDED: 1974.
OWNER: Diageo. METHOD: Pot stills.
CAPACITY: 819,000 gallons.

GLENTAUCHERS FOUNDED: 1898.
OWNER: Allied Distillers Ltd. METHOD: Pot stills.
CAPACITY: 542,000 gallons.

CRAIGELLACHIE FOUNDED: 1888.
OWNER: John Dewar & Sons Ltd. METHOD: Pot stills.
CAPACITY: 734,000 gallons.

THE SPEY *wanders through Speyside to the sea. Its banks are home to some of Scotland's greatest malts.*

AUCHROISK, *built in 1974, is a relatively young distillery reminiscent of a Californian winery.*

AUCHROISK

The Burn of Mulben enters the Spey 12 miles (19 km) inland, but prior to that it passes a white-painted collection of buildings with the air of a Californian winery. This is Auchroisk (pronounced "oth-rusk"), built in 1974 by IDV mainly to supply fillings for J&B. Its eight stills also gave the market a malt called the Singleton, which was launched amid considerable hype, but now plays a minor role in Diageo's extensive portfolio. The adjoining warehouses hold stock from many of the firm's Speyside sites.

GLENTAUCHERS

Farther up the burn toward Keith is Glentauchers. Built in 1898, it represents the time when blenders began to move into malt distilling. Originally, Glentauchers was a joint venture between broker William P. Lowrie and his eventual partner James Buchanan of Black & White fame, who took advantage of the new rail link to secure supplies. A substantial upgrade took place in the mid-1960s, and although DCL closed it in 1985, it was bought five years later by Allied-Domecq. Its light, dry, almost dusty malt is available through Gordon & MacPhail as a single.

THE CRAIGELLACHIE HOTEL *has a comfortable, relaxing bar and an excellent selection of malts.*

CRAIGELLACHIE

At Craigellachie, the Spey enters its gently meandering stage, casting great loops around the valley, laying down a high-banked flood plain dotted with ghillies' fishing huts. This is where the salmon run, surging up the fast-flowing stream, and seen as flashes of silver glinting under Telford's elegant iron bridge. This is Speyside's geographical heart.

The village of Craigellachie itself has two great whiskey bars. In the Craigellachie Hotel, you are stunned into silence by the serried ranks of bottles on every shelf. It is crepuscular, discreet, elegant. Across the road, The Highlander has a similarly extensive range in more down-to-earth surroundings.

Needless to say, there is a distillery close by. Craigellachie is one of those intriguing mixes of ancient and modern. It has computer control, but the spirit is transformed from vapor to liquid in worm tubs, just as it would have been when the distillery opened in 1888. This is a big whiskey, one of Speyside's heavyweights, in a similar vein to Glenfarclas, Mortlach, Benrinnes, and Dailuaine. One suspects that Diageo was sorry to see this and Aberfeldy slip away when it was forced to dispose of John Dewar & Sons Ltd.

TASTING NOTES

FROM LIGHT COASTAL malt to the lush, oily richness of the interior, the Spey valley distilleries offer a malt to suit every palate.

INCHGOWER

INCHGOWER
14-YEAR-OLD, 43 VOL.

Color Straw.
Nose Light and very fresh. Sea breezes, then cut grass, daffodil, and green apple. Some chocolate malt at the back.
Body Light. Slightly liquorous.
Palate Distinctly salty coupled with perfumed notes. Delicate, with jasmine and tangerine. Fresh.
Finish Tart, acidic, clean.

AUCHROISK

AUCHROISK
10-YEAR-OLD, 43 VOL.

Color Gold. Amber glints.
Nose Light, soft, and creamy. Cream soda, custard. Bread-and-butter pudding with nutty malt underneath.
Body Soft and sweet.
Palate Direct. Cereal. Hint of soft fruits.
Finish Soft.

CRAIGELLACHIE

CRAIGELLACHIE
14-YEAR-OLD, 43 VOL.

Color Gold
Nose Touch of smoke. Rounded, baked fruitiness. Crisp malt.
Body Medium. Oily.
Palate Ripe and full-bodied. Chewy with soft fruits and citrus peel. Good malt/oak structure.
Finish Smoke returns.

MACALLAN

IDIOSYNCRATIC, ICONOCLASTIC, AND ARISTOCRATIC: MACALLAN IS ALL OF THESE. IT HAS FORGED A HIGHLY INDIVIDUAL PATH THROUGH MALT WHISKEY AND ITS EVOLUTION IS ONGOING.

On the banks of the Spey, near Aberlour, peeking out from a grove of deep green conifers, is a white-painted house built in the austere Scottish baronial style. The house, Easter Elchies, is home to the Speyside heavyweight, Macallan. Here, in the late 1970s, the plan was hatched to change this whiskey from a respected filling malt into a single malt; the plan was a success.

It is difficult to imagine what Macallan's founder, Alexander Reid, would have made of this. Another of the band of tenant farmers who took out a license in 1824, Reid and his immediate successors appear to have been less ambitious than many of their neighbors. Macallan has the dubious accolade of being the distillery with the shortest entry in Alfred Barnard's *The Whisky Distilleries of the United Kingdom*; seven throwaway lines that describe an "old fashioned" establishment, "similar to other Speyside distilleries." That has changed. Today, Benromach is the only other Speyside distillery that approaches whiskey production in a way similar to Macallan.

Macallan has achieved the potential seen by the distiller who first put it on the map, Roderick Kemp, who sold his stake in Talisker (*see pp. 126–7*) to buy it in 1892.

MACALLAN'S BARRELS *are made of European oak. They are created to specification in Jerez, Spain, before being seasoned with sherry and later shipped to Speyside.*

DISTILLERY DETAILS

MACALLAN FOUNDED: 1824.
OWNER: The Edrington Group. METHOD: Pot stills.
CAPACITY: 1.6 million gallons.

THE DISTILLATION PROCESS

Every distillery has its peculiarities—that is what makes the whiskey of each one unique. Macallan has more than most. It is one of two distilleries (Glengoyne is the other) that continue to use a percentage of Golden Promise barley in every mash. Benromach and Bruichladdich have also run trials with this strain, which in the 1960s was the industry standard. Today, it is both expensive and low-yielding and has been dropped by every other distiller. Macallan, however, claims it gives extra weight to its spirit. In addition, two yeasts are used (most distillers use only one). That said, the days of Macallan being made with 100 percent Golden Promise and fermented with five yeast strains disappeared in the mid-1990s.

The core of Macallan's individuality lies in its still-house and warehouses. Its 21 stills are minuscule, less than 13 feet (4 meters) high, with necks that start to curve almost as soon as they leave the body. They are compact flavor engines, and their shape and utilization creates Macallan's personality. The smallness of the stills means that there is less contact between vapor and copper, which results in a heavier spirit. It would be easy for a spirit made in this way to be one-dimensional. To build in complexity, the Macallan stills are run very slowly, thereby maximizing the contact between the copper and vapor, and are also directly fired. This necessitates the use of rummagers (metal flails inside the still) to stop any liquid from burning on to the still. These, in turn, clean up the copper, making more available to the vapor.

THE IMPORTANCE OF OAK

Macallan whiskey is not just about distillation. It is also influenced by the European oak casks. As the spirit matures, the flavors of clove, resin, and dried fruits within the oak begin to embrace the whiskey. Tannins rise, and the color shifts from gold to mahogany; only a weighty whiskey can cope with the assertive personality of oak.

No one has obsessed as much about European oak as Macallan; it is the only single malt to be aged exclusively in this type of oak. The distiller has casks made to its

THE SIGHT OF HIGHLAND COWS *is a familiar one in this traditional farming area of Scotland.*

specification in Jerez, Spain, before they are seasoned with sherry by Gonzalez Byass. This has been Macallan's unique selling point. The manor house and the unrivaled stocks dating back to the early 20th century have allowed the distillery to promote itself as the château of malt. In 2003, the Fine & Rare range of vintage whiskeys aged in the distillery's own warehouses was launched. Sadly, Macallan was also duped into buying bottles purporting to come from the 19th century that have subsequently proved to be fakes.

In an even more surprising move, in 2004, a new range, Fine Oak, was launched, consisting of whiskeys aged predominantly in American oak. Although the whiskeys are superb, the old unique selling point no longer applies. Macallan, however, has never done things by the book. This is just another chapter in its long evolution.

TASTING NOTES

MACALLAN HAS established itself as one of the leaders among the top single malts. The fruity, rich, and complex 18-year-old has become a standard for lovers of single malts.

THE MACALLAN

18-YEAR-OLD, 43 VOL.

Color Mahogany. Red flashes.
Nose Dried fruits, Christmas cake, raisin, and clove. Figgy. Hint of smoke. Concentrated and richly oaked.
Body Heavy, slight oiliness.
Palate Resin, bitter chocolate, cumin, and fig. Bitter orange peel. Light tannins.
Finish Dry. Spicy. Malt.

THE MACALLAN FINE OAK

15-YEAR-OLD, 43 VOL.

Color Light gold.
Nose Aromatic, complex, and elegant. Juicy fruits, orange peel, ripe melon, mango, vanilla pod. Hot sawdust. Hazelnut. Light smoke.
Body Rich, sweet, and oily.
Palate Honey, nutty oak, sweet orchard fruits. Caramel toffee, oak, bracken, malt, and dark chocolate.
Finish Very complex fruits with a spicy tingle.

18-YEAR-OLD MACALLAN

MACALLAN'S SMALL STILLS *are unique to the distillery. There were originally six; on expansion, rather than build larger ones, the number grew to 21.*

West of the River

A GLIMPSE INTO THE START OF THE MODERN WHISKEY INDUSTRY, HOW SPEYSIDE GREW INTO THE GOLDEN TRIANGLE OF MALT PRODUCTION, PLUS A SPANISH CONNECTION AND "L'AFFAIRE CARDHU."

Speyside's evolution into malt whiskey's preeminent region occurred in three distinct stages. First, in the aftermath of the 1823 Wash Act, came the farm distilleries. The second wave appeared in the 1860s when the Strathspey railroad was built along the banks of the Spey between Boat of Garten and Craigellachie. The final part of the process came at the very end of the 19th century. The region was not the only thing to change in 70 years; whiskey itself had been transformed.

The farm distillers had started by making a malt whiskey in much the same way as they always had done; as a single malt to be consumed by their friends, neighbors, and, thanks to the smugglers, some customers in the Lowlands.

The distillers in the second and third waves, however, were primarily men of capital. They, too, were making single malt, but by this time they were making it to suit the palates and needs of a new breed of whiskey men—the blenders.

The four distilleries on the central Spey's north bank are an illustration of this development and remain important contributors to major blends. The first speaks of whiskey's shift from Highland peculiarity to global spirit. Its name is redolent of Victorian confidence: Imperial.

DISTILLERY DETAILS

IMPERIAL FOUNDED: 1897. OWNER: Allied Distillers Ltd. METHOD: Pot stills. CAPACITY: 660,000 gallons.

KNOCKANDO FOUNDED: 1898. OWNER: Diageo. METHOD: Pot stills. CAPACITY: 343,000 gallons.

TAMDHU FOUNDED: 1897. OWNER: The Edrington Group. METHOD: Pot stills. CAPACITY: 1.1 million gallons.

CARDHU FOUNDED: 1824. OWNER: Diageo. METHOD: Pot stills. CAPACITY: 608,000 gallons.

IMPERIAL

Imperial has always been too big. Any distillery with enormous stills can run well during times of high demand, but it will be the first to close when the industry hits lean times. Imperial has been closed four times. For all its great expectations, it ran for only six months when it was first opened in 1897. DCL operated it briefly before running it as

TAMDHU'S TRADITIONAL *buildings are overlooked by its modern Saladin maltings.*

TASTING NOTES

KNOCKANDO'S and Tamdhu's single malts are both light and lemony. Cardhu, with its colorful history, fittingly produces a very complex dram.

KNOCKANDO

KNOCKANDO
1990
43 VOL.

Color Straw to gold.
Nose Light and nutty/malty with some green pear, straw. Dusty. Estery and crisp.
Body Light. Dry.
Palate Nutty. Lots of malty notes (malt bins). Lemon. Milk chocolate in the middle of the palate.
Finish Crisp, very short, and dry.

TAMDHU

TAMDHU
NO AGE STATEMENT
40 VOL.

Color Yellow gold.
Nose High-toned citric notes. Ethereal. Hayloft. Cereal.
Body Light.
Palate Dusty and light. Malty. Straw. Bland.
Finish Distant flowers.

CARDHU

CARDHU
12-YEAR-OLD
40 VOL.

Color Gold moving into amber.
Nose Dried grasses and chocolate. Kumquat peel. Fresh and young. Charred, smoky notes.
Body Light to medium. Soft.
Palate Clean, lightly malty. Coconut, milk chocolate (fruit and nut). Light mixed-peel note.
Finish Mixing sweet and dry.

12-YEAR-OLD CARDHU

a maltings between the 1920s and 1950s. Although it then made whiskey for the next 30 years, it was mothballed in 1983. It was bought by Allied-Domecq six years later, although they closed it in 1998.

KNOCKANDO AND TAMDHU

The Strathspey branch railroad line closed in 1968, and its stations are long deserted. The distilleries, however, are in better shape. The pair that sit next to the river, Knockando and Tamdhu, remain major contributors to blends. The former was built a year after Imperial and was acquired by the wine and spirit firm W & A Gilbey. It has always played a key role in blends, most notably in J&B, in which Knockando's light, dry, malty notes sing out. The largest-selling brand in Spain, J&B has a fresh, crisp character that makes it ideal for drinking long.

Although Tamdhu is virtually opposite Knockando, it is hidden from sight. Part of Highland Distillers almost from its birth in 1897, it is a large, modern, six-still distillery that also has a "Saladin" maltings, making it one of a select band of distilleries to supply all its own needs. The maltings also supplies Highland's other distilleries, including Highland Park. A no-age-statement single malt is available, made in much the same malty vein as Knockando.

CARDHU

A short way uphill is the oldest of the quartet, Cardhu. This has its origins in the smuggling era, when tenant farmers John and Helen Cumming made illicit hooch and sold it through their kitchen window. It is quite probable that Helen was the whiskey-maker of the pair; traditionally, women took responsibility for distilling in rural communities, and the history of Scotch features many famous female distillers. Their farm also functioned as an early warning station. Helen was able to raise a red flag to warn the distillers farther up the glen that the gaugers (excise officers) were on the prowl.

KNOCKANDO'S MAIN OFFICE, *built in 1898, typifies the distillery's well-preserved Victoriana.*

It was John and Helen's daughter-in-law, Elizabeth, who put Cardhu on the map. In 1880 she expanded the distillery, selling her old stills to William Grant, who at the time was looking for plant for his newly built Glenfiddich distillery. The bulk of Cardhu's output was sold to John Walker & Sons in 1893, although Elizabeth remained in charge.

Today, Cardhu has six stills and is home to the Johnnie Walker brand. Its malt has a grassy note to it, alongside hints of chocolate and orange. As well as providing fillings for the Walker stable, it is also a successful single malt. By 2003, demand in Spain was growing so fast that Diageo realized supply could not keep up. Its solution was to retain Cardhu as a brand name, but change the whiskey from a single malt to a vatted. Although this made commercial sense, the decision provoked an outcry from the rest of the industry, who argued, correctly, that a vatted product could not take on the name of a single distillery. Diageo withdrew the product soon after, and Cardhu reverted to being a single malt. "L'affaire Cardhu" did, however, have one lasting benefit: it forced the industry to address the issue of whiskey definitions and labeling. A new set of regulations and clearer terminology were introduced in 2005.

East of the River

THE RIVER SPEY AND THE NORTHERNMOST OUTCROP OF THE CAIRNGORMS COMBINE TO PROVIDE IDEAL CONDITIONS FOR SOME OF SPEYSIDE'S MOST TRADITIONAL DRAMS.

The concentration of distilleries in central Speyside is a result of two significant geographical features: the river Spey, which has smoothed out a low, level valley, and Ben Rinnes. This mountain dominates central Speyside and is the source of the water for many of the distilleries here.

Although there is a similarity among many of these distilleries, this is not linked with the mountain water, but with tradition; these older distilleries make whiskey in the original, weightier Speyside style.

DISTILLERY DETAILS

ABERLOUR FOUNDED: 1879.
OWNER: Chivas Brothers. METHOD: Pot stills.
CAPACITY: 845,000 gallons.

BENRINNES FOUNDED: 1834.
OWNER: Diageo. METHOD: Pot stills.
CAPACITY: 687,000 gallons.

DAILUAINE FOUNDED: 1851.
OWNER: Diageo. METHOD: Pot stills.
CAPACITY: 845,000 gallons.

GLENFARCLAS FOUNDED: 1836.
OWNER: J. & G. Grant. METHOD: Pot stills.
CAPACITY: 793,000 gallons.

CRAGGANMORE FOUNDED: 1869.
OWNER: Diageo. METHOD: Pot stills.
CAPACITY: 423,000 gallons.

TORMORE FOUNDED: 1958.
OWNER: Allied Distillers Ltd. METHOD: Pot stills.
CAPACITY: 476,000 gallons.

ABERLOUR

The first of the Ben Rinnes stills is Aberlour. Built on the site of a chapel established by St. Drostan, an early Christian monk, Aberlour's layout makes it easy to miss, since its narrow, gated entrance sits on a bend in the road. The large distillery is hidden farther up a dark little glen.

Originally built to take advantage of the Strathspey railroad, thanks to its French ownership (Pernod Ricard), Aberlour has always been a big seller in France, where a large number of expressions are available. It has a medium- to full-bodied style that typifies this part of the region. Aberlour's large stills also provide its signature notes of toffee and mint, and it has the weight to be able to cope with European oak. Chivas Brothers also owns nearby Glenallachie, another distillery that draws its water from Ben Rinnes. Built in the 1960s, it rarely releases its sharp, fresh make as a single malt.

CRAGGANMORE'S *strangely shaped spirit stills are responsible for creating this complex malt.*

BENRINNES

The next distillery is located 700 ft (200 m) up the mountain's slopes and is appropriately named after it. Although it is one of Diageo's lesser-known single malts, Benrinnes is prized by blenders, thanks to its rather idiosyncratic "two-and-half times" distillation system. Part of each filling is distilled twice, while another portion is distilled three times. It is this, together with the very cold water used in its worm tubs, that gives Benrinnes its rich, somewhat meaty punch.

DAILUAINE

From its entrance, you can see clouds of steam rising from the Spey valley, marking the site of another of Diageo's big boys: Dailuaine is a distillery that has been constructed on a substantial scale. At one point this was the largest distillery in the Highlands and the first to sport a pagoda.

These days, its six stills (this time coupled to condensers) make a beefy, rich malt for blends, although the little that appears as a single malt shows how much it also likes being paired with European oak.

GLENFARCLAS

Another of the Ben Rinnes heavy hitters lies at the base of the mountain's southwestern shoulder. Glenfarclas was originally a farm distillery established (as Rechlerich) by its tenant George Hay in 1836. In 1865, the farm was sold to a cattle-breeding family named Grant, and has remained in their ownership ever since.

Glenfarclas distillery has the largest stills in Speyside, and it produces a weighty, substantial make. When direct firing was taken out for a period as an experiment, the distiller felt that the guts had been taken from the spirit, and so the fires were reinstated. Once again, European oak is the approved partner for this malt.

CRAGGANMORE

Farther toward the Spey lies Cragganmore, established in 1869 by one of the great distillers of his day, John Smith. His legacy lives on in the curiously shaped spirit stills. Small and narrow-necked, they have a flat top and a lyne arm that sticks out of the side. This was a deliberate design, intended to produce a specific flavor of whiskey. Worm tubs give it weight, the shape maximizes reflux, and the lyne arm ensures that only specific flavors come across. One of Diageo's Classic Malts, it is a complex, fluxing mix of dark fruits, leather, fruitcake, toffee, and perfumed notes.

TORMORE

The final member of the group could not be more different. Architecturally, most distilleries are functional. Tormore is something else. Built in 1958, it is a green-roofed modernist extravagance, complete with a musical clock, making it look like a Baltic seaside resort. Its eight stills produce a tight, lean, nutty malt, equally untypical of the area.

GLENFARCLAS *is situated on farmland beneath Ben Rinnes, the water source for the distillery's weighty malts.*

TASTING NOTES

THESE MOSTLY rich, full drams typify the local Speyside style. Ranging in color from mahogany to light gold, all these excellent malts are fragrant, complex, fruity, and warming.

ABERLOUR

ABERLOUR
10-YEAR-OLD, 40 VOL.

Color Light gold.
Nose Green melon balls, ginger, a hint of cream, raisin, and sherry. Malt.
Body Light to medium.
Palate The fruitcake/sherry notes beginning to emerge. Bracken. Nutmeg.
Finish Slightly astringent.

ABERLOUR SHERRY MATURED
12-YEAR-OLD
40 VOL.
Color Amber.
Nose Mellow, sherry-dominant nose. Tobacco leaf, orange pekoe tea, walnut, caramelized fruit. Mint, leather, toffee, and butter.
Body Creamy. Sweet.
Palate Silky with integrated European oak notes overlaying the creamy/minty character. Black fruits.
Finish Light chocolate and some dried fruit.

12-YEAR-OLD ABERLOUR

BENRINNES

BENRINNES
15-YEAR-OLD, 43 VOL.

Color Russet with red glints.
Nose Rich. Hint of leather, meat stock. Molasses and raisin. Ripe and full.
Body Heavy. Grippy.
Palate Sweet sherry notes, fine tannins. Toasted fennel, Dundee cake. Long, slightly oily feel.
Finish Long, lingering.

DAILUAINE

DAILUAINE
16-YEAR-OLD
43 VOL.
Color Mahogany. Green rim.
Nose Spicy oak with fig rolls, soft baked fruit, Dundee cake, and roasted walnut. Hint of rubber.
Body Soft but weighty.
Palate Rich, ripe, and very fruity. Dried fruits. Heavy European oak character. Deep and resonant. Assertive wood.
Finish Tight and a little tannic.

GLENFARCLAS

GLENFARCLAS
15-YEAR-OLD, 46 VOL.

Color Amber.
Nose Succulent malt. Raisin bread, cake mix, suet. Allspice. Has richness and good weight.
Body Full, beefy.
Palate Firmer than nose suggests. Good grip. Ripe, dried/cooked fruit. Molasses toffee.
Finish Malty. Long.

CRAGGANMORE

CRAGGANMORE
12-YEAR-OLD, 40 VOL.

Color Rich gold.
Nose Complex mix of flowers, fruit (dried and caramelized), cooked plum, baked apple, currant, honey, roasted chestnut, leather, and toffee.
Body Medium, soft, and silky.
Palate Complex. Black fruits mixed with light honey and cooked peach.
Finish Soft with a hint of smoke.

12-YEAR-OLD CRAGGANMORE

TORMORE

TORMORE SIGNATORY VINTAGE
1989, 46 VOL.

Color Gold.
Nose Firm. Lightly peated with cookie-like malt (bran flakes). Particularly fragrant with the addition of water.
Palate Medium. Quite dry.
Palate Dry start. Dried pear. Crisp malt and toasty oak.
Finish Lightly creamy.

The Upper Spey

THE JOURNEY TOWARD THE SPEY'S SOURCE BRINGS TOGETHER ONE OF THE OLDEST DISTILLERIES IN SCOTLAND, ONE OF THE NEWEST, AND A VERY COLD, HIGHLAND OUTPOST.

Following the parallel tracks of rail and river leads you toward the woods that surrounds Grantown-on-Spey. On your right is a wilder landscape where an upthrust of high hills separates Strathspey from Strath Avon. These are the Cromdales, the highest point of which, Creagan a Chaise, is 2,200 ft (670 m) above sea level.

BALMENACH

The village of Cromdale itself is home to the Balmenach distillery. It is a magnificent location. Distilleries look their best when set against wild, isolated scenery; they seem timeless, and part of the natural landscape. This is appropriate for Balmenach, which took out a license as long ago as 1824.

Balmenach is also the setting for a section of Sir Robert Bruce Lockhart's excellent 1951 book, *Scotch*. His family owned the distillery, and he recalls vividly the old ways of self-sufficient distilling, giving a first-hand account of malting, fermenting, and how the stillman—"a splendid type of man, with a sturdy belief in his own art and scarcely concealed contempt for chemistry"—was the ultimate arbiter of quality. Bruce Lockhart would recognize the family retreat today. The people might not speak Gaelic, there are certainly more cars, and Balmenach has gained another pair of stills, but its worm tubs still work, and its muscular, chewy whiskey is as well-suited to European oak today as it was in the 1950s.

DISTILLERY DETAILS

BALMENACH FOUNDED: 1824.
OWNER: Inver House Distillers Ltd. METHOD: Pot stills.
CAPACITY: 660,000 gallons.

SPEYSIDE FOUNDED: 1991.
OWNER: George Christie. METHOD: Pot stills.
CAPACITY: 159,000 gallons.

DALWHINNIE FOUNDED: 1897.
OWNER: Diageo. METHOD: Pot stills.
CAPACITY: 343,000 gallons.

SPEYSIDE

The Spey continues to throw gentle loops as it runs toward Broomhill. Here you can catch a steam train that takes you down the last remaining part of the Strathspey railroad as far as Aviemore. The river's flood plain widens as it runs through the glacier-scoured pass that separates the Cairngorms to the east from the Monadhliath mountains to the west. Small towns cling to its bank, dwarfed by the massifs that contain some of Great Britain's highest peaks. Close to Kingussie, the Tromie adds its small contribution. Just before the confluence is one of Scotland's newest distilleries.

It would not seem unreasonable to expect a distillery called Speyside to be a considerable concern. Instead, this is one of

TASTING NOTES

A PLEASING CONTRAST between the old and the new is evident: the spicy, smoky Balmenach and Dalwhinnie are rich and smooth; the yet still young Speyside is charmingly fresh, perfumed, and slightly grassy.

BALMENACH

BALMENACH
12-YEAR-OLD, 43 VOL.

Color Amber with red glints.
Nose Ripe, full, and sherried. Pipe smoke, antique shop. Beeswax polish. Dried fruits, heavy syrup.
Body Medium/full.
Palate Rich and powerful. Hard heather honey. Chestnut. Toasted/charred to the finish.
Finish Round and soft.

SPEYSIDE

DRUMGUISH
NO AGE STATEMENT, 40 VOL.

Color Gold.
Nose Perfumed, jasmine, intense, slightly oily. Young.
Body Medium. Softening.
Palate A creamy core but with dry (grassy) edges. Still knitting together.
Finish Short.

DRUMGUISH

DALWHINNIE

DALWHINNIE
15-YEAR-OLD
43 VOL.

Color Gold.
Nose Soft and sweet. Honeyed with a touch of peat, hint of sulfur. Tangerine and cream. Lightly spiced.
Body Smooth.
Palate Good weight. Fills the mouth. Honey again, florist's shop. Ripe.
Finish Tickle of smoke. Long.

Dalwhinnie is the coldest *settlement in the UK. The local icy cold water is essential in creating the unique character of Dalwhinnie's whiskey.*

the smallest distilleries in the country, housed in a beautifully designed, traditional-looking building. It took owner George Christie over 30 years to get from drawing board to producing spirit, but the two small stills have now been operating since 1991, and the whiskey (sold as Drumguish) is maturing nicely into a gently sweet dram.

DALWHINNIE

Sitting on another Spey tributary, the Tromie, Dalwhinnie is often thought of as a "Highland" distillery. In fact, it is a case unto itself. Although it was called Strathspey when it opened in 1897, it soon took on the name of the small settlement close to the Drumochter Pass. This is the coldest settlement in Great Britain, with an average temperature of 43°F (6°C), sufficiently cold to make most people wonder why anyone would choose to build a village here. The answer is cattle.

A map of the Highlands shows how difficult it is to get from west to east. One of the few passes linking the western Highlands and islands with the center is Glen Spean, which runs from the Great Glen to just north of Dalwhinnie. In the days when vast herds of black cattle were driven from the northern lands to the markets at Falkirk, Glen Spean was one of the main highways. The drovers from Speyside would have done the same, although by pushing their beasts down the Spey valley. Dalwhinnie was the meeting place; a crossroads before the hard slog over Drumochter into Perthshire.

It is conceivable that there could once have been an illicit still here, although the current distillery was built here because Dalwhinnie had a railroad station. Part of the DCL portfolio since 1919, its whiskey has not only played a major role in blends such as Black & White and Buchanan's, but has been the Highland representative in Diageo's Classic Malts, a subtle dram with good depth and texture. The character is partly the result of condensing in the wooden worm tubs that sit like giant Jacuzzis on the front of the distillery. The icy water from the Allt-an-t'Sluic burn minimizes the contact between copper and vapor, resulting in a weighty, sulfury new make. The sulfur soon dissipates and a honeyed note emerges.

The worm tubs were installed recently as part of an aesthetic makeover of the distillery, replacing some ugly square ones made of cast iron. What Diageo had not realized when it did this was that the change from square to round tubs would affect the flow of water and as a result would impact on the character of the spirit. Adjustments had to be made to bring it back rapidly. In whiskey distilling, you change things at your peril.

Speyside distillery *might look old, but in fact it is one of the newest, only producing its delicate and creamy malt since the early 1990s.*

THE AVON AND THE LIVET

THE GHOSTS OF MOONSHINERS AND THE FIRST LEGAL DISTILLERS CONTINUE TO HAUNT THE WILDER PARTS OF THIS HIGH RIVER VALLEY, ONE OF THE BLEAKEST, YET MOST BEAUTIFUL, LANDSCAPES IN SCOTLAND.

The river Avon (pronounced "A'an") is the Spey's main tributary. It flows from the loch at the foot of Cairn Gorm, before heading to Inchrory and then north toward the Spey at the foot of Ben Rinnes.

TOMINTOUL

This distillery's home country was wild up until the early 1800s, a notorious haunt of moonshiners. Not all the illicit stills became legal or were an immediate success. One of the sites, on the side of the Balnellan burn, 5 miles (8 km) north of Tomintoul, had to wait until the 1960s to be revived as a legal distillery. Today, Tomintoul is part of the Angus Dundee stable and its new owner is nurturing its potential as a single malt.

TAMNAVULIN

Were you to walk due east, you would find yourself on the banks of the river Livet, next to a modern Whyte and Mackay-owned distillery. Tamnavulin has been mothballed since 1996. Its 12-year-old is a definition of maltiness with a hint of perfume.

THE MOONSHINERS

To comprehend, even vaguely, what the life of an illicit distiller would have been like, head south from Tamnavulin toward Chapeltown. The road passes a conical hill called the Bochel ("shepherd") and enters a high plain that sits in the lee of the Ladder Hills. This is the Braes of Glenlivet. Its isolated

DISTILLERY DETAILS

TOMINTOUL FOUNDED: 1965.
OWNER: Angus Dundee Distillers PLC.
METHOD: Pot stills. CAPACITY: 819,000 gallons.

TAMNAVULIN FOUNDED: 1966.
OWNER: Whyte and Mackay Ltd. METHOD: Pot stills.
CAPACITY: Not currently in production.

THE GLENLIVET FOUNDED: 1824
OWNER: Chivas Brothers. METHOD: Pot stills.
CAPACITY: 1.6 million gallons.

TAMNAVULIN, *"mill on the hill" in Gaelic, was mothballed in 1996 by JBB, its owners at the time.*

TASTING NOTES

THE GLENLIVET is famously floral. Tomintoul is slightly nutty with some haylike sweetness, and is at its best in its mid-teens.

TOMINTOUL

TOMINTOUL
10-YEAR-OLD, 40 VOL.

Color Pale gold.
Nose Cereal with some nutty/toffee notes and baked fruits.
Body Light- to middle-weight.
Palate Nutty and spicy. Lots of malt, vanilla, and coconut.
Finish Heathery.

10-YEAR-OLD TOMINTOUL

12-YEAR-OLD TAMNAVULIN

TAMNAVULIN

TAMNAVULIN
12-YEAR-OLD, 40 VOL.

Color Straw.
Nose The definition of maltiness: wheat/bran cereal, flour sacks. Whole milk.
Body Light and soft.
Palate Light, slightly lemony, then a firm, nutty maltiness.
Finish Short.

THE GLENLIVET

THE GLENLIVET
12-YEAR-OLD, 40 VOL.

Color Pale gold.
Nose Lifted. Applewood, heather, baked soft fruits mixed with cereal, flowers, citrus, and pear. Freshly sawn wood.
Body Medium. Gentle.
Palate All the notes on the nose come through on the palate.
Finish Dry and clean. Short.

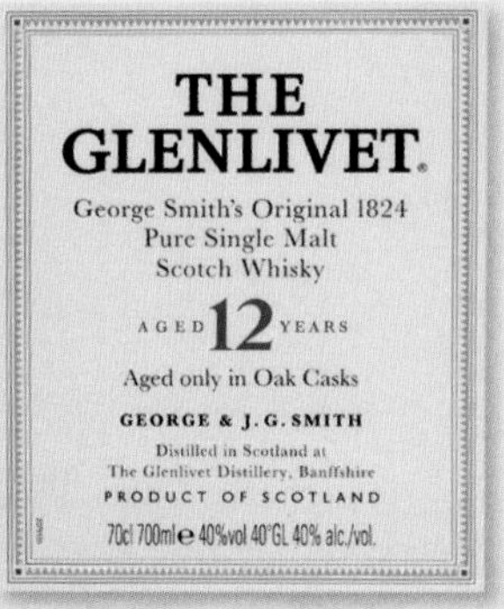

12-YEAR-OLD GLENLIVET

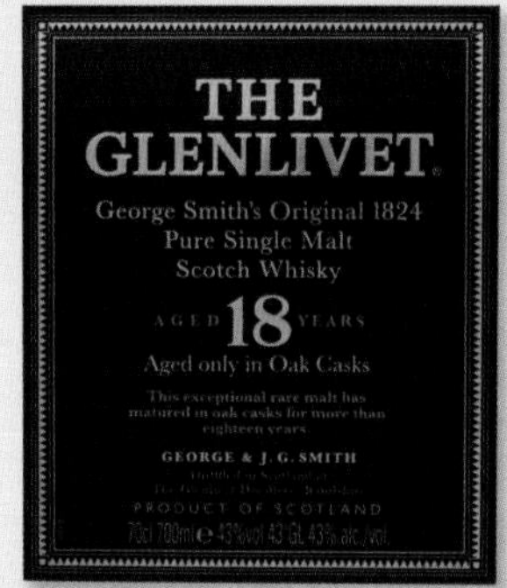

18-YEAR-OLD GLENLIVET

THE GLENLIVET
18-YEAR-OLD, 43 VOL.

Color Amber.
Nose Aromatic. Unrefined sugar, cut flowers (lilac), cooked pear, quince, and anise. Some smoke.
Body Medium. Rich.
Palate Semidried fruits, sandalwood, cedar. Dried orange peel. Fruity and long.
Finish Very long. Light smoke.

location made it the perfect place for moonshiners to practice their craft. It has been reported that, until recently, the men of the Braes refused to drink legal whiskey, especially that made at Glenlivet, seeing it as betrayal of their culture. True or not, it took until 1973 for the Braes to have a legal distillery—Braeval, now mothballed.

THE GLENLIVET

The alleged local resistance to Glenlivet occurred because this was the first distillery in the area to take out a license, in 1824. The original distillery was up the Gallow Hill, at Upper Drumin farm. The lease had been taken by the Smith family in 1783, and by the 1810s it was being run by James Smith and his nephew (or possibly cousin) George. This farmer—like a purported 200 others in Glen Livet—made the bulk of his income from illicit distilling. However, the passing of the Wash Act in 1784 coincided with the end of the lease on Drumin, and consequently George was persuaded by the estate factor, James Skinner, to take out the license.

Smith's Glenlivet prospered. By the 1880s, if a distillery tacked "Glenlivet" on to its name, no matter how far away it was, it could charge a higher price. Prolonged legal action concluded that Smith's Glenlivet could call itself "The Glenlivet," but others, including Glen Elgin and Glen Moray, were permitted to use a Glen Livet suffix, which many did until relatively recently.

The present distillery has a new-looking, almost brutal exterior; inside, it is as modern as any distillery in Scotland. The whiskey has kept some of the features that earned it its reputation in the 19th century; it is appley and floral. The No. 1 malt in the US since the 1970s, Glenlivet was bought by Seagram in 1978, and then by Chivas Brothers in 2001. It has expanded its range recently with a superb 18-year-old, and has explored finishing, vintage releases, and single barrels.

BRAEVAL *opened in 1973, but was closed in 2002 by its owner, Pernod Ricard. At well over 1,000 ft (300 m) above sea level, it is the highest distillery in Scotland.*

THE GLENLIVET *now has a modern distillery, and continues to produce some of Scotland's finest whiskey.*

The Fiddich

GLENFIDDICH WAS THE DISTILLERY THAT FIRST BROUGHT SINGLE MALT WHISKEYS TO INTERNATIONAL ATTENTION IN THE EARLY 1960S. DECADES LATER, THREE WILLIAM GRANT DISTILLERIES CONTINUE TO MAKE WHISKEY ON THE FIDDICH RIVER.

Rather than following the Avon on its course to the Spey, the whiskey trail now heads northeast, up quiet Glen Rinnes by the banks of the Dullan Water. The slopes of Ben Rinnes emerge once more, as does the last of the glen's distilleries, at the modernist shed of Allt-a-Bhainne. This is one of the filling distilleries closed by Pernod Ricard when it bought Seagram's whiskey interests. We are now heading to another town with a claim to being Speyside's whiskey capital, Dufftown.

DISTILLERY DETAILS

GLENFIDDICH FOUNDED: 1887.
OWNER: William Grant & Sons Ltd. METHOD: Pot stills.
CAPACITY: Not given.

BALVENIE FOUNDED: 1892.
OWNER: William Grant & Sons Ltd. METHOD: Pot stills.
CAPACITY: Not given.

KININVIE FOUNDED: 1990.
OWNER: William Grant & Sons Ltd. METHOD: Pot stills.
CAPACITY: 1.7 million gallons.

GLENFIDDICH

Dufftown's most famous distillery takes its name from the river Fiddich, which joins with the Dullan in the small glen below the town. The vast site comprises three distilleries, a bottling hall, a cooperage, a coppersmith, and 45 warehouses. This is whiskey-making on a grand scale. Glenfiddich may not have been the first malt whiskey distillery, but it was the brand that kick-started the category.

Glenfiddich is still owned by the same family that established it in 1886. William Grant was a Dufftown man who came of age at the time when whiskey was transformed into an international drink. He worked as a clerk at Mortlach and learned the whiskey business, saving money for his own project. In 1886, he bought a field close to Balvenie Castle, and with the rest of his funds he and his family built the distillery. On Christmas Day, 1887, the first spirit ran from Glenfiddich's stills.

The Grants moved into blending, and for most of the 20th century operated much like every other whiskey firm. Then, in 1963, the family fell out with DCL, which cut off supplies of grain whiskey. Although the family promptly built its own grain plant at Girvan (*see p. 102*), the altercation showed how precarious the whiskey business could be. The Grants' solution was innovative. They took eight-year-old Glenfiddich (until then bottled in limited quantities as five-year-old, and sold only in Scotland), put it in a triangular green bottle, and sold it into the new duty-free store that had opened at Shannon Airport in Ireland. The malt whiskey category was born, and Glenfiddich continues to be the world's top-selling whiskey brand.

In 1969, Glenfiddich became the first distillery to welcome the public. Today, nearly 20,000 people each year visit the plant. What they see is a large, airy plant with two huge still-houses housing 29 stills, some of which are directly fired. The stills have retained the small size and shape of the original pair that William bought from Cardhu. Normally, the smaller the still, the heavier the spirit, but not here. When it is young, Glenfiddich is a light-bodied, clean, slightly malty, and gently citric dram, but it really only hits its stride at 18 years, when other whiskeys are over the hill.

In recent years, Glenfiddich has launched its Solera Reserve 15-year-old. This is made by first maturing whiskey for 15 years in three types of wood: European oak, ex-bourbon barrels, and new oak, before being blended together in the enormous Solera vats that, in common with those in Jerez, are always kept at least half-full. This method of fractional blending gives consistency between bottlings and builds in extra layers of flavor. More conventional finishing has also been tried, most notably with the 21-year-old Havana Reserve that is finished in Cuban rum casks.

THE GLENFIDDICH LABEL *refers to "Special Reserve"; this used to read "Special Old Reserve."*

THE TRIANGULAR BOTTLES *of Glenfiddich helped to create a revolution in the malt whiskey industry.*

BALVENIE

The Glenfiddich site also encompasses the Balvenie distillery, which the Grant family built in 1892 to help offset a rise in demand for Glenfiddich, as well as to guarantee control of the water supply. Any notion that

Glenfiddich *stands as a landmark in the history of single malt. Still owned by the Grant family, who built it in the 19th century, the site is huge.*

there is such a thing as a Dufftown *terroir* can be dismissed at this point. Balvenie, with its small-floor maltings (the malt comes from the family's neighboring farm), and fat, bulbed, long-necked stills, makes a complex, fruity, honeyed dram that has earned its place in Speyside's premier league.

KININVIE

The last of William Grant & Sons' trio of distilleries is Kininvie. Opened in 1990, this is little more than a still-house, because all the mashing and fermenting takes place at Balvenie. The whiskey is not available as a single malt, but tasting shows it to be in a light, soft style, roughly in the Glenfiddich mold but probably earlier-maturing. It is used for blends in the Grant range.

At the Glenfiddich site, innovation is the recurring theme. Balvenie Double Wood was the first malt to be finished in a previously used cask, followed by a 21-year-old Port Wood, and more recently an Islay Cask finish. In addition, every year a venerable single barrel is bottled. There is no resting on their laurels where the Grants are concerned.

TASTING NOTES

Balvenie sits comfortably by Glenfiddich, deservedly the UK's most popular malt.

GLENFIDDICH

GLENFIDDICH

12-YEAR-OLD, 40 VOL.

Color Pale gold.
Nose Light and malty. Citric notes. Water reveals crispbread with dry grass and apple.
Body Light.
Palate Soft with vanilla, malt, a light nuttiness, and a soft mid-palate.
Finish Soft, lightly fruity, a hint of chocolate.

GLENFIDDICH SOLERA RESERVE

15-YEAR-OLD, 40 VOL.

Color Amber.
Nose Rich, cakelike (chocolate). Crisp malt. Liquorous.
Body Light. Slick.
Palate Smooth and rounded. Chocolate, walnut nougat, mocha.
Finish Caramel. Soft and soothing.

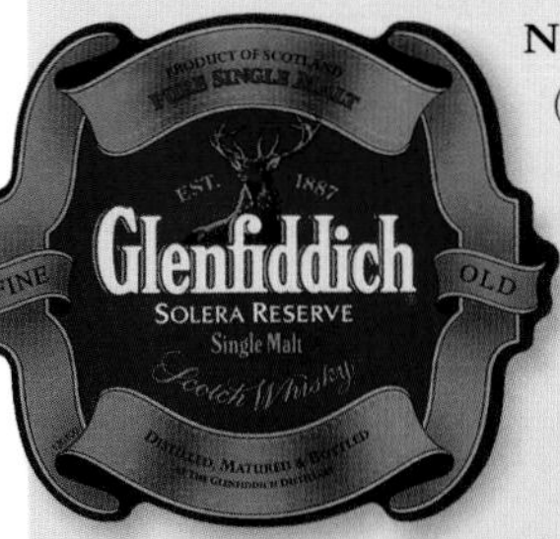

GLENFIDDICH SOLERA RESERVE

BALVENIE

BALVENIE FOUNDER'S RESERVE

10-YEAR-OLD, 40 VOL.

Color Light gold.
Nose Clover honey, jasmine, cumin powder, and other exotic spices.
Body Light to medium. Soft feel.
Palate Gentle and soft. Honey again. Sandalwood and light raisin notes.
Finish Long, softening.

10-YEAR-OLD BALVENIE

BALVENIE DOUBLE WOOD

43 VOL.

Color Gold.
Nose Rich, with toasted almond, raisin, dried apricot, honey, and flamed orange peel.
Body Medium. Silky feel.
Palate Gentle and complex. Wisp of smoke. Date, cinnamon, nutmeg. Elegant.
Finish Long, soft, spiced.

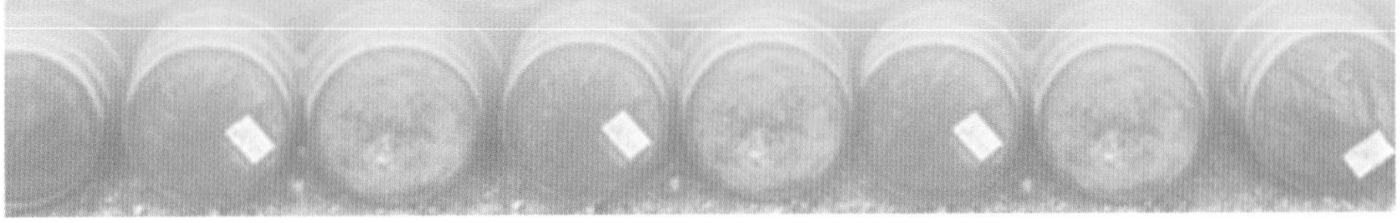

DUFFTOWN

THREE MORE GIANT DISTILLERIES LURK IN THE NEIGHBORHOOD OF THE QUIET TOWN OF DUFFTOWN AND THE RIVER FIDDICH: GLENDULLAN, DUFFTOWN, AND MORTLACH—THE BIGGEST AND BEEFIEST MALT WHISKEY OF ALL.

Dufftown is a neat, quiet town, the main street of which is dominated by a large, square sandstone clock tower. Legend has it that an illicit still once stood on this spot. The first legal distillery was established in Dufftown in 1823 by James Findlater and his two partners, Donald Macintosh and Alexander Gordon. They built a grand distillery on the banks of the Dullan river by Mortlach Church. It was sold to the Walker family in 1923, and is now part of the large Diageo portfolio.

MORTLACH

Mortlach is everything that Glenfiddich is not (*see p. 162*). Its entrance is easy to miss, on a sharp bend of the back road that heads down to the river. There is no visitor's center, and its malt is, stylistically, the polar opposite of that of its famous neighbor. The only thing this distillery has in common with Glenfiddich is its enormous size. Mortlach seems to have been built into a cliff, and the height of its interior, together with the enormous size of its distilling equipment, makes any visitor feel small.

DISTILLERY DETAILS

MORTLACH FOUNDED: 1823.
OWNER: Diageo. METHOD: Pot stills.
CAPACITY: 740,000 gallons.

DUFFTOWN FOUNDED: 1896.
OWNER: Diageo. METHOD: Pot stills.
CAPACITY: 1.1 million gallons.

GLENDULLAN FOUNDED: 1897.
OWNER: Diageo. METHOD: Pot stills.
CAPACITY: 977,000 gallons.

THE DISTILLATION PROCESS

The impact of the colossal scale of the distillery is all the greater as you enter the still-house. You walk through the entrance straight onto a high platform, from which you can see the oddest collection of copper stills in the industry. It is as if the distiller bought out a coppersmith that had gone bust: they are all different sizes and shapes. All have lyne arms that head through the wall to a group of worm tubs. This setup seems counterintuitive. Most distilleries have one shape of wash still, and one shape of spirit. Because the shape of the still

MORTLACH'S SELECTION OF *different stills is fundamental in creating its meaty flavor.*

affects the flavor of the spirit, consistency of shape is the simplest way to ensure consistency of character. Each of Mortlach's stills will produce a different flavor of spirit, but this is exactly what is wanted. Like Springbank and Benrinnes, Mortlach operates a two-and-a-half times distillation regimen (*see p. 156*), but its process is the most complex of all.

Taste Mortlach and you are assailed by notes of meat stock, roasting pans, chestnut, and smoke. This rich, robust character is achieved solely through the complicated distillation process, and, to the best of Diageo's knowledge, has always been done like this—in-house tasting notes in the distillery's archives talk of "Oxo cubes" (bouillon cubes) and "Bovril" (beef broth).

There are six stills in total: three wash and three spirit. One pair of wash and spirit stills works in tandem as in a normal distillery. The other two wash stills run as a pair. The bulk of their low wines run is collected as "tops," which are passed on to the larger of the remaining two spirit stills. The weaker end

DUFFTOWN DISTILLERY'S *appearance still shows traces of its original function as a mill, but its pagoda gives away its current status.*

of the low wines run is used as the charge for the tiniest still of all, "The Wee Witchie." This is run, and all the distillate is collected. It is then returned to the still, and the process repeated. Only on the third charge does the stillman separate the middle cut from the foreshots and feints.

The result is that three different strengths (and therefore flavors) of spirit are collected from the three spirit stills. Each filling of Mortlach must contain one charge from the Wee Witchie because that is where the characteristic weight and meatiness of the Mortlach spirit is created.

This beast of a dram is one that demands European oak and revels in it. Mortlach is unlike any other malt, and has a character that gives grip, weight, and structure to a blend. The result is that blenders from across the industry all want it, with the consequence that virtually none is available as a single malt, although it is definitely worth looking for the 16-year-old single.

DUFFTOWN/GLENDULLAN

Fiddichside is home to another two Diageo distilleries. Dufftown distillery was built in 1896 on the site of an old mill. Although it briefly made an appearance as a single malt in the 1970s, it has spent most of its life providing fillings for Bell's, and as such, conformed to the nutty and malty house style. In recent years, there has been a subtle change to the way in which it has been run, and the make is now lighter and more grassy.

The second of the plants is the slightly unfortunately named Glendullan. In 1962 DCL built a new distillery alongside it (as happened with Clynelish and Linkwood), and the two ran in tandem until the 1980s, when the original building was demolished.

Although virtually unknown to most malt lovers, Glendullan is Diageo's largest site, capable of producing close to 4.8 million gallons (18 million liters) of very light, slightly perfumed make each year; most of it is destined for blends.

The rest of Dufftown's old stills have all disappeared. Pittyvaich only ran from 1975 to the mid-1990s, while Convalmore has been absorbed into the William Grant site; you can still see its name on one of the old warehouses. Parkmore's warehouses are still used, but it has been silent since 1931.

GLENDULLAN'S *fragrance may derive from the yeast. Here its performance is being checked during fermentation.*

TASTING NOTES

MORTLACH'S meatiness is in stark contrast to the perfumy, dry firmness of Glendullan. Pittyvaich is rarely found but is well worth the search.

MORTLACH

MORTLACH

16-YEAR-OLD, 43 VOL.

Color Polished walnut.

Nose Huge and meaty (beef broth, roasting pan, oxtail soup). Molasses. Singed, slight smoke. Concentrated.

Body Robust and powerful. Earthy.

Palate Big impact of flavor. Tanned leather, meat, molasses cake. Roasted nut and charred dried fruits. Licorice sweetness.

Finish Long, nutty.

16-YEAR-OLD MORTLACH

15-YEAR-OLD DUFFTOWN

DUFFTOWN

DUFFTOWN

15-YEAR-OLD, 43 VOL.

Color Light gold.

Nose Bowl of nuts (almond, hazelnut, and Brazil). Marzipan and whole-wheat maltiness. In time, a toffee note.

Body Mid-weight.

Palate Good feel with a spicy nuttiness. Softens as it moves in the mouth.

Finish Nutty with decent length.

PITTYVAICH

PITTYVAICH

12-YEAR-OLD, 43 VOL.

Color Reddish amber.

Nose Dry amontillado sherry. Resin, clove, savory notes. Roasted almond, smoked tea, toffee.

Body Medium weight. Oily yet tannic.

Palate Heavy sherry flavors, almond especially. Perfumed smoke. Beefed up by the European oak.

Finish Smoked cheese.

GLENDULLAN

GLENDULLAN

12-YEAR-OLD, 43 VOL.

Color Very pale.

Nose Dry. Crisp malt, some floral notes, fruit (lemon, quince, and dried fruit), and a suggestion of smoke.

Body Light. Firm.

Palate Dry and clean, opening to show mid-palate sweetness, balancing a slightly firm structure.

Finish Soft and gentle.

12-YEAR-OLD GLENDULLAN

KEITH

THIS ANCIENT DROVERS' TOWN WAS OVER TIME EXPANDED AND TRANSFORMED INTO A HOME FOR WEAVING, BREWING, KILT-MAKING, AND, OF COURSE, DISTILLING WHISKEY.

The last of Speyside's whiskey towns sits on the banks of the river Isla. Keith takes its name from the Gaelic word *ceiteach*, meaning "forest." From the 12th century onward, this was a cattle town and a center for drovers who massed their herds here for the journey to the southern markets. Mills ground locally grown cereal crops, and the drovers slaked their thirst on local beer, which was made at the town's monastery. Today, one of Keith's distilleries still uses the same water source as these early ecclesiastical brewers. By the 18th century, "Old" Keith was a typical, bustling, narrow-streeted Highland town.

Keith grew substantially in 1755 when the Earl of Findlater designed a new "model" town on the opposite bank of the river. The urban expansion involved laying out "New" Keith's wide streets in a grid system and developing local industry. New textile mills were constructed (the Isla Bank Mill houses the world's only kilt school), as was a distillery; the first of three that are still producing today.

STRATHISLA

The Milton (later renamed Milltown) distillery received its license in 1786, making it one of the first licensed distilleries in Scotland. Today, the distillery is known as Strathisla, the name under which its malt has always been sold. It is, without doubt, the prettiest distillery in the Highlands. With a cobbled courtyard, subtly shaded gray stone walls, soaring pagodas, and a water wheel, Strathisla typifies the romantic idea of a Scottish distillery. Its reservoir, locals told Barnard, was "haunted every night by fays and fairies," which only adds to the fantastical atmosphere.

The impression of a Victorian idyll is reinforced inside. Strathisla operates the industry's first (and only) self-guided tour. You can play at being the owner, relax in the lounge, and browse through the papers and books before wandering at leisure through the distillery, asking the workers questions. Like most old distilleries, every part of the process is contained in a different room, which adds to the intimacy.

Although the stills are relatively small, they are barely contained in the barnlike buildings, and their necks rise into the rafters. There was at one time a plan to raise the roof, but it was felt that this might alter the ambient temperature of the room and perhaps change the character of the whiskey.

DISTILLERY DETAILS

STRATHISLA FOUNDED: 1786.
OWNER: Chivas Brothers. METHOD: Pot stills.
CAPACITY: 555,000 gallons.

STRATHMILL FOUNDED: 1891.
OWNER: Diageo. METHOD: Pot stills.
CAPACITY: 449,000 gallons.

AULTMORE FOUNDED: 1897.
OWNER: John Dewar & Sons Ltd. METHOD: Pot stills.
CAPACITY: 317,000 gallons.

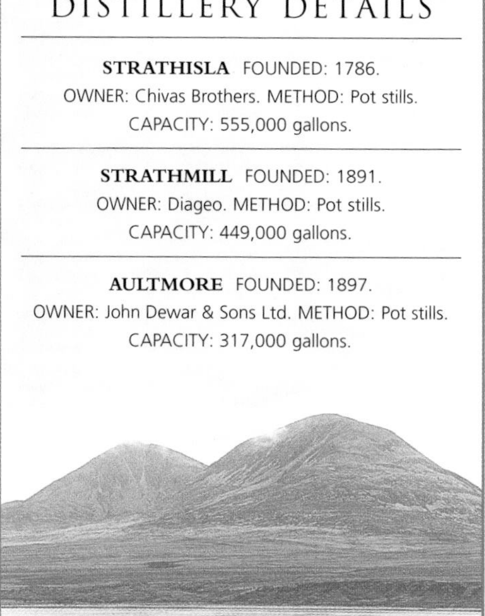

THE STRATHISLA SPIRIT-SAFE, *although small, is only just squeezed into Strathisla's cozy still-house.*

STRATHISLA *is one of Scotland's most charming distilleries, and also its oldest. Its water comes from a nearby spring, used by Dominican monks in the 13th century to brew beer.*

CHIVAS REGAL BLEND

Today, Strathisla doubles as the home of Chivas Regal. Seagram's bought the distillery in 1951 (when its name was changed from Milton), immediately after the purchase of the blend. Due to its important role in Chivas Regal, Strathisla cannot be heavily pushed as a single malt. It is a strange, almost frustrating spirit, lean and tight when young, but patience and good casks allow the secondary, mature aromas of flowers and light fruits to develop. Gordon & MacPhail have the best bottlings of Strathisla single, which fully encapsulates its complexities.

GLEN KEITH

Like any blender, Seagram's needed to control as much of its own supply as possible, and so in 1958 it built a sister distillery virtually next door to Strathisla on the banks of the Isla in one of the town's old mills.

Originally, triple distillation was used at Glen Keith, and even after that procedure was abandoned, the distillery's very tall and slender stills, with their upward-angled lyne arms, produced a very light style of whiskey. Glen Keith installed the first gas-fired still in Scotland and also pioneered the use of computers in the industry. Seagram's experimented with a heavily peated version, called Glen Isla, for filling purposes (the firm also did the same at Caperdonich and Benriach). It appeared as a single in the Heritage Selection, which was halfheartedly pushed by Seagram's in the 1990s. The range was dropped quietly, and the still has been mothballed for some years.

Glen Keith *also used to be one of the town's many mills. Sadly, even triple distillation could not save it.*

STRATHMILL

The name of Keith's third distillery gives a clue as to its first use. Strathmill was a corn mill and a brewery before being converted at the end of the 19th century into a distillery. It was soon bought by W & A Gilbey, and has always played a significant part in that company's J&B blend. A classic late-Victorian distillery, its sweet, slightly oily make is not widely seen as a single malt.

AULTMORE

Heading due north out of Keith takes you on to the coastal floodplain and to Aultmore. The Moray Firth can be seen, and Portgordon and Inchgower are not far away. Aultmore was one of a group of three distilleries (the others being Benrinnes and Craigellachie) that were bought by Dewar's in 1923. It is similar in looks to Craigellachie and was sold with it to Bacardi when Diageo was forced to dispose of Dewar's. Bacardi has not given much indication of what its plans for malt whiskey are, and no bottling has yet emerged, although there are rumors that one might appear soon.

TASTING NOTES

Although seen relatively rarely as single malts, these drams from one of Scotland's earliest centers of distillation do not disappoint. Strathisla's complexity is done justice in the fine 12-year-old.

STRATHISLA

STRATHISLA

12-YEAR-OLD, 40 VOL.

Color Full gold.

Nose Fragrant with citrus, flowers (freesia), and spice, and a touch of cream puff. Water pulls out weighty straw/malty notes.

Body Medium weight. Soft.

Palate Crannachan, soft baked fruits, fruitcake, syrup, apricot, and malt. It dances on the tongue.

Finish Bursts into spicy life.

STRATHMILL

STRATHMILL

12-YEAR-OLD, 43 VOL.

Color Gold.

Nose Dry, nutty, and airy. Dried banana on granola, green grassy notes, tea leaves, walnut.

Body Very soft.

Palate Attractive and floral. Medium-sweet with some vanilla and nut notes.

Finish Soft.

12-YEAR-OLD STRATHMILL

AULTMORE

AULTMORE

1989, SIGNATORY VINTAGE, 43 VOL.

Color Pale. Straw. Green glints.

Nose Clean and light. Slightly austere, green grapes, olive. Touch of smoke.

Body Light but gently soft.

Palate Sweet start, white fruits, pear. Hint of malt. All very light.

Finish Tingle of spice.

1989 AULTMORE

Bogie Deveron/Aberdeen

OVER TO THE EAST, SPEYSIDE'S CHARACTERFUL MIX OF COASTAL AND RURAL DISTILLERIES SLOWLY GIVES WAY TO THE LARGE BLENDING DISTILLERIES OF ABERDEENSHIRE.

Leaving Keith and heading toward the coast takes you past the first of the final group of Speyside distilleries.

AN CNOC

An almost conical hill dominates the landscape here. Knock Hill gets its name from the Gaelic *cnoc*, meaning "hill." Not only has the distillery recently changed ownership, but its whiskey has also changed name. New owner Inver House decided to switch the name from Knockdhu to An Cnoc and avoid confusion with Knockando. Although their names were similar, the whiskeys are very different—An Cnoc is soft, gentle, and appealing, very much in the Inver House style.

GLENGLASSAUGH AND BANFF

The easterly boundary of Speyside is drawn by the rivers Bogie and Deveron, the latter of which reaches the sea between the towns of Banff and Macduff, which face each other. Portsoy's Glenglassaugh, a bone-dry malt, has been mothballed by Edrington, while the story of Banff's eponymous distillery is even sadder. Founded in 1863, it was burned down in 1877, was bombed in World War II, and has now been demolished. The third and only remaining working distillery is Macduff.

DISTILLERY DETAILS

KNOCKDHU FOUNDED: 1894.
OWNER: Inver House Distillers. METHOD: Pot stills.
CAPACITY: 238,000 gallons.

GLENGLASSAUGH FOUNDED: 1875.
OWNER: The Edrington Group. METHOD: Pot stills.
CAPACITY: None.

MACDUFF FOUNDED: 1962.
OWNER: Bacardi. METHOD: Pot stills.
CAPACITY: 660,000 gallons.

GLENDRONACH FOUNDED: 1826.
OWNER: Allied-Domecq. METHOD: Pot stills.
CAPACITY: 238,000 gallons.

ARDMORE FOUNDED: 1898.
OWNER: Allied-Domecq. METHOD: Pot stills.
CAPACITY: 925,000 gallons.

GLEN GARIOCH FOUNDED: 1797.
OWNER: Morrison Bowmore. METHOD: Pot stills.
CAPACITY: 264,000 gallons.

MACDUFF

It is better news for Macduff, which sits across the Deveron. This is a big, modern, five-still site, built in 1962 on the site of Duff House's orchard, that has been part of what is now the Bacardi stable since 1972. The bulk of its whiskey goes into the William Lawson blend, while its single malt is sold as Glen Deveron. It is a sweet, slightly oaky, ten-year-old. Older expressions contain a drier, maltier note.

GLENDRONACH

The route now heads back inland, past arable lands, and through Turriff to Glendronach. This strikes you immediately as a traditional place, little changed since it was founded in 1826. The maltings, although not currently operational, are capable of being reopened, and there are coal fires under the stills, but the distillery was mothballed between 1996 and 2002. After dabbling with different expressions, owner Allied-Domecq

ARDMORE *stands as a symbol of the grand ideas of the late-Victorian blending business. Solid and powerful, it produces a rich, peaty malt.*

TASTING NOTES

Blending country this may be, but the single malts in all their variety are well worth seeking out.

KNOCKDHU

AN CNOC
12-YEAR-OLD, 40 VOL.

Color Full gold.
Nose A light, "airy" nose. Gentle, heathery, and fragrant. Delicate.
Body Dry with soft mid-palate.
Palate Grows well in the mouth building in sweetness and juiciness. Some elegance.
Finish Sweet and quite long with a hint of raisin.

GLENGLASSAUGH

GLENGLASSAUGH
25-YEAR-OLD, CADENHEAD, 60 VOL.
Color Pale straw/light gold.
Nose Very appley—flesh and seeds. Straw, grass, and herbs.
Body Medium-bodied. Spiky.
Palate Ripe pear, caramel apple, and wild herbs. Smoky oak toward the finish.
Finish Firm, dry, a little short.

MACDUFF

GLEN DEVERON
10-YEAR-OLD, 40 VOL.

Color Full gold.
Nose Malt bread spread with butter. A slightly slick, caramel/peanut brittle note. Floor wax and honey. Oak.
Body Light to medium.
Palate Juicy red grapes to start, then it's nuts. Spice. Soft and slightly sweet mid-palate. Butterscotch.
Finish A little short.

GLEN DEVERON

GLENDRONACH

GLENDRONACH ORIGINAL
12-YEAR-OLD, 40 VOL.

Color Gold/orange.
Nose Oak. Autumn fruits: medlar and pear. Orange crates, vanilla pod, butter toffee. Nutty.
Body Silky.
Palate Pecan pie, soft fruits, nutty maltiness. Becomes almost vinous with water.
Finish Firms up. Nut bowl.

ARDMORE

ARDMORE
1990, GORDON & MACPHAIL, 56.8 VOL.

Color Pale gold.
Nose Sweet eating apples, warm crusty bread, banana, and fresh sage. Light smoke and a vegetal note.
Body Soft. Medium-bodied.
Palate Cooked apple, lemon and lime zest, and sweet spices.
Finish A wisp of peat smoke.

GLEN GARIOCH

GLEN GARIOCH HIGHLAND TRADITION,
NO AGE STATEMENT, 40 VOL.

Color Light gold.
Nose Youthful nose with sandalwood, bracken, malt, heathery touches. A sharp, lemon zest note.
Body Light. Fizzy.
Palate Fresh and lively with dry, burlap-sack flavors and a refreshing citric lift.
Finish Fairly short, starting quite mellow, and then drying.

GLEN GARIOCH

has changed its strategy, and not only is a new Glendronach on the market, but serious investment is going into the plant. Sadly, that includes replacing the coal fires with steam coils.

ARDMORE

Adam Teacher built the Ardmore distillery near Kennethmont in 1898. He was a house guest of Colonel Leith-Hay, whose home Leith Hall is nearby, and it was he who persuaded Teacher that this location, with its ready supplies of barley, peat, and water and the rail link, would be a good spot for a distillery. Ardmore is big, solid, and imposing. Its buildings have confidence, their interiors speak of quality engineering, none more so than its still-house, which used to bear a striking resemblance to the engine room of an old Atlantic liner. The stills stood on a tiled pedestal, with coal fires raging below, watched over by two stillmen. The fires have gone recently, but Ardmore has retained its old-style peatiness and complex, orchard fruitiness. It is a complex, little-known malt.

GLEN GARIOCH

To the east of Kennethmont, the land broadens into a fertile valley, the Garioch (pronounced "Geerie"), at whose head is the market town of Oldmeldrum. Oldmeldrum's distillery, Glen Garioch, was licensed in 1797, although there is an allusion to a licensed distillery on this site in 1785. It is an impressive setup; the neat little still-house is dwarfed by thick, stone-walled maltings that sit at right angles to it. It was mothballed between 1995 and 1997, but owner Morrison Bowmore has reinvested in the distillery and changed the character of the whiskey. For years, this was the heaviest-peated mainland whiskey; now there is no trace of the dark stuff to be seen.

Glendronach *is enjoying something of a revival after being plunged into silence for six years.*

Deeside & the Eastern Highlands

DESPITE ITS WILD WHISKEY-SMUGGLING PAST AND A NUMBER OF ROYAL CONNECTIONS, WHISKEY PRODUCTION IN THIS REGION HAS BEEN DECIMATED.

Queen Victoria and Prince Albert, it could be said, initiated the shift in Scotland's image from the mid-1800s onward. What had been seen as a barbaric country was now a pleasure ground for the great and the good of the United Kingdom, and so it has stayed. So it seems appropriate that the distillery closest to Balmoral, the Royal Family's summer residence, remains in full production, and looks much the same as it must have been when Queen Victoria visited in 1868.

ROYAL LOCHNAGAR

Given the tourist potential, you might expect Royal Lochnagar to be as busy as Glenfiddich or Glenlivet. Instead, in the late 1990s, it took the interesting step of restricting visitor numbers, stopping bus tours and large parties, and ceasing to sell shortbread and tartan items. The spend, however, has increased—the shop now sells Diageo's full range of Rare Malts, and the tours are personalized, slower, and more detailed. Small stills are often the most satisfying to visit. It is easier to understand the whiskey-making process, and the subtle differences that make each whiskey unique.

Royal Lochnagar was owned originally by John Begg, a smuggler and illicit distiller who—perhaps mindful of his new neighbors—took out a license in 1826. His fellow smugglers did not take kindly to this, and his first distillery was burned to the ground. The new site was licensed in 1845.

DISTILLERY DETAILS

ROYAL LOCHNAGAR FOUNDED: 1845.
OWNER: Diageo. METHOD: Pot stills.
CAPACITY: 106,000 gallons.

FETTERCAIRN FOUNDED: 1824.
OWNER: Whyte & Mackay. METHOD: Pot stills.
CAPACITY: 423,000 gallons.

GLENCADAM FOUNDED: 1825.
OWNER: Angus Dundee. METHOD: Pot stills.
CAPACITY: 343,000 gallons.

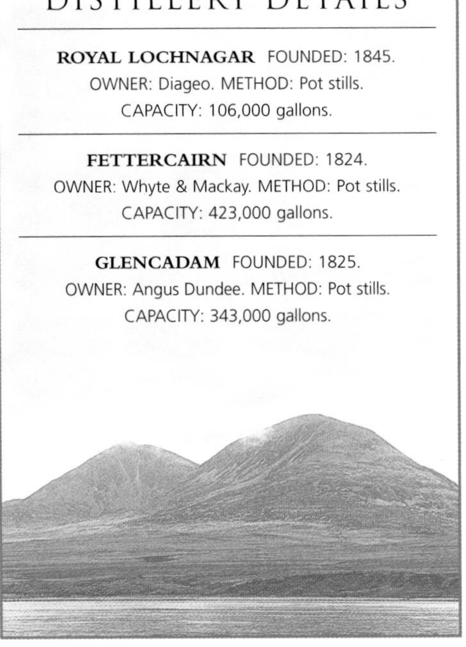

FETTERCAIRN, *situated on moorland at the foot of the Grampians—once a whiskey-smuggling area, was originally run as a farm distillery.*

Royal Lochnagar is one of the most traditional stills that Diageo owns. It has an open-topped mash tun with rakes, rather than the normal lauter, meaning skillful mashing is needed to ensure that no solids get drawn through into the washback; that would alter the character. The ferments are long and the pair of stills have worms attached. Normally, all this would give a heavy style of whiskey, and Lochnagar was set up to produce that, but today, its make has a grassy aroma with the worms giving just a touch of extra weight on the palate. This is achieved by resting the stills between distillations and keeping the worm tubs warm, thereby maximizing the amount of copper available to the spirit vapor and lightening the character.

FETTERCAIRN

Queen Victoria makes an appearance at Fettercairn distillery as well, in the shape of a rather ostentatious, red stone arch over the road, commemorating her brief visit. Another traditional site, Fettercairn has an open-topped, cast-iron mash tun, and stills with purifiers on the side. It is a neat place, full of nooks and crannies, and it makes a fresh, cereal-like malt with a hint of freshly turned soil.

GLENCADAM

The sole other working distillery on the east coast is Glencadam, in nearby Brechin. Its two stills were saved in 2003 by Angus Dundee from a short silent period. No malt has been released, but a recent bottling from Signatory has a very lively, spicy character.

DISTILLERIES FROM THE PAST

Glencadam's neighbor, North Port, is now a shopping center, while Montrose's two stills at Glenesk (a.k.a. Hillside) failed to survive the purges of the early 1980s. The town's other distillery, Lochside, which occupied the old Deuchars brewery, has also gone.

The seaside resort of Stonehaven used to have a regal distillery of its own, Glenury-Royal, but its four stills fell silent in the 1980s. All of Aberdeen's distilleries are long gone, while Peterhead's Glenugie has been dismantled. To pick up the whiskey trail once more, you have to head inland to Perthshire.

ON A BRIGHT DAY *the old malt barn and kiln at Royal Lochnagar are reflected in the distillery pond.*

BABY LOCHNAGAR *sees the light of day—clear new make spirit is ready for aging in the barrel.*

TASTING NOTES

THERE ARE ROYAL connections aplenty in this vast and disparate region, but are the drams regal?

ROYAL LOCHNAGAR

ROYAL LOCHNAGAR

12-YEAR-OLD, 40 VOL.

Color Gold.

ROYAL LOCHNAGAR

Nose Light, slightly grassy and citric. Good depth, as if hidden behind some gentle soft orchard fruits.
Body Medium. Succulent.
Palate Clean and fresh with ripe fruits in center. Grassy again. Sweet.
Finish Clean and dry. Balance.

ROYAL LOCHNAGAR

SELECTED RESERVE

Color Russet/mahogany.
Nose Hugely sherried. Fruity cake, molasses, roasted chestnut. Black cherry sweetness.
Body Rich and full. Liquorous.
Palate Jamaican ginger cake, Dundee cake. Chewy and ripe.
Finish Long and lingering.

FETTERCAIRN

OLD FETTERCAIRN

10-YEAR-OLD, 40 VOL.

Color Light gold.
Nose Freshly turned soil, moss. Hay loft. crisp maltiness, Light rubbery note.
Body Light.
Palate Cookie-flavored and crisp. Some sweet maltiness.
Finish Clean, crisp, quite short.

GLENCADAM

GLENCADAM 1979

SIGNATORY SILENT STILL RANGE, 56 VOL.

Color Golden.
Nose Aromatic and very spicy. Honey, caramel apple, malt.
Body Medium. Mature but lively.
Palate Venerable but has a spiky energy still with gentle softness underneath: cinnamon, toasted marshmallow.
Finish Crisp. Rose petal.

10-YEAR-OLD FETTERCAIRN

Edradour

THE MANAGEMENT OF SCOTLAND'S SMALLEST DISTILLERY DEMONSTRATES HOW OLD WAYS OF MAKING WHISKEY CAN BE BOTH A REMINDER OF THE PAST AND A SIGNPOST TO FUTURE OPPORTUNITIES.

To place Edradour in the correct context, it is best to approach it from the north rather than through Pitlochry. The road through Strathardle takes you up into high moorland, dotted with isolated farms. Glenshee is to your north, the bulk of Ben Vrackie in front. The narrow road bucks and twists, then suddenly spins you out of the heather, laying out in front of you the wide, lush valley of Strath Tay. Before you get to Moulin (and its microbrewery) there is a turn on your left and the suggestion of a white building. Go down into this deep valley, one of many which run through this landscape, and you reach Scotland's smallest and undoubtedly cutest distillery.

If you look at that geography again, you can see why it was perfect moonshining territory. Like so may of today's legal sites, Edradour started life as a hidden bothy. But in 1825 a group of eight local farmers banded together and started a cooperative distillery—very similar to what happened at Lagavulin *(see pp. 115–16)*.

Their legal venture was a success, unlike other local distilleries that failed to ride out the first few tough years. Quite how it survived when larger plants collapsed is hard to say. Maybe it was luck, but more likely its whiskey was of a higher quality. Unusually, however, while other distilleries expanded, Edradour stayed the same size.

Today, little has changed. A burn (which is prone to winter flooding) runs through the middle of the site. On one side there is a neat office and visitor center; on the other is a cluster of low-slung, white-painted buildings that house the distillery and warehousing. The place may look small, but some very serious whiskey-making is taking place inside.

DISTILLERY DETAILS

EDRADOUR FOUNDED: 1825.
OWNER: Signatory Vintage Scotch Whisky Co. Ltd.
METHOD: Pot stills.
CAPACITY: 24,000 gallons.

TASTING NOTES

THE SWEET, RICH malt from Scotland's smallest distillery justifies all the interest in Edradour's old-fashioned whiskey-making.

EDRADOUR STRAIGHT FROM THE CASK
11-YEAR-OLD, 60.2 VOL.

Color Amber.
Nose Rich, almost meaty nose when straight, with notes of chocolate, toffee, prune, spice and tea leaves. Appetizing.
Body Soft. Spreads well across the palate.
Palate Nutty (almond) sherried notes, but they never overpower the inherent sweetness of the spirit.
Finish Minty.

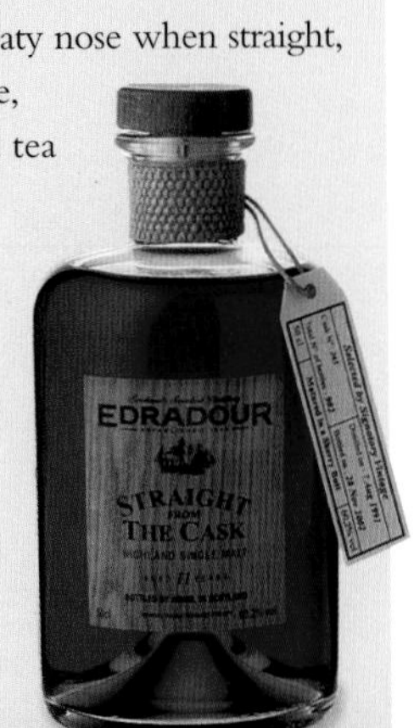

EDRADOUR

THE WHISKEY-MAKING PROCESS

Edradour was considered too small to have its own mill, so grist was bought in to supply its one-ton-capacity mash tun. The worts are cooled in an open-topped contraption called a Morton's Patent Refrigerator, as advertised at the back of Alfred Barnard's 1887 book, *Whisky Distilleries of the United Kingdom.* There are two small wooden washbacks and a pair of almost hunchbacked stills whose stubby, curved lyne arms go into tiny worm tubs. Everything is contained in one room.

TAKEOVERS AND CHANGES

In 1925, Edradour was bought by the Glasgow-based blender William Whitely, who used it in such blends as House of Lords and Kings Ransom (at that time the priciest Scotch in the world). Later on, it was absorbed into Campbell Distillers and then Pernod-Ricard. Still nothing changed; Edradour was caught in a time warp. Pernod was happy to keep its little oddity as it was, which in turn gave the whiskey visitor the opportunity to understand how an early Victorian distillery operated.

Then in 2002, following Pernod's acquisition of Seagram, Edradour was put on the market. Always an anomaly, it was now too small for a giant firm—Edradour had been lost in the Pernod portfolio. The single malt was sold either at the distillery or in France. There were only 24,000 gallons (90,000 liters) for sale every

EDRADOUR'S WORM TUBS *look like tiny hip baths, all part of the distillery's diminutive scale of operation.*

year; the rest went for blending. But that has changed. Edradour was immediately snapped up by Andrew Symington of independent bottler Signatory Vintage; it was one of a series of distillery purchases by independent bottlers that also included Glengoyne, Bruichladdich, and Benromach.

Behind these purchases lies simple economics. The independent-bottler sector has built itself on selling unusual, hard-to-find, high-quality whiskeys from distilleries either sold, closed, or removed from the front-line portfolios of their owners. Without the bottlers, the whiskey-lover would not have heard of cult whiskeys such as Longmorn, Strathisla, Mortlach, Caol Ila, Port Ellen, Dallas Dhu, and Ardmore. But many coveted whiskeys are becoming scare, either because stock is running low or because they have been returned to their parent company's portfolio. In other words, Signatory Vintage needed their own brand in order to survive.

A NEW WAY FORWARD

Since Edradour's change of ownership, there have been dramatic changes. Iain Henderson, the former manager of Laphroaig, has taken over production and used his engineering and whiskey-making experience to get the distillery running smoothly, while using the same old-fashioned equipment. It is truly a hand-crafted whiskey. That is not to say Edradour is a museum. In its bottlings it is contemporary. The range has expanded dramatically, with a standard bottling, cask strength variants, different age statements, a growing range of finishes, and even a cream liqueur. New make has been filled into Tokaji wine casks, and Iain has used his years on Islay to make a peated whiskey that takes it name from a long-defunct local distillery, Ballechin.

While such a move seems blasphemy to many whiskey-lovers, Iain and Andrew point out that the early records of the original Ballechin speak of how its whiskey was smoky. Heavily peated mainland malts are unusual these days, but it was a common style in the early days of whiskey production.

Inevitably, Edradour attracts tourists, 100,000 of whom annually spend nearly $2 million in the shop. It all amounts to a good way of building a new, revived, brand.

A CLASSIC FARM DISTILLERY, *Edradour is the proud possessor of the cutest still in Scotland.*

PERTHSHIRE

PIPERS, GIANT BIRDS, AND A RETAIL PARK; WELCOME TO PERTHSHIRE'S LATEST SPECIALTY—THE WHISKEY EXPERIENCE.

It may just be a tiny village missed by most southbound travelers, but at Calvine a subtle geographical change takes place. From this point, rivers begin to flow south and the landscape alters. The hills no longer loom over the road, there are more broad-leaved trees, and grass replaces heather and bare rock. Blair Castle, with its wide lawns and arboretum, sits on the side of the road, and the valley begins to broaden.

Perth is nearby, and with it comes a discreet shift in the concerns of distillers. Perth was one of the great blending centers, home to John Dewar, Matthew Gloag, and Arthur Bell. All of them were wine merchants who, in the mid- to late 19th century, saw the commercial opportunities in making blended whiskeys with mass consumer appeal.

Given this, it is surprising that there are so few distilleries in this part of the country. Although Perthshire was awash with illicit stills in its time, few went legal, and of those that did, few survived: Grantully, Pitillie, Auchnagie, Ballechin, and Stronachie are no more. Blenders were not interested in single malts, so distilleries ultimately prospered or died according to the suitability of their make for blending.

DISTILLERY DETAILS

BLAIR ATHOL FOUNDED: 1798.
OWNER: Diageo. METHOD: Pot stills.
CAPACITY: 500,000 gallons.

ABERFELDY FOUNDED: 1898.
OWNER: John Dewar & Sons Ltd. METHOD: Pot stills.
CAPACITY: 317,000 gallons.

GLENTURRET FOUNDED: 1775.
OWNER: The Edrington Group. METHOD: Pot stills.
CAPACITY: 90,000 gallons.

TULLIBARDINE FOUNDED: 1949.
OWNER: Tullibardine Ltd. METHOD: Pot stills.
CAPACITY: Not known.

DEANSTON FOUNDED: 1965.
OWNER: Burn Stewart Distillers Ltd. METHOD: Pot stills.
CAPACITY: 793,000 gallons.

BLAIR ATHOL

The Blair Athol distillery is not in Blair itself, but a little farther south, in the pretty Victorian town of Pitlochry. Maybe one of the distillery's early owners felt that the grand name would give his whiskey some aristocratic credibility. Blair Athol's first incarnation was not a success, but by the mid-19th century, Alexander Connacher had built up regular business with a salesman, Arthur Bell, from the Perth wine merchant Sandeman & Roy. Bell eventually took over the wine merchant's and, in 1933, his company, now called Bell's, bought the distillery.

Bell's eight-year-old continues as Great Britain's top blended Scotch, and Blair Athol remains at its heart. There is a definite "Bell's style" of malt whiskey, which uses four plain stills. The whiskey moves quickly through mashing, fermenting, and distilling, and the result is a crafted, nutty character.

The Blair Athol distillery is a popular tourist destination for those visiting Pitlochry each summer. If the Perthshire distilleries differ in style, they all share a similar commercial aim; to attract as many visitors as possible, something that is evident in the growing number of whiskey "experiences"

VIRGINIA CREEPER *and ivy clothe Blair Athol's beautifully maintained stone distillery buildings.*

THE HIGHLANDER *who has marched on countless Dewar's whiskey labels greets visitors to Aberfeldy. The distinctive malt house, or pagoda, no longer supplies malt to the distillery.*

offered in the area. An increased interest—in blends or malts—can only be good for Scotland's steadily rejuvenating industry.

ABERFELDY

Built by Tommy Dewar in 1898 to provide fillings for his fast-growing blend, the Aberfeldy distillery sits on a hill overlooking the river Tay. Dewar was the first true marketing genius in the whiskey trade, and his legacy is celebrated at the distillery today. The malt is excellent in its own right, but given Dewar's volumes (in excess of one million cases a year), it is not widely available. The four wide-bottomed plain stills have traditionally made a whiskey that has a mouth-coating waxiness; this is seen to great effect in a 25-year-old that Bacardi released recently.

Not that the tens of thousands of visitors each year necessarily know this. Many have come to visit Dewar's World of Whiskies, a $3.8-million extravaganza. The attention is on the brand, and with so many American tourists in the region, creating the attraction made commercial sense. Tommy Dewar no doubt would have approved.

GLENTURRET

Somewhat overshadowed by the nearby Famous Grouse Experience, which attracts 200,000 visitors each year, all of them eager to understand more about Scotland's famous blended whiskey, Glenturret distillery has a one-ton mash tun and two stills. It looks like a farm with all the animals removed and distilling equipment installed in their place, because that is exactly what happened.

Glenturret had a license in 1775, and traded intermittently before grinding to a halt in 1923. In 1950, James Fairlie bought it and spent a decade getting it up and running again. This floral, lightly honeyed whiskey is often overlooked, which is a real shame, since it's a fine dram.

TULLIBARDINE

The theme-park idea has inspired another local distillery, Tullibardine, in Blackford. The distillery was mothballed by Whyte and Mackay when it bought Invergordon, and over the years its warehouses have grown increasingly decrepit. In 2003, however, Tullibardine was bought by a consortium and placed, wisely, at the center of a retail park that will generate extra income.

DEANSTON

Deanston, the final distillery in the area, has not yet set up a themed visitor center, although it is located close to a safari park should any cross-merchandising be needed in the future. It is a modern distillery (although one with an open-topped mash tun), but situated in an 18th-century cotton mill. Although not widely available, Deanston single malt shares a soft, honeyed charm with many of its neighboring whiskeys.

TASTING NOTES

PERTHSHIRE has embraced "whiskey experience" marketing, and its subtle and varied whiskeys underlie the razzmatazz.

BLAIR ATHOL

BLAIR ATHOL
12-YEAR-OLD, 43 VOL.

Color Deep. Dried orange skin.
Nose Solid, quite dense, and wooded. Nutty: powdered mixed nuts. Stewed tea.
Body Slippery.
Palate Cakelike with lots of nuts on the top. Light mixed peel.
Finish Dry. Hint of smoke.

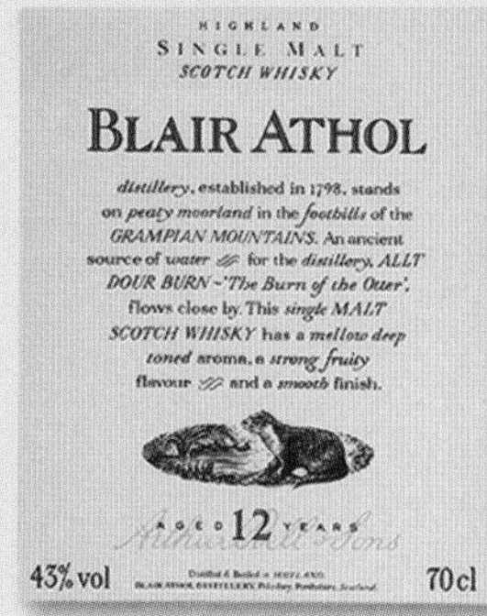

12-YEAR-OLD BLAIR ATHOL

ABERFELDY

ABERFELDY
12-YEAR-OLD, 40 VOL.

Color Gold.
Nose Wisp of turfy smoke. Tangerine, juicy malts, peach cobbler. Light nutmeg notes.
Body Oily.
Palate Mouthwatering and fresh. Mandarin, nectarine. Zesty and silky.
Finish Slowly drying.

12-YEAR-OLD ABERFELDY

GLENTURRET

GLENTURRET
10-YEAR-OLD, 40 VOL.

Color Straw. Green glints.
Nose Lightly flowery. Salad leaves. Fragrant. Parmesan cheese.
Body Light. Vaporous
Palate Light and lacy. Very delicate.
Finish Short and snappy.

TULLIBARDINE

TULLIBARDINE
10-YEAR-OLD, 40 VOL.

Color Light gold.
Nose Shredded Wheat with warm milk. Lightly perfumed. Some lime zest.
Body Medium.
Palate Decent weight. Butter, cooked pear. Malt.
Finish Long and sweet.

DEANSTON

DEANSTON
6-YEAR-OLD, 40 VOL.

Color Light gold.
Nose Lightly perfumed, grass, cream, granola, slightly nutty.
Body Soft and light.
Palate Cereal-like with a soft mid-palate and a malty note. Slightly hard.
Finish Green grape. Immaturity still there.

6-YEAR-OLD DEANSTON

Vatted Malts

BLENDING SINGLE MALTS IS HARDLY A NEW INVENTION BUT IT MAY PROVIDE THE SOLUTION TO ENSURING THE CONTINUED GROWTH OF THE WHISKEY INDUSTRY.

Quite simply, a "vatted malt" is a blend (or vatting) of single malt whiskeys from more than one distillery. When, in 1853, vatting of whiskeys was permitted under bond (that is, before duty was paid), the doors were opened, legally, for greater experimentation by blenders. This change in the law ultimately paved the way for blended whiskey, but it is entirely probable that they were preceded by vatted malts. In 1853, Andrew Usher launched his Old Vatted Glenlivet (OVG), which, although widely accepted as the first blended "brand," is likely in its first incarnation to have been a vatted malt.

The same thing was happening in groceries across Scotland: in Glasgow, Aberdeen, Perth, Kilmarnock, and Leith, where in 1853 Charles Mackinlay used his stocks of single malts to create his Old Vatted Ben Vorlich brand.

The advent of vatting demonstrates an understanding of maturation and shows how the first blenders were trying to impose quality and consistency in their product. They were also looking to create new flavors that would be acceptable to the British (and global) palate.

PRODUCERS

BLUE HANGER
AS WE GET IT
MACDONALDS OF GLENCOE
POIT DUBH
GORDON & MACPHAIL "PRIDE OF ..."
BALLANTINE'S PURE
JOHNNIE WALKER GREEN LABEL
GROUSE VINTAGE MALT
BELL'S SPECIAL RESERVE
COMPASS BOX
THE EASY DRINKING WHISKY COMPANY

Vatting was widely practiced in private homes, and is likely to have been an ancient custom. In 1864, Charles Tovey wrote of how, "in a gentleman's cellar," one would find a hogshead containing four or five malts that would be replenished with "any whisky that is particularly approved [of]" when the volume dropped below a certain level. This solera method of vatting was expanded upon by Professor George Saintsbury in his *Notes on a Cellar Book* (1920). The Professor's cask contained Clynelish, The Glenlivet, Glen Grant, Talisker, and an Islay. The idea has been revived by Richard Joynson at Loch Fyne, whose "Living Cask" has been evolving since 1998.

The appreciation of vatting seems to have been restricted to the gentry, however. In his book *Whisky* (1930), Aeneas Macdonald writes that, in 1909, following a hike in duties and a collapse in sales, malt distillers tried to sell vatted malts to get rid of stocks. The attempt failed in spite of a vigorous advertising campaign because, he claims, the public did not like the stronger flavor, having become accustomed to blends.

Vatted malts did not disappear, although they did recede into the shadows. There are old established brands such as Blue Hanger, As We Get It, Macdonalds of Glencoe, Poit Dubh, and the Gordon & MacPhail regional range, "Pride Of ...". There was an attempt at wider commercial credibility in DCL's 1982 six-strong "Ascot Malt Cellar," which contained Buchanan's and Haig's vatted brands, Strathconon and Glenleven, but that was soon scrapped. It did, however, sow the seed of the idea for Classic Malts; a collection of malts from each of Scotland's whiskey regions.

Vatted malts had to wait until the late-1990s before they reappeared fully. A number of firms saw vatting as a way of extending their blended range; some of the best-known include Ballantine's Pure, Johnnie Walker Pure (now renamed Green Label), Grouse Vintage Malt, and Bell's Special Reserve.

"NEW WAVE" WHISKEYS

At the same time, a number of new whiskeys have appeared from firms such as Compass Box (Eleuthera and Juveniles), and The Easy Drinking Whisky Company (Rich Spicy, Smoky Peaty, and Smooth Sweeter), both of whom have looked at vatted malts as a way of getting new flavors to a new audience. For Compass Box, it has involved crafting boutique whiskeys that have a flavor profile likely to find favor with a younger consumer and packaging them in bottles that do not conform to people's traditional idea of what a whiskey should look like. Easy Drinking, meanwhile, has studied how the wine market has attracted a new type of consumer by simplifying its labeling and

Andrew Usher *is the father of both blending and vatted malts. The son of an Edinburgh spirit merchant, he started blending in the mid-19th century.*

naming the grape varieties used. Vatted malts are more than just blends without the grain. Vatted malts are about combining different levels of complexity to create different flavor combinations. In other words, when making a blend, the grain is used to calm the more overt characteristics of the malts as well as pulling out new flavors. In a vatted malt, however, all the parts are competing on more or less equal terms. This means that technically it is difficult to make a complex, balanced, vatted product. No single component should be allowed to dominate, but the end result should be a drink that is more than just the sum of its parts. That said, blenders love vatted malts because they offer an opportunity to create a wider range of flavors.

WHISKEY'S FUTURE

Vatted malts have another function in the 21st century. In many mature markets, the blended sector is static at best, and younger drinkers, if they drink whiskey, are going straight to malt. However, there can never be a single malt that can sell in the same volume as Johnnie Walker, for example. Each distillery is restricted ultimately by the size of its stills and stock. But if a new, vatted category of whiskey could be created, it would offer an opportunity for new, high-volume, quality products appealing to the consumer who wants malt whiskey. That was the logic behind the proposed launch of Cardhu Pure Malt (now abandoned), and while no vatted malt should ever carry the name of a single distillery, the intention was sound. "L'affaire Cardhu" has, thankfully, forced the industry to tighten its previously loose labeling definitions. As of 2005, vatted malts will be labeled as "a blend of malts." Maybe, finally, vatted malts will achieve the recognition they deserve.

The Easy Drinking *Whisky Company offers a new angle and is attracting a new market in vatted malts with its straightforward labeling.*

TASTING NOTES

The rise of vatted malts is evident in the new bottlings appearing on the market.

BALLANTINE'S PURE MALT
12-YEAR-OLD
40 VOL.

Color Gold.
Nose Fresh. Malty vanilla, grass, and nut. Some elegance. Nougat with coconut, cream, and fresh fruits. Water shows a woody edge.
Body Medium. Mellow.
Palate Sweet and slightly bitter. Nut, cream, and light smoke.
Finish Nutty, a hint of smoke.

JOHNNIE WALKER GREEN LABEL
40 VOL.

Color Rich gold and amber.
Nose Smoky, slightly marine, then moss. Sweetens to Seville orange, stewed peach, and cherry. Rich, with good balance between sweet fruits and dry, nutty oak. Drifting peat smoke.
Body Medium to full.
Palate Soft and gentle with central sweetness. Clover honey, banana, loganberry, baked apple, butterscotch, cream, sweet spices, and a nutty note.
Finish Spicy with notes of cocoa, cedar, and cigar smoke.

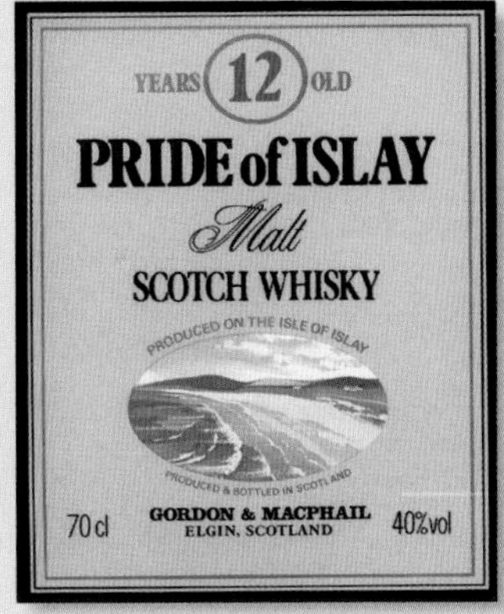

GORDON AND MACPHAIL

THE LIVING CASK
40 VOL.

Because of the nature of its production every bottling will be subtly different.

Color Light gold.
Nose Complex. Sooty smoke, sugared almond. Seaside. Perfumed notes, green olive, bracken.
Body Medium.
Palate Immediate sweetness then smoke. Vibrant. Orange muscat, citrus oils, and peat smoke.
Finish Long, smoky.

ELEUTHERA, COMPASS BOX
43 VOL.

Color Pale gold.
Nose Oily and slightly waxy. Canned peaches, honey, ginger, and subtle pancetta notes.
Body Medium. Silky.
Palate Sweet, quite luscious fruits, then a bite of smoke weaving its way around the palate. Well integrated.
Finish Ripe. Long.

PRIDE OF ISLAY, GORDON & MACPHAIL
40 VOL.

Color Light gold.
Nose Herring, heather blossom, cookie-like malt, and baked apple. Delicately smoky.
Body Medium. Soft.
Palate Juicy and well-balanced with a prickle of heathery smoke halfway through.
Finish Dry.

Great Blends

TASTE THE TALISKER IN JOHNNIE WALKER, THE ARDBEG IN BALLANTINE'S, THE ABERFELDY IN DEWAR'S? THESE MALTS WOULD NOT HAVE SURVIVED WERE THEY NOT KEY ELEMENTS IN BLENDS.

What most of today's malt whiskey enthusiasts tend to forget is that 90 percent of Scotch whiskey sold is blended. If it were not for blends, many, if not, most, of the distilleries that people love so much would not survive. Blended whiskey made the Scotch whiskey industry what it is today, and will continue to drive it forward. No single distillery could produce the millions of cases sold by Johnnie Walker, Ballantine's, and Dewar's. In other words, whiskey needs blends. Equally, the notion that taking a selection of malts and mixing them with a selection of grain whiskeys produces a drink that is somehow inferior is an erroneous one. A top blend is every bit as complex and rewarding as a single malt. It is time to rediscover them.

THE TOP SELLERS

1 JOHNNIE WALKER RED LABEL
2 J&B
3 BALLANTINE'S FINEST
4 WILLIAM GRANT
5 JOHNNIE WALKER BLACK LABEL
6 DEWAR'S WHITE LABEL
7 CHIVAS 12-YEAR-OLD
8 THE FAMOUS GROUSE
9 BELL'S 8-YEAR-OLD
10 CUTTY SARK
11 100 PIPERS
12 TEACHER'S HIGHLAND CREAM
13 CLAN CAMPBELL
14 CLAN MACGREGOR
15 LABEL 5

EARLY BLENDED WHISKEYS

Many of the most famous blended whiskeys started life in Scottish stores, where grocers experienced in blending tea, rum, and wine changed whiskey from a local specialty into a drink with global appeal.

Early malt whiskeys had a local appeal, but were not to everyone's taste. The invention of the continuous still in 1827 led to a new, lighter style of whiskey, but although some was certainly consumed on its own, the bulk was used to make gin. In 1853, a change in law meant that whiskeys could be mixed (vatted) while still in bond. Initially, this allowed distilleries to mix different casks and ages together, to make more palatable, consistent whiskey. Following a further relaxation of the law in 1860, mixes of malt and grain whiskeys began to appear.

Whether the first blender was a publican, a wine merchant, or a grocer, what is certain is that the first blended whiskey brand was called OVG [Old Vatted Glenlivet] and was created by Andrew Usher. Although it is probable that OVG started life as a vatting of The Glenlivet, for which Usher was the sole agent, by the 1860s, OVG had become a popular blend in its own right.

Very few traditional grocers blend whiskey today, although Gordon & MacPhail's shop in Elgin (*see p. 146*), and Valvona & Crolla's deli in Edinburgh keep up the tradition.

THE APPEAL OF BLENDS

Blending brought new consistency to whiskey. Vatting ironed out differences between casks, while blending took the whiskey a step further; a grocer could create whiskey with a consistent flavor, even though its component parts might vary from one year to the next.

BELL'S WHISKY, *an everyday favorite in the pubs of England, is blended in the picturesque heart of Scotland.*

R. Paterson, blending—*the role of a master blender is part artist, part technician.*

Blended whiskey also appealed to a wider market than single malts, with its lighter personality. This was particularly important to Scottish whiskey producers in the late 1800s, since Irish whiskey was then more popular than Scotch in the English market. The Speyside railroad provided a good transport link to England, meaning that the new blended whiskeys were more readily available, as were tourists to Scotland, who were able to try the new blends.

John Walker opened his grocer's shop in the Ayrshire town of Kilmarnock in 1819; John Dewar in Perth opened in 1846; and Glasgow-based William Teacher entered the grocery trade in 1836. By the 1850s, Teacher had established Glasgow's largest chain of "dram shops" selling his own wares. He also supplied George Ballantine, who started his own grocery and wine merchant business in Edinburgh in 1827, and James and John Chivas in Aberdeen, whose King Street store was known as the "Harrod's of the North." They supplied everything imaginable—from staff, donkeys, and table linen to provisions and whiskey—to the great houses of the north,

Yamazaki's Hibiki *is one of Japan's most popular blended whiskeys. The whiskey market is flourishing in Japan, with popularity in both single malts and blends ever increasing.*

including Balmoral. Although the Chivas brothers started blending in the late 1850s, it was not until 1909 that the firm's Chivas Regal (then a 5-year-old) was launched.

By the 1860s, it was the descendants of these famous men who exploited the opportunities for blended Scotch by producing whiskeys that appealed to the mass market. The first to be conquered was London, thanks to men like James Buchanan and Tommy Dewar. James Buchanan toured the capital, promoting his House of Commons (later Black & White) and Buchanan's Blend. Tommy Dewar went in for huge neon signs and movie-theater ads. In time, their blends spread across the world, first through the Empire, and then to the US. It was in the US where the final stylistic shift took place.

Chivas Regal *is one of the best-selling quality blends in the world today, but its origins are much like those of many other blends—a grocer's shop. Brothers John and James were extremely successful.*

US AND JAPANESE BLENDS

During, and then after, Prohibition, the American palate lightened. Two London wine merchants, Berry Bros. & Rudd and Justerini & Brooks, responded by creating new, paler, light-tasting blends. By the 1960s, Cutty Sark and J&B were both selling in excess of a million cases in the US, although Dewar's is now the clear market leader. Chivas Regal reappeared in 1954, as a 12-year-old, courtesy of its new owner, Seagram's.

The Scottish template for blended whiskeys is also used in Japan, where Suntory's Hibiki is the best-known brand internationally. Also like Scotch, blends account for the bulk of sales in the Japanese domestic market.

THE TOP 15 BLENDS

The family-owned blending dynasties are virtually all gone, yet the majority of the biggest global sellers, all of which sell more than one million cases a year, are from the original, pioneering grocers. Number one is Johnnie Walker's Red Label, selling vast quantities in Greece, the US, Dubai, Australia, and also the duty-free market. Second comes J&B—more of a European choice, and the best-seller in Spain and France, but also in South Africa. Another European favorite is Ballantine's, the third top seller. Next is William Grant, again big in France, but also in the UK and Portugal. Johnnie Walker's Black Label, number five, sells well in Dubai, as well as in the Far East and the US. Next is Dewar's White Label, big in Venezuela and Greece, followed by Chivas 12-year-old, its biggest markets including Europe, the Far East and the US. At number eight, The Famous Grouse is ever-popular in the UK, and also Greece. It is followed by Bells 8-year-old, a huge seller in Scandinavia, South Africa, and Brazil. Cutty Sark has its biggest sales in the US, Iberia, and Latin America. 100 Pipers lists Spain, Venezuela, and Thailand as its main markets. Teacher's Highland Cream, a major UK seller, comes next, followed by Clan Campbell and Clan MacGregor, big sellers in France and the US, respectively. Last in this list comes Label 5, also a French favorite.

Glasgow *and its surrounding area is home to some of the world's most popular blended whiskeys, many of which had humble beginnings in grocer's shops such as Teacher's.*

TASTING NOTES

THE POPULARITY OF blends is essential in the whiskey industry, and many of today's are fine drams in their own right, not the poor relative of single malt. From moist, rich, and fruity to gently smoky, there is a blend to suit every palate. This is a selection of some well-known, and some not-so-well-known, blends.

BALLANTINE'S

JOHNNIE WALKER RED LABEL

Color Gold.
Nose Fresh, lively with light vanilla, peat, and toasty oak.
Body Crisp, assertive.
Palate Balanced mix of soft fruit, vanilla, heathery peat. Vivacious.
Finish Lightly perfumed smoke. Crisp.

J&B

Color Pale straw
Nose Very light and floral. Estery top notes: flowers, cut pear, banana, light woodiness. Pretty. Young.
Body Light.

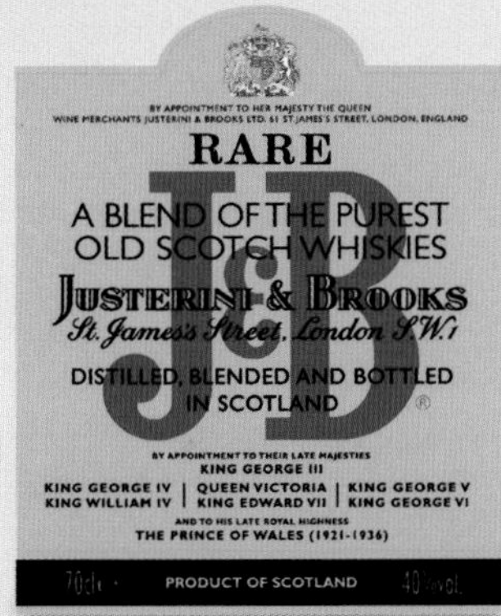

J & B

Palate A sweet start, then anise/fennel seed, spice and light grain with a slightly bitter edge.
Finish Crisp and short.

BALLANTINE'S FINEST

Color Gold.
Nose Cream toffee. Sweet, lightly grassy.
Body Soft. Medium weight.
Palate Gentle and sweet, crunchily crisp in the center.
Finish Dry, fresh.

WILLIAM GRANT'S FAMILY RESERVE

Color Light gold.
Nose Fragrant. Clover honey, lime, pear, and delicate smoke.
Body Medium. Silky.
Palate Soft to start, creamy. Brazil nut, nutmeg, soft fruits, vanilla pod.
Finish Gentle and sweet.

JOHNNIE WALKER BLACK LABEL

Color Amber.
Nose Ripe and fruity. Peat, nutmeg, vanilla, baked apple and raisin. Peaches, heather honey, orange peel.
Body Supple and chewy.
Palate Syrup, white pepper, orange blossom, honey. Peat underneath it all. Deep.
Finish Long, rich, and smoky.

DEWAR'S WHITE LABEL

Color Straw.
Nose Quite delicate. Malty. Lemon meringue pie, honey.
Body Light to medium. Soft.
Palate As nose suggests, gentle and sweet but with a tingle of gingery spice.
Finish Clean and sweet.

CHIVAS 12-YEAR-OLD

Color Gold.
Nose Light. Perfumed and floral. Nutty. Orange and mint.
Body Clean and light.
Palate Soft and grassy. Vanilla, milk chocolate, apple, lemon and orange peel.
Finish Short, dry.

THE FAMOUS GROUSE

Color Light gold.
Nose Dry but with good weight. Melting chocolate, hay, toast with honey.
Body Firm. Medium.
Palate Stewed prune, dark chocolate, caramel. Dried fruits.
Finish Light smoke.

THE FAMOUS GROUSE

BELL'S 8-YEAR-OLD

Color Rich amber.
Nose Sweet and fragrant but with deep ripe fruitiness. Moist fruitcake, chocolate cereal.
Body Soft and generous.
Palate Chewy and soft. Raisin, toffee, soft leather, and fruits. Light smoke.
Finish Gentle and warming

CUTTY SARK

Color Pale lemon.
Nose Light, floral, lemon, oat, butter, confectioner's sugar, fresh raspberry.
Body Delicate, light.
Palate Sweet and light. Cream, grassiness, soft fruits.
Finish Lemon sherbet.

WHYTE & MACKAY

Color Rich amber
Nose Full and sweet. Cooked fruits (raisin, date, fruitcake). Good grain elements.
Body Rich.
Palate Soft and gentle with an almost liquor quality. Black currant, heather, vanilla pod.
Finish Dry.

TEACHER'S HIGHLAND CREAM

Color Gold/amber.
Nose Ripe, full, and generous. Dried fruits, molasses toffee, cinnamon, smoke.
Body Medium to full.
Palate Spices galore alongside creamy toffee, raisin.
Finish Sooty.

TEACHERS

CLAN CAMPBELL

Color Gold.
Nose Rigid, spiritous, quite young. Crisp cereal.
Palate Grain dominant, some red fruits, hard candy. Young.
Finish Oak.

BLACK BOTTLE 10-YEAR-OLD

This is the only blend to contain every malt from Islay.

Color Gold
Nose Phenolic: tarry rope, seashell, salami, smoked peppered mackerel. With water-dried herbs, seaweed, cereal notes. Coal scuttle.
Body Medium. Explosive.
Palate Smokiness balanced by a silky soft mid-palate. Seashore aromas, fish oil, light ginger, lavender. Sooty. Balance.
Finish Smoke and ginger.

IRELAND

The charm, the welcome, the *craic*, the songs and stories...
lubricated by the pure pot still

BEAUTIFUL BARLEY
A rare tribute, in stained glass, at Bushmills. To the true whiskey-lover, a field of barley can give the same sensuous delight as the sight of a vineyard gives to a wine-drinker.

THE MAGIC OF AN IRISH POT STILL

MICHAEL JACKSON

Both of Ireland's national drinks, dry stout and whiskey, are made from barley. Both use a proportion of unmalted barley, and it is this ingredient in the most Irish of whiskeys that creates aromas of linseed and oil, reminiscent of leather and saddlery.

One could argue that the charm of Ireland is revealed in its approachable whiskey, while Scotch can appear more complex and harder to know. Ireland and Scotland are the two great, original whiskey nations; the surprise, perhaps, is that while Scotland has almost 100 distilleries, Ireland nowadays has only three, albeit producing 25 to 30 different whiskeys. Although the geography of Ireland is very peaty, its whiskeys are not, perhaps because both brewing and distilling became large industries in Ireland early on, long before peat-cutting was mechanized, and so the distilleries used wood or coal.

THE CHARM OF IRELAND IS REVEALED IN ITS APPROACHABLE WHISKEY, WHILE SCOTCH CAN APPEAR HARDER TO KNOW

The Romans or Normans may have brought to Ireland a grape distillate called *aqua vitae* (water of life), translated by the Irish as *uisce beatha*. This term is said to have been corrupted by the invading soldiers of England's King Henry II to "ushky," and later to "whiskey." In the early 1800s, a tax on malt led some distillers to use large proportions of raw barley, and this has remained a defining element in the flavor of today's Irish whiskeys.

As distillers sought to improve their product, double and triple distillation systems came into use, but the latter came to be more common in Ireland. The Irish distillers that grew and prospered were in the city-ports: Cork, Dublin, Belfast, and Londonderry.

BLUE HIGHWAYS
The greeny-blue haze on the hills of County Antrim. Presbyterians from Scotland settled here and in Londonderry, and then crossed the Atlantic to Maryland and Pennsylvania.

IRELAND'S DISTILLERIES

IRELAND WAS ONCE the greatest whiskey-producing nation, shipping the drink to a thirsty export market—especially the US—from its many ports. Many of its famous labels survive, or have been revived, each with its own specification.

Bushmills
LONDONDERRY
NORTHERN IRELAND
BELFAST
ATLANTIC OCEAN
Cooley
REPUBLIC OF IRELAND
IRISH SEA
GALWAY
KILBEGGAN
TULLAMORE
DUBLIN
SHANNON
WATERFORD
CORK
Midleton
CELTIC SEA

Key

◆ working distilleries

LIVING LEGEND
This flesh-and-blood distillery mascot is a successor to the legendary Brown Bull of Cooley, over which a battle was fought almost 1,000 years ago.

TEMPLE BAR, DUBLIN
The Temple Bar is the name of a pub and a nightlife neighborhood in the city's center. The Temple Bar pub is known for its selection of whiskeys.

WHEEL OF FORTUNE
The big wheel at Midleton rolls in retirement, recalling the days when Irish whiskey-making was a major industry.

The technique that revolutionized all distillation, the column still, was perfected by an Irishman, Aeneas Coffey, in the early 1800s (*see p. 64*), but his countrymen were ambivalent about it. This new still appealed to those who wanted to mass produce whiskey, but it threatened to undermine a product that had luxury status. The Irish distillers' devotion to pure pot-still whiskeys was still very evident until the mid-1960s, when the incorporation of blends started to become more common.

More recently, Irish whiskey has gained a connoisseur following with a "retro" taste for pure pot-still whiskeys, such as Redbreast and Green Spot. The Bushmills distillery produces only malt whiskey, but did not bottle a single malt until 1987. Since then, a single cask expression and versions either finished or wholly aged in unusual woods have begun to emerge.

In 1989, a new independent producer, Cooley distillery, reequipped a former distillery on the Cooley peninsula. It matures its whiskey at Locke's of Kilbeggan; has revived names like Tyrconnel; and has introduced a peated Irish whiskey, Connemara, which is possibly the most robust Irish whiskey in living memory.

NOSING AND TASTING
The differences between Irish whiskeys begin with the proportions of raw and malted barley.

Midleton

SOME SAY THE ART OF DISTILLATION CAME FROM MOORISH SPAIN BY SEA TO IRELAND. IF SO, IT WOULD HAVE ARRIVED IN THE SOUTH. CORK, THE CAPITAL OF IRELAND'S SOUTHERNMOST COUNTY, IS HISTORICALLY A CENTER OF BREWING AND DISTILLING.

What they call "the flavor of the Republic" resides in one small town. All pure pot-still Irish whiskey currently produced in the traditional manner is made in one extraordinary distillery in Midleton, County Cork, which also produces all the blends based on pure pot-still whiskey.

The town of Midleton is less than 15 miles (24 km) from Cork city. Near the church in Midleton, a short road leads to the original Midleton distillery, first opened in the 1820s. On the hill behind them is the current Midleton distillery, opened in 1975.

DISTILLERY DETAILS

MIDLETON FOUNDED: 1825.
OWNER: Irish Distillers Group.
METHOD: Pot and column stills.
CAPACITY: 5.3 million gallons.

WHISKEY STYLES

Some of Midleton's whiskeys have a southern flavor—for example, Hewitt's *(see p. 189)*, formerly made at the Watercourse distillery; the local Cork whiskey, Paddy; and the bar brand, Murphy's, named after the original owners. Two minor products have also emerged. One is Dunphy's, a blend with a high content of grain whiskey; another is Erin Go Bragh ("Ireland Forever"). This is something of an oddity: a single malt, matured mainly in bourbon barrels and bottled quite young, but given character and sweetness by a dash of older, sherry-aged malt. It is a rare creature sighted occasionally in Irish bars or specialty whiskey bars in the United States. A vintage-dated blend called Midleton Very Rare was added to the range when the new distillery opened. Early vintages contained some whiskey from the old distillery; that is all gone now, and all of the Very Rare is from the new distillery. At the beginning of the 21st century, the whiskeys included ranged from 12 to 25 years old. The emphasis is on first-fill bourbon casks. The aim is to produce a whiskey that is complex in aromas and flavors, but relaxed and approachable. It varies slightly from one vintage to the next, but tends to be elegantly sweet.

JAMESON RANGE

The label of Midleton Very Rare bears (in very small type) a reference to John Jameson and Son. Crested Ten is another whiskey that proclaims its own brand name, but is discreetly labeled as part of the Jameson range. Then there is Jameson itself, with other versions, such as the 1780 (12-year-old) Jameson Gold. The Jamesons, Power's, Redbreast, and Green Spot whiskeys are produced at Midleton, although historically all have their origins in Dublin. Even the Tullamore whiskeys are now made in Midleton.

The mergers that housed many of these products under one roof had already taken place before the present still-house was commissioned. It was therefore designed with an eye on flexibility. No other distillery produces so many styles of spirit.

VERSATILE DISTILLERY

Nowhere else in the world of whiskey is there such a stark contrast between old and new as at Midleton. On adjoining sites you can see a distillery so old that it once ground its grain with millstones (and still has them), and another so high-tech that it routinely produces a dozen spirits in one still-house. In fact, it could do far more. These 12 spirits are blended in different ways to produce more than 20 principal products.

The old distillery looks up at the new one, which stands at a respectful distance, screened by poplars, on the hillside behind. The new distillery is a steel-skin structure,

MIDLETON *was acquired by the Murphy family in the mid-1820s. This attractive site housed the original Midleton distillery. It is now the visitor center, bar, restaurant, and museum.*

THE BIG STILL *at Midleton is the world's largest still. Built in 1825, and retired from use with the old distillery, the mighty beast—a wash still—could accommodate 40,409 gallons (152,966 liters).*

which resembles a small power station or a missile silo. Inside, a row of four pot stills follows the line of the structure. Behind them, set against the wall, is a row of modernist spirit-safes. Opposite these, against the other wall, is a row of six column stills. These are large stills, capable of holding 19,800 gallons (75,000 liters) each.

It is not unknown for pot and column stills to live together on one site like this, but it is unusual, and nowhere else in the world is there cohabitation on this scale. No other whiskey distillery is so versatile.

THE POT STILLS

Given the company's emphasis on triple distillation, a configuration of three pot stills might better tell the story, at least visually. However, there are four pot stills, of which two act as wash stills for the first run. The other two (the feints still and the spirits still) are used for the second and third runs.

The first run turns wash into what are called low wines, at 22–50 vol. These low wines are then run through a second distillation in the feints still. They emerge as pot feints, at 50–78 vol. These pot feints, in turn, run through the third distillation, emerging as new spirit at 63–85 vol. Midleton is quite unconventional in that runs are collected at different strengths in order to produce spirits of different character. As might be expected, spirits at the upper end of the alcohol range are lighter in body and flavor. Those at the lower end are heavier in body and fuller in flavor. The differences are very evident in new spirit, but they evolve further during aging. Once aged, these Midleton whiskeys are used in most of the Irish blends. The blender's specifications refer to light, medium, and heavy versions of whiskey from Midleton. There are also intermediate variations.

The giant wash still in the old distillery might sneer at the more manageable size of the four pot stills in the new one, but they are still bigger than anything in Scotland. They are a broad-based onion shape, with a slight downward angle on the lyne arm. The wash stills carry a confusion of additional plumbing. First, there is a small chamber with no plates or tubes that spins the vapor to remove solids. This is called a cyclone. Next comes a very small rectifying column, with a reflux pipe linked back to the pot. Finally, a third chamber can again link back to the pot or to the column stills. A further refinement on the pot stills is a valve to vent aldehydes. All of this hardware can be used to fine-tune the flavor of the spirit.

The pot stills are occasionally used to produce pure malt whiskey, providing the blender with an alternative to Bushmills. More usually, the pot stills are charged with a wash made from a blend of raw and malted barley. This is the pot-still whiskey of Irish tradition. The two forms of barley meet in the mash tun. The company regards 40–50 percent malted barley as traditional, but as little as 20 percent is used in some products.

Midleton's light pot-still whiskey can be more assertive than it sounds. The body is light, but the flavors can be leafy, dry, spicy, and peppery. Heavier styles develop more of a cereal-grain character, an oiliness, and estery flavors from cedar to lemon, among others.

THE COLUMN STILLS

The grain whiskey distilled at Midleton is usually produced from corn, though

MIDLETON *was one of the first companies to stack casks upright on pallets, which is done in both the old and new warehouses. Three original warehouses at the old distillery are still in use.*

TASTING NOTES

AS WELL AS producing its own whiskeys, Midleton also continues to distill a range from the south.

HEWITT'S WHISKEY

NO AGE STATEMENT, 40 VOL.

A sociable, soothing whiskey, with an addictive dryness, found mainly on the west coast of Ireland.

Color Refractive gold.
Nose Floral, melony, slight earthiness.
Body Light, lively.
Palate Very lively. Sweet maltiness. Honeydew melons. Touch of vanilla, developing to a perfumy spiciness.
Finish Falls away somewhat, but saved by a grainy, nutty firmness.

DUNGOURNEY 1964

PURE POT-STILL, 40 VOL.

A single cask from the Old Midleton distillery. The cask was found in a warehouse in 1994.

Color Pale, shimmery gold.
Nose Light, flowery. Surprisingly fresh for its age.
Body Silky.
Palate Very flowery indeed.
Finish Drying. Thinnish. Woody. Shows its age here.

MURPHY'S

NO AGE STATEMENT, 40 VOL.

As a bar brand in the United States in the 1970s and 1980s, Murphy's was often used in Irish coffee. Perhaps it was given its malty emphasis to meld well with the coffee flavors. A relatively high malt content for its price. It is now available only in Ireland.

Color Warm gold.
Nose Lightly malty. Fudgy.
Body Smooth.
Palate Light butter and toffee.
Finish Peanut brittle. Crisp, refreshing.

PADDY

NO AGE STATEMENT, 40 VOL.

A classic Irish, although the blend includes a touch of malt whiskey from Bushmills. Not much vanilla or oak character; mainly second-fill bourbon barrels.

Color Lemon marmalade.
Nose Very linseedy and flowery.
Body Firm and oily.
Palate Smooth, perfumy.
Finish Mustardy and appetizing.

MIDLETON VERY RARE

40 VOL.

While the other whiskeys in the range all have a history elsewhere, this one was devised at the new distillery. It is also the product of the new wood policy. It is intended to be

MIDLETON VERY RARE

"the best of the new." This note is based on tastings of vintages since the year 2000.

Color Subtle, attractive, amber.
Nose Leather armchairs. Victorian kitchens. Spices. Ginger. Apricot.
Body Medium, smooth.
Palate Light, sweetish, delicate. Vanilla pods. Walnut bread. Walnut oil. Peach kernel. Fresh peaches.
Finish Toasty, cookie-like flavor and dryness.

unmalted barley and wheat are both used occasionally. A proportion of malted barley is also used, to contribute the necessary enzymes. This varies from 5 to 20 percent, depending on the rest of the grist.

The grain whiskey is also triple-distilled. Three different types of column stills are used. The first run is through a beer column. Confusingly, the distillate collected from this, at about 70 vol., is called high wines. The second run is through an extractive column, to remove fusel oils and other unwanted higher alcohols. In this process, water is introduced, and the alcohol level drops back to 20 vol. The final run is through a rectifying column, which produces spirit at 94.5 vol. The grain whiskey is matured at 63 vol., like the malt and pot-still whiskeys.

MATURATION

Sherry wood is an essential element in some regular products, notably versions of Jameson, and the company supervises the production in Spain of sherry casks made to its own particular specification of size and shape. In recent years, the company has been buying port pipes, madeira drums, and marsala casks with a view to future special bottlings. A small proportion of virgin oak is used in the casks of Jameson Gold.

The overwhelming majority of casks are former bourbon barrels, acquired in a complete restocking of cooperage that began in the late 1970s and early 1980s and was completed in the 1990s. Most of these barrels were acquired from the Wild Turkey or Heaven Hill distilleries. There are also some Tennessee whiskey barrels from Jack Daniel's. There are more than 25 warehouses, most with a capacity of over 30,000 casks.

HEWITT'S WHISKEY

Hewitt's is the one whiskey specifically associated with the city of Cork, and is available only in three or four southern counties. Hewitt was the name of one of the founders of Cork's defunct Watercourse distillery. The Midleton distillery still makes a malt specifically for this blend, with no peating but with some cedary oiliness. The blend also includes a malt whiskey from Bushmills and the house grain.

SILOS AT MIDLETON *store corn, the main ingredient in Midleton's triple-distilled grain whiskey.*

Tullamore and Kilbeggan

THESE NEIGHBORING TOWNS GIVE THEIR NAMES TO WHISKEYS FROM RIVAL COMPANIES. CONFUSINGLY, TULLAMORE'S ORIGINAL STILLS ARE NOW AT KILBEGGAN, AND THERE IS KILBEGGAN WHISKEY MATURING IN TULLAMORE.

Tullamore (the name derives from *Tulach Mhor*, meaning Big Hill) is in barley-growing country in the Midlands, and the town already had distilleries by 1790. Its whiskeys are well established in several European countries, most notably France, Germany, and Denmark.

The original distillery was founded in 1829. The company passed to the family of its general manager, Daniel E. Williams. His initials formed a useful acronym and the company's whiskey became known as Tullamore Dew. Its advertising slogan was "Give every man his Dew."

DISTILLERY DETAILS

TULLAMORE FOUNDED: 1829.
OWNER: The Daly Family.
METHOD: Now produced at Midleton.

KILBEGGAN FOUNDED: 1843.
OWNER: The Locke Family.
METHOD: Now produced at Cooley.

THE WHISKEYS

The original Tullamore Dew was triple-distilled, and was said to have been one of the lighter pot-still whiskeys. The pot-still character may also have been masked, though probably not hidden, by the sherry butts and port pipes used in maturation.

Tullamore Dew was a big name in the heyday of Irish whiskey, and the first to offer a change of style when it seemed appropriate. As a result of a visit to the US in 1947, D. E. Williams' grandson added a new product, Tullamore Dew Blended Whiskey. It had a relatively high proportion of pot-still whiskey (60 percent) but was the first blended Irish. However, it was not in time to give the distillery a reprieve. Within seven years, the distillery closed. Given that the grain whiskey for the blend had to be matured for at least three years, this was hardly time to establish a new product. There were, as well, other considerations: the company had an excess of stock; much of the equipment was old and in need of replacement; and the company had begun to have more success with a heathery, honeyish, whiskey liqueur—Irish Mist.

Stocks of whiskey lasted until 1963, at which point the brand name Tullamore Dew was sold to John Powers & Son. Three years later, Powers had merged with Jameson and the Cork Distillers Company. Less than a decade after that, the merged companies, under the name the Irish Distillers Company, were producing all their whiskeys, including Tullamore Dew, in Midleton, County Cork.

The town of Tullamore still had one product. The Williams family's liqueur, Irish Mist, continued to be produced in the town until the 1990s. It had been acquired by an old established distributor of drinks, Cantrell & Cochrane, who in turn were once jointly owned by Guinness and Allied-Domecq. A management buyout subsequently restored its independence, and Irish Mist is now blended at Clonmel. In 1994, Irish Distillers Company, which continues to produce the Tullamore Dew whiskeys, sold the rights to Cantrell & Cochrane. Thus the whiskey and the liqueur are reunited, though neither is produced in the town.

LOCKE'S KILBEGGAN DISTILLERY

It can be quite a shock coming around a bend on the road from Dublin to Galway and seeing the force with which the waters of the

Locke's Kilbeggan *distillery has the power to surprise. It is one of Ireland's ghost distilleries, but it can hardly be described as silent. That clanking, roaring, and screaming… is the spirit walking?*

TASTING NOTES

WITH A NAME that sounds in French like a pledge of love, "*tout l'amour,*" Tullamore does well in France, one of the world's best markets for whiskey. A distillery may die, but love for its products is eternal.

TULLAMORE DEW

TULLAMORE

TULLAMORE DEW

NO AGE STATEMENT, 40 VOL.

A very light-bodied, easily drinkable blend, with just a touch of Irish pot-still oiliness. Linseedy.

Color Pale gold, white wine.

Nose Meadow flowers. Grass. Sweet.

Body Light but smooth.

Palate Grainy. Linseedy. A hint of seed cake. Light syrup.

Finish Lemon grass. Drying. Gently appetizing.

A 12-year-old Tullamore Dew is slightly fuller in color, body, and flavor, with suggestions of vanilla, peanut brittle, and dates. A 2000 bottling to celebrate the opening of a Heritage Center was even spicier, with hints of nutmeg and ginger.

KILBEGGAN

KILBEGGAN IRISH WHISKEY

NO AGE STATEMENT, 40 VOL.

A blended whiskey for everyday drinking. Bestseller in the entire range of whiskeys distilled at Cooley (see pp. 194–5). *Flavors are restrained, and beautifully dovetailed.*

Color Pale gold.

Nose Lemon grass. Lime.

Body Light but firm.

Palate Firm, smooth, sweetish; very toasty, malt character. Satisfying flavors.

Finish Nice balancing, with a leafy dryness.

KILBEGGAN IRISH WHISKEY

LOCKE'S

NO AGE STATEMENT, 40 VOL.

A maltier, and slightly more mature, blend. The malt whiskey component includes a tiny touch of peat. Estery and expressive flavors.

Color Old gold.

Nose Grassy. Lemon grass. Lemons.

Body Smooth, oily.

Palate Spearmint. Becoming sweet. Mint toffee.

Finish Minty, fruity, estery.

Brusna hurl the water wheel at Kilbeggan. Despite this assault, John Locke's building stands defiant, as it has done since 1757. At that time, there were several local distillers, working on a very small scale, in the area. The peaty water, rising from limestone, was one attraction, argues Andrew Bielenberg in *Locke's Distillery: A History*. Another was the plentiful corn grown in the area. According to Bielenberg, small whiskey-makers in this period would employ a single still, but run each batch through it three times.

The distillery was leased by the Locke family in 1843, and later purchased. John Locke married into the Smithwick brewing family of Kilkenny, and later used their yeast at Kilbeggan. The distillery was developed considerably between the 1860s and the 1880s, and much of the equipment dates from that period.

Distilling stopped in 1953, during the time when all Irish whiskeys were experiencing difficulties. The stills were sold for scrap, but three sets of millstones survive, as well as four wooden washbacks and other pieces of machinery. Kilbeggan became one of Ireland's several ghost distilleries. Around the country, there are vestiges of 20 or more. Some are recognizable distillery buildings, abandoned, overgrown, or converted to incongruous purpose. Kilbeggan refuses to go gently. This ghost of a distillery is still restless, and inside, the power of the wheel—the roaring and clanking noises, the creaking of the building's timbers, the screams of pulleys when they are engaged, the clatter of cogs—cannot be escaped. There has been considerable investment in its restoration, and in the yard are the three stills that once produced Tullamore Dew. They were acquired by entrepreneur John Teeling, the driving force behind Cooley and Kilbeggan, with a view to their one day working again, at Kilbeggan. That hope is still cherished.

Meanwhile, the Cooley distillery (*see p. 194*) sends its spirit—malt and grain—to Kilbeggan for maturation. There are four damp stone warehouses, one of which still has a dirt floor. All the warehousing is full. "It's spirit when it comes to us," says Kilbeggan's manager, Brian Quinn, reminding visitors (of whom there are nearly 40,000 a year) of the regulations concerning age. "After three years here, it is whiskey. That is what we do here. We make whiskey."

MIDLANDS' MIDDAY: *Morrissey's of Abbeyleix is a delightful example of a pub that also serves as a liquor store and grocery store. Some packaged foods from the 1950s are on display.*

DUBLIN

ONCE THE HOME TO SUCH GREAT NAMES AS JOHN POWERS & SON AND JAMESON, DUBLIN NO LONGER HAS ANY DISTILLERIES, AND THE OLD POWERS DISTILLERY IS NOW THE NATIONAL COLLEGE OF ART AND DESIGN.

DISTILLERY DETAILS

POWERS FOUNDED: 1791.
OWNER: Irish Distillers Group.
METHOD: Now distilled at Midleton.

JAMESON FOUNDED: 1780.
OWNER: Irish Distillers Group.
METHOD: Now distilled at Midleton.

One of the most memorable aromas of Dublin is the sweet smell of success: malt being kilned or infused at the Guinness brewery, on the south bank of the river Liffey, in an area known as The Liberties.

Where cities grew on one side of a river, industries like the milling of grain, malting, brewing, distilling, and tanning were often banished to the opposite bank. Perhaps the city government did not control that side of the river. If the area was free to make beer and whiskey as it wished, it probably also had taverns and unbridled entertainments. The Liberties was the name for such a quarter in the English-speaking world. The Dublin Liberties once accommodated the Powers distillery, producer of the biggest-selling whiskey in Ireland. The distillery looked across the river at its rival, Jameson, which was always more oriented toward exporting.

James Power founded his distillery in 1791, and it flourished under his son, John, who was knighted despite being a friend of the Irish patriot Daniel O'Connell. Its great local rival was founded in 1780 by John Jameson, a Presbyterian from the brewing town of Alloa in Scotland. The Jameson family had connections with the Haigs and the Steins—it was a Scottish-Irish distilling dynasty. One of the most successful Jamesons was a unionist who subsequently served in the Senate of the Free State. Today, the scale of the former distillery buildings recalls the industry at the height of the Victorian era, when all 32 counties were part of the United Kingdom. In the 1880s, the Jameson distillery covered five acres (two hectares), and made 1.2 million gallons (4.5 million liters) of spirit per year. Jameson is now the biggest-selling Irish whiskey worldwide, and is growing. The names of Powers and Jameson still appear on labels, though the whiskeys are now both distilled in Midleton, County Cork, and both are distinctive in character.

POWERS

The Irish favorite, Powers Gold Label, highlights the character of the distillate, rather than the wood. It has been a blend since the 1960s, but retains a notable pot-still accent. About three-quarters of the blend is pot-still whiskey, albeit of the medium rather than the heavy style. Gold has no age statement. There has been the occasional 12-year-old special.

JAMESON

The Jameson whiskeys appear as a range. They are accented toward pot-still whiskey, again of medium intensity, but with 50:50 being a more typical ratio. An especially significant Jameson characteristic is the interplay between spirit and wood. This is emphasized throughout the range. First-fill bourbon is very influential, and a certain amount of sherry wood is used. Jameson Gold employs some virgin oak.

REDBREAST

Until a very late stage—the 1960s—Jameson sold all of its whiskey in the cask to bonded warehouse companies or independent bottlers. The distillery made a whiskey called Redbreast for the Irish branch of the wine and spirits company Gilbey's. Perhaps due to benign neglect, Redbreast remained an "old-fashioned" pure pot-still whiskey. When Gilbey's was lost in a sequence of takeovers, the Irish Distillers Group acquired Redbreast

DUBLIN'S TEMPLE BAR *pub is an oasis for many of the tourists who throng the city's Cultural Quarter. An impressive choice of whiskeys is available.*

TASTING NOTES

THESE WHISKEYS all originally came from Dublin, but most are now made in Midleton as copies of the original styles.

POWERS GOLD LABEL
NO AGE STATEMENT, 40 VOL.

Color Gold with a tinge of orange.
Nose Pronounced pot-still esters. A hint of peppermint.
Body Oily.
Palate Dances lightly on to the tongue and off again. The middle palate is brief but big and tasty. Nutty, cereal grains. Some underlying malty sweetness.
Finish Toast and honey, but also herbal. Bittersweet.

JAMESON IRISH WHISKEY
40 VOL.

Color Pale gold.
Nose Aromatic. Waxy orange skins. Linseed oil. Leather.
Body Light, but smooth.
Palate Creamy, smooth, sociable.
Finish Delicate. Peppery. Addictive.

JAMESON IRISH WHISKEY

JAMESON RESERVE
12-YEAR-OLD, 40 VOL.
(Dublin)
There are two excellent versions of Jameson, one available at the old distillery in Dublin, and the other in Midleton. This one has suggestions of older whiskeys and some cellar character.

Color Bronze.
Nose Cedary. Fresh sweat. Sensuous.
Body Medium to full.
Palate Firm. Full flavors. Fruity. Apricot-like.
Finish Spicy. Slight sulfur.

JAMESON RESERVE
12-YEAR-OLD, 40 VOL.
(Midleton)
Sold at the Midleton distillery gift shop. A more elegant expression, with some sherry.

JAMESON RESERVE

Color Warm bronze.
Nose Sweet, oily, aromatic.
Body Medium to full.
Palate Very creamy taste. Cream toffee. More nuttiness. Like freshly ground almonds.
Finish Nutty. Slightly toasty.

REDBREAST
12-YEAR-OLD, 40 VOL.
Delicious, soothing, contemplative. A great whiskey.

Color Bright bronze.
Nose Clean, fresh. Hint of linseed. Nuts. Cake.
Body Expansive.
Palate By far the biggest of this selection. Assertive and complex, with lots of development and seemingly infinite dimension. Ginger cake. Brazil nuts. Molasses.
Finish Licorice-like sherry notes.

GREEN SPOT
NO AGE STATEMENT, 40 VOL.

Color Pale, shiny gold.
Nose Astonishingly lively aromas. Fresh hay. Sappy wood. Oil. Peppermint.
Body Lightly teasing.
Palate Firm, developing spicy, minty, characters. Dry. Assertive.
Finish Long. Leafy. Rooty. Medicinal. Warming.

GREEN SPOT

and relaunched it as a 12-year-old. This is traditional Irish pot-still whiskey at its richest: well matured and with a generous slug of sherry. For some lovers of the style, Redbreast approaches perfection.

GREEN SPOT

For those who prefer a younger pot-still whiskey that flaunts its muscle, look to Green Spot. This whiskey survives from a range produced for the Dublin wine and spirits merchant Mitchell & Son. There was once a variety of ages, each coded on the label with a spot of a different color. Now, only Green Spot remains; a vatting of whiskeys from seven to 12 years old. For decades, it made a living as a staple of country clubs, but Green Spot was rescued from obscurity by whiskey writer Jim Murray. Soon, people were traveling from North America and the far corners of Europe and Asia to buy the whiskey. The Georgian shop of Mitchell & Son is on Kildare Street, just around the corner from the Shelbourne Hotel, favored by politicians, writers, and rock stars. The shop premises have been there since 1776; Mitchell's has occupied it since 1880, but not until the late 1990s did anyone kiss the carpet as a preliminary to buying a Green Spot.

THIS ELEGANT GEORGIAN BUILDING *is the home of Mitchell & Son, destination for the whiskey pilgrim in search of his bottle of Green Spot.*

COOLEY

THE MOUNTAINS OF MOURNE, IN NORTHERN IRELAND, LOOK ACROSS AT CARLINGFORD LOUGH, WHICH FORMS PART OF THE BORDER. ON THE OTHER SIDE, IN THE REPUBLIC, IS THE COOLEY PENINSULA.

Cooley distillery is masked by a thicket of spruce trees and high iron gates—a traveler chancing upon it, and unaware of its good work, might easily believe it to be some sinister installation. Any wariness felt on approaching might be heightened by the presence of a bull in an adjoining field. This is the distillery mascot; the beast is intended as a successor to the Brown Bull of Cooley, over which a bloody battle was fought with the Queen of Connaught long ago. More recent wars helped shape the distillery itself. The buildings are softened by a coat of green paint, but they are in an industrial style, with steel-framed windows that speak of the period interrupted by World War II.

DISTILLERY DETAILS

COOLEY FOUNDED: 1987.
OWNER: Cooley Distillery PLC.
METHOD: Pot and column stills.
CAPACITY: 859,000 gallons.

THE COOLEY MOUNTAINS *are the source of the distillery's soft water, which is piped from a reservoir.*

A BRAVE NEW ENTERPRISE

While studying for a doctorate at Harvard in the early 1970s, John Teeling had made an analysis of the state of the whiskey industry in his native Ireland, and decided there was a niche he could exploit. His opportunity finally came when he and his business partners were able to acquire the Cooley distillery in 1987, but it needed adapting. The distillery had originally produced alcohol as a fuel to supplement gasoline, using potatoes as the raw material, and later had made alcohol for, among others, Smirnoff Vodka.

The Cooley mountains can be seen from the distillery, which is built around a series of metal platforms and stairs, linked by walkways. The rectifying column that made Smirnoff is still used, but a wash column has been added, along with a pair of pot stills previously used at the Old Comber distillery in Belfast and the Ben Nevis distillery in Scotland.

THE REVIVALS

Cooley has thus far not produced a pure pot-still whiskey in the Irish sense of mixing raw and malted barley. Its pot stills are used to produce malt whiskey, and its column stills to make grain whiskey. Teeling has explained that, faced with the challenge of a monopoly, in the form of the Irish Distillers Company, he wanted to take as few chances as possible. He opted for the simplest distillation system, and bought stills that had been proven to work well; doing so was also less costly.

In its previous incarnations, Cooley did not require capacity for maturation. Partly as a solution for this, Cooley bought Locke's Kilbeggan distillery *(see pp. 190–1)* and now uses the distillery's 200-year-old stone warehouses for that purpose. Since Cooley distillery is not especially attractive as a showpiece, Kilbeggan fulfills that role, too.

The Cooley name was unknown in Irish whiskey, but buying Locke's at Kilbeggan provided an instant heritage; both names have been used for Cooley whiskeys, two of several revived by the firm. Another is Millar's, a blend that until 1988 was offered by Millar's bonded warehouse in Dublin. A further, vigorous ghost is the single malt, Old Tyrconnell, originally made by the distillery in the city and county known to republicans as Derry and to unionists as Londonderry. This also revives the name of an ancient kingdom and a previous owner's celebrated racehorse of the 1870s, depicted on the label.

THE NEW NAMES

As Cooley has gained a more confident foothold, the company has begun to create its own brand names. The most distinctive of these newer products is Connemara, launched in 1995–6. It is not the first peated Irish whiskey, but certainly the first revivalist one. Connemara is named after the rugged region of western Galway—distiller David Hynes went peat-cutting there in his youth. Malt from both Ireland and Scotland has been used. The peating level is modest, at 15 parts per million, but the nose and palate of the whiskey suggest more.

Another of Ireland's rugged corners, Inishowen in Donegal, gives its name to a blend that also has a touch of peat, albeit a far gentler one. Despite its Irish name, this whiskey is intended to be in a more Scottish style. Although Donegal is a western county, and in the Republic, it leans north, as though reaching for Scotland.

The shading of characteristics in a blend is not easy, even in the case of well-established whiskeys. Making blends from just one malt distillery and one grain is much more difficult. And there is a further challenge at Cooley: it is a new distillery. Yet despite the fact that it has not yet built up a stock of mature whiskey, Cooley has used skilful vatting and blending to produce whiskey of roundness and complexity.

BULL-HEADED *determination brought the independent whiskey distillery at Cooley into being; the distillery mascot is a reminder of this.*

This house character is evident over an ever-increasing range, including products for marketing companies and retailers. These include a sweetly spicy single malt to augment the range offered by another drinks company of Irish origin (albeit several centuries ago)—the Cognac house of Hennessy. In another helping hand across the sea, Cooley supplies "The Smooth Sweeter One" in a range of styles marketed by the Easy Drinking Whisky Company of Scotland. Inexhaustibly, Cooley also produces a malt, a blend, and a Tennessee taste-alike; these are packaged in three interlocking flasks. The new company's brand name is Clontarf, in honor of the famous battle. Their product's novelty does not detract from the enjoyable flavors of the whiskeys.

TASTING NOTES

THIS NEW DISTILLERY'S range embraces a single grain whiskey (which includes a version at 59.6 vol.) and an intense smoky one.

CASK STRENGTH CONNEMARA

CONNEMARA PEATED SINGLE MALT

NO AGE STATEMENT, 40 VOL.

Made entirely with peated malt.

Color Full gold with a greenish tinge.

Nose Pungent. Smoky, rather than peaty. Aromas and flavors are young and fresh.

Body Light to medium. Firm.

Palate Mouth-filling. Sweet grass. Roasted nuts. Earthy. Some phenol.

Finish Dry. Toasty. Sesame oil. Spicy.

GREENORE

8-YEAR-OLD, 40 VOL.

A single-grain whiskey. The whiskey itself is very light in flavor, leaving the wood to do the talking. Bourbon casks are used, and their vanilla character is quite assertive.

Color Soft gold.

Nose Sweetly appetizing. Toasty, lemony.

Body Light, smooth.

Palate Clean, sweet. Vanilla. Some resiny, lemon peel notes. Honey.

Finish Firm, dryish.

INISHOWEN

NO AGE STATEMENT 40 VOL.

A blended whiskey that gives the impression of having a touch of peated malt. Intended to have a Scottish accent. Quite full in flavor and very well balanced.

INISHOWEN

Color Pale and bright gold.

Nose Light, perfumy, smokiness. Linseedy, cereal-grain.

Body Oily.

Palate Firm, smooth, sweetish. Touch of peaty rootiness.

Finish Faint balance of orange peel dryness.

TYRCONNELL SINGLE MALT

NO AGE STATEMENT, 40 VOL.

This whiskey has developed considerably since its Cooley launch. First-fill bourbon and recharred barrels are both important influences.

Color Gold with a tinge of lime green.

Nose Fruity. Lime skins. Very scented.

Body Grainy, oily.

Palate Grainy. Vanilla pods. Creamy. Oily. Slightly smoky, like roasted peppers.

Finish Crisp. Herbal. Vine leaves. Parsley. Mint.

TYRCONNELL SINGLE MALT

BUSHMILLS

ONE OF THE BEST-KNOWN NAMES IN IRISH WHISKEY IS FOUND NORTH OF THE BORDER, NORTH OF BELFAST, IN THE NORTHEASTERN TOWN OF BUSHMILLS IN COUNTY ANTRIM, A STONE'S THROW FROM THE GIANT'S CAUSEWAY.

It's Irish, and triple-distilled in pot stills. So why isn't Bushmills an Irish pot-still whiskey? Because it's an Irish malt whiskey. Here, in the northeastern corner of Ireland, beyond the university city of Coleraine, is what might be the oldest known distillery.

The northeast of Ireland has the boldest Gaelic legends, and the strongest associations with St. Patrick and St. Columba, and this is especially true of County Antrim. It is also, significantly, the county geographically and culturally closest to Scotland. It is less than 2 miles (3 km), as the gull flies, to the sea, and, across the water, it is 25 miles (40 km) to Scotland. The nearest points are synonymous with Scottish whiskey: the island of Islay and the peninsula of Kintyre.

If you had legs long enough, you could walk across the Giant's Causeway to the Scottish islands a little farther north: to Staffa and Fingal's Cave; to Iona where an abbey was founded by St. Columba; and to Mull, which still has a distillery. Fingal was a giant—also known as Finn the Gael and Finn MacCool—and romantics say that he built the causeway so that he could visit a lady giant in Scotland. Some believe he took the recipe for whiskey with him. There is indeed an astonishingly human-made appearance to the Giant's Causeway. Yet its smooth surfaces were, in reality, given their gleaming polish by the sea, and what look like tall, dark, molded bricks are actually basalt columns.

DISTILLERY DETAILS

OLD BUSHMILLS
FOUNDED: 1608. OWNER: Irish Distillers Group.
METHOD: Pot stills.
CAPACITY: 793,000 gallons.

The distillery at Bushmills is named after the town, and itself has the appearance of a tiny, smartly whitewashed village or hamlet, leaning into a slope just above the town and to the east. More than 120 people are employed there year-round, and this number can swell to 150 in the summer.

Bushmills was once dedicated to the Irish style of pot-still whiskey, but has for more than a century now specialized in malt whiskey made by triple distillation. For decades, this malt whiskey remained a secret, and was used in Irish blends, famously one called simply Bushmills Malt, and a maltier big brother labeled Black Bush. However, in recent years, the secret has been exposed with the bottling of several single malts.

In this far northeastern region of Ireland, the colors of town and country seem less rich and dense, more cautious. Presbyterian churches are more in evidence, as are church halls. Alongside whiskey production, the traditional industries in Antrim are tourism, linen, and farming. The farmers' fields are larger, shared with fewer siblings, and the countryside open and undulating as a result.

STAIRWAY TO THE SEA. *Follow the stepping stones to Staffa, and enjoy a giant-sized whiskey in Fingal's Cave.*

ANCIENT DISTILLERY

A stream known as St. Columb's Rill flows for 10 miles (16 km) over basalt rock and peaty land before filling the distillery's dam, and then joins the river Bush shortly before it passes through the town and reaches the sea. "Rill" is an old word for a rivulet, and is a term still used by geographers and water engineers to identify a particular shape of watercourse formed by erosion.

The word may be of Gaelic, French, or Germanic origin: etymologists agree only on the Indo-European root *rei*. In the French Alps, a mountain stream identified as Ruis de St. Bruno flows through the site of the monastery that produces the liqueur Chartreuse. "Ruis" relates to our word "rush." The river Bush itself is not much more than

HOLY WATER? *St. Columb's Rill flows into the distillery's dam (opposite), then joins the river Bush in search of the sea.*

a creek, but good, clean, fast-flowing water was valued even 1,000 years ago. A Gaelic saga of about AD 1100 describes the river as one of the "king waters" of Ireland.

Other historical references were in the past appropriated by Bushmills to support its claims to great antiquity. These included a reference to aqua vitae (water of life) in the 1400s, and the granting of a license to distill in Antrim in 1608. The licensee does indeed seem to have been in the right part of Antrim, but the link with Bushmills is far from clear.

There were certainly watermills by the river Bush in the early 1600s, and some watermills existed here relatively recently; and at least one of today's buildings in the town formerly accommodated a mill. There is also evidence of illicit whiskey-making on the Bushmills site since about 1743. The distillery was formally registered in 1784. So, on that basis, it is the oldest working distillery in Ireland, if not, as some claim, the oldest whiskey distillery in the world.

CASKS *are stored vertically (background) at Bushmills. The more common horizontal posture is assumed when they are dumped (emptied). The names of the sizes, from left, are: hogshead, butt, barrel.*

DRAMATIC HISTORY

Almost every distillery has in its history a fire, for whiskey is a highly flammable product, and there are endless dramatic stories of exploding barrels and of blazing whiskey flowing down the millrace. Bushmills' fire occurred in 1885, and it was in the subsequent rebuilding that the Scottish influence on the distillery became more pronounced. It may also have been at this time that Bushmills switched to malt distillation.

The former maltings, in Tyrone red brick, predate the fire, while the pagodas affecting the classic design of Scottish architect Charles Chree Doig were added much later. Barley of the Irish variety Fractal is used, as well as the more widespread Optic variety, grown in Tipperary and Carlow, and malted in Cork and Kildare.

During maintenance in 2001, a stained glass window was uncovered and restored in the mash house, a small building with open, metal beams. Here, a red-painted, cast iron mash tun, with brass trim and a copper hood, accommodates 9.3 tons of malt. A three-water system is used. Each water is 11,360 gallons (43,000 liters), with the third becoming the first of the next run. The last wooden washbacks were retired in 1994, and replaced with stainless steel. Only one yeast is used, the former DCL "M" strain.

TRIPLE DISTILLATION

Although Bushmills makes a point of triple distillation, this is not clear from the layout of the crowded still-house. There are four wash stills down one side of the room, and five spirit stills down the other, with receiving vessels in the middle. Linking walkways and platforms are painted in red oxide. Both types of stills are tall and elegant, but the spirit stills are slightly slimmer and higher, producing a great amount of reflux.

The wash stills are heated by calandrias (external heaters), and the spirit stills by steam pans. Of the five spirit stills, three are used for the second run, and two for the third. From an original gravity of 1,060, the fermented wash has reached 8.5 vol. when it enters the first (wash) still. There, its strength is increased to 20–22 vol., at which point it is known as low wines. All the low wines are sent on to the second still.

The products of the second still are deemed either weak feints, at 30–32 vol., or strong feints, at around 70 vol. The weak feints are run into a receiver, or holding tank. If the distiller were a cook, he might say that

A touch of tradition *in the mash tun, with rotating forks instead of knives.*

these had been "set aside"—prepared ingredients waiting to be reincorporated in the dish at the right time. They are, in fact, added to the subsequent batch of low wines and given a second run through this still.

Meanwhile, the strong feints have gone on to the third still, which produces weak feints at 32 vol., strong feints at 70 vol., and new spirits at 83 vol. Once again, the weak feints are set aside and reincorporated in a further run in the third still.

LOCAL RIVAL

The Bushmills distillery has eight warehouses, containing 22,000 barrels each, racked 12 high. All the spirit is triple-distilled, exclusively from malt. For many years, Bushmills had a local rival in malt whiskey, also triple-distilled, from Coleraine, a distillery that had begun life as a mill and been converted to a distillery in 1820. In the 1930s, the two distilleries had the same owner; in 1964, Coleraine stopped distilling malt, but continued to produce grain whiskey in a Coffey still. This was used in the Bushmills blends. There was an occasional bottling of the 34-year-old, at cask strength (57.1 vol.) still available at the beginning of the 21st century. A whiskey with a big, assertive, oily, and complex palate, it still had that Irish leather-linseed note, despite its being all malt. Production of grain whiskey at Coleraine distillery finally ceased in 1978 with the opening of the new Midleton distillery. By the mid-1980s, there was no Coleraine whiskey in the Bushmills blends. However, today, a small amount of a standard 40-vol. whiskey is still produced by Bushmills and labeled as Coleraine. It is a pleasant blend, for everyday drinking, with a fruity, honeydew melon flavor.

THE WHISKEYS

There is no Irish-style pot-still whiskey in the Bushmills' blends; they nonetheless do not quite taste "Scottish." They are unusual, although not unique, in being blends of whiskeys from only two distilleries. Such a duopoly is not exclusive to Ireland, although these two distilleries are deeply rooted, north and south, in their native island.

In general, Irish grain whiskeys are on the light-bodied side. They are also less malty than some of their Scots counterparts, but are arguably more floral and fragrant. The idea is that they should harmonize with the gentler character of modern Irish pot-still whiskeys, especially those used in blending.

THE BLENDS

The Bushmills Irish Whiskey blend comprises 35–40 percent malt whiskey, all of which comes from its own distillery. This component is mainly six to seven years old. The remainder of the blend is composed of just one grain whiskey, from Midleton distillery. Of the several grain whiskeys produced there, this is a lighter example, with an emphasis on floral, fragrant notes. The grain whiskey is aged for four or five years, mainly in bourbon casks from Wild Turkey. The wood imparts some excellent vanilla notes and some toastiness.

Black Bush is very unusual, even as a deluxe blend, for its high proportion of malt—80 percent at eight or nine years. Again, this is all from Bushmills distillery. This time, there are two grain whiskeys, both a little sweeter than average, and one has a touch of malty, butterscotch character. The intention is that the sweetness and butterscotch will help the grain stand up to the somewhat hefty 80 percent of well-matured malt.

Such an uncommon, malty blend deserves the devoted following that it has. Over the years, Black Bush has inspired many myths and legends, especially in the days when drinks companies were more secretive about the properties of their products. As its malty magic became better understood, whiskey-lovers began to wish for a single malt, and their prayers were answered when one finally appeared in the form of Bushmills 10-year-old.

Pretty but restrained. *Shops and bars are a shade less colorful in the most Protestant county.*

THE OLD MALTINGS *afford the most Scottish-looking view of Bushmills.*

THE SINGLE MALTS

Perhaps the long wait had heightened expectations, but this Bushmills Malt seemed to lack excitement. The distillery manager at the time explained later that the idea was to let the house character shine through, and not to be too elaborate with wood. It is an easily drinkable, gentle, well-balanced malt, perhaps with half an eye on the Irish market. Bushmills might have a conservative following in Ireland, but its supporters elsewhere in the world are more likely to see themselves as individualists, and for this reason the distillery needed to develop and export a single malt that was more robust.

AN ICON? *Stained glass trinity, from which the spirit ascends.*

Since it first put its toe into the water, Bushmills has made giant strides in its offering of single malts. These have included: in its core range, a 16-year-old matured in three woods (sherry, bourbon, and madeira casks); in some markets, an intensely sweet, heavily sherried, Cask Strength edition; a rich, expressive, madeira finish; and very flavorsome "single wood" versions (sherry and bourbon casks).

The rarest vintage of Bushmills is surely that laid down in 1975, in 350 first-fill Bourbon barrels, and bottled for the Millennium. The mature whiskey was rich and sweet, with notes of apple and citrus. Each cask sold for $5,000 and was bottled without vatting.

KNAPPOGUE CASTLE

Lending its name to a slight oddity in the Bushmills canon, Knappogue Castle is a tourist attraction near Shannon Airport, in County Clare, in the southwest of the Republic. In the 1930s, an American enthusiast bought the property and subsequently decided it should have its own whiskey; he gave the castle name to the bottlings. Its first vintage was a 1951 Tullamore pure pot still. More recent vintages have been single malts from Cooley and, latterly, Bushmills.

Even on a small island like Ireland, it seems incongruous that the label and the contents indicate opposite corners of the country. The current version is a rare opportunity to taste Bushmills entirely bourbon-aged, with no sherry contribution. As might be expected, it has a pronounced vanilla flavor—but there are also undertones of rose-water and a briarlike dryness. It is a delicate, elegant whiskey.

TASTING NOTES

UNTIL RECENTLY Bushmills concentrated on two principal products, but, overcome by the might of malt, it now has an ever-increasing range.

BUSHMILLS BLENDS

BLACK BUSH

NO AGE STATEMENT, 40 VOL.

Demonstrates how malt can sometimes be enhanced by a leavening of grain.

Color Very full gold.
Nose Fresh, oaky, vanilla, softened with sherry. Toffee nut crunch.
Body Rounded.
Palate Full of flavors. Fudgy, buttery, with that Bushmills rose-water character.
Finish A grainy, but addictive, dryness. Long and lingering.

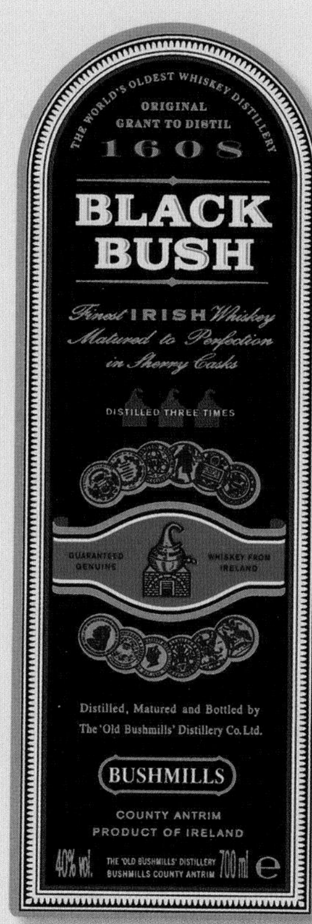

BLACK BUSH

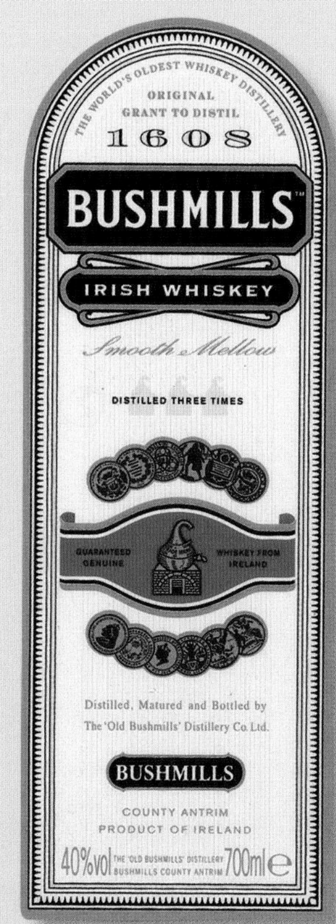

BUSHMILLS IRISH WHISKEY

BUSHMILLS IRISH WHISKEY

NO AGE STATEMENT, 40 VOL.

Well-balanced and easily drinkable, but with plenty of flavor.

Color Bright, pale gold.
Nose Fresh linen. Toast. Lemon.
Body Lightly syrupy.
Palate Lively, sweetish. Rose-water. Turkish delight. Marzipan.
Finish Becoming drier. Nutty. Pistachio nuts.

BUSHMILLS 1608 SPECIAL RESERVE

12-YEAR-OLD, 43 VOL.

A version with 90 percent malt whiskey, and a lighter-than-usual grain whiskey. Very rich and sweet, but still a Bushmills.

Color Bronze.
Nose Distinctly roselike. Sandalwood. Spicy.
Body Full-bodied, soft.
Palate Syrupy, sherryish. Nutty. Almondy.
Finish Hard licorice. Late rootiness.

BUSHMILLS SINGLE MALTS

BUSHMILLS DISTILLERY RESERVE

12-YEAR-OLD, 40 VOL.

More personality than the Bushmills Irish Whiskey at 10 years old. Drinkable and sociable.

Color Bronze.
Nose Warm. Toasted wood. Cedar.
Body Light but viscous.
Palate Toasted almonds. Fruity. Flowering currant. Good flavor development.
Finish Apricot-like, oily sweetness.

BUSHMILLS IRISH WHISKEY

16-YEAR-OLD RARE, MATURED IN THREE WOODS, 40 VOL.

A proportion of Bushmills malt matured in bourbon casks is married with a slightly smaller amount aged in oloroso sherry butts. Both are 16 years old. They are then recasked in port pipes for six to (more often) 12 months. The whiskey fights hard to make itself heard above the powerful wood. Gradually, the Bushmills flavors emerge, each time the glass is raised. Wonderfully complex.

Color Bronze.
Nose Suggestion of anise. Fragrant. Hint of smoke.
Body Soft, velvety.
Palate Mouth-filling, tongue-coating, soothing, soft. Marshmallow. Burnt toffee.
Finish Fruity again. Raspberries, prunes, raisins. Winey. Some balancing dryness.

BUSHMILLS 21-YEAR-OLD

MADEIRA FINISH, CASK STRENGTH, 51.4 VOL.

As the only distillery in Northern Ireland, with a long history, and distinctive styles of whiskey, Bushmills had no difficulty in achieving market visibility. There was a sustainable argument for concentrating on Bushmills and Black Bush and avoiding anything that might distract either producers or consumers. This whiskey is an example of how it is now branching out.

Color Full copper.
Nose A hint of mint. Pronounced madeira "toffee" character. Some winey acidity.
Body Irish cream.
Palate Hot buttered toast and apricot jam. Strawberry shortcake.
Finish Ginger snaps. Spicy dryness.

BUSHMILLS 21-YEAR-OLD

CANADA

The secret giant of American whiskeys comes from north of the border.
Is the giant asleep… or stirring?

A CHOICE OF WOOD
Canadian distilleries use new wood and bourbon, sherry, and brandy barrels. The whiskey must be aged for a minimum of three years, with premium Canadian whiskeys aged on average from six to eight years.

CANADA'S BLEND OF OLD AND NEW

STUART RAMSAY

Populated with a citizenry drawn from a rich range of nationalities, Canada embraces the history of many cultures, including those of the early French, Irish English, and Scottish inhabitants.

Ontario was probably the birthplace of whiskey distilling in Canada. Although not well documented, the industry seemed to begin at the end of the 1700s, in the area around Kingston, which is between Toronto and Ottawa, and on the route to Quebec. In *Canadian Whisky*, William Rannie notes there were 200 distilleries in the 1840s. Today, there are about ten companies and twelve producing distilleries. Of the distilleries that were operating 30 years ago, all of them except Canadian Mist (owned by Brown-Forman) are under new and mostly foreign ownership.

CANADA IS A LAND OF DIVERSITY, EMBRACING THE HISTORY OF MANY CULTURES

Canadian distillers developed a huge market across the US border, especially during Prohibition. For a time, the Canadian whiskey distiller Seagram was the world's biggest drinks company, owning some of Scotland's famous distilleries. Scottish blends were clearly an inspiration for Canadian whiskey. Canadians often point to this affinity of technique, but their whiskeys are lighter, sweeter, and fruitier than Scotch.

CANADIAN STYLE

The classic method is to blend rye, and perhaps other whiskeys, with a relatively neutral, base spirit. These are blended rye whiskeys, quite different from the traditional straight rye of the United States. The use of malted rye provides a smoothness and fullness of flavor. Most blends include more than one

HARVEST TIME
The heavier-bodied flavoring whiskeys that give character to Canadian whiskey (and make up around 10 to 20 percent of the blend) are typically produced from spicy, bittersweet rye grain.

rye whiskey, and for this purpose a single distillery may produce different ryes. Canadian distilleries also produce their own bourbon-type whiskeys, as well as corn whiskeys, and they even distill unmalted barley, all for use in blends.

EQUIPMENT AND TECHNIQUES

Although all Canadian whiskey is column-distilled, the distilleries are inclined to have very complicated still-houses. The level of aging of the various whiskeys for blending is also of importance. In the case of rye, aging tends to smooth out the whiskey, but also to make it heavier. Flavorings, such as sherry or other fruit wines, also add to the character of a particular whiskey, as can the wood used for maturation. Canada uses new wood and bourbon, sherry, and brandy barrels. As with Scotch, aging must be for a minimum of three years. Despite all these variables, the differences between the whiskeys are subtle, and they all display characteristics unique to Canada.

Canadian Club
CLASSIC
100 PROOF
RESERVE

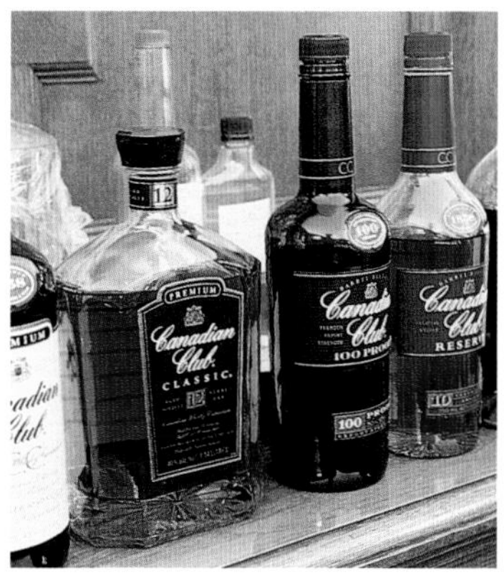

CANADIAN CLUB
A pioneer brand launched in 1884, Canadian Club is the biggest-selling Canadian whiskey in its homeland.

CANADA'S DISTILLERIES

THE OLDEST whiskey distilling companies in Ontario, and therefore Canada, had their roots in farming and grain milling in the mid-1800s. The western stills came later, taking advantage of the prolific prairies. In palate, the best Canadian whiskeys have at least some of the spicy, bittersweet character of rye, which is lightened with the blending spirit.

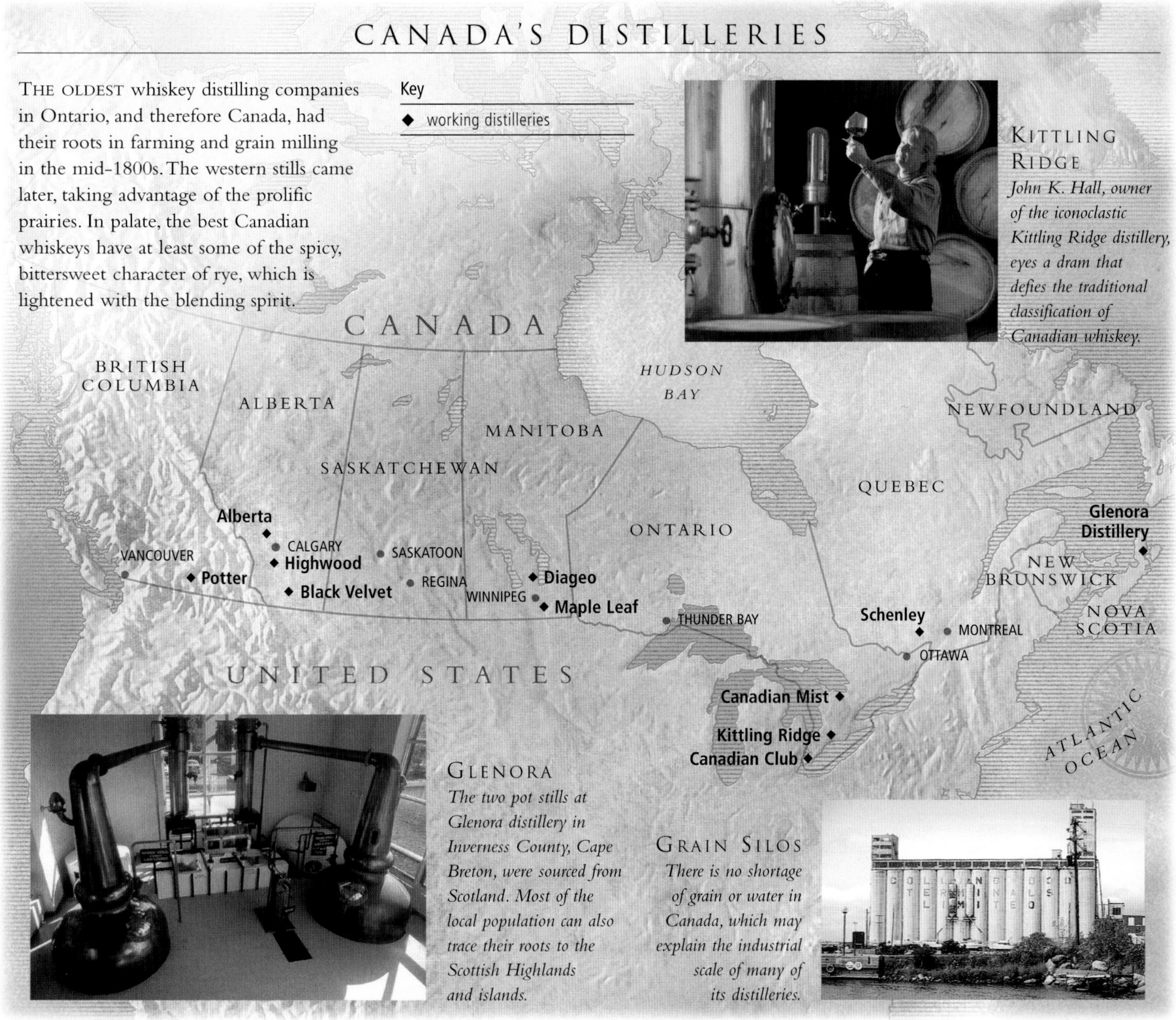
Key
◆ working distilleries
CANADA
BRITISH COLUMBIA
ALBERTA
SASKATCHEWAN
MANITOBA
HUDSON BAY
ONTARIO
QUEBEC
NEWFOUNDLAND
NEW BRUNSWICK
NOVA SCOTIA
UNITED STATES
ATLANTIC OCEAN
Alberta
CALGARY
Highwood
VANCOUVER
Potter
Black Velvet
SASKATOON
REGINA
WINNIPEG
Diageo
Maple Leaf
THUNDER BAY
Schenley
MONTREAL
OTTAWA
Glenora Distillery
Canadian Mist
Kittling Ridge
Canadian Club
COLLINGWOOD TERMINALS LIMITED

KITTLING RIDGE
John K. Hall, owner of the iconoclastic Kittling Ridge distillery, eyes a dram that defies the traditional classification of Canadian whiskey.

GLENORA
The two pot stills at Glenora distillery in Inverness County, Cape Breton, were sourced from Scotland. Most of the local population can also trace their roots to the Scottish Highlands and islands.

GRAIN SILOS
There is no shortage of grain or water in Canada, which may explain the industrial scale of many of its distilleries.

Nova Scotia

OF ALL THE LANDS SETTLED BY SCOTS, CANADA—AND NOVA SCOTIA IN PARTICULAR—DISPLAYS THE DEEPEST HERITAGE. A POT-STILL, SINGLE-MALT DISTILLERY IN CAPE BRETON HAS MADE ITSELF QUITE AT HOME.

On Cape Breton Island (named by Celts from France), in the province of Nova Scotia (Latin for "New Scotland"), a distillery just 16 years old is changing Canada's tradition of distillation. It is making malt whiskey, but in much the same way as the Scots do.

Of all the different Canadian landscapes, it is the mountain streams, icy rivers, peninsulas, and archipelagoes of Nova Scotia that fire the imagination of the drinker elsewhere in the world. Canada's beers, both the Pilsner and ale types, and its whiskeys, are known far beyond its borders, and especially by the inhabitants of its southern neighbor, the United States. Within Canada itself, the choice of drink and the circumstances in which it is purchased will vary depending upon the exact location. The real Canada is eclectic and highly multicultural, its people forming an ethnic jigsaw puzzle.

DISTILLERY DETAILS

GLENORA FOUNDED: 1989.
OWNER: Lauchie MacLean. METHOD: Pot stills.
CAPACITY: 66,000 gallons.

In the Maritime Provinces, dark rum is popular, no doubt a holdover from a tradition shared with neighboring New England. But it is the Scots, the Highlanders in particular, who have influenced Canadian spirit the most with their whiskey-making heritage, first introduced to Canada about two centuries ago.

TWIN WHISKEY PRODUCERS

Canada and Scotland have a lot of shared history. They also have similar issues of geography and identity, each sometimes feeling as though it has been subsumed by larger neighbors to the south. In each case, the northern country has a surprisingly large land area, a very small total population, and a mountainous landscape. The northern

THE ARCHITECTURE, *distilling equipment, people, and landscape of Glenora would fit easily into a Scottish West Highland glen.*

As in the islands of the Hebrides, *the sea is the lifeblood of Cape Breton.*

countries feel dismissed by their southern neighbors, although their identities have become stronger in recent years. But this has not inhibited Scotland from selling endless casks of whiskey to England. An early group of Scots, many displaced by the Highland Clearances, left their imprint on the geography of Canada, and in politics and culture. They also established distilleries, and ancestors of these Highland Gaels have come full circle in the most Gaelic of Canada's provinces.

GLENORA DISTILLERY

This young distillery in Glenville, Cape Breton, was the dream of Canadian businessman Bruce Jardine. He chose the site in Inverness County, for the same reason as so many Scottish single-malt distilleries have done, for the water source. MacLellan's Brook is a sparkling burn that flows over granite and is fed by 20 springs. Anecdotal reports of illicit stills in these Cape Breton Highlands helped point the way.

The copper stills are true pot stills from Scotland, a wash and a spirit still, with the capacity to produce 66,000 gallons (250,000 liters) a year, although they are running at a modest 13,000 gallons (50,000 liters) at present. Lightly peated barley from Scotland makes up the wash, although experiments are being carried out with more heavily peated barley. The new make spirit is aged in once-used bourbon barrels. Wood warehouses with earth floors are surrounded by orchards; in autumn, the aroma of fermenting apples mingles with the dank, deep alcohol of sleeping casks.

In the same area, there is a nine-room country inn that predates the distillery, a country garden, and an array of Highland chalets overlooking the glen where eagles soar. The Glenora pub hosts Highland ceilidhs with local fiddlers and entertainers from May to October. In the gift shop, Smuggler's Cove dark, white, and amber rums are sold alongside whiskey; both are produced by the distillery. Outdoor recreation, ranging from whale-watching to horse-riding, can be enjoyed. And in the local community, the lilt of Gaelic confirms the Highland heritage.

A NEW MALT

The whiskey launched in 2000 bears the proud descriptor Glen Breton Rare Canadian Single Malt Whisky. It is currently a nine-year-old, 46-vol. dram sold primarily in Nova Scotia and Ontario. At CAN$75 a bottle, the whiskey is promoted as rare and expensive; the owners release only 2000 cases a year.

At nine years, the whiskey has come into its own. Pale gold in color, earthy and sweet heather honey in the nose, this light- to medium-bodied dram has butterscotch and sweet caramel flavors with hints of toasted wood, almonds, and marzipan, finishing round with fruit and honey and a tickle of smoke.

The early years for any startup whiskey distillery are likely to be lean ones. So it was for Glenora. Bruce Jardine passed away, and the current owners took over in 1994. The president of the company is Lauchie MacLean, whose ancestors settled the area 200 years ago. They came across the wild seas from the Hebridean island of Barra. Their hearts are still Highland, and at last they have their spirit.

TASTING NOTES

After a somewhat rocky beginning in both taste and financial stability, the pot-still malt whiskey of Glenora has finally found its way.

GLENORA DISTILLERY

GLEN BRETON RARE
9-YEAR-OLD, 46 VOL.
100% barley malt. Pot-still single malt.

Color Pale gold.
Nose Heather honey sweetness, earthy tickle of smoke.
Body Light to medium.
Palate Sweet caramel, butterscotch, toasted oak, almonds, orange, and marzipan.
Finish Round, lingering sweetness, soft smoke, and honeysuckle sweetness.

QUEBEC

CANADIAN WHISKEY CAME OF AGE UNDER THE CANNY GUIDANCE OF THE QUEBEC-BASED BRONFMAN FAMILY. THEIR LA SALLE DISTILLERY IS NOW CLOSED AND THEIR WHISKEY DYNASTY OVER, LEAVING SCHENLEY TO FLY THE QUEBECOIS FLAG.

The story of Canadian whiskey must pay due homage to the Seagram and Bronfman distilling families, their spirits now dispersed to the highest bidders in the marketplace of conglomerate machinations. During the 1920s, Scotland's distilling giant Distillers Company Ltd. (DCL) acquired Seagram, of Waterloo, Ontario. The Seagram family were British immigrants. The first Canadian-born generation, brought up with a background of farming and innkeeping, moved into grain-milling and distilling, and eventually became Canada's biggest producers of rye whiskey, with brands like 83 and VO.

DISTILLERY DETAILS

SCHENLEY FOUNDED: 1945.
OWNER: Barton Brands, Inc. METHOD: Column stills.
CAPACITY: 6.3 million gallons.

SEAGRAM AND BRONFMAN

DCL not only acquired Seagram, but also accepted an invitation to be partners in a company being set up by another Canadian family, the Bronfmans. This family had been successful as liquor distributors in Canada during Prohibition in the United States, and had now established a distillery at La Salle, a suburb of Montreal. At the time, DCL's bosses felt they could progress better in the North American market by utilizing the experience of the Seagrams and Bronfmans, but as the shadow of Prohibition in the US lifted, they changed their minds and decided to go it alone. DCL's share of Seagram was sold to the Bronfman family—a fateful decision.

The Bronfmans, refugees from Czarist Russia, became a dynasty comparable with the Rothschilds. With them, Canadian whiskey came of age. It was Seagram, under the Bronfmans' control, that would prosper most in the US. Indeed, Seagram went on to become the biggest distillers not only in North America, but also worldwide, with substantial interests in Scotland.

The company's portfolio included Ronrico and Captain Morgan rums, Sir Robert Burnett and Boodles gins, Wolfschmidt vodka, and Leroux liqueurs. The Bronfman family also had extensive interests in oil and property. There were ironies in Seagram's success, however. Wishing to erase the memories of bootleg liquor, Sam Bronfman became obsessed with quality distilling, in particular the art of blending, which he saw as key to producing whiskeys that combined character, cleanness, and consistency. In a similar vein, he also preached moderation, with Seagram's buying advertising space to dissuade the consumer from excess.

THE SCHENLEY DISTILLERY *in Valleyfield dates from 1945. It produces Black Velvet and two brands solely for the Canadian market: Golden Wedding and OFC.*

SEAGRAM WHISKEYS

Seagram's Canadian whiskeys were, in general, well-rounded, with a touch of sweetness, usually delicate in palate, with a slightly oily body, and with a clean, faintly oaky, finish. No flavorings were used, and the master rye was sometimes blended with whiskey made from unmalted barley. A high proportion of charred new oak was used, although the whiskeys in any one blend were drawn from a complex matrix of different cooperages. The super-premium brand was Crown Royal, created to honor King George VI and Queen Elizabeth when they visited Canada in 1939. Then, in order of quality, came VO, followed by 83 (named after the date when Joseph Seagram became the sole proprietor of his Waterloo distillery), and Five Star, a bar brand sold only in Canada.

All these whiskeys are now owned and produced by Diageo at their Gimli plant in Manitoba. Seagram's Waterloo distillery in Ontario has been demolished and the La Salle distillery in Montreal is closed and likely to be disposed of. It currently serves as a bottling and office facility for Diageo. The Bronfman and Seagram dynasties, Canadian to their core, are over.

THE SCHENLEY DISTILLERY

Schenley is another proud name in Canadian whiskey with a heritage in Montreal and Quebec. Schenley's distillery was built in 1945 in Valleyfield, a city of about 35,000 Québecois, an hour's drive west of Montreal. Schenley Canada was sold in 1981 to a group of Canadian businessmen, then passed to the

THE FRENCH-SPEAKING *staff of Schenley jokingly refer to non-French Canada as ROC (Rest of Canada).*

TASTING NOTES

In addition to the ubiquitous Black Velvet, Schenley supplies Canada only with two quite decent 3-year-olds.

SCHENLEY OFC
3-YEAR-OLD, 40 VOL.

Available in Canada only. OFC stands for Original Fine Canadian.
Color Light gold.
Nose Soft, sweet toffee and caramel, notes of fruit and citrus.
Body Balanced, firm, medium-body.
Palate Sweet, lots of vanilla, background rye spice and toffee.
Finish Smooth, delicate vanilla and caramel.

SCHENLEY GOLDEN WEDDING
3-YEAR-OLD, 40 VOL.

Available in Canada only.
Color Medium gold.
Nose Rich, fruity, and sherry, pears, honey, spice, and vanilla.
Body Light to medium, smooth.
Palate Full fruit and vanilla, round with sherry notes.
Finish Sweet caramel, vanilla, and apples.

Guinness/United Distillers consortium in 1990. In 1999, it changed hands once more, to US-based Barton Brands.

Valleyfield today is home to the lightly sweet Black Velvet Canadian whiskey, destined for the markets of the eastern United States and Europe. Its sister distillery in Lethbridge, Alberta, makes Black Velvet for the west. The base whiskeys for Black Velvet are aged for a minimum of three years and the flavoring whiskeys for six years. Black Velvet Reserve, an 8-year-old Canadian, is also produced at the Valleyfield plant, as is the light, 3-year-old Golden Wedding, and the complex, well-balanced OFC, a 4-year-old dram.

The substantial column *stills at the Schenley distillery produce not only the company's Canadian whiskeys, but also vodka and rum for Diageo.*

ONTARIO

THE OLDEST WHISKEY-DISTILLING COMPANIES IN ONTARIO, AND THEREFORE IN CANADA, ARE THOSE THAT HAD THEIR ROOTS IN FARMING AND GRAIN-MILLING IN THE MID-19TH CENTURY.

One 19th-century mill distillery was the beginning of an entire chapter in the history of whiskey. In what is now a district of Windsor, a mill and distillery was founded in 1858 by Hiram Walker.

HIRAM WALKER

Walker's launch of Canadian Club in 1884 represented the beginning of a national style of whiskey. Because of his distinctive method of production, Canadian Club combined some of the full flavor and fruitiness of North American whiskeys with a much cleaner and lighter palate than was common at the time. These characteristics have been associated with Canadian whiskeys ever since.

Walker adopted a twofold approach. He used an unusually long and intense distillation process to produce a master whiskey that was as clean as possible. Then he blended this with neutral spirits. By the time Canadian Club was launched, there were growing cities to provide a market for such a product, including Detroit—just across the US border.

DISTILLERY DETAILS

HIRAM WALKER & SONS FOUNDED: 1858.
OWNER: Allied Domecq.
METHOD: Column and pot stills.
CAPACITY: 11.9 million gallons.

CANADIAN MIST FOUNDED: 1967.
OWNER: Brown-Forman. METHOD: Column stills.
CAPACITY: 4 million gallons.

KITTLING RIDGE FOUNDED: 1992.
OWNER: John K. Hall. METHOD: Pot stills.
CAPACITY: Not given.

Today, Canadian Club remains a classic name in whiskey. The flagship six-year-old has a dry, rye fruitiness and a crisp, faintly smoky finish, which might be regarded as the house style of Hiram Walker's Canadian whiskeys. The distillery produces a worthy portfolio of differently aged Canadian Club bottlings, including the full, creamy Classic 12-year-old, with a higher percentage of barley malt; the spicy Reserve 10-year-old, which has a higher rye distillate; and an exotically fruity Canadian Club Sherry Cask, which is eight years old.

Hiram Walker & Sons also produces and bottles the range of Corby whiskeys, their original home the old-fashioned distillery at Belleville on the Moira River, Ontario. Corby's two most important brands fall under the Wiser's label and are 40-vol., full-flavored whiskeys redolent with fruit and oak. Wiser's products are mostly aged for a little longer ("Wiser and Older" was the classic slogan). The De Luxe bottling has ten years' maturation, and Wiser's Very Old has 18 years and is a robust, oaky dram. Special

THE CANADIAN CLUB *brand dates back to 1884. Its crisp and fruity style has been adopted by many distilleries, and it has become a Canadian benchmark.*

Blend rounds out the Wiser's portfolio. Another seven, including Walker's Special Old, all fly under the Corby premium whiskey banner.

BROWN-FORMAN

Canadian Mist, a light, 40-vol., clean-tasting whiskey, is produced in the resort community of Collingwood, Ontario, about 90 miles (145 km) north of Toronto on Georgian Bay. A modern distillery, built in 1967 and owned by Brown-Forman of the US, it is one of the few Canadian distilleries that does not produce other spirits. It is a major bulk brand at three years old in the American market, and is exported to Kentucky in bulk to be bottled.

KITTLING RIDGE

The most revolutionary whiskey in Canada may well be Forty Creek, produced by the independent Kittling Ridge distillery in Grimsby. Owner John K. Hall has brought a handcrafted, wine-making sensibility to whiskey production and in doing so has broken the barriers of whiskey classification. Forty Creek is a delightful and well-crafted whiskey with international, timeless appeal.

Midway between Buffalo, New York, and Toronto, Grimsby is 40 miles (65 km) from Niagara Falls, as is Forty Mile Creek, which empties into Lake Ontario. Hall has been making and marketing wines for 33 years, and he treats the grain whiskeys that make up Forty Creek as he would a varietal wine, distilling and then aging each grain spirit in casks that are suited to each particular whiskey character.

The flagship Forty Creek is blended from a selection of 6- to 10-year-old rye, barley, and corn whiskeys, after they have aged individually. The blend is then finished for six months in a sherry cask, the sherry having been made by Hall himself. The end result is an ethereal whiskey with good body, a flavor of apricots and black walnuts from the rye, and a lingering, gentle finish.

FORTY MILE CREEK, *the home of the innovative Kittling Ridge distillery, empties into Lake Ontario.*

TASTING NOTES

ONTARIO'S whiskeys cover a broad spectrum of flavors, from fruity to ethereal.

CANADIAN CLUB

CANADIAN CLUB
6-YEAR-OLD,
40 VOL.

Color Bright gold.
Nose Fresh, soft. Sweet, nutty.
Body Light, smooth.
Palate Vanilla, caramel, pleasant oil, spicy oak, soft fruit.
Finish Dry, clean, with soft oak and spice.

CANADIAN CLUB

CANADIAN CLUB CLASSIC
12-YEAR-OLD, 40 VOL.

Color Deep gold.
Nose Full, creamy, toffee, vanilla.
Body Full, round.
Palate Pepper and allspice, balanced oak and vanilla, smooth and rich.
Finish Lingering, dry, vanilla, and spicy caramel.

CANADIAN CLUB CLASSIC

WISER'S

WISER'S DE LUXE
10-YEAR-OLD,
40 VOL.
Blended and bottled at Hiram Walker & Sons distillery, Walkerville, Ontario.

Color Deep amber.
Nose Soft, floral, fruity, and toffee caramel, spice notes.
Body Full, round, balanced.
Palate Butterscotch, rich, toasted oak.
Finish Warm, lingering, smooth, with sweet caramel notes, soft plum, and mild spice.

WISER'S VERY OLD
18-YEAR-OLD
40 VOL.
Blended and bottled at Hiram Walker & Sons distillery.

Color Deep amber.
Nose Dry, fresh, floral, soft fruit, and balanced oak.
Body Full, heavy.
Palate Rich, caramel and vanilla, apple and spice.
Finish Deep, lingering oak.

CANADIAN MIST

CANADIAN MIST
AGED THREE YEARS
40 VOL.

Color Deep gold.
Nose Fragrant soft fruit and spice, sweet, toffee and caramel. Notes of sherry and honey.
Body Light to medium, soft.
Palate Delicate sweetness, builds to toffee, hard edge.
Finish Soft sweet caramel.

KITTLING RIDGE

FORTY CREEK BARREL SELECT
40 VOL.
Pot-still Canadian distilled from rye, barley, and corn. Aged in a selection of charred oak and finished in sherry casks.

Color Amber gold.
Nose Fragrant, soft aromas of honeysuckle, vanilla, plums, with nuts, spice, and toasted oak.
Body Rich, round.
Palate Complex evolution of vanilla, honey sweetness, oranges, cocoa, walnuts, and spice. Notes of leather and marzipan.
Finish Smooth, lingering fruit, vanilla, and pecans.

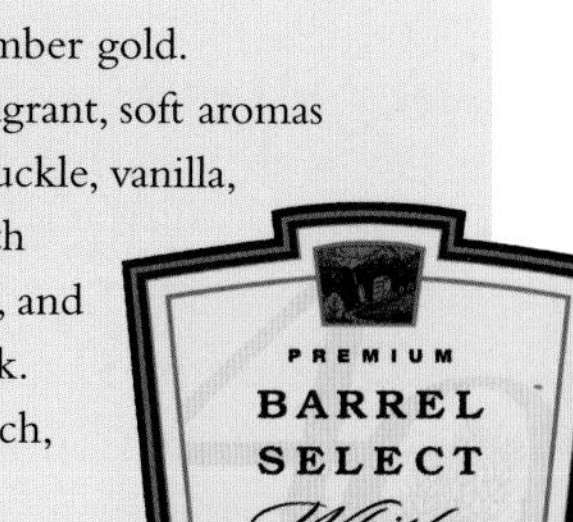

FORTY CREEK BARREL SELECT

THE WEST

THE VAST PRAIRIES OF THE CANADIAN WEST PROVIDE IDEAL GROWING CONDITIONS FOR GOLD-GREEN SEAS OF RYE, CORN, AND WHEAT. THEY ARE NATURAL LOCATIONS FOR A PAIR OF INDUSTRIAL-SCALE DISTILLERIES AND FOR RARE ALL-RYE WHISKEY.

The one distillery in Canada that has consistently remained true to its rye roots is Alberta Distillers in Calgary, Alberta. It was founded in 1946, in large part to take advantage of the sweeping rye country of the Canadian prairie. The distillery has been owned by US-based Jim Beam Brands since 1987, and three of its 40-vol. whiskeys—Alberta Premium five-year-old, Alberta Springs 10-year-old, and Tangle Ridge 10-year-old—exemplify what true Canadian rye whiskey can be, in particular the singular, 100 percent rye grain Alberta Premium.

The distillery does batch cooking and distillation with 100 percent unmalted rye mash and a 60-hour fermentation. Primary distillation is in a beer still, secondary distillation can be made in a continuous rectifier or batch rectifier, and pot-still distillation is used for specialty spirits. Ten percent of the whiskey is flavoring whiskeys that go through a beer still and into new, charred oak or once-used bourbon barrels.

DISTILLERY DETAILS

ALBERTA FOUNDED: 1946.
OWNER: Jim Beam Brands.
METHOD: Beer, column, and pot stills.
CAPACITY: 5.3 million gallons.

BLACK VELVET FOUNDED: 1973.
OWNER: Barton Brands. METHOD: Column stills.
CAPACITY: 4.9 million gallons.

HIGHWOOD FOUNDED: 1974.
OWNER: Highwood Distillers. METHOD: Column stills.
CAPACITY: Not given.

GIMLI FOUNDED: 1968.
OWNER: Diageo. METHOD: Column stills.
CAPACITY: 8.8 million gallons.

MAPLE LEAF FOUNDED: 1997.
OWNER: Maple Leaf Distillers. METHOD: Column stills.
CAPACITY: Not given.

ALBERTA WHISKEYS

Sweet and decidedly mellow Tangle Ridge, which was launched six years ago to compete with Crown Royal, has a base of 100 percent rye. After 10 years in oak, it is dumped and blended with a hint of sherry and other natural flavors, then recasked to allow the flavors to mingle. Alberta Premium is a complex, serious dram, a delightful balance of stewed fruit, vanilla, and rye spice—a real Canadian character. The 10-year-old Alberta Springs is softer, sweeter, and rounder; a grand sipping whiskey by itself. Two other Canadian whiskeys produced at the plant, Windsor Deluxe five-year-old and Lord Calvert, are value-priced brands.

BLACK VELVET DISTILLERY

The Black Velvet Distilling Company, Barton Brands' second distillery in Canada, is in Lethbridge, Alberta, a two-hour drive from the US border. Built in 1973 for IDV/Gilbey when Canadian whiskey was booming, this distillery is the major producer of Black Velvet for the world market. Two million cases of the light, sweetly round Canadian whiskey are dispatched each year. The flavoring whiskeys, aged for an average of six years, pass through a one-column still, and the base neutral spirit, aged for a minimum of three years, comes from a three-column still. In a process the company calls "blending at birth," the aged flavoring whiskey is blended with the new make.

HIGHWOOD DISTILLERY

Highwood Distillers, located in the Alberta township of High River, opened in 1974. It was originally named Sunnyvale but in 1984 was renamed Highwood after the dramatically beautiful Highwood region in the foothills of the Rocky Mountains. A producer of liqueurs and spirits, the distillery claims to be the only Canadian distillery using lighter wheat alcohol. Highwood's Canadian whiskeys, all 40 vol., are Centennial 10-Year-Old Rye Whisky, a Limited Edition version of the same, and Highwood Canadian Rye Whisky, made with rye and wheat distillates and aged in charred oak for a minimum of five years.

GIMLI DISTILLERY

Diageo's only Canadian distillery is in Gimli, Manitoba, on the western shore of Lake Winnipeg and about 100 miles (160 km) north of the city of the same name. Gimli and the surrounding communities account for the largest Icelandic community outside the island itself. Diageo Global Supply, Gimli Plant, is the official distillery name. It is responsible for supplying Crown Royal and several other former Seagram's whiskeys for international consumption.

The distillery was built by Seagram's in 1968, and much of their grain, especially the corn, is sourced from the vast Manitoba prairie. A substantial 20 percent of the whiskey blends are made up of rye and bourbon flavoring whiskeys, the majority of which go into new, charred American oak. There are three primary beer stills and a four-column rectifier; the flavoring whiskeys pass through a two-column Coffey still.

Crown Royal, at 40 vol., is a quintessential Canadian: soft and sweet, with a tantalizing aroma, rich, full body, and fruity with spice notes. The older Special Reserve and Limited Edition Crown Royal add an intense depth to the Crown Royal character. Seagram's Canadian VO shares the soft sweetness of the flagship brand but is more subdued. Seagram's 83, a lighter, drier dram, and fruity, sweet Five Star round out the Gimli family.

MAPLE LEAF DISTILLERY

Maple Leaf Distillers, affiliated with Vinco Beverages Europe, is one of Canada's newer distilleries. Founded in 1997, it specializes in vodkas, fruit liqueurs, and coolers. Based in Winnipeg, Manitoba, this distillery produces a standard three-year-old Canadian Cellars Rye Whisky for the Canadian market.

POTTER DISTILLERS

British Columbia's sole distillery company is, sadly, currently a silent one. Potter Distillers is based in Kelowna in the beautiful Okanagan valley, an area better known for its wineries than its distillery, and is owned by Cascadia Brands of Vancouver, British Columbia. It bottles Potter's Special Old Rye Whisky and a portfolio of well-aged whiskeys under the Century Reserve label.

Some of this whiskey has been brought in from other distilleries and subsequently aged at Potter Distillers, and some was previously distilled at the old Potter distillery. The oldest of the whiskeys is 21 years, an intensely oaky dram with leather and tobacco notes. The 15-year-old is a single cask, vintage-dated, 100 percent rye whiskey, rich with butterscotch and whiffs of smoke. The 13-year-old displays spicy, deep fruity rye character, and the eight-year-old is the softest, with sweet vanillins, malt, and oak.

Gimli is the home *of the global brand Crown Royal, and several former Seagram's whiskeys. Now owned by Diageo, it was built by Seagram's in 1968.*

TASTING NOTES

The whiskeys of the west range from softly sweet and fruity Crown Royal, a quintessential Canadian, to assertive, rye-based Alberta drams.

ALBERTA

TANGLE RIDGE DOUBLE CASKED

10-YEAR-OLD, 40 VOL.

100 percent rye base; whiskey is recasked after 10 years in oak.

TANGLE RIDGE DOUBLE CASKED

Color Amber.
Nose Sherry and vanilla, subtle oak.
Body Medium, soft.
Palate Slightly sweet. Fruit and oak.
Finish Medium long, sweet, smooth.

ALBERTA PREMIUM

5-YEAR-OLD, 40 VOL.

Color Deep gold.
Nose Toffee, fruit, citrus, honey, and soft vanilla, spicy tickle.
Body Medium.
Palate Fruit—apples and plums, honey, marzipan, vanilla and rye spice.
Finish Stewed fruit, hints of leather, and chocolate mint. Orange liqueur at end.

BLACK VELVET

BLACK VELVET

40 VOL.

Color Pale gold.
Nose Grain spirit, pepper spice, sweet toffee.
Body Light, jagged.
Palate Grainy; caramel and chocolate notes.
Finish Short and sharp.

CROWN ROYAL

CROWN ROYAL

40 VOL.

Color Amber gold.
Nose Rich fruit, toffee, sweet honey, and hints of spice.
Body Soft, delicate.
Palate Full, silky, balance of fruit and oak, sweet, touch of binding oil.
Finish Delicate fruit and spice, softly sweet.

UNITED STATES

Small-batch bourbons are changing the spirit of the South. They are smart, sophisticated, and successful

CELEBRATING THE CORN SPIRIT
Ceramic crocks and designer bottles take their place among a gathering of modern whiskeys. They sit on that great influencer of US liquors, the American white oak barrel.

THE UNITED STATES

STUART RAMSAY

For a country that celebrates Happy Hour with hedonistic zeal and bombards its citizens with alcohol advertisements, the United States has a drinking history with a surprisingly puritanical streak. America gave birth to bourbon and the cult of cocktails, lifting the martini to legendary status; but it also allowed an extreme experiment with Prohibition in the 1920s to obliterate saloons and taverns, decimate indigenous whiskey styles, and corrupt its drinking culture.

Although the evangelical movement casts a prohibitive shadow over swaths of Middle America and the South, this next decade could well witness the rebirth of American spirit. There are whiskey men in Kentucky who say bourbon is only now recovering from the pummeling of Prohibition. Also, there are enlightened whiskey-drinkers who say that rye whiskey is ripe for resurrection, for a well-aged rye, although hard to find, is a dram bursting with character. Some whiskey-makers are now rediscovering ryes, whiskeys, and a plethora of other spirits.

THIS NEXT DECADE COULD WELL WITNESS THE REBIRTH OF AMERICAN SPIRIT

In the late 1980s, the American consumer, becoming tired of mass production and the dumbing down of US food and drink, began to rediscover the quality and complexity of aged American whiskey. Following on from the success of Scottish single malts, distillers started to select their finest whiskeys and bottle them as premium spirits. Distilleries lured tourists with handsome visitor centers, and began to integrate their whiskeys into foods and quality cocktails.

IF THE RIVER WERE WHISKEY
The great river systems that course through Kentucky and its neighboring states brought many frontier settlers, and provided easy transportation, on flatboats, for the frontier spirit.

DISTILLERIES OF THE UNITED STATES

UNTIL THE ONSET of Prohibition in 1920, whiskey-making thrived in many American states. Kentucky remains the state with the most stills, with 10 (there were 55 in 1960). The popularity of premium bourbon at an affordable price has marked a resurgence in the native spirit.

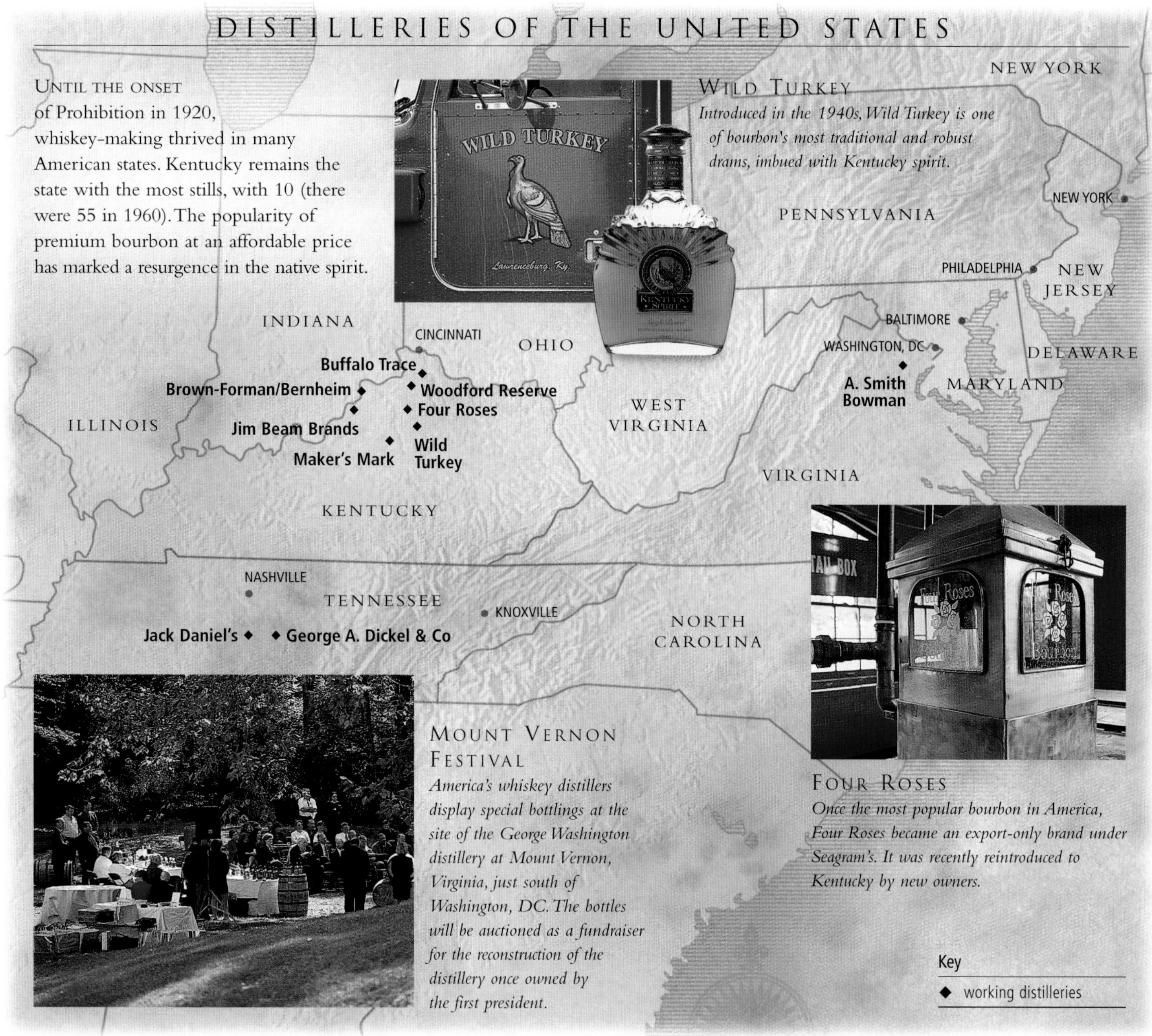

WILD TURKEY
Introduced in the 1940s, Wild Turkey is one of bourbon's most traditional and robust drams, imbued with Kentucky spirit.

MOUNT VERNON FESTIVAL
America's whiskey distillers display special bottlings at the site of the George Washington distillery at Mount Vernon, Virginia, just south of Washington, DC. The bottles will be auctioned as a fundraiser for the reconstruction of the distillery once owned by the first president.

FOUR ROSES
Once the most popular bourbon in America, Four Roses became an export-only brand under Seagram's. It was recently reintroduced to Kentucky by new owners.

The way American self-confidence with alcohol has matured is perhaps symbolized by the current reconstruction of George Washington's distillery at Mount Vernon, Virginia. The first President of the United States and Revolutionary Commander-in-Chief, Washington was also proprietor of one of the largest commercial distilleries in the new republic. His pioneer instinct sits well with the new breed of craft distillers in the US, who have shaped a distilling micro-revolution. The market for these alchemists includes visionary restaurateurs and educated consumers in progressive city-states such as San Francisco, Seattle, and Portland, where interest is gathering pace.

Regional pride and sustainable agriculture are often integral to the craft distillers' production philosophy, and focus groups are blessedly ignored. Small is beautiful in this culture of good food and drink. American spirit has truly been born again.

Virginia

WITH THE HISTORIC GEORGE WASHINGTON DISTILLERY SCHEDULED TO BEGIN PRODUCTION IN 2006, AND THE SOLE SURVIVING DISTILLERY PRODUCING PARTIAL DISTILLATION, VIRGINIA CLINGS, BARELY, TO ITS WHISKEY HERITAGE.

George Washington, the greatest of all Virginians, somehow found the time, despite his many military and political duties, to be a successful farmer, fisherman, miller, and owner of one of the largest commercial distilleries in colonial times.

Indeed, whiskey seemed always to be touching his life in one way or another, although that may be testimony to the social and economic importance of the spirit in those times. As a general, Washington emphasized the importance of troops being supplied with spirits to sustain them against tiredness or the weather. During the American Revolution, he held the view that whiskey was "essential to the health of the men," and commended it as "very refreshing and salutary."

WASHINGTON'S DISTILLERY

Washington inherited the Mount Vernon estate in Fairfax County, Virginia, from his brother's widow in 1761, and expanded it to a plantation of 8,000 acres (3,200 hectares)

DISTILLERY DETAILS

A. SMITH BOWMAN FOUNDED: 1935.
OWNER: Sazerac Company.
METHOD: Column still and copper doubler.
CAPACITY: Not given.

comprising five farms, each a complete unit with overseers, slaves, and other laborers. His Mount Vernon plantation was a model of efficiency, and wheat was at the heart of his diversified farming operation.

The gristmill for Washington's milling enterprise was built in 1771 on a piece of land about 2½ miles (4 km) south of the Mount Vernon mansion. Visitors to Washington's home today can see an impressive working reconstruction of the mill on the original site, its water wheel, and two sets of milling stones powered by Dogue Creek, which wraps around the property. Today the site is also home to a project that exemplifies the integral role that spirits played in colonial America—the reconstruction of Washington's distillery. Archaeologists and historians have unearthed a fascinating story of George Washington, commercial distiller.

In October 1797, Washington recorded in his weekly farm journal that carpenters began "hewing the timber for the still house." According to the archaeologists on site, the distillery was a one-story stone building with a loft. Its floor area measured 75 by 30 feet (23 by 9 meters). There were 50 mash tuns and five copper stills, the smallest of which had a 127-gallon (480-liter) capacity. John Anderson, the son of Washington's Scottish farm overseer, James Anderson, ran the distillery with five or six slaves. The mashbill for Washington's rye recipe was 60 percent rye, 35 percent corn, and 5 percent barley, giving an indication of the established regional whiskey style at the end of the 18th century. The distillery produced 13,000 gallons (50,000 liters) of rye- and corn-based whiskey in 1799, the year of Washington's death, yielding a substantial profit of $7,500. The whiskey was sold unaged both at the distillery, where customers included some of Virginia's most prominent families, and to local whiskey merchants.

THE SECOND DISTILLATION *of Virginia Gentleman takes place in an elaborate copper doubler still at the Bowman distillery.*

The archaeological dig has received financial backing from the Distilled Spirits Council of the United States, a trade and lobbying group that represents many of the large liquor producers. Whiskey and rum distillers have created special bottlings that will be auctioned off to raise funds for the project, and in 2003, several distillers produced a batch of whiskey in a replica of an 18th-century still and using Washington's rye mashbill. This whiskey is now maturing at Mount Vernon. The reconstructed distillery is scheduled to start production in the summer of 2006, making Mount Vernon the only historic site in the US capable of showing the distilling process from crop to finished product.

A. SMITH BOWMAN DISTILLERY

Despite its heritage of whiskey-making (legal and otherwise), Virginia currently has only one, partial, distillery in operation. The A. Smith Bowman distillery sits in an industrial park by the charming colonial town of Fredericksburg, in Spotsylvania County. Virginia Gentleman Bourbon has a pedigree going back to the end of Prohibition, when the distillery was founded by the Smith Bowman family. It was sold to the Sazerac Company of New Orleans in 2003, owners of the Buffalo Trace distillery in Frankfort, Kentucky.

TASTING NOTES

WITH A HIGHER percentage of corn in the mashbill compared to other bourbons, Virginia Gentleman has a sweet, round character.

VIRGINIA GENTLEMAN
STRAIGHT BOURBON WHISKEY, 90 PROOF (45 VOL.)

Aged six years. The mash bill has 85 percent corn. Buffalo Trace distillery does the first distillation, and A. Smith Bowman distillery carries out the second distillation.

Color Red copper.
Nose Sweet, vanilla, oak, hints of honey, soft pepper spice; lovely oak perfume.
Body Full, round.
Palate Flavorful balance of oak and vanilla sweetness.
Finish Smooth, mature, soft spice.

VIRGINIA GENTLEMAN

For 16 years, since Smith Bowman moved to its current site at Fredericksburg, the Buffalo Trace distillery (formerly Ancient Age) has been fermenting and distilling the first run of Virginia Gentleman. The second run, a slow one through a copper doubler still, is carried out in Fredericksburg by Joe Dangler, distiller at the A. Smith Bowman distillery for over 26 years. Dangler also supervises the whiskey cuts and the maturation in Virginia.

The bottling Dangler is most proud of is the round and sweet six-year-old 90-proof (45-vol.) Virginia Gentleman. "There's a synergy between the proper age and the proof," he says. "You get rid of the young corn smell and start to pick up the wood." With a mashbill of 85 percent corn, 8 percent rye, and 7 percent barley malt, the whiskey has a higher corn content than most bourbons, and just enough rye to give a ticklish character and depth to its sweet corn whiskey character. The A. Smith Bowman distillery also bottles a four-year-old, 80-proof (40-vol.) Virginia Gentleman.

AMERICAN WHISKEY DISTILLERIES *have rallied around the fundraising campaign for the reconstruction of the George Washington distillery by producing special bottlings.*

Pennsylvania and Maryland

ONCE THE HEARTLAND STATES OF AMERICAN RYE WHISKEY, PENNSYLVANIA AND MARYLAND NO LONGER PRODUCE A DROP OF THIS APPETIZING AND FORMIDABLE DRAM.

It was rye whiskey that forged a patriotic identity during, and just after, the Revolutionary War, and its cradle was the Pennsylvania Dutch country in southeast Pennsylvania. The German settlers brought with them a heritage of distilling rye-based schnapps, and they discovered that rye grain adapted well to the rich farmlands they settled. By the time of the Revolutionary War, a distilling community was well established, with copper pot stills produced by skilled craftsmen in the thriving manufacturing towns.

By the end of the war, whiskey from the Monongahela Valley in western Pennsylvania had also established itself as a highly respected dram in Philadelphia and down the Ohio River. Just south of Pittsburgh, where the Allegheny and Monongahela rivers meet to form the great Ohio, the valley farmland was filled with Scots-Irish and Pennsylvania Dutch settlers in the early 1770s. A full-bodied rye whiskey, Monongahela "Red" fetched a dollar a gallon in Philadelphia and was considered as good as currency by the frontier farmer distillers. The Monongahela farmers planted corn in addition to rye, and it is likely that this grain was added to the mashbill, softening and sweetening the rye whiskey. That it was termed a "red" whiskey indicates at least a minimum aging period in charred oak casks. (Burning the inside of an oak cask was an early and effective method of sanitation.)

A DEFINING FLAVOR

What the rye grain gives to bread, it also imparts to whiskey. Rye whiskey has that same hint of bitterness. It is reminiscent of a bittersweet fruit—perhaps a hint of apricot—spicy, a little oily, almost peppermint. The bitterness arouses the appetite, like that of quinine in tonic water, or hops in beer. The peppermint palate, which adds a digestive quality, is especially evident in samples of rye whiskey from the first two or three decades of the 20th century.

DISTILLERY DETAILS

MICHTER'S
FOUNDED: 1753.
OWNER: Dwight Hostetter.
CLOSED: 1989.

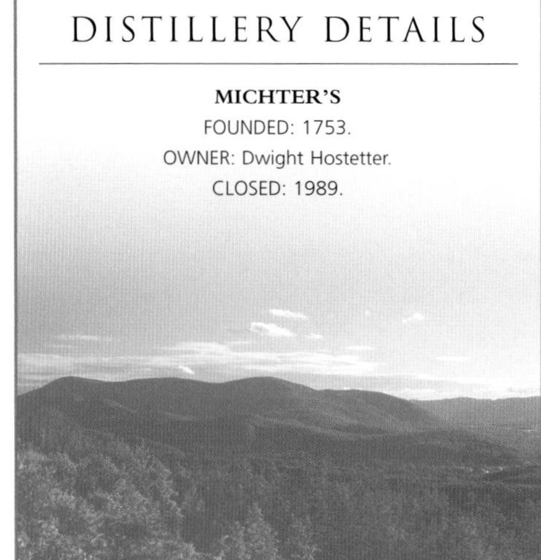

PENNSYLVANIA DISTILLERIES

One or two "Pennsylvania" ryes survive, as products of Kentucky. The once-famous Rittenhouse Rye, associated with Philadelphia, is alive and well and being produced by Heaven Hill's Bernheim distillery in Louisville. Bottled at 100 proof (50 vol.), Rittenhouse (51 percent rye, 37 percent corn, and 12 percent barley) is a bold, emphatically spicy example of the style. The most widely recognized product in this category is four-year-old, 80-proof (40-vol.) Old Overholt, named after Abraham Overholt (1784–1870), one of the "fathers" of American distilling. Jim Beam Brands produces Old Overholt as a genuine straight rye at their Clermont and Boston distilleries in northern Kentucky.

There is no sadder prospect to a serious drinker than a silent distillery that most likely will never produce whiskey again, more so if the distillery has a heritage of producing some outstanding whiskeys. So it is with Michter's distillery in Schaefferstown, in the heartland of Pennsylvania Dutch country. The distillery is a National Historic Landmark and encompasses the historical sweep of distillation in America. From 1753 there was a farm distillery on the site, and a commercial plant was built in 1861. Although it introduced column stills, Michter's persisted with pot-still distillation long after other distilleries abandoned this method.

Upkeep and maintenance of the distillery is a labor of love for the current owner, Dwight Hostetter, who also runs a furniture company. There are two column stills and a pot still in place, and all the pipes and boilers are intact, but Hostetter says time is running out for Michter's and anxiously waits for a spiritual savior who can start up the stills once more. A prospective buyer will not be able to call the whiskey Michter's, however. As with so many small distilleries that have closed their doors or merged, the brand name was sold on, in this case to a New York company that sources its current Michter's bottlings from Kentucky warehouses. They are not bad whiskeys at all, but they are not made in Schaefferstown.

Whiskeys that have passed through a Michter's pot still are a dwindling breed. The last of the pot-still straight bourbon whiskey made at Michter's is the 16-year-old AH Hirsch Reserve, owned by Preiss Imports of California. A rare gem of a bourbon, multilayered and robust, it was distilled in 1974, then put into stainless steel tanks in 1990 at Buffalo Trace distillery in Kentucky to halt the aging. The last of the whiskey, a few thousand cases of an American icon, was bottled in 2003.

MARYLAND WHISKEYS

If the spirit of Pennsylvania rye languishes in mothballed silence, distant memories of place are all that is left of Maryland's proud heritage. Chesapeake, Preakness, Pimlico, Baltimore, and Cockeysville ryes were all imbued with Maryland character and whiskey tradition. But Kentucky once again saves face with Pikesville Supreme Rye whiskey, named after the community just outside Baltimore and distilled by Heaven Hill distilleries of Bardstown. An 80-proof (40-vol.) straight whiskey with 51 percent rye, it is a lighter, fruitier "Maryland" rye, with touches of spice, mint, and vanilla.

WHISKEY ADVERTISING *has moved on since this huge jar was perched on the roof of Michter's still-house, but the sight certainly asserts the brand.*

Prohibition and a predilection for lighter whiskeys thereafter pummeled the robust ryes of Pennsylvania and Maryland, but there is life in the spicy grain yet, and hope for properly mixed Manhattans, Old Fashioneds, and Sazeracs. Two formidably sturdy straight ryes have been made in Kentucky since the 1940s: Jim Beam Rye is the world's best-selling straight rye and has over 80 percent rye in the mashbill; Wild Turkey straight rye faithfully delivers its trademark kick at 101 proof (50.5 vol.).

Well-aged ryes come in limited bottlings and are more difficult to track down, but they are certainly worth the effort. Seek out Van Winkle's splendid 13-year-old Family Reserve Rye, and Buffalo Trace's limited-release Sazerac 18-year-old—a mountain of a whiskey. And then there are Fritz Maytag's Old Potrero bottlings in San Francisco. Made from 100 percent rye malt in a pot still, these rebellious, rambunctious whiskeys have turned the category inside out.

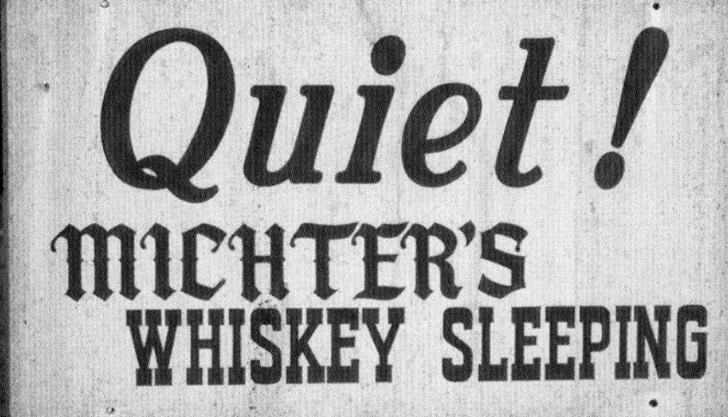

WISHFUL THINKING: *Michter's whiskey stocks have all been bought and sold.*

CERAMIC KEEPSAKES *highlight aspects of Michter's past as the oldest operating US distillery.*

Kentucky: Frankfort

WHERE BUFFALO ONCE ROAMED, A SPLENDID RANGE OF SPECIALTY BOURBONS HAVE FOUND THEIR SPIRITUAL HOME IN ONE OF KENTUCKY'S OLDEST FRONTIER SETTLEMENTS.

Stony Point, an elegant limestone mansion, overlooks the whiskey landscape of Buffalo Trace distillery, formerly known as Ancient Age. The distillery site is located on an ancient buffalo crossing, where the animals forded the Kentucky River. It was part of the Great Buffalo Trace, a pathway or trail carved out by the buffalo as they thundered from salt lick to salt lick through the wilderness.

The present distillery site became a settlement in 1775 when Hancock and Willis Lee established a camp here. The Leestown settlement eventually became an established stopping place for travelers and by 1790 was home to a thriving population.

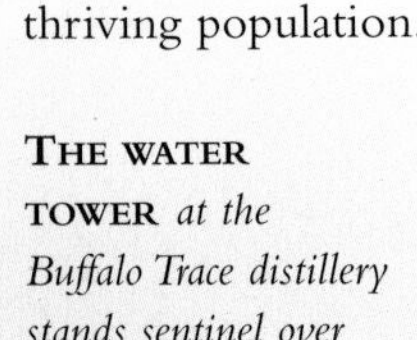

THE WATER TOWER *at the Buffalo Trace distillery stands sentinel over 200 years of whiskey production and 300 years of American frontier history.*

DISTILLERY DETAILS

BUFFALO TRACE FOUNDED: 1787. OWNER: Sazerac Company. METHOD: Column stills. CAPACITY: 14.3 million gallons.

The first modern distillery was built on the Buffalo Trace site in 1857, and was the earliest to incorporate steam power in the production of bourbon whiskey.

E. H. Taylor Jr., one of Kentucky's original bourbon aristocrats, bought the distillery in 1886 and introduced a number of innovations, including the first use of steam pipes to heat the warehouse in winter.

The Buffalo Trace site encompasses 110 acres (270 hectares) and 110 buildings, representing three centuries of American history, and 200 years of whiskey production.

COLONEL BLANTON

On the way down the hill from the mansion to the distillery courtyard is a stone statue of a dapper Kentucky gentleman, Colonel Albert Bacon Blanton. Starting as an office clerk in 1897, Blanton became distillery manager and eventually part owner with George T. Stagg.

Colonel Blanton retired in 1952, after 55 years of service, and the distillery has been using the same recipes ever since. Buffalo Trace bourbons are rich in corn (and thus in sweetness) and a high priority is placed on sanitation. The barrels have a heavy char, with a 55-second burn, and the mature spirit is chill filtered before bottling, rather than using activated charcoal. This leaves more flavor in the spirit, according to the distillery.

In 1984, master distiller Elmer T. Lee, now retired, was given the honor of selecting individual barrels for the introduction of Blanton's, a full-bodied, honey-sweet whiskey regarded as the world's first commercially marketed single barrel bourbon.

The distillery's namesake whiskey, Buffalo Trace Kentucky Straight Bourbon, is destined to become the company's flagship brand and a competitor to the likes of Maker's Mark, Woodford Reserve, and Knob Creek. Launched in August of 2001, the sweet, fruity and spicy Buffalo Trace, a 90-proof (45-vol.) bourbon, has been allocated to specific markets until production levels can meet the demand.

SPECIAL COLLECTIONS

As well as Blanton's, Buffalo Trace's Single Barrel Collection includes six other bourbon brands, each one different by recipe, by proof strength, or by warehouse aging. The six are: Eagle Rare 10-year-old, a caramel-sweet favorite with the distillery employees and the most widely marketed, which is made with rye as the small grain; W. L. Weller, a wheated bourbon (meaning wheat is the small grain used, along with malted barley and the majority corn); Rock Hill Farm is bottled at 100 proof (50 vol.); Hancock's Reserve; Elmer T. Lee, named for the distiller; and Charter Proprietor's Reserve 13-year-old.

Each autumn, Buffalo Trace also produces a limited and much-anticipated Antique Whiskey Collection of individual brands that change annually. They have included W. L. Weller 19-year-old Bourbon, a delicious Sazerac 18-year-old Straight Rye Whiskey and 15-year-old, barrel-proof George T. Stagg, an outstanding dram. The Antique Collection bottlings are selected from a small batch of around 27 barrels each, enough to make 300 cases of whiskey.

The company's premium brands are W. L. Weller 12-year-old, W. L. Weller 7-year-old (107 proof/53.5 vol.), W. L. Weller 7-year-old (90 proof/45 vol.) and Old Charter 8-, 10-, and 12-year-old. Their standard brands are Ancient Age 10-year-old and Ancient Age McAfee's Benchmark.

Colonel Albert Bacon Blanton *was the manager and part-owner who gave 55 years of service to the distillery, and his name to a fine single barrel whiskey.*

VAN WINKLE

Buffalo Trace also acts as distributor and partner in the US for Julian Van Winkle's sophisticated range of aged whiskeys. The grandson of whiskey aristocrat Pappy Van Winkle, Julian makes truly small-batch bourbon whiskeys—only about three or four barrels per bottling. His first Van Winkle Family Reserve was introduced in 1984. It was designed to be an after-dinner sipping whiskey. He only chill-filters bourbons and ryes that are under 100 proof (50 vol.). His bottlings include well-aged bourbons and some stunning straight ryes, but they are in very limited supply. Van Winkle Special Reserve, a 12-year-old, 90.4 proof (45.2 vol.) whiskey, is widely available, alongside Old Rip Van Winkle 10-year-old (90 and 107 proof—45 and 53.5 vol., respectively), and his deeply formidable 15-year-old, 107 proof (53.5 vol.).

TASTING NOTES

Buffalo Trace has made a concerted effort in recent years to become a leader in specialty whiskeys. Today, the distillery's portfolio offers a wide range, including single barrel, well-aged, rye and wheated whiskeys.

BUFFALO TRACE

BUFFALO TRACE

BUFFALO TRACE
90 PROOF (45 VOL.)
Introduced 2001; named after the Great Buffalo Trace, a trail carved out by buffalo.

Color Light bronze with streaks of gold.
Nose Complex aroma of vanilla, mint, and molasses.
Body Medium.
Palate Sweet, notes of brown sugar and spice, oak, leather, toffee, and fruit.
Finish Long, dry, and deep.

BLANTON'S SINGLE BARREL

BLANTON'S SINGLE BARREL
93 PROOF (46.5 VOL.)
Introduced 1984; the first single barrel to be marketed commercially. Named after Colonel Albert Bacon Blanton, distillery manager and co-owner.

Color Deep amber.
Nose Balanced, sweet, soft spice and mint, caramel.
Body Full and firm, round.
Palate Honey sweetness, spice, and vanilla.
Finish Sweet caramel, spice; hint of mint; lingering.

VAN WINKLE

VAN WINKLE SPECIAL RESERVE
12-YEAR-OLD, 90.4 PROOF (45.2 VOL.)
A wheated bourbon.

Color Bright gold.
Nose Sweet honey, soft caramel and oak, gentle vanilla.
Body Full, round.
Palate Balanced, deep flavors of caramel, vanilla, soft wheat, and toffee.
Finish Gently sweet, balanced, lingering.

PAPPY VAN WINKLE'S FAMILY RESERVE
15-YEAR-OLD, 107 PROOF (53.5 VOL.)
A wheated bourbon.

Color Deep gold.
Nose Deep oak aromas, heavy sweetness, charcoal, caramel, vanilla, and soft wheat.
Body Full, round, smooth.
Palate Complex. Vanilla sweetness and toffee, wheat.
Finish Delightful deep oak sweetness of caramel, vanilla, and toffee, spices and fragrant hints of orange.

PAPPY VAN WINKLE'S FAMILY RESERVE

Kentucky: Lawrenceburg

THE WHISKEYS AND DISTILLERIES OF ANDERSON COUNTY ARE A CONTRAST IN STYLE AND ARCHITECTURE, FROM THE ASSERTIVELY TRADITIONAL AND ROBUST WILD TURKEY TO THE SOFT AND DANGEROUSLY EASY FOUR ROSES.

Home of Wild Turkey, the plain and functional buildings of Boulevard distillery, although not the prettiest in Kentucky, make a serious and traditional full-bodied dram. The distillery sits on Wild Turkey Hill, in the little town of Lawrenceburg in Anderson County.

According to distillery sources, the Wild Turkey name originated in the early 1940s when Thomas McCarthy, president of the New York–based Austin Nichols company, selected some straight, 101-proof (50.5-vol.) bourbon from his company stocks as his contribution to a wild turkey hunting trip. After years of success, the company bought the distillery in 1970. Austin Nichols, in turn, was taken over by a French drinks company, the Pernod Ricard Group, in 1980.

Wild Turkey does not disclose its mashbill recipe, but according to Jimmy Russell, master distiller, 50-year whiskey veteran, and true Kentucky gentleman, "Of all the distilleries, we use the lowest amount of corn for our bourbon recipe. There is more rye and malted barley and all the grains are premium. We use more rye and malt to get more flavor and body in the whiskey."

DISTILLERY DETAILS

WILD TURKEY FOUNDED: 1869. OWNER: Pernod Ricard USA. METHOD: Column stills. CAPACITY: Not given.

FOUR ROSES FOUNDED: 1860s. OWNER: Kirin Brewery Co. METHOD: Column stills. CAPACITY: 2.1 million gallons.

Wild Turkey's beer (or what Scottish distillers would call wash) ferments out at around 13 proof (6.5 vol.), and is pumped into a 40-foot- (12-meter-) tall continuous still. Both stills are copper. The column still has 19 stripper plates and the beer is fed on to the 18th plate. Wild Turkey is distilled at around 112 to 115 proof (56 to 57.5 vol.) to get more flavor and body congeners coming over. Most importantly, the barrels are given a heavy char at the cooperage.

THE WILD TURKEY WHISKEYS

All the richly colored bottlings of Wild Turkey, with the exception of their rye whiskey, use the same grain mashbill and yeast strain. The flagship whiskey is Wild Turkey, 101-proof (50.5-vol.) Kentucky Straight Bourbon, a traditional, full-bodied, and uncompromising southern dram, smooth and heavy with vanilla and caramel flavors in the aroma and taste.

When the distillery released Wild Turkey Rare Breed Straight Bourbon in 1991, it bottled the whiskey at an even higher strength than the 101. Rare Breed, a seamless ultra-premium bourbon, is a marriage of 6-, 8-, and 12-year-old stocks from Wild Turkey, bottled

Wild Turkey *whiskey is aged in deeply charred barrels in traditional, ironclad warehouses dotted on Kentucky hilltops.*

at the strength it comes out of the barrels.

In 1995, Wild Turkey launched Wild Turkey Kentucky Spirit, a single barrel, ultra-premium bourbon. Jimmy Russell hand-selects Kentucky Spirit to be fuller-bodied, with a rich vanilla flavor and a hint of sweetness. Wild Turkey's family of 101-proof (50.5-vol.) straight bourbons is rounded out with the superb ten-year-old Russell's Reserve, a smooth and silky, dark amber whiskey with intense depth and caramel flavor. The distillery is one of the few in the United States to make a rye whiskey, admirably bottled at 101 proof (50.5 vol.).

FOUR ROSES DISTILLERY

Across State Highway 127, on the other side of Lawrenceburg, is the Four Roses distillery, in as pretty a production site as you will find in Kentucky. Its fruity, creamy whiskey is a soft counterpart to its robust neighbor on the hill. In 2002, the Kirin Brewery Company of Tokyo, Japan, bought the distillery from Seagram Americas. In 2004, with a redesigned yet still distinctive label, the bourbon was reintroduced to Kentucky and a visitor center was added to the plant.

THE FOUR ROSES WHISKEYS

According to master distiller Jim Rutledge, the Yellow Label is aged for a minimum of five years, usually six. Yellow Label is soft and easy because that was the Bronfman (Seagram) style. This lightness and smoothness make it different from other bourbons. A spicy, floral, and slightly dry Four Roses single barrel is also produced, at 86 proof (43 vol.). The distillery has a five-year contract to make Bulleit bourbon for Diageo; it has a little more rye in it than Four Roses.

Four Roses is the only company that uses five different yeasts and two mashbills. One mashbill recipe has 60 percent corn and 35 percent rye. The yeasts were chosen specifically to give soft, smooth flavors, like a blended whiskey. Instead of bottling ten individual bourbons with the different yeasts and mashbills, the distillery mingles the ten to create one constant flavor.

The California *mission-style architecture of the Four Roses distillery dates back to 1910.*

Four Roses bourbon is matured in medium-charred barrels off-site, in 20 low, single-story warehouses by Cox's Creek, north of Bardstown.

TASTING NOTES

Anderson County's two distilleries offer two very distinct styles of bourbon: robust, heavy drams from Wild Turkey; soft and light from Four Roses. They exemplify the range of the flavor spectrum found in Kentucky whiskey.

WILD TURKEY 101

WILD TURKEY DISTILLERY

WILD TURKEY 101
101 PROOF (50.5 VOL.)

Color Deep amber.
Nose Vanilla and caramel, peaches, peppery spice, and leather.
Body Full, robust, heavy.
Palate Profound bourbon flavors, balanced; vanilla, spice, oak, and fruit.
Finish Toasted oak and fruit.

WILD TURKEY RARE BREED
108.4 PROOF (54.2 VOL.)
Barrel proof bourbon. A marriage of 6-, 8-, and 12-year-old stocks.

Color Deep amber.
Nose Complex, fruity, flowery, spicy, and nutty.
Body Full, rich.
Palate Big, smooth, rich, with notes of peppermint and citrus, tobacco, and vanilla.
Finish Lingering, toasty, spicy.

WILD TURKEY RARE BREED

FOUR ROSES DISTILLERY

FOUR ROSES
80 PROOF (40 VOL.)

Color Pale russet.
Nose Soft, delicate, fruity. Notes of vanilla, nutmeg, and citrus.
Body Medium, round.
Palate Rich, creamy. Pleasant balance of honey, caramel, and oak.
Finish Soft, smooth.

FOUR ROSES

FOUR ROSES SINGLE BARREL
86 PROOF (43 VOL.)

Color Red amber.
Nose Full, rich. Fruitcake spices, vanilla, and fruit.
Body Full, fruity.
Palate Fruit and honeysuckle, oak, and vanilla.
Finish Emphatic, spicy, mellow.

Kentucky: Versailles

CONCEIVED AS A TRIBUTE TO HANDCRAFTED BOURBON, WOODFORD RESERVE'S THOROUGHBRED DRAM IN THE HEART OF BLUEGRASS HORSE COUNTRY IS THREE TIMES DISTILLED IN COPPER POT STILLS.

The agricultural bounty of this farming state is gathered in the autumn: corn is harvested for whiskey, tobacco and hams cure in wooden barns, and the Kentucky communities celebrate their festivals and fairs.

WOODFORD RESERVE DISTILLERY

About an hour's drive from Louisville, the journey through Woodford County to Woodford Reserve distillery is a tranquil one. The landscape is dotted with substantial farmhouses and corrals enclosed by white wooden fences. Thoroughbred racehorses graze on the fertile Kentucky bluegrass, shaded by white oak, maple and dogwood trees.

In this horse country heartland, on the banks of Glenn's Creek, are the limestone buildings of the Woodford Reserve distillery, a National Historic Landmark. Reborn on 17 October 1996, Woodford was conceived by its owner, Louisville-based Brown-Forman Company, as a tribute to the history and tradition of handcrafted bourbon distillation in Kentucky. The refurbished distillery was called Labrot & Graham until October 2003.

The smallest distillery currently operating in Kentucky, Woodford creates "small batch" whiskey from start to finish, producing 45–50 barrels a day. It is the only bourbon distillery to use copper-pot stills exclusively, and employs the rare method of triple distillation to do so. Crafted in Scotland, the pot stills are just one of several historic links between the spirits of Kentucky and Scotland at this unique distillery, where Scottish and Scots-Irish roots run deep.

DISTILLERY DETAILS

WOODFORD RESERVE FOUNDED: 1812. OWNER: Brown-Forman. METHOD: Pot stills. CAPACITY: Not given.

THE "CRADLE" OF BOURBON

Elijah Pepper, whose hilltop home overlooks the distillery, began making whiskey on the Glenn's Creek site in 1812. Elijah brought his distilling skills from Virginia in 1797, settled in Versailles (pronounced "Versales"), the Woodford County seat, and began making corn whiskey behind the county courthouse. In need of abundant, pure limestone water for a growing business, he moved the operation and built his cabin on the site nearby at Glenn's Creek.

The distillery site has been called "the cradle of bourbon" due, in large part, to the pioneering scientific achievements of James Christopher Crow, a Scottish physician and chemist. Elijah Pepper's son, Oscar, hired Crow as head distiller in the 1830s, and he spent most of his career perfecting the craft of bourbon distillation at the distillery. Dr Crow recognized the importance of producing a consistent and reliable product from batch to batch. His scientific training helped him understand the sour mash process used by all bourbon distillers today, and the benefits of charred oak barrels for maturation.

A visitor centre and crafts shop overlooks the distillery, housing informative displays and photos outlining the history of the distillery and Kentucky bourbon. The distillery has also become an important culinary and educational destination for tourists and whiskey drinkers, but the glory of Woodford lies in the wood and limestone distillery buildings of Glenn's Creek hollow, a hundred yards down the hill.

New barrels *of raw whiskey are rolled to the limestone warehouse of Woodford Reserve by Glenn's Creek.*

TRIPLE DISTILLATION

The mashbill for Woodford Reserve is 72 per cent corn, 18 per cent rye and 10 per cent barley malt. The cooked grains ferment in small, 5 cm- (2 in-) thick cypress wood fermenters for five to seven days, creating a beer of around 18 proof (9 vol). As you descend the steps from the brew house to the spacious still-house, the bonny sight of three graceful pot stills working away would make a single-malt lover, or maker, catch their breath. Built in Scotland by Forsyth's, the coppersmiths of Rothes in Speyside, they produce America's only triple-distilled whiskey. The long, slender-necked stills stand nearly 5 metres (16 feet) tall, and comprise a beer still, a high wines still and a spirit still. They are heated by live steam injection. Most Scottish single malt distillers would be content with the spirit that comes off the second, high wines still, but Woodford distils it one more time, in the spirit still. The spirit from the third still comes off at 158 proof (79 vol), just two points below the legal limit.

The still house overlooks the cask filling station, where the spirit goes into medium-charred oak barrels at 110 proof (55 vol), using demineralized water. The barrels are rolled a short distance to the distillery's limestone warehouse. The walls are just under a metre (2 feet) thick, and embedded in the limestone blocks are thousands of fossilized sea creatures; a prehistoric reminder of the ancient inland sea underneath Kentucky's soil. There are four floors inside, with three barrel tiers on wooden ricks per floor.

Woodford Reserve is mostly 6 to 7 years old and handsomely packaged at 90.4 proof (45 vol). This distillery whiskey is now mingled with a good proportion of choice Old Forester whiskey from the Brown-Forman Distillery in Louisville. Robust "honey" barrels from upper floors and sunny exposures are the ones destined for Woodford, where they are cut with water and aged. Woodford Reserve is a robust and spicy whiskey with sweet maple fullness and a lingering finish.

A whiskey aged in the bluegrass alongside stud farms would not be complete without a racehorse connection. Woodford is the official bourbon of US racing's two premier events: the Kentucky Derby and the Breeder's Cup. A thoroughbred dram, indeed.

THE WOODFORD STILLS *are made of copper and comprise a beer still, a high wines still and a spirit still. They were crafted in Speyside, Scotland.*

TASTING NOTES

WOODFORD RESERVE is a revolutionary whiskey, breaking with column still production to produce spirit in Scottish pot stills. And it goes one step further, distilling the spirit three times. The site's pioneering whiskey maker, James Christopher Crow, would no doubt be impressed.

WOODFORD RESERVE DISTILLER'S SELECT

90.4 PROOF (45.2 VOL)

A mingling of triple-distilled bourbon from Woodford Reserve and straight bourbon from Brown-Forman Distillery in Louisville.

Colour Soft golden amber.
Nose Sweet, maple fullness, hints of vanilla and honey.
Body Full and robust.
Palate Complex. Citrus notes, spice, floral, balanced and round.
Finish Long, spicy and smooth.

KENTUCKY: BARDSTOWN

KENTUCKY'S "WHISKEY CAPITAL" MIGHT WELL BE BARDSTOWN, A HISTORIC NELSON COUNTY TOWN IMBUED WITH BOURBON HERITAGE AND ITS OWN FESTIVAL CELEBRATING THE CORN SPIRIT.

My Old Kentucky Home, fondly remembered in the song by Stephen Foster, is a substantial Georgian building in its own grounds, the most visited attraction in Bardstown. A community of about 7,000 people, Bardstown sits along the Blue Grass Parkway from Lexington, and south of Louisville. The second and third attractions in Bardstown are the 1785 Talbott's Tavern and the Oscar Getz Museum of Whiskey History. They have been joined by Heaven Hill Distillery's new and informative visitor center. September is the time to visit, since Bardstown is host to an annual, week-long Kentucky Bourbon Festival, the greatest whiskey celebration in America, and a mandatory experience for devoted followers of the corn spirit.

Whiskey is the lifeblood of Bardstown and Nelson County, and this area has perhaps the best claim to be the center of Kentucky's distilling industry, not only geographically but also historically. Nelson County once had over 20 distilleries, and the whiskey archaeologist can explore a handful of silent distilleries in and around the town.

DISTILLERY DETAILS

HEAVEN HILL FOUNDED: 1890.
OWNER: Constellation Brands, Inc.
METHOD: Column stills. CAPACITY: Not given.

BARTON FOUNDED: 1890.
OWNER: Constellation Brands, Inc.
METHOD: Column stills. CAPACITY: Not given.

The whiskey museum is a few blocks from the courthouse, in a former college building called Spalding Hall. It is open all day, Monday to Saturday, and also on Sunday afternoons, and is well worth a visit for its documentary material, whiskey displays, and early advertising. The collection was created by Oscar Getz as chairman of the board of Barton distillery, where it was originally on display.

HEAVEN HILL

The Heaven Hill company was founded in 1935 by Gary, Ed, George, Mose, and David Shapira and is operated today under the direction of second- and third-generation family members. The distillery itself was

ALL OF THE HEAVEN HILL *whiskeys are now produced at the efficient Bernheim distillery in Louisville, bought by the company in 1999.*

TASTING NOTES

HEAVEN HILL specializes in higher-proof, older whiskeys packed with body and spicy sweet character. Barton leans toward younger, drier bourbons.

BARTON BRANDS

VERY OLD BARTON
6-YEAR-OLD,
90 PROOF (45 VOL.)

Color Russet brown.
Nose Fresh, fragrant, berry fruits, apples, toffee, hints of pepper.
Body Medium, smooth.
Palate Rich, caramel oak, nutmeg and pepper, oranges and apples.
Finish Rich, spicy.

KENTUCKY TAVERN
4-YEAR-OLD,
80 PROOF (40 VOL.)

Color Pale amber.
Nose Apple pie, citrus, oak, and honey.
Body Medium, dry.
Palate Honey oak, allspice, apples, pears, and rye.
Finish Medium, austere, but warm.

HEAVEN HILL

EVAN WILLIAMS BLACK LABEL
7-YEAR-OLD,
86 PROOF (43 VOL.)

Color Deep gold.

EVAN WILLIAMS

Nose Complex. Sweet butterscotch, caramel, vanilla, peppermint.
Body Medium, balanced.
Palate Spicy, sweet vanilla, toasted oak, toffee.
Finish Warm leather and tobacco.

ELIJAH CRAIG
12-YEAR-OLD, 94 PROOF (47 VOL.)
Introduced in 1986. Named after Reverend Elijah Craig, Kentucky bourbon pioneer.

Color Burnt gold.
Nose Classic bourbon, caramel sweetness, vanilla, spice, and fruit.
Body Full, gutsy.
Palate Rich, warming. Sweetness and oak, caramel and rye, in robust harmony.
Finish Heavy sweetness, licorice, vanilla, and spice; emphatic finale.

ELIJAH CRAIG

founded many years previously, in 1890. Heaven Hill is the nation's largest independent, family-owned marketer and producer of distilled spirits products. It is the second-largest holder of aging bourbon whiskey in the world, with over 600,000 barrels currently in its traditional, ironclad warehouses in and around Bardstown. Heaven Hill's storage, bottling, and distribution, as well as sales and marketing offices, occupy the same farmland in Bardstown that was once owned by the company's namesake, William Heavenhill. In 1999, the company bought the historic Bernheim distillery in Louisville from Diageo, and this 300-barrel-a-day plant is the sole location for the production of its bourbons.

THE HEAVEN HILL WHISKEYS

Heaven Hill specializes in higher-proof, older bourbons packed with complexity, full traditional body, and a spicy, sweet character. Their extensive portfolio of splendidly affordable specialty bourbons includes whiskeys that belong in the cabinet of every serious drinker: a new 86.6-proof (43.3-vol.) bottling of Evan Williams Single Barrel Vintage is launched each year from "honey" barrels selected by master distiller Parker Beam, a seventh-generation Beam. Super premium Elijah Craig 12-year-old was launched in 1986 and is a gem of a whiskey—full-bodied, honeyed, and redolent with spice and caramel.

Other Heaven Hill whiskeys include Evan Williams 7-year-old Black Label (the second-biggest-selling bourbon after Jim Beam); Evan Williams 1783 10-year-old (Parker Beam's favorite); Elijah Craig Single Barrel 18-year-old; Rittenhouse and Pikesville Supreme ryes; Fighting Cock; Very Special Old Fitzgerald 12-year-old (a "wheated" bourbon); and Henry McKenna Single Barrel 10-year-old.

THE HEAVEN HILL SIGN *may be weathered, but the distillery opened a state-of-the-art Bourbon Heritage Center in Bardstown in 2004.*

THE BARTON DISTILLERY

The whiskeys from Barton are notably dry and aromatic. The company's main national label is Very Old Barton, which is available at 90, 80 and 86 proof (45, 40 and 43 vol.) as a six-year-old. Very Old Barton is the premium brand, although it is very competitively priced, and is well-regarded in the industry. Barton produces several other standard straight bourbons, including four-year-old, 80-proof (40-vol.) Kentucky Gentleman and four-year-old, 80-proof Kentucky Tavern. Tom Moore (four-year-old, 80-proof), is named after the man who founded the distillery, in 1890.

The present distillery, largely built in the 1940s, has the red-brick industrial style of the period. It uses its own yeast, in a sour mash of backset, malt, and rye. Despite their flavorful palate, the whiskeys are also very clean, perhaps because the distillate is run through the column twice.

Kentucky: Loretto

AMERICA'S FIRST PREMIUM, SPECIALTY BOURBON OF THE MODERN ERA, A SOFT AND EASY DRAM, LIES HIDDEN IN THE ROLLING HILLS OF MARION COUNTY. THE DISTILLERY SITE IS ONE OF KENTUCKY'S OLDEST.

Amid the rolling hills of Marion County, in a broad and fertile hollow with sycamore trees standing sentinel, is the organic cluster of buildings that comprise Maker's Mark distillery.

Maker's Mark occupies one of Kentucky's oldest whiskey-making sites, dating back to 1805, and is designated a National Historic Landmark. The black and red-trim buildings straddle the banks of Hardin Creek, the stream that dissects the serene valley floor of Star Hill Farm. On the road leading down to the creek, the visitor passes "The Quart House," one of the oldest remaining US "retail package stores." In a period before the dark cloud of Prohibition, Marion County neighbors would swing by in their horse and buggy and have their quart jugs filled from the whiskey barrels inside.

A special southern alchemy takes place at Maker's Mark, an alchemy that creates a truly handmade whiskey, America's first premium, quality bourbon of the modern era.

DISTILLERY DETAILS

MAKER'S MARK FOUNDED: 1805.
OWNER: Allied-Domecq.
METHOD: Column stills followed by pot stills.
CAPACITY: 2.2 million gallons.

Bill Samuels Jr., a seventh-generation Kentucky bourbon maker, is president of Maker's Mark distillery. Samuels' ancestors are Scots-Irish, the fearless Presbyterian pioneers who settled the American frontier. The Reverend Elijah Craig, a Presbyterian turned Baptist minister, is often credited with "inventing" bourbon in 1780s Kentucky. According to Bill Samuels, however, "bourbon was not invented; it evolved out of these early Scots-Irish families. Elijah Craig was a neighbor in Pennsylvania of Robert Samuels, my great-great-great-great-grandfather. Robert migrated to Kentucky in 1780, and was a farmer by trade who made whiskey for himself and his neighbors."

PREMIUM BOURBON

In 1953, Bill Samuels Sr. bought the Star Hill Farm: 200 acres (80 hectares) of fertile farmland with an old country distillery on site, and a deep, spring-fed lake on the hill above it. Bill Senior had no interest in making and selling the "pedestrian" bourbon of his competitors, so he scrapped the old family recipe and set out to produce a premium sipping bourbon.

"My dad's goal was to create a bourbon that was more refined, palatable, and yet still flavorful," explains Bill Junior, "something that didn't have the hot aftertaste traditionally associated with bourbon. The purpose was not about money; it was about bringing good taste to bourbons, and he designed it for a palate of one—himself." Bill Senior experimented with different grains for his bourbon, developing a recipe based on locally grown corn, winter wheat (softer and gentler in flavor than traditional, spicier rye), and malted barley.

MAKER'S MARK *is one of the few distilleries that still painstakingly rotates barrels in their black and red-trim, metal-clad warehouses.*

MAKER'S MARK DISTILLERY *gleams with wood and copper; it is one of the most picturesque in Kentucky.*

TASTING NOTES

MAKER'S MARK USES red winter wheat instead of rye in its mashbill. The result is a softer, gentler whiskey. Maker's fresh distillate enters the barrel at a low 110 proof (55 vol.).

MAKER'S MARK
90 PROOF (45 VOL.)
The original, handmade, super-premium whisky, spelled without the "e." A "wheated" bourbon.

Color Bright amber.
Nose Sweet, caramel, vanilla, fruit, clean.
Body Medium, soft.
Palate Soft and round, buttery, seamless medley of sweetness, vanilla, and caramel.
Finish Smooth, clean, with gentle afterglow.

MAKER'S MARK BOTTLES

Mrs. Samuels, meanwhile, came up with the name, Maker's Mark, based on the tradition of English pewter-makers who put their mark on their finest pieces. The mark of Bill Samuels still decorates every bottle, as does another Mrs. Samuels innovation: the hand-dipped wax seal that spills down the neck of the Maker's Mark bottle.

By 1958, the first barrel of Maker's Mark handmade whisky (spelled without an "e" in tribute to the Samuels' Scots-Irish ancestry) was ready for the market. Sales of the early Maker's were gradual and local, spreading slowly by word of mouth among the whiskey connoisseurs of Kentucky. "By 1980, Maker's Mark had become a Kentucky icon," Bill Samuels says, "and then the *Wall Street Journal* ran a front-page article about us that year, and the phone rang off the hook. The article was huge for us; it created consumer interest outside Kentucky and gave the brand credibility."

THE DISTILLERY TODAY

Owned by the Allied-Domecq company, today Maker's Mark distillery is running at full capacity. The mashbill is 70 percent corn, 16 percent wheat, and 14 percent malted barley. Red winter wheat is preferred to rye, because, according to the distillery, wheat softens and mellows the whiskey. An old roller mill grinds the grain gently so as not to scorch it. The beer still is one of the smallest in the industry and a true double distillation with a lower 130 proof (65 vol.) takes place.

Maturation is in black, metal-sided warehouses ranging from three to six stories, and Maker's is one of the rare distilleries that rotates barrels in the same warehouse; a costly and labor-intensive process. The result is overall uniformity of flavor. The barrel wood staves are air-dried outdoors for nine months, which helps take the astringent tannins out, and the fresh distillate goes into the barrel at 110 proof (55 vol.) instead of the more common 125 proof (62.5 vol.) for bourbons. With the lower proof, Maker's gets more extractives from the wood.

To relieve the bottling-hall congestion caused by dipsomaniac tourists, the company has installed a dipping booth in their gift shop. Visitors who make the pilgrimage to Star Hill Farm can buy a bottle of whiskey and do their own wax dipping and sealing.

Kentucky: Clermont

THE BEAM FAMILY, A BOURBON DYNASTY, HAS WHISKEY ROOTS DATING BACK MORE THAN 200 YEARS IN NELSON COUNTY. TODAY, JIM BEAM IS THE BIGGEST-SELLING BOURBON IN THE WORLD.

No one seems to know any more from where in Germany the original Mr. "Boehm" came; when he emigrated to Maryland; or at what stage the name was Americanized to "Beam." We do know that the Beam family has supplied proprietors and employees for several of the best-known distilleries to be founded in the United States during the past 200 years.

The Beams' American roots are located in Bardstown, Nelson County, and two or three adjoining counties. The first distiller in the family was Jacob Beam, who set up in Washington County in 1795. His great-grandson, David Beam, established a distillery in the mid-1800s at Clear Springs, just up the hollow from the distillery that would bear the name of his son Jim, at Clermont in Bullitt County. The Jim Beam distillery at Clermont was established after Prohibition ended in 1933. Along the way, the company also acquired a distillery located about 9 miles (14 km) away, in Boston, Nelson County.

The James B. Beam Distilling Company was acquired, in 1967, by the conglomerate American Brands and is now part of Fortune Brands. Jim Beam itself is the biggest-selling bourbon by a fair margin, and among the top few brands of spirits of all types.

DISTILLERY DETAILS

JIM BEAM BRANDS CO. FOUNDED: 1795. OWNER: Fortune Brands, Inc. METHOD: Column stills. OUTPUT: 10.6 million gallons.

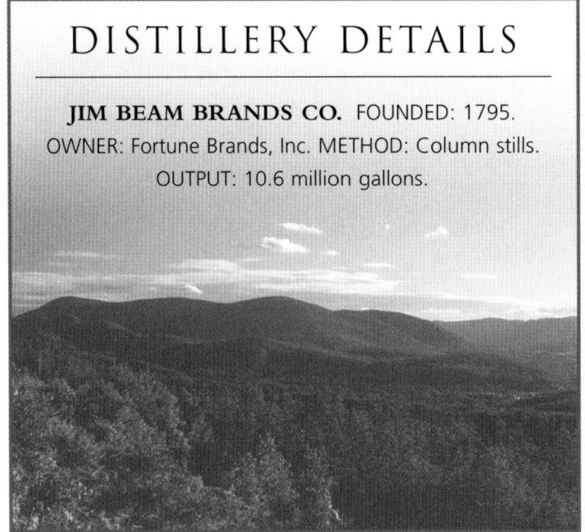

The plain, and somewhat industrial, Clermont distillery, a 30-minute drive south of Louisville, is a major tourist attraction, and home to Jim Beam's American Outpost, where visitors can learn about the Beam whiskey heritage and view the historic family home. The company uses its own "sweet" yeast, with hops. There is plenty of rye in the mash and backset in the cooker and, in an especially large proportion, in the fermenters. Beam distills and barrels at notably low proofs, the latter element making the most significant contribution to its taste character.

JIM BEAM WHISKEYS

The principal Jim Beam version is four years old, at 80 proof (40 vol.), and has a white label. It is an innocuous dram, soft, medium-bodied, with understated sweetness, vanilla, and spice. Jim Beam Black, aged for eight years and at 86 proof (43 vol.), is different and distinctive. It is complex and overflowing with oak, vanilla, and fruit, and is a long and balanced dram. Beam's Choice is an 86-proof (43-vol.) whiskey that is charcoal-filtered after aging.

In the early 1990s, Jim Beam launched the Small Batch Bourbon Collection, giving loose definition to a subcategory of bourbon that has energized the industry. The Small Batch Collection had the great good fortune to have Booker Noe, grandson of Jim Beam, as their roving brand ambassador. Booker passed away in early 2004 after 50 years of making and supervising the production of Beam whiskey; his son, Fred, has taken on the role of brand ambassador.

Booker Noe's eponymous whiskey was introduced in 1988 as an uncut, natural-proof, and non-chill-filtered bourbon. In 1992, the complex, oaky Booker's was joined by three more bourbons in the collection:

After a second distillation *the "high wine" is transferred directly to new oak barrels and set in hilltop rackhouses to be exposed to dramatic temperature changes.*

seven-year-old, 107-proof (54-vol.) Baker's, a fruity, toasty dram named after Clermont alumnus Baker Beam, Booker's cousin; Basil Hayden's, an 8-year-old, 80-proof (40-vol.), spicy, peppery whiskey with twice as much rye in its mashbill; and the balanced and robust Knob Creek, a 9-year-old, 100-proof (50-vol.) whiskey named after Abraham Lincoln's childhood home in Kentucky. Beam also has an excellent 6-year-old rye whiskey (without an age statement), 80 proof (40 vol.), with a yellow label.

A triumvirate of Kentucky's most historical bourbons are also produced at the Clermont and Boston distilleries, although less promoted than their Beam label cousins. Old Grand-Dad, which honors early whiskey distiller Basil Hayden on the label, is formulated with more rye in the mashbill. It is a gutsy, spicy 86-proof (43-vol.) whiskey. Old Crow, a 4-year-old bourbon named after Scottish chemist and pioneering 19th-century Kentucky distiller James Christopher Crow, is bottled at 80 proof (40 vol.). The current recipe, with citrus and spice dominating, dates back to the 1960s, and is not the one that received accolades from a plethora of early American poets and writers. Old Taylor, a traditional, robust 6-year-old bourbon, commemorates Colonel Edmund Haynes Taylor Jr., whiskey aristocrat and the force behind the Bottled-in-Bond Act of 1897. In a major victory over the adulterous rectifiers of the time, the Act guaranteed that any bottle with a government seal would be at least four years old, and a full 100 proof (50 vol.).

TASTING NOTES

THE BOURBONS from Jim Beam use plenty of rye in the mash and backset in the fermenters, and are put in the barrel at lower proofs.

JIM BEAM WHITE LABEL
80 PROOF (40 VOL.)

Color Straw gold.
Nose Soft notes of vanilla, sweet caramel, pepper, and allspice.
Body Light to medium, soft.
Palate Vanilla oak, hints of toffee and allspice, caramel.
Finish Grassy, short.

JIM BEAM WHITE LABEL

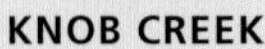

KNOB CREEK
9-YEAR-OLD, 100 PROOF (50 VOL.)
Introduced in 1992. Named after President Abraham Lincoln's childhood home in Kentucky.

Color Deep mahogany.
Nose Toasted nuts, maple, oak, balanced.
Body Full, rich.
Palate Classic, robust bourbon aromas; oak sweetness, spice, fruit, vanilla.
Finish Long, rich, glowing.

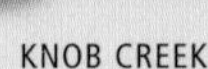

KNOB CREEK

THE VAST JIM BEAM *distillery in Clermont steams ahead. Fortunately, its visitor center is much more attractive.*

Kentucky: Louisville

LOUISVILLE IS THE LARGEST CITY IN KENTUCKY, AND WAS ONCE HOME TO A DOZEN IMPOSING DISTILLERIES PLANTED ALONG "DISTILLERY ROW." THE CITY STILL PRODUCES SPLENDID BOURBON AT ITS TWO REMAINING PLANTS.

Louisville is a busy riverport city on the Ohio River that has been described as the southernmost Northern city and the northernmost Southern city in the United States. In sailboat days, the city made rope from hemp, which grows wild in Kentucky; it grew on the trade in tobacco, not to mention the occasional Kentucky country ham; and down by the riverfront is a plaque honoring Evan Williams, in 1783 the city's first distiller, and perhaps the state's, too.

On the edge of town, to the southwest, past Churchill Downs and astride Dixie Highway, is the area known as "Distillery Row." The distilleries of Louisville were big industrial plants, the growth of which continued throughout the postwar recovery years of the 1950s. At the height of competition in the bourbon business there were half a dozen distilleries, and now there are just two, Brown-Forman and Bernheim, producing whiskey.

DISTILLERY DETAILS

BROWN-FORMAN FOUNDED: 1891. OWNER: Brown-Forman. METHOD: Column stills. CAPACITY: Not given.

BERNHEIM FOUNDED: 1992. OWNER: Heaven Hill Distilleries, Inc. METHOD: Column stills. CAPACITY: 2.2 million gallons.

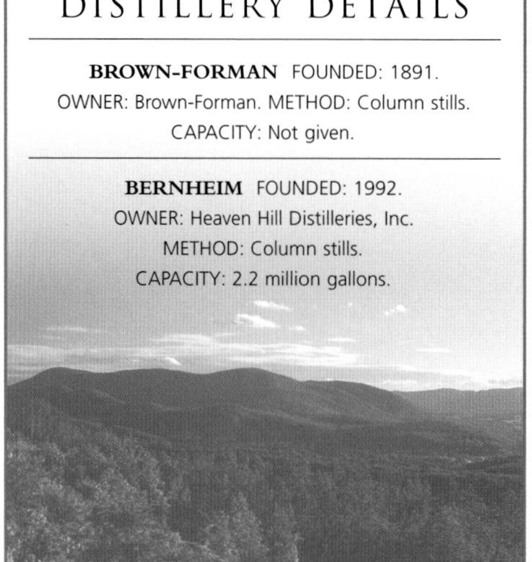

BROWN-FORMAN DISTILLERY

Formerly known as Early Times, the Brown-Forman distillery is home to Old Forester Bourbon and Early Times Kentucky Whisky (spelled, unusually for the US, with no "e").

In 1870, George Garvin Brown, a young pharmaceuticals salesman in Louisville, saw the need for a consistently high-quality whiskey that met medicinal standards. At this time, whiskey was the best anesthetic available, and was prescribed for a host of ailments. Branded barrels were sold in bulk, and some retailers adulterated this whiskey. In response, Brown and his half-brother, J. T. S. Brown, began selling their Old Forester Bourbon Whisky in sealed glass bottles to assure its quality.

Early Times was the name of a settlement elsewhere in Kentucky, and the label originated there in 1860 before finding its way to Louisville in 1933 after Prohibition ended. The mashbill for Old Forester is 72 percent corn, a substantial 18 percent rye, and 10 percent malted barley; it undergoes a five-day fermentation and has 12 percent sour. Early Times' mashbill is 79 percent corn, 11 percent rye, and 10 percent barley malt, with a three-day fermentation, and 20 percent sour. The yeast strains are different for each whiskey. New make or "white dog" (the spirit from the final distillation) of Early Times is grainy with some spice and very little fruit. The yeast strain for Old Forester produces a robust, fruity white dog, with spicy notes, and citrus and ripe cherry aromas.

After passing through the beer still, both are redistilled in a vaporous state in a thumper. Old Forester is poured into new, charred oak barrels and is a straight Kentucky bourbon, but some Early Times is partially aged in used oak, which is why it has "Kentucky Whisky" on its label, and not "Kentucky Bourbon." The spirit in used barrels ages for a minimum of three years, and this is mingled with five-, six-, and seven-year-old straight whiskey from new, charred barrels. The style of this whiskey dates back to 1981 to compete with lighter, popular Canadian whiskeys. Straight Early Times bourbon is exported to Australia and a few foreign markets as a four-year-old Yellow Label and a seven-year-old Brown Label.

THE BRICK WAREHOUSES *of the Brown-Forman distillery are steam-heated in winter to accelerate maturation.*

BROWN-FORMAN WHISKEYS

Old Forester is traditional, well-crafted bourbon, with lots of body up front, fruit in the nose and palate, and all the right notes of vanilla and oak. There is an 86-proof (43-vol.), six-year-old bottling, a complex cracker of a 100-proof (50-vol.) bottling aged over eight years, and limited edition vintage bottlings released in September to commemorate George Garvin Brown's birthday. All are handsomely packaged, which would no

THE DISTILLERIES *of Louisville in its glory days were large affairs. The column stills at Bernheim reflect the scale of their enterprise.*

doubt please the pioneer of bottled bourbon. Early Times, a soft and mixable 80-proof (40-vol.) dram, with notes of nuts and spice, is lighter on the palate than Old Forester.

BERNHEIM DISTILLERY

Over in the gritty 10th ward of the city is Heaven Hill's 300-barrel-a-day, equally efficient Bernheim distillery, named after Isaac Wolfe Bernheim. A considerable whiskey businessman at the turn of the 19th century, Bernheim was founder of I. W. Harper Bourbon, now owned by Diageo. Heaven Hill makes all their whiskeys here, but prefers to age them in Nelson County, rather than in the behemoth brick warehouses at Bernheim.

TASTING NOTES

THE MASHBILL, fermentation time, and yeast strains are different for Old Forester and Early Times, yet both are produced at the same distillery. Early Times is low in fruit character; Old Forester is fruity.

OLD FORESTER

OVER 8 YEARS OLD, 100 PROOF (50 VOL.)

Color Burnished deep copper.
Nose Complex, ripe fruit, vanilla, anise, mint, chocolate cream.
Body Full, creamy.
Palate Apples and peaches, caramel, oak, hint of nutmeg.
Finish Sweet, soft fruit, lingering.

EARLY TIMES KENTUCKY WHISKY

80 PROOF (40 VOL.)

Matured at least three years in reused cooperage; blended with five-, six-, and seven-year-old straight whiskey aged in new, charred oak.

Color Pale mahogany.
Nose Spicy, nutty (walnuts and pecan), clean, sweet.
Body Smooth, medium.
Palate Soft, clean, nutmeg, nuts, and honey.
Finish Sweet spice, brief.

Tennessee

PUMMELED BY PROHIBITION AND STILL "DRY" IN ALL BUT THREE COUNTIES, TENNESSEE MAINTAINS A PROUD WHISKEY HERITAGE AND A DISTINCT STYLE OF SOUR-MASH SIPPING WHISKEY AT JACK DANIEL'S AND GEORGE A. DICKEL DISTILLERIES.

Among those famous whiskeys that are always asked for by name, rather than being identified by their category, Jack Daniel's is a prime example. People always ask for a Jack Daniel's, not a Tennessee whiskey. In fact, Tennessee whiskey is a specific style, the essence of which is captured by Jack Daniel's. The distinctive feature of the Tennessee whiskey style is the filtration process, a leaching or mellowing of the raw spirit through vats of sugar maple charcoal before it is barreled. The significance of the mellowing's being done before barreling is that a cleaner whiskey goes into the wood. It is thus a different character of spirit that extracts flavors from the barrel, and the end result has its own distinctive balance.

DISTILLERY DETAILS

JACK DANIEL'S FOUNDED: 1866. OWNER: Brown-Forman. METHOD: Column stills. CAPACITY: Not given.

GEORGE A. DICKEL & CO FOUNDED: 1870. OWNER: Diageo. METHOD: Column stills. CAPACITY: 1.26 million gallons.

TWO MAIN DISTILLERIES

Within the Tennessee whiskey category, there are six products made by two distilleries: Jack Daniel's and George Dickel. In general, the whiskeys from Jack Daniel's are a little heavier, with a slight pleasant oiliness of body. The Dickel whiskeys are lighter, very aromatic, sweet with the typical vanilla bouquet of the barrel, and have a soft aftertaste. Jack Daniel's principal product, Old No. 7, with its familiar black label, is marketed at 86 proof (43 vol.). A green-label version is 80 proof (40 vol.). Both are between four and five years old but carry no age statement. Gentleman Jack, a soft, 80-proof (40-vol.) whiskey is charcoal-mellowed twice, before and after aging. The distillery's Single Barrel weighs in at 94 proof (47 vol.) and is a full-bodied, complex whiskey. George Dickel's No. 8 black label is a clean, slightly sweet dram at 80 proof (40 vol.), and the No. 12, in a parchment label, is aromatic and dry at 90 proof (45 vol.). Both bottlings currently have whiskey aged over 10 years, according to the distillery.

The two distilleries welcome visitors, and are very close—less than 10 miles (16 km) apart. They are very much a part of the tourist route that is centered on Nashville, the busy state capital and country music mecca. The landscape around the distilleries is dotted with horse farms, home to the famous Tennessee Walking Horses—instantly recognizable by their strange gait and cricked tails. This is Tennessee whiskey country, and yet visitors here may have to settle for a soft drink rather than savoring the local spirit, since most of the state is "dry"—and also very devout. The small towns are dotted with Primitive Baptist Churches: the First Presbyterian Church, the Church of the Nazarene, and the First Church of God.

Tennessee Walking Horses, *with their unusual gait, are common in the whiskey counties of Tennessee.*

In 1825, the first distillery is said to have been established in the area where Jack Daniel subsequently started his operations. By the 1890s, Tennessee was a major force in commercial distilling, but the shadow of Prohibition was spreading. One or two states had already gone dry, and in 1910 Tennessee followed suit, 10 years before national Prohibition. Distilling was not legal again in Tennessee until 1938, five years after the rest of the US, and only then to produce whiskey to be sold in other states. Tennessee's distilleries are in dry counties, although a little moistness creeps in here and there. You can buy whiskey in the towns of Tullahoma and Manchester in Coffee County, but not in the rural areas. In Tennessee, spirits may still only be made in just three of the 95 counties: Moore, Coffee, and Lincoln.

A third, micro, distillery produces rum in the community of Kelso in Lincoln County, about 13 miles (20 km) south of Jack Daniel's. The proprietor, Phillip Prichards, has plans to distill whiskey.

LYNCHBURG

The name Lynchburg seems incomplete without the parenthetical "(pop. 361). That was the town's population when it first featured in the famous series of advertisements for Jack Daniel's, and both parties have agreed that is how it will stay, regardless of births, deaths, and, a few years ago, a change of boundaries. Lynchburg and Jack Daniel's have helped make a name for each other. After all this time, they need each other, too. It is an interesting relationship.

Vignettes of life in Lynchburg, etched simply in modest monochrome spaces and evoking a life gone by, have been a running

In Lynchburg *they claim it was divine inspiration that led Jack Daniel to add "Old No. 7" to the name of his whiskey.*

JACK DANIEL'S
SINGLE BARREL

In the burning ceremony *at the Jack Daniel's distillery, planks of sugar maple are set ablaze with raw spirit. The smoke is sucked through the enormous canopy in order to cut down on pollution.*

story in glossy American magazines for decades. They have whimsically reminded people of the small-town foundation on which the United States is built, and that has struck a chord.

Lynchburg is little more than a square of shops set around Moore County Courthouse. The layout is that of any small town in the South. The shops mostly date from the 1920s, although there are some sun-faded 1940s brick buildings. The courthouse is a stylish small Georgian structure, with a memorial to the Confederate dead.

Three of the shops sell Jack Daniel's souvenirs. A fourth, the Lynchburg Hardware and General Store, is owned by the distillery. It sells branded clothing, whiskey paraphernalia, a plethora of golf and barbecue merchandise (including wood-smoking chips made from used barrels), whittling knives (and the wood for carving), tools, cooking equipment, and a wide range of country products. Jack Daniel's also owns the White Rabbit Saloon, which sells coffee and snacks but not alcohol.

JACK DANIEL'S DISTILLERY

Lynchburg stands in open country among high, sweeping hillsides. One rockface opens into a cave, about 20 ft (6 m) high and 25 ft (8 m) wide, which narrows so quickly that an explorer would have to crawl to get into it. The channel has been investigated as far down as 6,000 ft (1,800 m), but the water it provides has never been traced to a source. If it were an underground stream, it would have a big natural basin, which could be up to 5,000 acres (2,000 hectares) in area. The cave supplies the water used to make Jack Daniel's whiskey.

THE DISTILLATION PROCESS

A little backset is used in the atmospheric cooker; the yeast, of which Jack Daniel's is proud, is a very vigorous, two-cell strain, which is recovered from each fermentation, kept in jugs on ice, and mashed in rye and lactic malt. The 16 fermenters are all open, and made of stainless steel, and the original, pre-Prohibition still stands alongside four copper column stills, with doublers. The still-house, a narrow, red-brick, seven-floor building, is covered in ivy. The old mellowing house is overgrown, too. The wooden mellowing vessels are sunk into the floor. They are packed with 10 ft (3 m) of charcoal, resting on a wool blanket. Immediately above the top surface of the charcoal is suspended a crisscross of copper pipes about 1 in (2 cm) in diameter. These pipes are perforated, and the whiskey is fed onto the charcoal through the holes. It drips, never managing even a dribble, let alone a flow. There are several dozen of these vessels.

The wood mellowing vats *at Jack Daniel's contain 10 ft (3 m) of sugar maple charcoal.*

THE BURNING CEREMONY

After three months, the charcoal is unusable and more has to be made. To maintain an adequate supply, the distillery burns a batch of maple once or twice a week. First, the maple is cut into planks about 4 ft (1 m) long, like giant matchsticks. These are stacked neatly to a height of about 8 ft (2 m). Then the rick is set ablaze, and the flames roar into the canopy above. The canopy sucks away the smoke and afterburns it, as a measure against pollution. When the flames are at their highest and the wood is burning with a fierce red glow, the rick is thoroughly hosed with water. It stubbornly resists extinction, hissing in fury and spitting the smoke of a hundred dragons before it is extinguished. When they have cooled down, the black, crumbly remains of the planks are ground down into something resembling charcoal. They are then packed into the mellowing vats and given a grudging drink.

The burning ceremony is watched by tour groups standing in a semicircle at a safe distance. Behind them you can see the warehouses, full of whiskey slowly maturing. It is a phenomenon: the town, the distillery, the rites, and the shrewd way in which it has all been presented to the consumer.

The Louisville-based distillers Brown-Forman own the phenomenon, but cannot be said to have orchestrated it. They still list Lem Motlow, the nephew of Jack Daniel, as proprietor, and the rural climate of his family and friends prevails.

ROMANTIC HISTORY

The romantic story that is Jack Daniel's began with Joseph Daniel, an Englishman who worked as a coachman for a wealthy Scottish family. He fell in love with their 15-year-old daughter, and in 1772, the couple eloped to

America, where Joseph fought against the British in the War of Independence. They settled in North Carolina, then moved to Tennessee. Their grandson Jack Daniel, the youngest of a family of 10, was born around 1846. Jack didn't get along with his stepmother and left home at the age of seven and moved in with an uncle. He got work doing chores and making whiskey for 17-year-old Dan Call, a Lutheran lay preacher and farmer who ran the local store and sold corn whiskey made from a wooden still.

Call decided to become a full-time preacher and sold the whiskey business to 14-year-old Jack. Call's distiller was Nearest Green, a slave, and it was Nearest who taught Jack the art of making whiskey. Jack eventually moved his still to the Cave Spring Hollow by Lynchburg, the site of the present distillery. It was registered with the government after the Civil War, in 1866.

JACK DANIEL'S NO. 7

There are several stories about the origin of the Jack Daniel's No. 7 brand name, introduced in about 1887. The nearest to an authorized version is that Daniel was inspired by the success of a Jewish merchant whom he met, who had built a chain of seven retail stores. It would seem that seven was nothing more than an inspirational number. Daniel also used the designation "Old" for his whiskey. If he aged it, or affected to, that was unusual at the time, and may have helped him develop a certain cachet. Normally, whiskey was supplied to bars in the barrel and the aging was then their responsibility.

From his earliest days in the whiskey business, rather than selling from a store, Daniel favored distribution by horse and wagon. This undoubtedly helped spread the fame of his spirits. But his big breakthrough came when he took his whiskey to the 1904 World's Fair in St. Louis, Missouri; the Gold Medal for the best whiskey in the world went to someone pointed out as "that little guy from Tennessee in the stovepipe hat."

Jack Daniel's normal attire was a broad-brimmed planter's hat and a formal, knee-length frock coat; he was a dandy, but a tiny one, at only 5 ft 2 in (1.6 m). He was the most eligible bachelor in the county, but he never married. Toward the end of his life, Daniel became a Primitive Baptist, and he died in 1911, after a tragicomic incident in which he injured his foot while kicking a jammed safe. After Prohibition, which lasted 28 years in Tennessee, no one else in the state was interested in restarting production, but Daniel's nephew Lem Motlow, who was already 69, decided to extend and rebuild the distillery. He died in 1947, and passed the distillery on to his four sons. However, none of them had successors, and so the family sold the business to Brown-Forman in 1956.

TULLAHOMA

If the Tennessee whiskey business has a historic center, it is the town of Tullahoma (pop. 17,000). This was the home of Alfred Eaton, who is credited with developing the charcoal-leaching process in 1825. Then, as now, Tullahoma, which is in Coffee County, was the main town for a large stretch of countryside, and Eaton's distillery was in the hollow subsequently occupied by Jack Daniel's.

In the small towns that make up the heartland of the United States, there are several classic layouts: the town set around the courthouse; the one-street town; and the town where the railroad runs down the

The current George A. Dickel *distillery was built in 1958, about 1/2 mile (800 m) from its original location. It is dwarfed by its neighbor, Jack Daniel's.*

The George A. Dickel *distillery was first named Cascade distillery after its location, Cascade Hollow.*

middle of the main street, the way it still runs in Tullahoma Not only did the railroad offer people in Coffee and Moore counties access to Nashville and Chattanooga, it also helped make Tullahoma into a resort town. The railroad was itself a curiosity, but all the more so when a town was built around it. Tullahoma had a spa with limestone water, too.

GEORGE A. DICKEL

Among those attracted to the town was George A. Dickel, a successful merchant and German immigrant living in Nashville. He visited Tullahoma with his wife Augusta in the late 1860s and decided to stay and produce Tennessee whiskey. In 1870, he established the firm George A. Dickel & Co., and the Cascade distillery was founded in 1877. The original distillery owners named the distillery after its location, Cascade Hollow. Dickel marketed the whiskey through his business in Nashville. In 1888, Dickel's business partner and brother-in-law Victor Schwab acquired a controlling interest in the Cascade distillery, along with the exclusive right to bottle and sell what was then called Cascade Tennessee Whisky.

The distillery continued to operate after Dickel's death in 1894, and only then did the whiskey bear his name. It closed, along with a few other Tullahoma distilleries, in 1910, when Tennessee outlawed whiskey. Schwab moved the company to Louisville, Kentucky. After repeal, the Dickel and Cascade names were acquired in 1937 by the national drinks company Schenley. Then, in 1958, the company decided to reunite the brand with its geographic origins, and built the present distillery only about 2/3 mile (1 km) from its original location. Standing alone in a long, winding valley fringed with trees, the silence broken only by birdsong and the fast-flowing creek, the distillery is a charming place to visit.

Production began the following year using the same water and recipes as the original Cascade whiskey, and the first bottles reached the shelves in 1964. George Dickel remained a Schenley property until 1987, when it was acquired by Guinness, now part of Diageo.

THE DISTILLATION PROCESS

Dickel uses atmospheric batch-cooking and their own original yeast; a low-fusel-oil-producing culture developed by Schenley. There are three- and four-day, natural fermentations in stainless steel fermenters, and the whiskey is double-distilled, going into the doubler as a liquid. Before charcoal-mellowing in stainless tanks, the new spirit is cold-chilled.

The limestone water *and bucolic countryside turned Tullahoma into a spa town. George Dickel's country store, located above the fast-flowing creek, is still open for business today.*

The warehouses are made of galvanized metal on wooden frames, and are single-story with insulated roofs and walls. All the houses are on a hill, 1,000 ft (300 m) above sea level, and the distillery manager, David Backus, keeps the temperature inside at or above 55°F (12°C).

Outside the distillery, the hard sugar maple, from which the charcoal is produced, is piled up. Because the distillery is smaller than its famous neighbor (Dickel has 29 employees; Jack Daniel's has 400), Dickel has fewer bonfires, but the charcoal is used in the same way by both companies. Back in Tullahoma, Alfred Eaton would be pleased.

TASTING NOTES

All Tennessee whiskeys are mellowed through vats packed with sugar maple charcoal, removing some of the heavier fusel oils for a cleaner new spirit.

JACK DANIEL'S

JACK DANIEL'S
OLD NO. 7, 86 PROOF (43 VOL.)

Color Medium amber.
Nose Balance of caramel, vanilla, licorice, and toffee.
Body Medium, round.
Palate Oak, with soft fruit—stewed apples, caramel, and sooty vanilla.
Finish Dry, charcoal smoke.

JACK DANIEL'S SINGLE BARREL

GENTLEMAN JACK
80 PROOF (40 VOL.)
Charcoal-mellowed twice, once before and once after aging.

Color Light amber.
Nose Caramel and fruit—black currant and tangerine.
Body Soft, silky.
Palate Delicate, balanced, more caramel and fruit laced with vanilla and smoke.
Finish Gentle wisps of smoke and currants.

GEORGE DICKEL

GEORGE DICKEL
NO.8, 80 PROOF (40 VOL.)

Color Soft amber.
Nose Sweet, vanilla, and notes of chocolate and cocoa.
Body Clean, balanced, light to medium.
Palate Hint of sweetness, round, apples, pears, and vanilla oak.
Finish Abrupt, notes of spice and charcoal.

GEORGE DICKEL
NO.12, 90 PROOF (45 VOL.)

Color Russet amber.
Nose Aromatic, soft vanilla, fading charcoal.
Body Medium, delicate.
Palate Rich, dry, chocolate, soft fruit, apricots.
Finish Clean, crisp, fruity.

MERCHANDISE
U.S. POST OFFICE
PROVISIONS & GENERAL MERCHANDISE
DISTILLERY TOUR

MICRODISTILLERIES

"SMALL IS BEAUTIFUL" IS THE CREED OF THE MICRODISTILLERS OF THE WEST COAST. COMBINING TRADITIONAL EUROPEAN PRACTICES WITH A MODERN CULINARY APPROACH, THEY PRODUCE SMALL QUANTITIES OF WONDERFUL, HIGHLY INDIVIDUAL SPIRITS.

In the late 1980s, the American consumer, tired of mass production and the dumbing down of their food and drink, rediscovered the quality and complexity of aged American whiskey. The bourbon-makers and their specialty bottlings were joined around this time by a new breed of alchemist: the microdistillers of the West Coast.

Some of these micro-, or craft, distillers followed tradition, and like their microbrewing brothers and sisters before them, they had the pioneer instinct to break with tradition, creating a mini-revolution of distillation. Gin, rum, vodka, grappa, fruit brandies, and whiskey have been revisited and reconstructed in stills from Nantucket to San Francisco, and from Texas to Vermont.

They are at the tail end of a larger gastronomic revolution in the United States; their audience the visionary restaurateurs and educated consumers in the city-states of San Francisco, Seattle, and Portland. Regional pride and sustainable agriculture are often integral to their production philosophy, and focus groups are ignored. Small is beautiful in this culture of good food and drink.

MICRODISTILLERIES

CALIFORNIA

ANCHOR DISTILLING CO., DOMAINE CHARBAY WINERY & DISTILLERY, ESSENTIAL SPIRITS ALAMBIC DISTILLERIES, SAINT JAMES SPIRITS, ST. GEORGE SPIRITS.

OREGON

CLEAR CREEK, MCMENAMIN'S EDGEFIELD.

WEST VIRGINIA

ISAIAH MORGAN DISTILLERY, WEST VIRGINIA DISTILLING CO.

ST. GEORGE SPIRITS

Jörg (pronounced "Yorg") Rupf is the founder and master distiller of St. George Spirits, the first and foremost distiller of *eau-de-vie* in the United States. He began distilling *eau-de-vie* in 1982, and has acted as a mentor for many of the pioneer craft distillers. Born in the Alsace region of southeast France, he was raised in Germany's Black Forest and came to the United States in 1978 to study law at the University of California at Berkeley. He gave up a career in law to pursue the craft of distillation, and has enriched his adopted city of San Francisco with enormous skill and grace.

Rupf explains that his *eau-de-vie* philosophy is to use the best of European traditional practices and combine these with what he does in today's environment. "We have taken this philosophy into the production of our single malt," he explains. "I look on it from a totally culinary perspective." Jörg Rupf and distiller Lance Winters create both their *eau-de-vie* and their single malt from Holstein copper-pot stills that have a 77-gallon (292-liter) capacity.

Winters started working at the Alameda-based distillery nine years ago, and before that he was the brewer at two Bay Area brewpubs. The 86-proof (43-vol.) whiskey, floral, light, and fruity with an orange blossom signature, is distilled from an unhopped two-row barley malt beer. Five percent of the barley is heavily roasted and some is smoked over alderwood and beechwood.

After distillation, St. George Single Malt rests in a combination of different barrel types. To preserve the floral top notes and add oak and vanilla, 82 percent of the Single Malt has been aged in used bourbon (first refill) barrels, 12 percent is aged in new French oak for vanilla and mouth feel, and

THE ESSENTIAL SPIRITS ALAMBIC DISTILLERY *crafts schnapps in an all-copper Stupfler still from Bordeaux, France.*

6 percent in port casks to focus the cocoa flavor and add depth and a pleasant tint. The current, fourth, bottling has whiskey that has matured for over five years.

ANCHOR DISTILLING CO.

Fritz Maytag began distilling on Potrero Hill in 1994, but he has a gastronomic pedigree reaching back to 1965, when he bought the venerable Anchor Steam Brewery in San Francisco. His father created Maytag Blue cheese at the family-run farm in Newton, Iowa, and Fritz himself lives on a vineyard that straddles the prime wine counties of Napa and Sonoma, just north of San Francisco. Here, he makes wine and port under the York Creek label, and grows olives.

The Anchor distillery, tucked into the rear end of the brewery, produces the delightfully aromatic Junipero gin, which is made by hand and with a large number of special herbs and botanicals, and two barrel-strength, pot-distilled rye whiskeys. Both made from a mash of 100 percent rye malt, the current bottlings are Old Potrero Single Malt Whiskey, a peppery, oily dram with mint and chocolate notes, which is aged one year in new, uncharred oak; and Old Potrero Single Malt Straight Rye Whiskey, spicy, buttery, and sweet, which spends three years in new, charred oak barrels.

Maytag says the distillery is dedicated to creating very small batches of traditionally distilled spirits of many types and styles, and claims that his pot-style whiskeys are attempts to recreate the original spirits produced from grain in North America.

EDGEFIELD DISTILLERY *is next to the golf course, up the hill from the movie theater, brewery, and winery.*

LIKE MANY MICRODISTILLERIES, *Edgefield distills a variety of white and aged spirits.*

"It began as a research project and we had around 1,100 bottles," explains Maytag. "Our first whiskey was aged for barely one year and went into the barrel on December 9, 1994. We released it in February of 1996. The Old Potrero Single Malt is our primary brand, what we call our 18th-century style. We get our oak from a wine cooperage where they toast the barrel over oak chips to a medium level. The Straight Rye Whiskey is our 19th-century style. After the repeal of Prohibition, the federal government required that bourbon and rye whiskey had to be aged in new, charred oak barrels. We age ours for three years, and unlike other straight ryes, ours has 100 percent rye malt in the mashbill."

ESSENTIAL SPIRITS *may be in a high-tech location, but the methods are most definitely low-tech.*

ESSENTIAL SPIRITS ALAMBIC DISTILLERIES

Dave Classick's distillery lies between Palo Alto and San Jose in the heartland of high technology. Dave and his wife, Andrea Mirenda, began their family spirits business, Essential Spirits Alambic distilleries, while maintaining careers in Silicon Valley. He distills two versions of European schnapps, and is distilling grappa from cabernet sauvignon grapes. His dry, aromatic, Classick Original American Bierschnaps is distilled from his own, lightly hopped California pale ale, and the floral, spicy Sierra Nevada Bierschnaps is the distillate of generously hopped Sierra Nevada pale ale, supplied by the Chico, California, brewery. The heart of Essential Spirits is the all-copper Stupfler still, handcrafted by Bordeaux's Jean Luis Stupfler, one of France's premier alembic still-makers, and a third-generation craftsman.

SAINT JAMES SPIRITS

Jim Busuttil, owner and distiller at Saint James Spirits in Irwindale, California, has been distilling a single malt whiskey, Peregrine Rock California Pure Single Malt Whiskey, since 1997. A sweet, medium-peated whiskey, it is distilled in a 40-gallon (150-liter) Jacob Carl copper-pot still, and aged for a minimum of three years in bourbon casks.

DOMAINE CHARBAY

Charbay whiskey, distilled by the Karakasevic family at Domaine Charbay in the Napa Valley, is a toasty, herbal, floral whiskey bottled at barrel strength and unfiltered. Produced from 100 percent two-row, unpeated malted barley, with hops added to the wash, Charbay is double-distilled in an 800-gallon (3,000-liter) copper Charentais pot still. The spirit is aged in new, charred American white oak.

CLEAR CREEK DISTILLERY

In Portland, Oregon, Steve McCarthy's 18-year-old Clear Creek distillery is perhaps best known for well-crafted traditional European spirits, among them *eau-de-vie*. But a few years ago, he began distilling in his Holstein pot still a peated, unhopped barley wash made by the city's Widmer Brothers brewery. Aged for a minimum of three years in several kinds of oak, McCarthy's Oregon

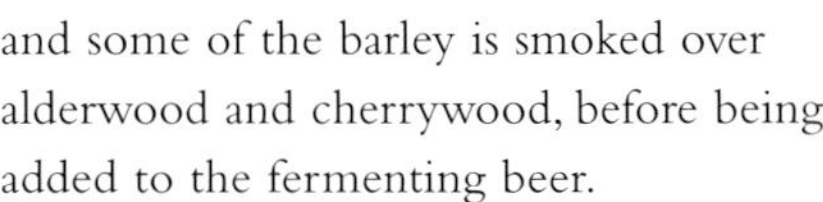

Single Malt Whiskey is one of craft distilling's earliest and boldest whiskeys; a dram that has come into its own.

EDGEFIELD

McMenamin's Edgefield is a hedonistic hotel/brewery/movie theater/winery destination just outside Portland. It is owned by Mike and Brian McMenamin, a pair of prolific, yet laid-back, publican-brewers. They added a distillery and yet another eclectic bar to Edgefield a few years back, up by the golf course, which they also own.

Lee Medoff is the distiller at Edgefield, and he started working there during the fall of 1998. "In the early days, we did lots of experimentation with grappas and brandies," explains Medoff. "But over the last few years, we've narrowed it down to what we're good at and what is in demand. Our gin is called Vintners, and it's a Dutch style with more aggressive aromatics and flavors than the drier, more austere, English-style gins. I'm most excited about our Hogshead whiskey. It is made from 100 percent unpeated barley malt and it's aged in American charred oak. Our still is a Holstein copper pot still and it's very versatile."

A pioneer *in the industry, Clear Creek's Steve McCarthy has been distilling for over 18 years.*

The Edgefield, Clear Creek, and St. George whiskeys are all coming into their fifth year of aging, and the effect of this additional contact with wood places them as serious contenders in the whiskey category.

STILLWATER DISTILLERY

There are a number of other American microdistilled whiskeys maturing across the country. Most of the distilleries also produce unaged vodkas, gins, and rums in order to provide an immediate cash flow.

Stillwater Distillers (formerly Sweetwater) of Petaluma in northern California distills unhopped, fermented wash from its sister brewery, Moylan's, 15 miles (24 km) away. The still has a 600-gallon (2,250-liter) capacity, and is custom-made by the venerable Vendome Copper and Brass Works in Louisville, Kentucky. The whiskey comes from 100 percent, two-row barley malt, and some of the barley is smoked over alderwood and cherrywood, before being added to the fermenting beer.

TRIPLE EIGHT

Across the country, Triple Eight distillery began spirits production in 2000 on the tiny island of Nantucket, Massachusetts. Their winery started in 1981, and their Cisco Brewery has been producing ales and lagers since 1995. One of these beers, Whale's Tale Pale Ale, is distilled in a 200-gallon (780-liter) Holstein pot still to make the whiskey. The unpeated spirit, called Notch ("not scotch") Whiskey, is maturing in bourbon casks, and the earliest stock is about four years old.

COLORADO WHISKEY AND WOODSTONE CREEK

In Denver, Colorado, Stranahan's Colorado Whiskey distillery uses a Vendome still. Owner Jess Graber conveniently gets his malted and roasted barley wash from George Stranahan's Flying Dog brewery, located right next door. The wash is filtered before distillation, and the spirit is currently aging in new, charred American oak. The first distillery to appear in Colorado, it opened in March 2004, and is now producing around three barrels a week.

In Cincinnati, Ohio, Donald Outterson of Woodstone Creek distillery, established in 2000, is aging a variety of whiskey styles, including corn, bourbon, and single malt.

WEST VIRGINIA DISTILLING CO. AND ISAIAH MORGAN

Two whiskey distilleries in West Virginia have capitalized on the area's illicit mountain whiskey heritage and sell unaged whiskeys. One example, Mountain Moonshine, a 100-proof (50-vol.) corn whiskey blended with corn grain neutral whiskey, is made in Morgantown by the West Virginia Distilling Co.

The Isaiah Morgan distillery, founded in 2002, is a true farm distillery in the hill-country community of Summersville. Unaged Southern Moon corn liquor and rye whiskey

Clear Creek's pot stills *are European* eau-de-vie *stills manufactured by the Holstein family. A third of all microdistillers use these versatile stills.*

are produced in a 60-gallon (225-liter) column still. The owner, Rodney Facemire, has operated Kirkwood winery for 13 years.

PIONEER DISTILLERS

One point that should be stressed about these youthful distillates is their extremely limited availability and distribution. St. George Spirits produces around one barrel a day and Anchor Distilling even less. Local citizens are the beneficiaries of most of the production, although bottles from some distilleries have been distributed in New York, Washington, DC, and London. Given the size of the stills, nationwide distribution is not going to happen soon. But that is not what these pioneer distillers are seeking. They want to make the best-quality spirit from the ingredients they choose, and not to be restricted by tradition. Many of the distillery proprietors talk about their spirits from a lifestyle and culinary perspective; they learn as they go and frequently experiment. They are connoisseurs in modern whiskey-making.

TASTING NOTES

Without Scottish or Kentucky traditions to hold them back, the whiskeys from the modern microdistilleries offer a revolution in flavor.

ANCHOR DISTILLING CO.

OLD POTRERO SINGLE MALT WHISKEY

62.1 VOL.

100 percent malted rye; aged one year in new, uncharred oak.

Color Pale brown.
Nose Nutty, vanilla, pepper, and cinnamon, floral, grassy.
Body Medium-full.
Palate Oily, smooth, sweet honey.
Finish Peppery rye, honey, soft, mint chocolate.

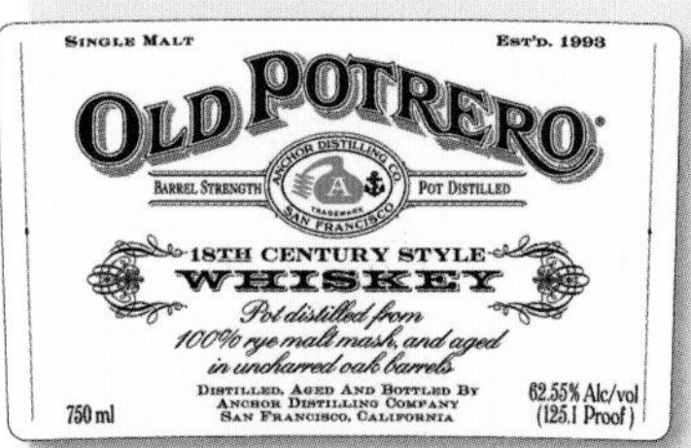

OLD POTRERO SINGLE MALT

OLD POTRERO SINGLE MALT STRAIGHT RYE WHISKEY

62.6 VOL.

100 percent rye malt; aged three years in new, charred oak.

Color Soft amber.
Nose Buttery, chestnuts, vanilla sweetness, oak, and pepper spice.
Body Full, complex.
Palate Sweet, spicy, some oil.
Finish Caramel oak, rye spice, sweetness.

CLEAR CREEK

MCCARTHY'S OREGON SINGLE MALT WHISKEY

40 VOL.

Distilled from fermented mash of peat-malted Scottish barley. Aged three years in old sherry casks and also Oregon oak.

Color Burnished yellow gold.
Nose Burning peat and heather, salt and pepper, earthy, touch of sulfur, and hint of honey, vanilla, and plums.
Body Firm, medium, meaty.
Palate Smooth, with earthy bite, profound smoke, with vanilla sweetness in background.
Finish Clean finish with lingering, seamless smoke, hint of vanilla and caramel. Splash of salt at end.

MCMENAMIN'S EDGEFIELD

HOGSHEAD WHISKEY

46 VOL.

Double-distilled from unhopped, unpeated Hammerhead Ale. (100 percent malted barley.) Aged a minimum of three years in new, heavy, charred American oak.

Color Pale gold.
Nose Sweet honeysuckle, grassy, floral. Vanilla and apricot notes.
Body Medium.
Palate Sweet caramel, malty, vanilla, malt/bourbon balance.
Finish Warming, lingering honey and floral.

EDGEFIELD: HOGSHEAD

ESSENTIAL SPIRITS ALAMBIC DISTILLERIES

CLASSICK, THE ORIGINAL AMERICAN BIERSCHNAPS

40 VOL.

Distilled from lightly hopped California pale ale.

Color Clear.
Nose Fruity, estery, dry, and aromatic.
Body Crisp, smooth.
Palate Light, fruity.
Finish Lingering malt and hop notes.

ST. GEORGE SPIRITS

ST. GEORGE SINGLE MALT

43 VOL.

Distilled from unhopped two-row barley malt beer. Aged three to five years in used bourbon, new French oak, and port pipes.

Color Burnished gold.
Nose Light floral notes, hazelnuts, strawberry, taffy, and oranges, soft coffee notes, vanilla, and background smoke.
Body Light to medium.
Palate Light and delicate, sweet, fruity, hazelnut, cocoa/chocolate. Some mint.
Finish Wisps of smoke, sweet honeysuckle, chocolate, lingering.

SAINT JAMES SPIRITS

PEREGRINE ROCK CALIFORNIA PURE SINGLE MALT WHISKEY

40 VOL.

Distilled in a 40-gallon (150-liter) Jacob Carl copper-pot still. Aged for at least three years in bourbon casks.

Color Green-gold.
Nose Floral and fruity, honeysuckle, apricots, peaches, tickle of smoke.
Body Light, fruity.
Palate Sharp, with more apricot and peach, grassy, malty, and soft smoke.
Finish Harvested hay, sweet malt and wisp of smoke.

JAPAN

From the land of quality in cars, computers, and cameras…
a new way with whiskey

WHITE ICON
The swashbuckling salesmanship of Scotland's Tommy Dewar made his White Label blended whiskey an international icon. The style was followed by Suntory for its early whiskeys in the 1930s. Products like this still exist in Japan. Compare this with the style of a current export label, such as the one shown on p. 253.

JAPAN

MICHAEL JACKSON

Such is the power of popular culture that a movie comedy introduced many Westerners to Japanese whiskey. *Lost In Translation*, directed by Sofia Coppola, had, as its storyline, the making of a commercial for a Suntory whiskey. Until the release of this movie in 2003, even bartenders were more likely to know Suntory for its Midori melon liqueur, a relatively minor product (albeit a very successful one) in the company's extensive range.

EMERGING FROM FUJI'S MOUNTAIN MISTS... NEW WHISKEYS TO TAKE ON THE WORLD

NEW-FOUND CONFIDENCE

Suntory is one of the world's biggest drinks companies. It has been in business for more than 100 years, and has been making whiskey for three-quarters of a century. In the film, both the Japanese and the Americans are the butt of its jokes and, by colluding in its making, Suntory risked loss of face—a fate worse than death in Japan. That the company was willing to take this risk was a sign of a new-found confidence. It was no coincidence that *Lost In Translation* coincided with the launch in the US, UK, and several other international markets of whiskeys from Suntory's two malt distilleries, Yamazaki and Hakushu.

Although most Japanese whiskey is made in the same way as its Scottish inspiration, the products of these two distilleries do not have a hint of tartan or bluebells in their packaging. The Kanji characters, in bold, calligraphic style on their

labels, stand out with a flourish on the shelves of back-bars. Their aromas and flavors are restrained but complex. For the first time, Suntory is talking about the nuances of tropical spice introduced by the use of homegrown Japanese oak in addition to the imported American and Spanish varieties. This is not sufficiently distinctive to qualify Japanese malt whiskey as being a style in its own right, but it has begun to assume a more evident local accent.

The company has been bottling single malts for about 20 years, but in the Western world they have been largely restricted to bars, restaurants, and shops with a Japanese flavor. In their own modest way, the Japanese knew they were making good whiskey but felt that in consumer perception they could never quite match their counterparts from Speyside and the islands. They deferred to Scottishness in the way that a great white jazz musician, however great, never forgets that he is working in a black culture.

BEST OF THE BEST AWARD

A year or so earlier, in 2001, the new confidence of the Japanese distillers was proven to be justified. Suntory's rivals, Nikka, saw a bottling of their Yoichi single malt judged "Best of the Best" in an international tasting organized by *Whisky Magazine*.

PAGODA POWER
This Buddhist temple, built in AD 730, is Yakushi-ji, not far from Yamazaki. Such temples inspired the appearance of the vents on Scottish maltings designed by Charles Chree Doig in the 1890s.

JAPAN'S DISTILLERIES

YOICHI IS A COASTAL distillery, on the northern island of Hokkaido. The rest are on the main island, Honshu; three are in the mountains surrounding Tokyo, and these are truly Highlanders.

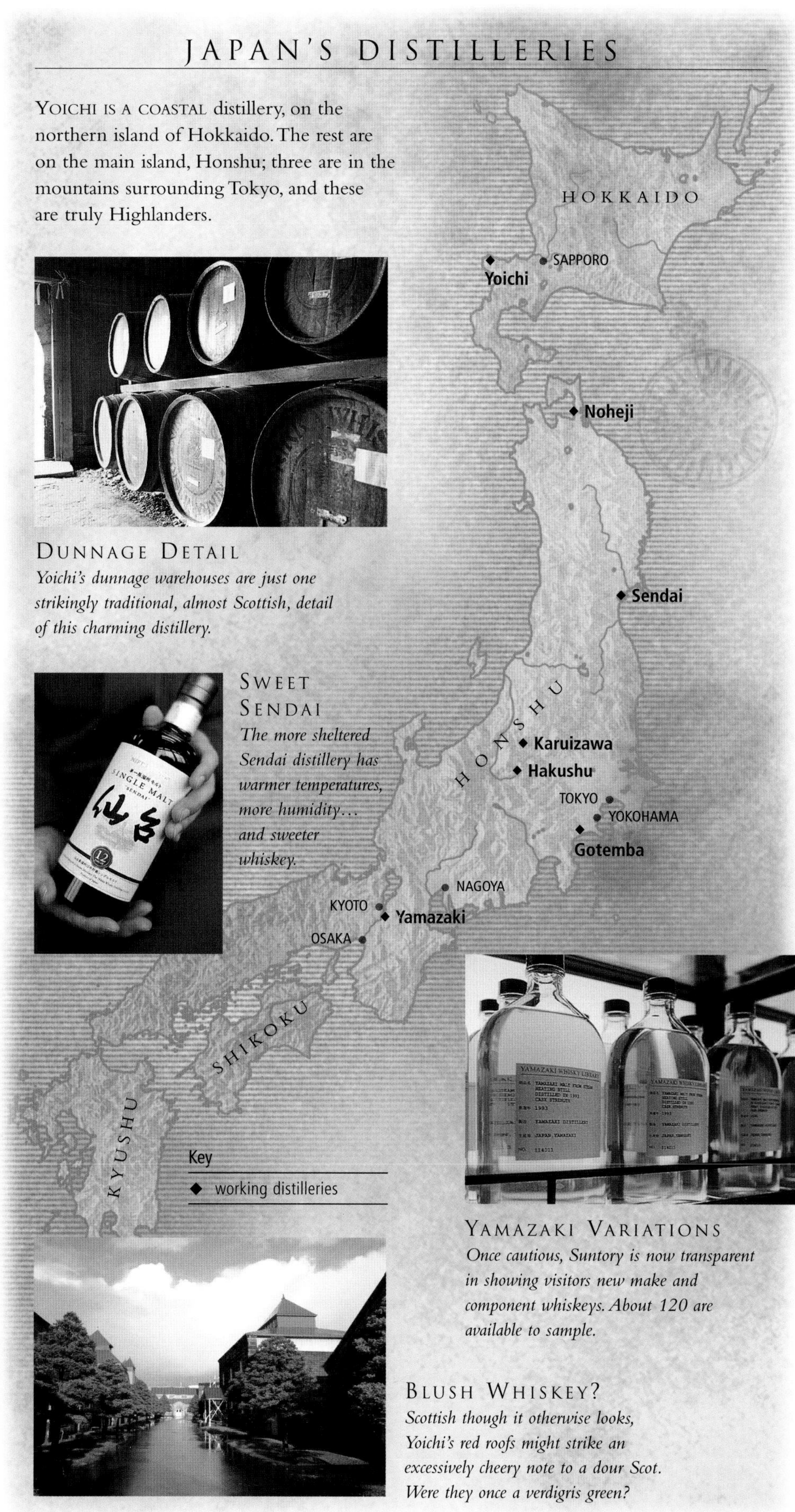

DUNNAGE DETAIL
Yoichi's dunnage warehouses are just one strikingly traditional, almost Scottish, detail of this charming distillery.

SWEET SENDAI
The more sheltered Sendai distillery has warmer temperatures, more humidity... and sweeter whiskey.

YAMAZAKI VARIATIONS
Once cautious, Suntory is now transparent in showing visitors new make and component whiskeys. About 120 are available to sample.

BLUSH WHISKEY?
Scottish though it otherwise looks, Yoichi's red roofs might strike an excessively cheery note to a dour Scot. Were they once a verdigris green?

The 100 whiskeys selected had been category winners in the magazine's regular tastings over a period of three years. They were assembled and tasted by panels in Scotland, Kentucky, and Japan.

The outcome was not quite as dramatic as the "Judgment of Paris" in the 1970s, in which, at a gathering in France, Californian cabernets outscored some of the most famous first-growth clarets (although this comparison did occur to some). In the tasting, each product competed only against others from the same region. Nonetheless, Yoichi's score was higher than that achieved by any other product in the competition. Soon afterward, a similar bottling from Yoichi was chosen as a monthly selection by the Scotch Malt Whisky Society.

THE START OF A LOVE AFFAIR

On the principle that the lands most devoted to spirits are in cold, northern countries, Japan is in the right place. Its northernmost island, Hokkaido, is often compared with Scotland. Japan's main island, Honshu, which accommodates all but one of the distilleries and by far the majority of people, is extremely mountainous. Only volcanic Kyushu and semi-Mediterranean Shikoku might argue for some other type of drink.

As a cereal-growing country, Japan has its own traditional, grain-based drinks. It grows rice, which is fermented to make saké and distilled to produce shochu. Buckwheat and sweet potatoes are also used to make shochu.

The introduction of drinks based on malted barley came during the steamship era, a time when Western nations began to seek commercial opportunities in what we now call the Pacific Rim. The most assertive manifestation of this was the visit of the United States Navy in 1853. The smoky vessels are still remembered in Japan as Commodore Matthew Perry's "Black Ships." This initiative led to a trading treaty between the two countries. A few years later, an American brewery was established in Yokohama, and this later became a Japanese enterprise under the name Kirin.

Japan became yet more open to Western ideas with the ascent of a new emperor and the beginning of the Meiji Restoration in 1868. While the US was admired as a bold modernizer, Western European countries, such as Great Britain, the Netherlands, and Germany, were respected for their culture. Perhaps the US and the UK were seen as the

BAMBOO TOO
High on the hillside, a backdrop of bamboo enwraps the Yamazaki distillery. Plane trees soften the line of the buildings. Down in the valley there are cherry trees, gingko, and magnolia.

SORCERER'S STILL?
It looks rather like a hat belonging to a sorcerer's apprentice, but this curiously conical 1963 still at Yamazaki has lost its magic and will be replaced.

modern Rome and Athens. It is hardly Greek tragedy, but the writing of Scotsman Arthur Conan Doyle is almost an obsession for many Japanese, as is rugby union with its arcane rules. Most of all, the Japanese remain inescapably bunkered in their love for the Scottish sport of golf. Would any of this be complete without a whiskey?

Early attempts at whiskey-making greatly frustrated the Japanese. No matter which herbs and spices they used, they could not produce the authentic aromas and flavors. This phase gave rise to stories of labels proclaiming whiskey "made with Scottish grapes," although they may be apocryphal.

IN SEARCH OF AUTHENTICITY

The man who revealed the secret of authentic whiskey was Masataka Taketsuru, the 25-year-old son of a saké-making family. He attended Glasgow University, and worked briefly at the Hazelburn distillery in Campbeltown and at Longmore, on Speyside. He lodged with the family of a doctor in Kirkintilloch, and befriended the family's daughter, Rita. World War I had just ended and her fiancé had died in Damascus. Masataka gave her a gift of perfume, and she responded with a collection of Burns' poems. Soon afterward they married, without the approval of either family. Masataka took his wife to Japan, where she worked as an English teacher and, through her clients, established many contacts that helped her husband's career.

WHISKEY IN JAPAN TODAY

Masataka Taketsuru helped Suntory establish its first whiskey distillery, and went on to create a distillery of his own: Nikka at Yoichi. Nikka is now owned by the brewer Asahi. The Kirin brewing company also owns a whiskey distillery, at Gotemba, near Mount Fuji. The wine company Mercian has a malt distillery in the mountains near Karuizawa, and there is a sprinkling of other smaller and intermittently active distilleries.

TAKETSURU'S DREAM
As the sun rises on Yoichi, the light casts a dreamlike aura. It is not a hallucination, nor is it a Disney replica. Yoichi is as solid as the stone from which it was built.

HIGHLIGHT

THE MAN WHO SAID: "MINE'S A DOUBLE"

One man brought to realization the Japanese dream of whiskey-making. After studying and working in Scotland, Masataka Taketsuru had the know-how to work with Suntory on the setting up of Yamazaki, Japan's first authentic whiskey distillery, on the island of Honshu. A few years later, he founded his own distillery, Nikka Yoichi. He thus played a critical role in establishing both of Japan's principal producers.

YAMAZAKI

JAPAN'S FIRST AUTHENTIC WHISKEY DISTILLERY HAS LONG COME OF AGE. MATURE AND VERSATILE, IT ROLLS FORWARD—NOT FAST LIKE THE SHINKANSEN, BUT GRADUALLY, WITH BUDDHIST PATIENCE.

The most familiar symbol of Japanese technology, the Shinkansen (Bullet Train), runs right in front of the country's first whiskey distillery, in the village of Yamazaki. Yamazaki is a remarkably rural location considering that it lies between two of the world's biggest urban agglomerations: Tokyo/Yokahama and the Kansai region (Kyoto, Osaka, and Kobe).

SITING THE DISTILLERY

The potential size of the market must have seemed very attractive when Suntory planned its distillery in the early 1920s. A further reason for the location was its proximity to Osaka, Japan's second city, a major port and commercial center, and the home of Suntory. The company's founder, Shinjiro Torri, was very much a child of the outward-looking Meiji Restoration. He began by importing Spanish wines and later built up a successful business making dessert drinks based on Japanese plums. Construction of the Yamazaki distillery began in 1923, and its first whiskey was marketed in 1929.

DISTILLERY DETAILS

YAMAZAKI FOUNDED: 1923.
OWNER: Suntory. METHOD: Pot stills.
CAPACITY: 1.8 million gallons.

Early photographs show a Scottish-looking but rather industrial site. Over the years, the Yamazaki distillery has evolved, and its present red-brick buildings have a 1950s appearance. On the façade, the huge gilt Suntory logo conveys a sense of that period. Rising behind the main building are what appear to be the giant loudspeakers of an Art Deco radio. They turn out to be the kilns of the former maltings.

As is the case with almost all of the distilleries in Japan, the site is kept beautifully. It is surrounded by flowerbeds and shrubberies, and each plant is identified by both its Japanese name and its Latin botanical name.

It is rare to visit a distillery without seeing tour groups, often including school children, being shown around. If there is a mere hint of rain, everyone is provided with an umbrella. Over the years, Suntory has become ever more aware of the value of these visits to the education of the consumer in the qualities of the products it makes. The visitor center at Yamazaki is lined with

ON A ROLL—*pushing a puncheon requires weight and muscle. This cellarman at Yamazaki is developing some momentum for Japanese oak.*

Art deco radio? *Even the villagers say the Yamazaki distillery looks like a giant radio surrounded by forest. Hakushu's location is even more sylvan.*

samples of malt whiskeys of various vintages, and there are opportunities to nose and taste and begin to understand the blender's art.

IMPORTED MALT

Although some malting barley is grown in Japan, much more is imported. Australia is a relatively convenient source, but imports also come from North America and Scotland. Peat from Japan, or Scotland, has occasionally been used, but more often ready-peated malt is imported. The Suntory whiskeys are, in general, very lightly peated.

Yamazaki stopped making its own malt in 1971. Its source of water is less likely to change. In its mineral content the water is comparable to that of Glenmorangie, and it is drawn from several wells amid the bamboo-forested hills behind the distillery. The hills are laced with small streams winding their way to the valley below, where the rivers Katsura, Uji, and Kizu meet. A temple once stood on the hillside, and there is still a shrine on the site of the distillery. Within the shrine, as an offering to the gods, are two casks of whiskey.

As in Scotland, distilleries in Japan have long been used primarily to create malt for blending. The Japanese blended whiskeys have for decades been of an excellent quality, but they have lacked complexity. The reason for this is quite simply that Japan has so few malt distilleries. Nor does the Japanese business ethic make it easy for rival companies to operate by swapping malts as the Scots do. As the first malt distillery in Japan, Yamazaki could add complexity only by using small amounts of imported Scottish malt whiskey.

HOME-GROWN COMPLEXITY

Small proportions of Scotch whiskey are still used in this way, but increasingly Yamazaki is adding complexity of its own creation. The distillery has been developed in such a way as to make it very flexible. For example, both traditional mash tuns and lauter systems have been used. The duality has operated in fermentation, with both wooden and stainless washbacks. The distillery has also experimented with different yeast cultures.

Such a regimen is not unusual, but in the early 1990s Suntory began to tackle the sizable subject of still design. Where once seven pairs of matching stills stood in symmetrical grace, there is now a selection of shapes and sizes to please the most earnest devotee of diversity. Each pair produces a spirit of slightly different character. Were a little partner-swapping to take place, there would be yet further offspring.

Even with the existing pairings, further variations can be achieved by the use of different woods in the casks. This was always true, but Suntory has developed a particular range, incorporating not only Spanish and American oak, but also Japanese oak. It also uses two distinct barrel sizes: American barrel and puncheon. With the possibility of using first, second, or third fill, and a modest amount of recharring, Yamazaki can produce a substantial range of mature whiskeys for its blends, and increasingly for bottling as single malt. And, since the 1980s, Hakushu is also available to contribute.

The traditions of consensus and gradualism that typified Japanese management for so long are changing. To the outsider, they may seem to be changing in a very consensual, measured way. To the Japanese, the changes seem dramatic, especially since the post-industrial era struck their shores. Attempts to harmonize taxes and duties during the late 1980s meant that the traditional Japanese whiskeys became less competitive on price in their local market. However, with a greater variety of malts emerging from Yamazaki's modified, flexible still-house, and more from Hakushu, new blends, such as Hibiki, have begun to make their mark, especially in the export markets.

TASTING NOTES

Yamazaki 12-year-old was a pioneering malt in Japan. Since then, a number of other bottlings have been tasted, including an 18-year-old with a juicy overlay of first-fill dry oloroso; a 1980 Japanese oak, with notes of cedar, orange, and maple syrup; and the big but elegant anniversary bottling reviewed below.

YAMAZAKI SINGLE MALT WHISKY

12-YEAR-OLD, 43 VOL.

In its early days, it was rounded and delicate, as though wary of offending anyone. Now it seems more intense, confident, and elegant.

YAMAZAKI 12-YEAR-OLD

Color Bright, warm, pale yellow.

Nose Flowery. Fresh herbs. Cookies.

Body Smooth. Lightly syrupy.

Palate Lightly clean and sweet. Honeyed. Intense.

Finish Burst of concentrated, perfumy sweetness, balanced by drier, cereal-grain notes, and Japanese oak.

YAMAZAKI 80TH ANNIVERSARY

43 VOL.

Color Deep, warm gold to bronze.

Nose Like walking into an expensive candy store. The sweets are all in boxes, even gift-wrapped, but the aromas of fudge, chocolate, mint, and Parma violets linger in the air.

Body Firm, smooth, rounded.

Palate Honeyed. Cinder toffee. Shortbread.

Finish Balancing flowery dryness.

HAKUSHU

THE WORLD'S BIGGEST MALT DISTILLERY AT FULL CAPACITY, HIGHER AND MORE REMOTE THAN ANY IN SCOTLAND... AND A BIRD SANCTUARY WITH MORE THAN 60 SPECIES.

For the half-century during which it was Suntory's only distillery, Yamazaki had no choice but to be versatile, feeding blends such as Suntory White Label, Reserve, Royal, and Old. During the height of demand for these products, in the postwar recovery period, the company decided it needed a second malt distillery, at Hakushu.

A SHOWPIECE DISTILLERY

Suntory was thinking big. The Hakushu distillery would be a showpiece, and the world's biggest malt distillery. It would occupy a spectacular site, in a beautifully managed environment, at the center of a plateau between the three mountain ranges that are known collectively as the Japanese Alps, just to the north and west of Mount Fuji, Japan's most sacred landmark.

Planned in the 1960s, Hakushu was built in the 1970s. From a purely geographical viewpoint, with no particular reference to the aromas and flavors of the whiskeys, Yamazaki might be deemed a Lowland distillery and Hakushu a Highlander. In fact, Suntory's technical team was expecting Yamazaki's honeyish whiskeys to gain a lighter partner from Hakushu. The water is much softer, and smaller, sleeker stills were installed.

DISTILLERY DETAILS

HAKUSHU FOUNDED: 1970. OWNER: Suntory. METHOD: Pot stills. CAPACITY: 1.6 million gallons.

THE INFLUENCE OF *TERROIR*?

The whiskey did turn out to be light in body, but it is very firm, and with a full flavor. No one is sure why, but there were several new circumstances, some of which had not been experienced before, such as the altitude, distance of the distillery from the sea, and the influences of the landscape in which it is set.

In terms of remoteness, Hakushu outdoes anything Scotland has to offer. From Tokyo (or from anywhere on the coast), it is a journey of about three hours. No Scottish distillery is more than about an hour from the sea. Throughout the journey, a striking feature of the scenery is the constant crossing of shallow rivers, their beds washed with sand, scree, and large pebbles, all sparklingly white on a sunny day. The name Hakushu means "White Sand Bank," an allusion to the source of water. How white is the sand? A little poetic license may have been used, but it is very pale indeed. The poetic license may be god-given: white is the most sacred color in Japan's blend of Shinto and Buddhism. Rivers carve an alluvial path over the local granite, with a notable absence of the peat that would be found in Scotland.

CHUNKY *lantern-style stills, then a tiny one, with a downward arm, line up at Hakushu.*

THE MALTINGS *at Hakushu were always ornamental. They contain an excellent small museum that recounts the history of Suntory and of the development of whiskey.*

At 2,300 feet (700 m), Hakushu is twice as high as the most elevated Scottish distillery. It is also higher than either of the distilleries built in this part of the mountains by its competitors, at Karuizawa and Gotemba.

When the company established the distillery, they bought a large area of the surrounding forest to ensure (in their words) "the purity of the water source and environment." The forest is dense with Japanese varieties of spruce, pine, maple, and sawtooth oak. Tarlike spruce, and resiny, leafy, herbal, "forest-floor" flavors seem to permeate the whiskey during maturation.

PRODUCTION METHODS

Hakushu uses a traditional mash tun, with copper hood; wooden washbacks; and stills heated by direct flame. The elevation of Hakushu makes a significant difference in terms of temperature and atmospheric pressure, and that in turn affects the work of the condenser in the distillery. This means that the new make of Hakushu may be even cleaner and creamier than those produced in the mountain distilleries in Scotland.

When Hakushu was built, with two distilling lines, it was the world's biggest producer of malt whiskey. It shortly became even larger with the addition of a second distillery on the site. The second distillery was initially known as Hakushu East. At the moment, the main distillery is silent, and only the second distillery is being used. The "East" part of the name has been dropped. As at Yamazaki, the original still-houses were uniform in design, and have since been restyled in order to achieve a variety of characteristics in aroma and flavor.

TASTING NOTES

HAVING STARTED EARLIER, Yamazaki has released more malts than Hakushu. Hakushu now has others in the pipeline, having begun with a 12-year-old.

HAKUSHU SINGLE MALT WHISKY

12-YEAR-OLD, 43 VOL.

A beautifully structured, appetizing whiskey. Interesting balance of sweetness and dryness, with the latter narrowly winning.

Color Bright gold.
Nose Honey, heather, chamomile. Perfumy. Some vanilla.
Body Light to medium. Slight viscosity.
Palate Firm. Honeyish. Heathery. Delicate touch of peat.
Finish Long, warming. Marshmallow. Sweet grass. Lemon.

HAKUSHU 12-YEAR-OLD

SUNTORY HIBIKI

21-YEAR-OLD, 43 VOL.

The creation of the Hakushu distilleries (original and East), and the subsequent developments in the design of the stills, greatly increased the range of aroma and flavor characteristics available to Suntory's blender. One result was Hibiki ("Harmony"), a beautiful blend for international sale. The 21-year-old in particular is a classic.

Color Subtle bronze.
Nose Chocolates in a cedar box.
Body Creamy. Oily.
Palate Flavors fused, as though bubbling under. Bittersweet chocolate, orange flower water, acacia honey.
Finish Passion fruit. Steely. Firm. Long.

YOICHI

WEST OF SAPPORO, THIS FAMOUSLY PRETTY DISTILLERY EMERGES FROM ITS ROMANTIC PAST, AND SCORES HIGHLY WITH A WORLD-CLASS PEATY WHISKEY.

Whiskey-lovers in Japan like to point out that the country's northern island, Hokkaido, is almost exactly the same size as Scotland in both land area and population. A further affinity is its tendency to have windy, cold, and snowy weather. In other respects, notably a pioneering spirit, Hokkaido more persuasively resembles its neighbor, Alaska. In the long history of Japan, the settlement of this island is comparatively recent, having taken place mainly after the Meiji Restoration.

Even by Japanese standards, Hokkaido island has a lot of coastline. Not only does Hokkaido reputedly have the best sushi, it also has Japan's most emphatically coastal whiskey. Given that sushi and whiskey are perfect partners, there is something to be said for enjoying them in their home country. It is also an island whiskey. The fishing port and seaside town of Yoichi has a population of fewer than 20,000. Recently, the town has begun to look more commercial, but it is well worth the journey for the whiskey-lover.

The debate between adopting and adapting was one of the reasons Masataka Taketsuru left Suntory and established the Nikka distillery in Yoichi, Hokkaido. The two companies make much of their difference in style. Suntory's adaptations make for an open freshness, and an airy aroma and flavor, and whiskey intended to be more Japanese than Scottish. Nonetheless, in blind tastings with Scottish whiskeys, Suntory's products have generally not been unmasked. Nikka's whiskeys were traditionally bigger and firmer in maltiness, peatier, and more robust in their esters. The Nikka whiskey that won "Best of the Best" was very much in this style, although the more readily available bottlings have been rendered less intense over the years.

DISTILLERY DETAILS

YOICHI FOUNDED: 1934.
OWNER: Nikka. METHOD: Pot stills.
CAPACITY: 40,000 gallons.

VISITING THE DISTILLERY

It is an extraordinary experience to look beneath the decorative battlements of a stone arch (inspired by Glen Grant?), and see the Yoichi distillery; it is the most attractive and distinctive distillery in Japan. Under the gatehouse arch, a path curves through a lawn dotted with miniature pines. To either side, at a respectful distance, a series of small, neat stone buildings follows the line of the path. Each building has a red roof (very un-Scottish), and all have ornamental pagodas. Each has, or had, its own whiskey-making function: steeping, germination, kilning, milling, mashing, fermentation, distillation, and maturation. Masataka and Rita lived in one of these buildings during his years of running this distillery.

THE PRODUCTION PROCESS

The maltings last worked in 1970. When they were in use, the malt was kilned over Hokkaido peat. A pile of the peat remains from those days. Today, malt is imported from Scotland. A well at the distillery provides very soft water. These two elements meet in a traditional mash tun, which seems set to work for some time; it was given a new hood in 2000. The four wash stills are coal-fired, and the three spirit stills use steam. The stills are buxom, but with curves in the right places. The Scottish-style warehouses contain bourbon casks and Japanese oak, with the latter lightly charred.

THE HISTORY OF YOICHI

The creation of the Yoichi distillery as a transplanted slice of Scotland has its poignant aspect. Founder Masataka Taketsuru had a whirlwind romance during his brief stay in Scotland, when lodging with the widow of a doctor in the small town of Kirkintilloch. In a matter of months, he fell deeply in love with her daughter Rita, whose fiancé had recently died in World War I. They married in 1920, without seeking the approval of either family. Masataka, well-educated, handsome,

YOICHI *has its own repair cooperage. There are as many as 20,000 casks on site.*

and from a prosperous family, would have been expected to accept an arranged marriage, and Rita knew nothing of a woman's position in Japanese society, nor did she speak the language. The couple did their best to tackle these problems, but their years at Yoichi were difficult.

As Japan approached war with China, and subsequently the Western allies, Rita found herself living in a country in conflict with her own. In addition, there was a shortage of supplies, and barley was rationed. These constrictions put the couple under enormous strain just at a time when Masataka was trying to realize his dream: his own distillery, making authentic whiskey, in Japan. By the time the business was well established, Rita's health was failing, and she died in the early 1960s. Masataka died in the late 1970s. Their bungalow at the distillery is still maintained in their memory.

Their nephew Takeshi, whom they had adopted as a son, ran the business for a time. The company had the backing of the brewers Asahi, who eventually became its owners.

TASTING NOTES

NIKKA WAS SLOW to introduce single malts, but they were generally worth the wait. The two shown here were among a range of recent bottlings.

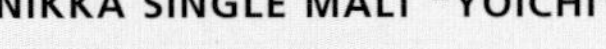

NIKKA SINGLE MALT "YOICHI"

10-YEAR-OLD, 43 VOL.

Like eating pralines in front of a log fire. This is a wonderful whiskey at 10 years old. I like the flavors best in this lively interplay. Others might prefer them to be melded with more maturity.

Color Full gold, with a hint of bronze.
Nose Pronounced, astonishingly fresh, dry, peat. Extremely appetizing.
Body Medium
Palate Mint creams, then orangey.
Finish After the creaminess, the peat surges back. Clean, sweetish, soft smokiness.

NIKKA SINGLE MALT "YOICHI"

NIKKA SINGLE MALT "YOICHI"

15-YEAR-OLD, 45 VOL.

Creamier than the 10-year-old, but that softens the peatiness, Between these two, I preferred the 10.

Color Full gold, with a hint of bronze.
Nose Polished oak, then smoky.
Body Medium, firm, oily, creamy.
Palate Lots of malt. Chewy.
Finish More crisply peaty.

A RAINY DAY IN YOICHI. *Even the weather reflects the Scottish influence. The former maltings, with two kilns, are in the right foreground. Behind are the mash house and the tun room. On the left is the still-house.*

SENDAI

MORE HINTS OF SCOTLAND... THE TOPOGRAPHY COULD BE SPEYSIDE, BUT THE WHISKEYS TASTE MORE LIKE LOWLANDERS. THEY ARE MALTY, SWEET, AND DESERVE TO BE BETTER KNOWN.

The romantic story that led to the making of whiskey in Yoichi, the remarkably pretty appearance of the distillery there, and its location in a fishing village tend to overshadow Nikka's second distillery at Sendai. Sendai is also in the north of Japan, but on the main island, Honshu. While not as famous for high gastronomy as Kyoto, this northern region has an elaborate cuisine, and local delicacies include oysters and flatfish.

Although Sendai is not especially well-known to the rest of the world, it is one of Japan's major cities. It was a fort in the 1600s, became a city in the Meiji Restoration, and was largely destroyed in World War I, after which it was rebuilt with a new harbor. It has more than a million inhabitants, is a center for education, and is the regional capital for a large northern slice of Honshu. The city is roughly halfway between Tokyo and the tip of Honshu. It has, over the years, absorbed half a dozen surrounding towns.

Although the distillery is in Greater Sendai, it is about half an hour's drive west of the city itself, in the broad, wooded valley of the Hirose river. The countryside here has some parallels with Speyside. The Ou mountains give rise to a system of rivers that flow between rolling hills and across plains until the land descends to the Pacific.

DISTILLERY DETAILS

SENDAI FOUNDED: 1969
OWNER: Nikka. METHOD: Pot and column stills.
CAPACITY: 528,000 gallons.

SITING THE DISTILLERY

Masataka Taketsuru spent three years in the area, looking for a site. He is said to have been persuaded when he tasted the water of the Nikkawa River, and a plaque marks the spot where this historic draft was enjoyed. Taketsuru also felt that the humidity generated by the adjoining rivers would be conducive to good maturation. Like Suntory's Hakushu distillery, which it preceded, Sendai was intended to produce large volumes of mildly malty whiskey to bulk up the company's blends. The distillery was established in 1969, and expanded in 1979 and 1989.

Although Taketsuru had already made a tribute to the architecture of Scottish distilleries when he built Yoichi, he obviously continued to hold them in awe. The greater size of Sendai, and the recent construction, create a more industrial impression, but it is clear that every effort was made to sustain a sense of Scottish tradition and rural ambience. An imposing entrance off the road continues down a winding drive fringed with oak trees. To add to the rural charm, a grassy slope leads to a lake with swans.

The distillery itself is a sizable, chunky construction of handsome, dark red brick, with a decorative malting kiln in traditional style. After the bright red rooftops of Yoichi, the more restrained russet of Sendai makes a very distinctive impression.

THE PRODUCTION METHODS

The site has both pot and column stills, in separate buildings. The pot stills are, as might be expected, used to produce malt whiskeys. More than one style is made, to provide different notes for the blender. The columns also produce a malt distillate for blending, but their principal function is as a grain distillery.

The malt distillery has two full-lauter tuns, which are operated to different degrees of clarity, depending upon the style of whiskey that is being made. Fermentation is in stainless steel, and a number of different yeasts are used. The pot stills are wide-bottomed and bulbous, with a boil ball, fat neck, and short condenser. In the original configuration, two pairs of stills are mounted on a red brick platform set in a marble-floored still-house. This arrangement was repeated when the distillery was expanded.

The well-designed grain distillery is very sharp-looking: in a square-sided tower, with its galleried walkways protected by bright

RURAL OR URBAN? *Sendai attracts 200,000 visitors a year.*

green railings, it has a Coffey still and two rectifying columns. There are also further columns for the production of grain-neutral alcohol. Sendai has more than 20 warehouses, maturing spirit mainly in American oak hogsheads. American barrels and sherry butts are also used. The butts are stacked only two high, and a handful of the warehouses are in traditional dunnage style.

THE WHISKEYS

Sendai's malt whiskeys have a good cereal-grain character, a notably honeyed sweetness, and some estery floweriness. Despite their northerly origin, and the comparisons with Speyside, they are perhaps more reminiscent of some of the great Scottish Lowland whiskeys when at their best.

TASTING NOTES

SENDAI PRODUCES a light, fresh, clean, grain whiskey, and a bigger, oilier example. Some older malts, from sherry, are deliciously creamy, flowery, and even slightly smoky.

NIKKA SINGLE MALT "SENDAI"
12-YEAR-OLD, 45 VOL.
Totally different in style from the Yoichi malts. A very enjoyable, sweet pick-me-up—after a round of golf?

Color Full gold. Very slight hint of bronze.
Nose Faint tobacco. Autumn leaves. Hint of pine.
Body Very creamy and oily.
Palate Sweet. Cereal grains. Almost like crunching on malt.
Finish Very sweet. Cookie-like. Light, perfumy dryness.

THE NIKKA WHISKY
34-YEAR-OLD, 43 VOL.
Seems to contain a high proportion of Sendai's grassy, grainy, nutty maltiness.

Color Full amber-red.
Nose Succulent. Powerful.
Body Maple syrup.
Palate Ground almonds. Marzipan. Cakey.
Finish Oatmeal bitterness and chewiness. Dark grass. Subliminal suggestion of peat.

SENDAI SENTRIES. *Well-polished, muscular stills stand as smart as sentries. The distinctive boil ball, between the bulbous base and the neck, helps to cool the vapors slightly so that the heavier volatiles fall back. This contributes to Sendai's delicate character.*

Gotemba, Karuizawa, & Toa Shuzo

KIRIN'S DRAGON-HORSE RIDES INTO KENTUCKY, TOA SHUZO'S GOLDEN HORSE ENTERS THE RACE, AND KARUIZAWA BETS ON VINTAGE.

After the big two, there are three smaller whiskey-makers in Japan. One is a subsidiary of a major brewer, another grew out of a wine-making company, and the third has its origins in saké.

GOTEMBA

The main base for visitors to Mount Fuji is the town of Gotemba. A distillery was established there in 1973, the result of a joint venture between the Canadian international giant Seagram and the Japanese brewer Kirin—known to beer-lovers for its "Dragon-Horse" logo, drawn from Confucian myth.

At the time of the original cooperation, Seagram also owned some of Scotland's most famous distilleries and blends (the Glenlivet and Chivas Regal, for example), and the Kentucky distillery Four Roses. Some of these products gained distribution in Japan through Kirin. At the same time, the Japanese venture into whiskey-making benefited from Seagram's breadth of experience in distilling and blending whiskey.

DISTILLERY DETAILS

GOTEMBA FOUNDED: 1973.
OWNER: Kirin. METHOD: Pot and column stills.
CAPACITY: 1.9 million gallons.

KARUIZAWA FOUNDED: 1955.
OWNER: Mercian. METHOD: Pot stills.
CAPACITY: 40,000 gallons.

TOA SHUZO FOUNDED: 1941.
OWNER: Mr. Kazuki Onishi METHOD: Pot stills.
CAPACITY: Not currently producing.

Four Roses whiskey was especially successful in Japan, and when the Seagram company withdrew from the whiskey market, Kirin acquired Four Roses. As a result, the Japanese now have a stake in American whiskey. Kirin also became sole owners of the Gotemba distillery. This distillery produces both malt and grain whiskeys, in separate pot and column still-houses.

Malt is imported from Ireland and Scotland, at various levels of peating. Emphasis is placed on achieving as clear a wash as possible. The mash tun, with its unusually high dome, is stainless steel, as are all the washbacks. The wash stills are pear-shaped and the spirit stills have a boil ball. Both wash stills and spirit stills have a lyne arm that tilts upward slightly. The condensers are very large and are found inside the still-house. An adjoining still-house produces grain whiskey. It has a copper beer still, with further columns to separate aldehydes and rectify the distillate.

The house character of the new make is clean and estery, with notes of sweet plums and orange flower water. Maturation is mainly in bourbon wood, and warehousing is in a modern, racked block. Now that the establishment is wholly Japanese, new products are awaited with interest.

TASTING NOTES

Each of these distilleries produces a full range of whiskeys. Those shown here are representative examples.

GOTEMBA

FUJI GOTEMBA PURE MALT
NO AGE STATEMENT, 43 VOL.
This is an all-malt whiskey, but with a difference. Two types of spirit are used. One is a conventional malt whiskey produced in the normal way in a pot still. The other is all malt, but produced in the distillery's column still.

Color Deep gold.
Nose Fruity. Apples and oranges. Apples dominate.
Body Light but firm.
Palate Malt-accented. The maltiness is both dry and sweet, with an interesting interplay between these two elements.
Finish Gently dry. Polished oak.

KARUIZAWA

KARUIZAWA SINGLE MALT
17-YEAR-OLD, 40 VOL.
This single malt is pleasant as a dessert whiskey, but unfortunately lacks complexity.

KARUIZAWA SINGLE MALT

Color Tan/orange. Bright.
Nose Slow to open. Earthy. Riesling. Linseed oil. Eventually pears, strawberries, gumdrops.
Body Smooth.
Palate Sweetish. Chocolatey. Sliced toasted almonds.
Finish Warming. Soothing.

TOA SHUZO

GOLDEN HORSE CHICHIBU SINGLE MALT
12-YEAR-OLD, 50 VOL.
Bittersweet and sophisticated.

Color Distinctly fuller. Gold to pale orange. Ripe (but not dried) figs.
Nose Fruitier. Orange. English clotted cream. Vanilla. Sponge.
Body Cakey. Chewy.
Palate Candied citrus peels. Zest of orange and lemon.
Finish Marmaladey bitterness. Sophisticated.

MERCIAN KARUIZAWA

Of all the inland resorts near Mount Fuji, the most elevated socially is Karuizawa. The power-brokers and financiers of Tokyo vacation and retire here. Between the two locations are the vineyards around Yamanashi.

The wine producer Mercian has owned the Karuizawa distillery for four decades, but only added the Mercian name to its whiskeys in the 1990s. The original name, Sanraku Ocean, is still used on lower-priced products.

The oldest buildings at Karuizawa distillery were part of a vineyard before distillation was introduced in the late 1950s and early 1960s. The first products were blends, and today there are also vattings. Vintage casks from 1970 to 1989 can be bottled to order via the Internet, although any whiskey-lover visiting Japan would want to see the distillery. It has a rustic appearance, and likes to compare itself to Edradour, the smallest distillery in Scotland.

The Japanese mash tun is at least 40 years old. Its washbacks are made from Oregon pine, and the stills look like milk churns or, perhaps, early space rockets. The stills have always been steam-heated, but they have fake fireboxes. Leaded windows add a final flourish of rustic eccentricity. Karuizawa whiskeys tend toward a firm maltiness, with a cedary, citric sweetness.

A VIEW FROM ABOVE. *More utilitarian than beautiful, Toa Shuzo is the most urban of the Japanese whiskey distilleries.*

THESE TWO STILLS *were installed at Toa Shuzo distillery in 1981, and are responsible for the Golden Horse single malt range.*

TOA SHUZO

The Toa Drinks Company has existed since the 16th century, but only started producing whiskey after World War II. Its best-known whiskey, Golden Horse, was released in 1999. The 21st generation of the Toa family is currently in charge.

Toa began as a brewer of saké, in the town of Chichibu, northwest of Tokyo. The company opened a distillery in nearby Hanyu to produce shochu, and added whiskey after World War II. Initially, the whiskey was produced in a single still, through which first and second runs were made. A two-still system was introduced in 1981. As soon as the distillates were running smoothly, the company started laying them down, for release in the 1990s and 2000s.

The distillery at Hanyu makes shochu and whiskey, although it has been silent recently. It looks very different from any of the other malt whiskey distilleries in Japan; it is a down-to-earth distillery, rather than state-of-the-art.

The whiskey is made from imported British malt, with light-to-medium peating, and with water from a nearby spring. The steel washbacks, which are cooled with water jackets, were formerly used for saké. The pot stills are of the lantern type, with a fat neck and a lyne arm that floats slightly downward. The whiskeys in the Golden Horse range are single malts, with a touch of peat and some grassy, vegetal, sweetly fruity notes.

THE REST OF THE WORLD

Innovative newcomers from Finland to Australia are expanding the universe of whiskey-making

Europe

Jürgen Deibel

SCOTLAND'S FELLOW CELTS IN BRITTANY, AS WELL AS OTHER EUROPEAN DISTILLING ENTHUSIASTS, HAVE SHOWN THAT THEY TOO CAN MAKE VERY ENJOYABLE WHISKEYS.

From an occasionally uncertain start, a healthy number of whiskey distilleries have become established in mainland Europe.

GERMANY

For centuries, Germany was famous primarily for its excellent beers and wines, and distilling was used only in the production of schnapps. However, after World War II, Scotch, Irish, and American whiskeys became more widely available, and interest grew. In the late 1950s, a blended whiskey called Racke Rauchzart became very popular, selling up to three million bottles a year during the late 1960s. The whiskey was made by A. Racke in the town of Bingen, and remains popular.

A few other whiskeys also appeared after the war, but none of them lasted. They included Jacob Stück, a brand simply called Whisky, and Private Whisky. There were also whiskey distilleries in the former East Germany, among them VEB Edelbrände in Luckenwalde, the maker of Der Falckner. However, production ceased after the fall of the Berlin Wall in 1989.

The real boom in modern German whiskey distillation started in 1984, when Robert Fleischmann, from Eggolsheim, near Bamberg, began production. In 1994, he marketed his first whiskey, called Piraten Whisky. Originally only made for small-scale consumption, it quickly developed a name for itself. The whiskey was the first in Germany to be distilled according to Scottish production methods, and was made from malted barley. These days, Fleischmann makes a number of other malt whiskeys, including Spinnaker, Krottentaler, and Grüner Hund.

DISTILLERIES

GERMANY
BLAUE MAUS DESTILLERIE, GRUEL, LANTENHAMMER, VOLKER THEURER, ZAISER, ERICH SIEGEL, WEINGUT MÖßLEIN.

AUSTRIA
REISETBAUER, WEIDENAUER, WALDVIERTLER ROGGENHOF, SIGGI HERZOG, WOLFRAM ORTNER.

SWITZERLAND
HOF HOLLE, BRENNEREIZENTRUM BAUERNHOF.

FRANCE
WARENGHEM, CLAEYSSENS, MENHIRS, GUILLON.

EASTERN EUROPE
CZECH REPUBLIC: OLOMOUC (1 & 2).
POLAND: ZIELONA GÓRA.

Inge and Christian Gruel from Owen/Teck, near Stuttgart, were inspired to start making Gruel Single Grain Whisky after a visit to Scotland, and have won a number of awards for their product. It is the only grain whiskey made in Germany. Unusually, it is sold in wine-shaped bottles.

In 1990, Rainer Mönks of the Sonnenschein distillery in Witten (near Dortmund) produced a one-off single malt whiskey to celebrate the 125th anniversary of the distillery. It was made from imported malt from Scotland, and was matured in Scottish whiskey casks for 10 years, prior to a finishing period in sherry casks for a further two years. Sonnenschein Single Malt is no longer available.

Slyrs, a Bavarian malt whiskey, distilled in Schliersee, is made from malted barley. It was first released in 2002, after the legal maturation period of three years, and continues to generate much interest. There are several other German whiskeys, including Ammertaler from Tübingen; Zaiser's Schwäbischer whiskey; Dettinger whiskey; and

Slyrs malt whiskey *is distilled at the pretty town of Schliersee, on the Bavarian Lakes in Germany.*

Slyrs, *from Lantenhammer distillery in Germany, has recently been introduced to the market with great success.*

Fränkischer whiskey. Most use a mixture of different grains. Bierbrände, which are spirits distilled from beer, are an interesting new development, but due to the fact that they are not left to mature for long, cannot strictly be called whiskeys.

AUSTRIA

In 1995, the Reisetbauer distillery in Axberg, near Linz, released almost 1,000 bottles of their first whiskey. The spirit, matured in Chardonnay and Trockenbeerenauslese ("TBA") casks for six years, was a success, and sold out quickly. The whiskey is made from local malted barley, and is not peated.

A new venture from the Weidenauer distillery (established in 1838) is Waldviertler oat whiskey, which is distilled twice, and matured in selected medium-toasted oak barrels. Oats were probably used in early whiskey-making in Scotland, but are not often used today.

Johann Haider produces several styles of whiskeys in his Waldviertler Roggenhof distillery, situated halfway between Vienna and Salzburg in the Wachau region. His range includes a rye whiskey, two rye malt whiskey—one called "Nougat"—and two barley malts—with one called "Karamell." The names reflect the key flavor characteristic in each case. They are matured on site in selected oak barrels made from Manhartsberger summer oak, and all are single-barrel bottlings.

Other producers include Siggi Herzog from Saalfelden, who makes a special whiskey from spelt (a type of wheat), and Wolfram Ortner from Bad Kleinkirchheim, who produces Nock-Land whiskey.

SWITZERLAND

The pioneer of whiskey-making in Switzerland is Ernst Bader. In 1999, as soon as using barley for making spirits was permitted by law, he started making Holle Single Malt whiskey at Hof Holle distillery, located at

Rye is the *main ingredient in Haider's whiskeys, which are matured in oak barrels for three to six years.*

Ernst Bader, *one of the prime innovators of Swiss whiskey-making, is seen here at his Hof Holle distillery.*

Lauwil, close to Basel. The distillate is produced with malted barley from southern Germany, and is matured in white wine casks from Burgundy, in France. The water used in the process comes from the local area and is well known for its softness.

A new variety of whiskey is now being made with rauchmalz, a traditional malted barley from Bamberg, in southern Germany. Examples are Swissky and St. Moritzer Single Malt, made by Edi Bieri and Kurt Uster of Brennereizentrum Bauernhof in the town of Baar.

Reisetbauer

FRANCE

This is a country better known for its wine, Cognac, and champagne, but its best-known whiskey is probably Amorik, from the Warenghem distillery in the town of Lannion, in Brittany. The region is proud of its Celtic traditions. First released in 1999, Amorik is a single malt whiskey, distilled and matured in the Scottish style. It is light and fruity, and slightly woody and dry in the mouth. Warenghem also makes Whisky Breton, a blended whiskey, which is similarly light, with pronounced vanilla notes on the nose.

La Distillerie des Menhirs in Plomelin, Brittany, uses partly malted buckwheat to produce its Eddu whiskey—named after the Breton word for buckwheat (*blé noir* in French). The whiskey has distinct fruity berry notes on the nose.

Warmbrechies, in the northwestern corner of France, is home to the Claeyssens distillery. Warmbrechies single malt is distilled in a combination of column and pot still. It is dry, very strong on the nose, and is not a typical whiskey.

The Guillon distillery, in the Champagne region, released its first single malt in 2002. Guillon is produced in a small *eau-de-vie* still, Smoke from beech and oak leaves is used to dry the malted barley for this whiskey.

EASTERN EUROPE

In many Eastern European countries, what was called whiskey was for many years a neutral spirit that had been artificially colored. European Union regulations have put a stop to this, and real whiskey is now starting to replace it.

Of all the Eastern European countries, the Czech Republic has been making whiskey the longest, having started in the 1970s. Today, the center of whiskey distilling is the town of Olomouc, where the two distilleries produce both malt and blended whiskey. The best known are King Barley (also available, confusingly, as a blend) and Gold Cock; both of these single malts are matured for six years. Several other brands are marketed as well, although they are mainly blends.

Although vodka is universally regarded as the national spirit of Poland, Dark Whisky and Old Family Whisky are made by the Zielona Góra distillery. Dark Whisky is an extremely light single malt, with fruity notes and a soft, round palate.

Asia and Australasia

Willie Simpson

JAPAN SPEARHEADED EASTERN WHISKEY-MAKING IN THE EARLY 20TH CENTURY, BUT IT WAS NOT UNTIL DECADES LATER THAT OTHER PARTS OF ASIA AND AUSTRALIA FOLLOWED SUIT.

Production of whiskey in Asia and Australasia derives, in part, from historical links with the UK, but each country has developed whiskeys with distinctive personalities.

DISTILLERIES

PAKISTAN & INDIA
MURREE (Pakistan); AMRUT (India).

THAILAND
MEKHONG.

AUSTRALIA
LARK, TASMANIA, WHISKY TASMANIA, BAKERY HILL, SMITH'S.

NEW ZEALAND
WILSON.

PAKISTAN

One of the Islamic countries that permits the production of alcoholic drinks "for visitors," Pakistan is home to the Murree brewery and distillery, near Rawalpindi, in the Punjab. The company began as a brewery in 1861, and started production of pot-still, matured, malt whiskey in the 1960s. Murree Single Malt bears no age statement, but is said to have eight to 10 years' maturation. It is bottled at 43 vol., and has a flowery aroma and finish, with a sugary, hard-candy character.

INDIA

There are about 10 dedicated whiskey distilleries in India. The first to enter the world market was the Amrut distillery, near Bangalore in Karnataka, which is one of the most liberal states in respect of alcohol availability and consumption.

Amrut Single Malt is named after an elixir of life in Indian mythology. Made from unpeated malt grown in the Himalayan foothills of the Punjab and malted in Jaipur, Rajasthan, it is matured in bourbon and virgin oak. Bottled at 40 vol. with no age statement, it has a fresh, grassy, aroma, with red apples, cereal grains, and caramel apples in the palate.

Beware: cheap Indian arrack made from molasses can be found labeled as "whiskey." The term "blended malt whiskey" is equally compromised; it needs to contain only four percent malt. A whiskey identified as pure or single malt is required to be just that.

THAILAND

The Scottish producer Inver House has some well-regarded distilleries, notably Old Pulteney (*see p. 132*), but no superstars. The principal shareholders, the Thai family of Khun Charoen, offer serious competition—the family's Mekhong whiskey commands 89 percent of the Thai market. The whiskey has a cream-toffee sweetness, contributed in part by generous use of new American oak, as well as spices. The family also has a new, Scottish-style distillery in Thailand, but the whiskeys have not yet been revealed.

AUSTRALIA

In the mid-1980s, pioneering whiskey producers Bill and Lyn Lark decided there was no reason why high-quality single malt whiskey could not be made in Tasmania. There was abundant pure mountain water and Franklin barley, a special strain developed for Tasmania's cool climate. A supply of peat was found in Tasmania's Central Highlands.

Having acquired a tiny, antique still, the Larks faced changing federal legislation covering distillation. The Commonwealth Distillation Act 1901 permitted only large-scale operations, stipulating a minimum wash-still capacity of 700 gallons (2,700 liters). The Larks approached their local parliamentary member, and, in a matter of weeks, the legislative regulations were amended; they were granted a general distiller's license, the first issued in Tasmania since the 1830s.

The first batch of Lark's Single Malt Whisky was released in 1998. It soon sold out, and subsequent production has struggled to match demand. The whiskey is bottled after a minimum of five years spent in 25-gallon

The purity *of the water collected by New Zealand's mountains (here near Porter's Pass, South Island) makes it perfect for use in whiskey distillation.*

THE LARK DISTILLERY *occupies a harborside site in Hobart, Tasmania, which has a cool climate closer to that of Scotland than mainland Australia. Lark pioneered the current Australian whiskey-making revival.*

(100-liter) casks. About 20 percent of the malted barley is smoked over peat. Lark's Single Malt Whisky (43 vol.) is complex, full-flavored with a distinctive smoky pepperiness.

Also located on the island, the Tasmania distillery opened in 1994, utilizing a replica 1860 French alembic Charentais-style pot still. Sullivan's Cove Premium Whisky was released in March 1997, at less than three years old, and it generally lacked finesse. After two changes of ownership, distillation ceased in 2002. The equipment (along with a large stock of aged whiskey) was relocated to a warehouse in Cambridge, some 12 miles (20 km) outside Hobart, in 2004. Currently, there are plans to recommence distilling and to release the aged whiskey as Hobart Single Malt and Old Hobart Cask Strength in 2005.

Whisky Tasmania, the most ambitious new whiskey venture in the Antipodes, has more than 2,500 casks (132,000 gallons/ 500,000 liters) currently maturing in its bond stores. The stainless-steel distillery produced its first whiskey run in 1999. The whiskey is matured in used bourbon barrels, and the company aims to produce 500 casks each year. A barrel sample (no name is available at press time) indicates a light, grassy spirit in the style of an Irish whiskey. The final range will include varying degrees of peat.

The Bakery Hill distillery in Melbourne produced the equivalent of just 5,000 bottles in its first three years of operation, but the subsequent whiskey, released in 2004, attracted widespread praise. David Baker uses a portion of peated malt, and the whiskeys mature in 15- and 25-gallon (50- and 100-liter) casks, which have been rebuilt from bourbon and French oak port barrels. Although less than three years old, the whiskeys benefit from an accelerated aging process that results from the use of smaller casks. The Bakery Hill range is unfiltered and bottled at 46 vol. Classic Malt is sweetish, with vanillin and hints of spice and ginger. Double Wood is deep gold and malty, with a dry, peppery finish. Peated Malt is fruity and complex, with hints of iodine and seaweed.

Smith's Angaston Whisky (Vintage 1997, aged seven years), released in September 2004, was a single batch resulting from 4,800 gallons (18,000 liters) of wash produced at Cooper's Brewery, Adelaide (made from Franklin barley and seeded with Cooper's Ale yeast). The wash was double-distilled at S. Smith & Sons' Angaston winery in the Barossa Valley, in their original 1931 (brandy) pot still. Similar batches were produced in 1998 and 2000. Smith's seven-year-old Angaston Whisky of 1997 is a medium-gold color. With hints of hay, toffee, and vanilla, it is clean, unpeated, and sweetish.

NEW ZEALAND

The first New Zealand distillery opened at Dunedin in 1974. The Wilson distillery first produced two blended whiskeys, Wilson's and 45 South. In 1984, a single malt was released, named Lammerlaw after its water source in the Lammermoor hills outside Dunedin.

The company was acquired by Seagram's in the 1980s, but production ceased in 1997 and the distillery was dismantled in 2002. Lammerlaw is still available in some New Zealand retail outlets, although it is becoming increasingly difficult to find. A large stock of mature whiskey produced between 1987 and 1993 was acquired by the New Zealand Malt Whisky Co., an independent liquor distributor, and is currently being marketed as Milford Single Malt. Bottlings include 10- and 12-year-old (43 vol.) plus a limited edition 16-year-old (46 vol.).

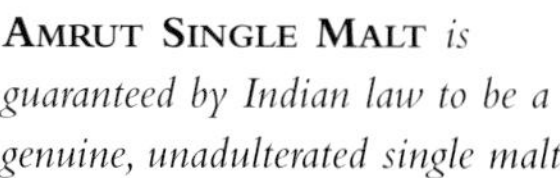
AMRUT SINGLE MALT *is guaranteed by Indian law to be a genuine, unadulterated single malt.*

JIM BEAM
HOUSE of
Glenfiddich
Scotch Whisky

ENJOYING WHISKEY

Whiskey Cocktails

Dale DeGroff

SINCE 1830, COCKTAILS OF ALL KINDS HAVE BEEN DEVELOPED, INCLUDING A WIDE RANGE USING WHISKEY AS THEIR BASE.

NIGHTTIME NEW YORK
The fleet-footed and friendly New York bartenders have made the Manhattan bar a popular destination for travelers for many generations.

The first cocktails appeared in the early 19th century. They were simple and direct, based on gin, brandy, or whiskey, flavored with bitters, and sweetened with curaçao. The first cocktail hour on record took place in the 1830s at the apothecary shop of Antoine Amadée Peychaud in New Orleans. Peychaud concocted a bitter flavor additive from herbs, spices, and alcohol, which he called Peychaud's Bitters, and which is still available today. He mixed the bitters with Sazerac brandy and served the drink in a two-sided egg cup called a *coquetier*. This was the birth of the Sazerac cocktail. Some believe that *coquetier* is the source of the English word "cocktail" but, in fact, "cocktail" first appeared in print in 1806, when Peychaud was only three years old.

NEW YORK USED TO BE A RYE TOWN, AND THE MANHATTAN WAS THE PREMIER WHISKEY DRINK

Until 1803 the Louisiana Territory, to which New Orleans belonged, was owned by the French, and the names Peychaud and Sazerac are French. Sazerac was one of many French brandies with the same *-ac* word ending, which dates back to the Roman conquest: Armagnac, Cognac, Jarnac, and Polignac are all at the heart of brandy culture.

THE SPREAD OF WHISKEY

By the middle of the 19th century, the Sazerac cocktail was being made with American rye whiskey rather than French brandy. After the sale of Louisiana to the United States, New Orleans became steadily more American: links with France decreased and communications with the rest of the US gradually increased. Consequently, American rye whiskey became more readily available and less expensive than imported French Cognac.

Rye whiskey was, in fact, made some distance away, in the more northerly states of Maryland and Pennsylvania. Before the advent of the railroads, local distribution was difficult, even within the same state. However, it was easy to send whiskey, and other products, by barge down the great rivers to the ports of the south—hence the rise of New Orleans as the cocktail capital it remains today.

With the industrial revolution came steam-powered river boats that could make the trip upstream against the strong currents as well as downstream, plus an expanding railroad system and a growing network of canals in the northeast. All this opened up big cities on the eastern seaboard, such as New York and Boston, to the western whiskey-makers, and business improved.

COCKTAIL HEYDAY

The period between 1880 and 1912 was the golden age of the cocktail, and during this time whiskey drinks became more ambitious and exotic. The Whiskey Daisy, from Harry Johnson's *New and Improved Bartenders Manual* of 1882, was a glorified whiskey sour, flavored with Chartreuse and decorated with a generous helping of fresh, seasonal fruits. New York was a rye town in those days, and the Manhattan was the premier whiskey drink. The original recipe called for a dash of absinthe or curaçao, along with angostura bitters, vermouth, and rye whiskey. In the late 1880s members of the Pendennis Club in Louisville, Kentucky (an exclusive social club established in 1881), nostalgic for the simplicity of the old-time whiskey cocktails, invented the Bourbon Old Fashioned. It was introduced in honor of Colonel James E. Pepper of Kentucky, proprietor of a celebrated whiskey of the period and a member of the Pendennis Club himself.

SCOTCH ENTERS THE MIX

In the late 19th century, Scotch found its way into many cocktails. In Europe, a phylloxera blight decimated vineyards in France, causing a shortage of French brandy, which had been the spirit of choice in England. The pioneers of blended Scotch whiskey saw an opportunity

EQUIPMENT

The necessary tools of the trade: a long-handled cocktail spoon, a three-piece cobbler shaker, the finely machined European milliliter jigger, and a hawthorn strainer.

SHAKER AND SPOON
The shaker, stirrer, and measuring cup or jigger are indispensable to the cocktail-maker.

STRAINER
The strainer is essential to filter out any herbs and fruit required in the preparation of some cocktails.

to expand their market, and they set about toning down the strong malt whiskey of Scotland to appeal to a wider audience. The milder flavor of blended whiskey was appreciated not only by the English but also by Americans. Scotch found its way into the cocktail culture of the United States, especially in hot whiskey drinks such as the Blue Blazer, Hot Whiskey Sling, and the Hot Scotch Whiskey Punch. Most were toddy-style drinks with hot water or tea, lemon, sugar, and nutmeg.

The 20th century brought Scotch drinks such as Blood and Sand, created to publicize the silent movie of that name starring Rudolph Valentino. It contained Robbie Burns Scotch whiskey in a Manhattan-style drink, with Benedictine as well as vermouth and whiskey. Other Scotch whiskey drinks, such as the Rusty Nail, were created simply to promote Drambuie and other new products.

SCOTCH OR AMERICAN?

Today, the distinctive smoke and peat character of Scottish whiskey, although greatly prized by many single-malt-lovers, presents a serious challenge to the cocktail bartender. Its flavors will never blend quietly into a cocktail, but instead shout out their presence. The solution is to find partners for the special flavors of Scottish whiskeys that enhance them, rather than trying to hide them among other strongly flavored ingredients.

American whiskey and its close relation, Irish whiskey, are sweeter whiskeys, which present more mixing options in cocktails. Even American straight rye whiskey with its pepper-and-spice, sour-mash characteristics is at home in the fruity setting of whiskey-punch-style drinks, such as the John Collins, and the official drink of Belmont Race Track on Triple Crown day, the Belmont Breeze.

HIGHLIGHT

THE PERFECT IRISH COFFEE

Make the coffee strong and sweet and lace it well with whiskey. Whip the cream lightly—if it is under-whipped it will mix in when floated; if it is too stiff, it will just sink. A stemmed Irish coffee glass will make it impossible to over-pour the coffee and drown the whiskey. The glass should contain between ¾ cup and 1 cup.

COCKTAILS *The classic V-shaped cocktail glass, first introduced at the Art Deco show in Paris in 1921, has today captured the imagination of a new generation of cocktail aficionados.*

TECHNIQUES

Preparing great cocktails needs the same attention to detail as preparing gourmet meals. Find a good recipe and follow it. Use fresh ingredients and quality spirits. Equip the bar with the proper equipment. Finally, practice before your party!

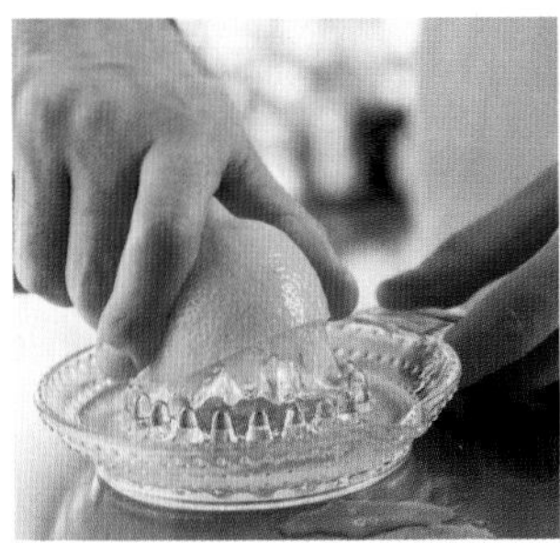

SQUEEZING LEMONS
There is no replacement for fresh lemon or lime juice. Remember, never squeeze cold fruit—you will not get much juice out of it.

MUDDLING
Muddling releases juices and oil from citrus fruit. Mix well and press the fruit firmly to extract sufficient quantities for the fruit cocktail.

BOOZE AND THE BIG EASY

The French Quarter of New Orleans is a window on an earlier time. The liberal laws controlling the sale and consumption of spirits set the scene for a nightly party in the Quarter all year round. And time seems to have stood still at 437 Royal Street, the apothecary shop where Antoine Amadée Peychaud sold Peychaud's Bitters, the secret ingredient in the legendary Sazerac cocktail, until his death in the 1880s.

Today, Steve Cohen and his son Barry operate the shop, selling old coins, antique firearms, and relics from sunken Spanish galleons. However, they are always quick to pull out the 19th-century Peychaud's Bitters bottles and to pay homage to their famous predecessor.

A night in the French Quarter can give you a swollen head the next morning. Never drink more than one of Pat O'Brien's Hurricanes, a seemingly innocuous drink, made with both light and dark rums and a selection of fruit juices. Never go near the Hand Grenade at Tropical Isle on Bourbon Street: it is made with a terrifying 190-proof (95-vol.) grain alcohol! And do not ever stop at a daiquiri shop, where even the headache remedies they sell are laced with alcohol.

WHISKEY COCKTAIL RECIPES

HERE IS A selection of recipes that represent the evolution of whiskey in cocktails. Belmont Breeze, Port Whiskey Punch, Whiskey Peach Smash, and Dubliner are all my invention.

WHISKEY SOUR

The art of using fresh lemon juice!

INGREDIENTS
1½ fl oz whiskey of choice
1½ Tbsp fresh lemon juice
2 Tbsp simple syrup (50/50 superfine sugar and water; mix, and use when the cloudiness clears)

PREPARATION
Shake all ingredients with ice and strain into an old-fashioned glass. Garnish with a cherry and a slice of orange.

MINT JULEP

This American classic dates from the 18th century, when it was concocted with brandy and peach brandy.

INGREDIENTS
1 Tbsp simple syrup
2 sprigs mint (use tender, young sprigs—they last longer and look better in the glass)
2 fl oz bonded bourbon

PREPARATION
Muddle one sprig of mint in a mixing glass with sugar syrup. Add the bourbon and strain into a highball glass filled with crushed ice. Swirl with a bar spoon until the outside of the glass frosts. Garnish with a sprig of mint.

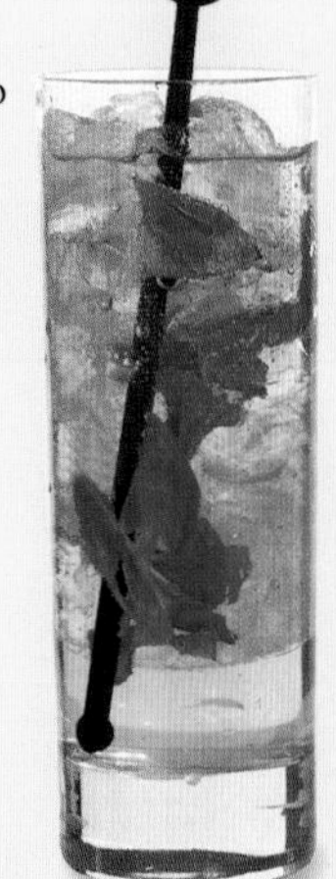

MINT JULEP

BELMONT BREEZE

The official drink of the Belmont Race.

INGREDIENTS
1½ fl oz Seagrams 7
¾ fl oz Harveys Bristol Cream sherry
1½ Tbsp fresh lemon juice
1½ Tbsp simple syrup
¼ cup fresh orange juice
¼ cup cranberry juice

PREPARATION
Shake all ingredients with ice and top with half lemonade and half soda water, approximately 2 Tbsp of each. Garnish with fresh strawberry, a mint sprig, and a lemon wedge.

DUBLINER

I created this drink for Molly Malone's Restaurant in the Czech Republic.

INGREDIENTS
1 fl oz Irish whiskey
1 fl oz Irish Mist liqueur
Lightly whipped unsweetened cream

PREPARATION
Pour the spirits into a mixing glass with ice and stir to chill. Strain into a small wine glass and top with 1 in (2.5 cm) of cream.

OLD FASHIONED

This standard was created in Louisville, at the Pendennis club.

INGREDIENTS
2 fl oz bourbon
6 dashes angostura bitters
1 tsp superfine sugar
2 orange slices
2 maraschino cherries
splash of soda water

PREPARATION
Muddle carefully in the bottom of an old-fashioned glass the sugar, angostura, one orange,

If there is such a thing here as the local brew, to use the term broadly, it is the whiskey-based Southern Comfort. Its origins lie in the 19th century, when New Orleans saloon-keeper M.W. Heron created the original version, which he called Cuff and Buttons, in a barrel of whiskey. He would pulled the bung from the top of a barrel of bourbon and stuff in chopped-up sweet Georgia peaches. He then added clover honey and a secret blend of spices.

The Sazerac is the ultimate New Orleans whiskey cocktail, and the Ramos Gin Fizz is definitely the ultimate New Orleans hangover cure.

There are very few rules in easy-living New Orleans, and the rules they do have are mostly ignored. Bars can operate 24 hours a day, seven days a week. According to the locals, they have the best politicians money can buy, and on a death certificate cirrhosis of the liver is listed as death by natural causes.

New Orleans has something that attracts musicians, artists, and all those who prefer not to live under the heavy hand of authority. People live and let live; in the Big Easy, there is only one real rule: be yourself but don't hurt me while you're being!

FROSTING
Frost only the outside of the glass rim. When using sugar, prepare the glasses in advance so that the frosting stays put.

one cherry, and a splash of soda water. Remove the orange rind and add bourbon, ice, and soda water or water. Garnish with a fresh orange slice and a cherry.

MARK TWAIN COCKTAIL
As described to his wife in a letter from London in 1874.

INGREDIENTS
- 1.5 fl oz Scotch whiskey
- 1½ Tbsp fresh lemon juice
- 2 Tbsp simple syrup
- 2 dashes angostura bitters

PREPARATION
Shake with ice and strain into a chilled cocktail glass.

SCOTCH WHISKEY

SAZERAC
This underappreciated drink was named after the cognac imported by New Orleans.

INGREDIENTS
- 2 dashes Peychaud's bitters
- 2 fl oz rye whiskey
- Splash of Ricard or Herbsaint
- ¼ tsp sugar

PREPARATION
Take two tumblers and chill one while preparing the drink in the other. Muddle the sugar and bitters in the second glass until the sugar is dissolved. Add the rye whiskey and several ice cubes and stir to chill. Toss the ice out of the first glass and splash in the Herbsaint. Swirl it to coat the inside of the glass, then pour out any remaining liqueur. Strain into the chilled rocks glass, and garnish with a lemon peel.

BLOOD AND SAND
This cocktail was created especially for the premiere of the 1922 silent movie of the same name, starring Rudolph Valentino.

INGREDIENTS
- ¾ fl oz Scotch
- ¾ fl oz Cherry Heering
- ¾ fl oz sweet vermouth
- ¾ fl oz orange juice

PREPARATION
Shake all ingredients well with ice and strain into a cocktail glass. Garnish with a flamed orange peel.

JIM BEAM

WHISKEY PEACH SMASH
Save this delicious, special drink for the height of the summer fruit season to enjoy the peaches at their best.

INGREDIENTS
- 2 fl oz bourbon
- 4 small peach quarters
- 3 mint leaves
- 1 sprig of mint
- 2 lemon wedges
- 2 Tbsp simple syrup

PREPARATION
Muddle all the ingredients except the whiskey in a bar glass. Add whiskey and shake with ice. Strain into an ice-filled tumbler and garnish with mint and a peach slice.

PORT WHISKEY PUNCH
The 19th-century tradition of punch-style whiskey drinks, prepared with fruits and topped with port, is ripe for revival.

INGREDIENTS
- 1½ fl oz Jack Daniel's
- 1½ Tbsp fresh lemon juice
- 2 Tbsp simple syrup
- 1 Tbsp fresh orange juice
- 3 Tbsp cranberry juice
- 1 fl oz ruby port

PREPARATION
Shake all the ingredients with ice and pour into a highball glass filled with ice. Top with ruby port. Garnish with orange slice.

MANHATTAN
Originally a rye whiskey drink, many barmen these days prepare the Manhattan using a good bourbon instead.

INGREDIENTS
- 2¼ fl oz blended whiskey
- ¾ fl oz Italian sweet vermouth
- 2 dashes angostura bitters

PREPARATION
Stir with ice to chill, and strain into a chilled cocktail glass. Garnish with a cherry.

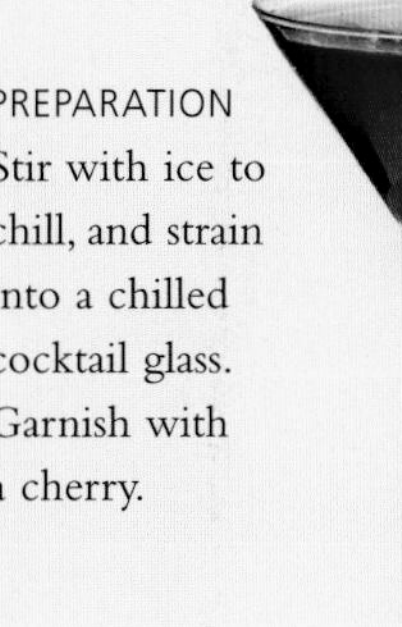

MANHATTAN

Whiskey with Your Meal

Martine Nouet

IF WELL PAIRED, WHISKEY AND FOOD PRESENT A WEALTH OF WONDERFUL NEW AROMAS AND FLAVORS TO ENJOY.

Celebrated Ritual

Whiskey is perfect with haggis, and not only as a drink on the side. Here's a tasty tip from the Highlands: pour a good dash of a colorful blend or a young malt on the steaming-hot haggis. After all, this custom had the approval of Robert Burns himself.

Choosing a whiskey to accompany a dish is exactly like choosing the right wine. You need to have some knowledge of the drink, experience of what works and what does not, and a reasonably educated palate. After that, just follow your personal preferences!

The fantastic range of tastes and aromas offered by single malts, pot-still whiskeys, bourbons, and rye whiskeys is just as wide as that offered by wine. There is absolutely no need to restrict your dram to before or after dinner. After all, there is an entire menu to be found in the descriptions that whiskey-tasters ascribe to whiskey flavors. Tastes that crop up include kippers, snow peas, peppered mackerel, bacon, apple crumble, crème brûlée, and hot cross buns. Such flavors cry out to be tried with food. Individually, a whiskey and a dish each have their own richness and personality; when the two are well-matched, they create additional character and introduce completely new flavors, which serve to heighten your enjoyment of the meal as a whole.

Serving whiskey with a meal is not just about having your favorite dram with your favorite dish. If you drink a highly medicinal single malt—say, a Laphroaig—along with an apple crumble, you will not appreciate either the whiskey or the dessert. Matching requires following some simple but essential rules. It is important to note the key aromas and the profile of the whiskey, then think of dishes that would echo or complement them. You can also play on contrasts: sweet with bitter, or sour or mellow with crunchy.

A Scottish Tradition?

Oddly enough, Scotland has no long-established tradition of drinking whiskey with a meal. According to most historians of the subject,

whiskey has never been a table drink, although some sources do record the consumption of large amounts of *uisge beatha* at mealtimes.

In fact, drinking habits seem to have varied according to social position and geography. While the Lowlands gentleman was partial to claret or rum punch with his food, the poor man would drink straight whiskey with his. In the Highlands, whiskey crossed social boundaries and was a warming drink to enjoy at any time. Elisabeth Grant of Rothiemurchus, in her *Journal of a Highland Lady*, observed at the beginning of the 19th century: "in our house, the bottle of whisky … was placed on the side-table with cold meat every morning. In the pantry, a bottle of whisky was the allowance per day, with bread and cheese in any required quantities." She adds that a decent gentlewoman began the day with whiskey!

"… A BOTTLE OF WHISKY WAS THE ALLOWANCE PER DAY …"

Whiskey for breakfast was, in fact, the special treat offered by the Glenfarclas distillery during the Speyside Whisky festival one year, although this was neither in the form of an accompanying dram nor, strictly speaking, an example of cooking with whiskey. Visitors were offered a dash of Glenfarclas 105 (60 vol.) in their porridge (oatmeal)—a tasty pairing of two traditional Scottish products. This was followed by kippers, smoked haddock, and bacon, all of which matched the whiskey equally well.

SEASONAL PAIRINGS

A glass of a rich, creamy, heavily aromatic whiskey goes particularly well with autumnal dishes in which ingredients such as duck, beef, foie gras, parsnips, leeks, raisins, apples, figs, ginger, or cinnamon feature, while it definitely does not complement light salads, red fruit, scallops, or veal. Younger, lighter-bodied, single malts marry well with spring and summer dishes featuring fish (salmon, red mullet), shellfish, herbs (basil and cilantro), broad beans, artichokes, spinach, fennel, rhubarb, red currants, and blackberries. These foods also go beautifully with a single malt matured in bourbon or refill casks, as opposed to sherry casks.

Many malt-lovers tend to associate smoked food with peaty single malts, but this is not, in fact, an ideal pairing, as the smokiness of the malt clashes with, and overpowers, the food. It would be better to choose a honeyed and malty whiskey for smoked foods.

WHISKEY AND SUSHI

These days, restaurants, bars, and supermarkets bring us a fantastic selection of international dishes. The worldwide success of Japanese sushi bars is a shining example, and whiskey and sushi are a perfect pairing. This combination works even better if the whiskey is slightly chilled. Japanese whiskeys work best of all: fruity blends and minty or malty single malts combine wonderfully with maki, sashimi, or sushi. So, experiment and explore, and let your nose and taste buds be your guide.

CHILLED OR UNCHILLED?

The temperature at which whiskey is served also matters. When accompanying seafood or smoked fish dishes, whiskey will be better appreciated if served chilled or simply refreshed in a chilled glass. This also affects the way aromas are displayed: fruit and floral notes will be noticeable first, then malty flavors will be released gradually as the whiskey reaches room temperature.

PRACTICE MODERATION

Many people who have not made a habit of drinking whiskey with food worry about the quantity of alcohol they will be consuming during the meal. Needless to say, only very small measures of whiskey (no more than about 2 tablespoons) should be served with each dish. In addition, when enjoyed with food, it is quite easy to dilute your whiskey with water. And, of course, you can drink a lot of water separately during the meal to quench your thirst. In short, due moderation is necessary to thoroughly enjoy whiskey with your meal!

SELECTING SUSHI
Sushi bars, such as the Sushi Hatsu in Central Florida, shown here, are a fantastic discovery land for Japanese whiskeys. You will learn that there are alternatives to saké; try a light, sweet, blended whiskey to accompany your sushi. Tuna, salmon, and shrimp go especially well with Japanese whiskeys.

FLAVORS

Whiskey aromas create a complex alchemy that enhances the aromatic profile of a meal. The success of the pairings is in the balance of flavors. One must not overwhelm the other.

SHELLFISH
Seafood dishes combine very well with sweet, light, vanilla-tinged malts matured in bourbon casks.

CINNAMON STICKS
Cinnamon, ginger, pepper, and star anise create a spice link between food and whiskey.

BASIL
Grassy malts shine through better when the dish contains herbs, such as basil, tarragon, mint, or thyme.

RED CURRANTS
Summer fruits prefer malty, floral Lowland whiskeys, while citrus fruits go well with peaty Islay malts.

SOUP WITH KICK
Whiskey in the broth does not spoil it! Martine Nouet likes to combine flavors and textures by adding a few teaspoons of Aberlour 10-year-old to a cream of sweet potato soup. The whiskey gives a kick to the otherwise mild character of the dish.

COOKING WITH WHISKEY

MARTINE NOUET

USING WHISKEY IN COOKING AS A SEASONING INGREDIENT CAN GIVE A WIDE RANGE OF DISHES EXTRA FLAVOR AND PUNCH.

Once you have appreciated the pleasures of a glass of whiskey with your food, it is time to take the next step and use whiskey as an ingredient in recipes: if it works on the table, it stands to reason it will work in the kitchen.

Strangely, few Scottish cookbooks mention the use of whiskey in the preparation of dishes, apart from in a few traditional sweet recipes such as cranachan or trifle, or remarking upon the Burns Night habit of pouring a shot of whiskey over the haggis. When alcohol is called for in a recipe, most cooks tend to reach for the brandy, sherry, or port. So, why is this the case? Is there no tradition of cooking with whiskey because the spirit was thought of as such a precious drink that it would have been considered a sacrilege to season a venison sauce with a dash of the house dram? Or is it for completely the opposite reason? Did cooks feel that the harsh and pungent "cratur" of old would spoil their fine broth?

> IF IT WORKS ON THE TABLE, IT WILL WORK IN THE KITCHEN

Contemporary cooking has no such qualms about experimenting with whiskey, sometimes with the active encouragement of the whiskey manufacturers themselves. Distillery restaurants, such as those at Ardbeg, Arran, and Glenturret, have whiskey dishes on the daily menu, as do some of the top restaurants in Glasgow and Edinburgh. In Kentucky, Jim Beam has launched a bourbon-style cooking school, which demonstrates its techniques at the Kentucky Bourbon Festival each September.

COOKING TECHNIQUES

Cooking with whiskey is about more than just adding any whiskey to any dish. As with pairing a dram with your food at the table, cooking with whiskey requires matching flavors as well as textures, working on the same aromatic scale *(see pp. 274–75)*. Just as important as a good balance of flavors—if not more so—is the way whiskey is incorporated into the food. The cook has to use methods that retain all the aromas while allowing the alcohol to evaporate.

MALTED STIR-FRY
Stir-fry mushrooms, carrots, celery, onions, soybeans, and red pepper in a wok with a touch of sesame oil. Add lemon grass, basil, ginger and chili pepper. Pour in half a glass of a light, young malt (peated or unpeated). Serve with noodles and pan-fried seafood.

SPEYSIDE MARINADE
To prepare a marinade: mix together grated ginger, lime juice, garlic, crushed peanuts, mixed spices and some Speyside malt whiskey. Pour it over the chicken and leave to marinate for 15 minutes. Grill the chicken, brushing with marinade at intervals until cooked.

FRUIT SALAD OF DISTINCTION
Whiskey gives a distinguished taste to the most ordinary fruit salad. Stir a good dash of a peated single malt in a little marmalade, gently melt in the microwave, and mix with peeled oranges and grapefruit. Add a few slices of kiwi fruit to provide a color contrast.

For the Sweet Tooth

Any dessert containing dried fruit, molasses, honey, or unrefined sugar works well with a heavily sherried malt. Try soaking brown and golden raisins in whiskey for a few days beforehand. Who can resist a rich whiskey fruitcake?

Single malts work particularly well in cooking, since their great range of aromatic profiles are the gateway to all sorts of preparations and bring out some extremely interesting flavors. However, Irish whiskeys and bourbons are characterful, if less varied, and also leave their signature in dishes. Think of the whiskey as an ingredient in its own right, and then use it in different ways.

Hallmark of many a French chef, the *flambé* method is probably the first cooking-with-alcohol technique that springs to mind. However, while the flame does burn off the alcohol, it also takes away most of the aromas. So, although a fine piece of showmanship, this method does nothing for the dish.

Much more rewarding is to use whiskey as a glazing liquid in place of *flambé*. For example, after taking sautéed scallops or langoustines off the heat, glaze with a few spoonfuls of an Islay malt and an equal quantity of lemon juice and honey. This ensures that none of the cooking juices are lost, while allowing the alcohol to evaporate. For a grilled piece of veal, a little double cream can be added after glazing the meat with whiskey; the fat acts as a flavor enhancer.

MARINADES

One of the best ways of combining whiskey with a meat or fish dish—especially if you are starting with raw ingredients—is to use it in a marinade. It is important to keep the marinating period quite short; after 15 minutes, alcohol tends to cook the fish or meat, giving it a grayish color. Whiskey acts as a meat tenderizer, but may break down the meat fibers if used to excess, and could make a steak unacceptably spongy. For a subtle effect, brush the surface of the meat with whiskey before serving.

Marinades do not consist simply of whiskey. A proper seasoning includes lemon, olive oil, spices, herbs, and perhaps teriyaki or Worcestershire sauce as well. Fresh ginger, honey, marmalade, and balsamic vinegar can also complement whiskey in some marinade recipes. The great thing is that, because marinades are so efficient in extracting flavors, you do not need to use much whiskey!

Marinades really come into their own with sweet courses. Fruit, such as pears or apples, can be soaked in whiskey and honey before being poached. Candied and dried fruit—whether raisins, dates, figs, or apricots—all soak up whiskey very effectively, too.

A DASH OF WHISKEY

A stir-fry is another great way to cook with whiskey. Quick, tasty, lightly cooked—all hallmarks of Asian cooking, which fits with whiskey so well. Try stir-frying vegetables in a wok, with shrimp or chicken, and a dash of whiskey.

Whiskey can also be used as a finishing touch, just like seasoning, and can be the crucial factor in the balance of aromas. To avoid cooking it and driving off some of the flavors, pour the whiskey on at the last minute, away from the stove. Drizzle it over roast or steamed fish, just to perk up the flavors. The same applies to sweet dishes.

The amount of whiskey to be used in a recipe depends on its aromatic profile, which is why single malts work better in cooking than blended whiskeys. You can be quite generous with a light and delicate malt, whereas a heavily peated or sherried one will only need a splash. It is really a matter of chemistry, but then that applies to all kinds of ingredients in cooking, *n'est-ce pas*?

HIGHLIGHT

BON APPETIT

Before cooking, brush fillets of salmon with a mixture of olive oil and whiskey, or brush with a honey-and-whiskey glaze right after cooking. The same technique can be applied to cakes. Just brush the surface of a freshly baked (and still very warm) chocolate cake with a rich, fruity Highland malt before frosting it. Be generous—the cake will soak up whiskey.

Further Reading

BOOKS

Appreciating Whisky
Phillip Hills
HarperCollins, Glasgow, 2000. Reprinted 2002.
The physiology, psychology, and chemistry of taste.

The Book of Bourbon
Gary Regan and Mardee Haiden
Chapters, Shelburne (Vermont), 1996.
Distillery guide with cocktail recipes.

Classic Blended Scotch
Jim Murray
Prion, London, 1999.
A rare study of this category.

Handbook of Whisky
Dave Broom
Hamlyn, London, 2000.
An excellent introduction to malts.

The Island Whisky Trail
Neil Wilson
Angel's Share, Glasgow, 2003.
An illustrated guide to all the Hebridean distilleries.

The Joy of Mixology
Gary Regan
Clarkson Potter, New York, 1923.
Cocktail manual from the most whiskey-friendly of famous bartenders.

The Making of Scotch Whisky
John R. Hume and Michael S. Moss.
Canongate, Edinburgh, 1981. Updated 2000.
A standard history of Scotch by respected academic authors.

The Malt Whisky Companion
Michael Jackson
Dorling Kindersley, London, 2004 (5th edition).
Internationally recognized as the definitive tasting guide.

Peat, Smoke and Spirit: A Portrait of Islay and Its Whiskies
Andrew Jefford
Headline, London, 2004.
A welcome study of the greatest whiskey island by an original and stylish writer.

Scotch Missed
Brian Townsend
Angel's Share, Glasgow, 2004.
A study of extinct Scottish distilleries.

The Scotch Whisky Book
Tom Bruce-Gardyne
Lomond Books, Edinburgh, 2002.
A well-written contemporary tour around Scotland's distilleries.

The Scotch Whisky Industry Record
Charles Craig
Index Publishing Limited, Dumbarton, 1994.
Includes a year-by-year chronology from 1494.

The Scotch Whisky Industry Review
Alan S. Gray.
Sutherlands, Edinburgh, (published annually).
Industry statistics, financial analysis, and commentary.

Scotch Whisky: A Liquid History
Charles MacLean
Cassell, London, 2003.
Social history and commentary by a whiskey specialist.

Scotland and Its Whiskies
Michael Jackson with Harry Cory Wright (landscape photographer)
Duncan Baird, London, 2001.
From the sea-spray to the scorched moorlands: treading the *terroir* that shapes the whiskeys.

Vintage Spirits and Forgotten Cocktails
Ted Haigh
Quarry Books, New York, London, 2004.
Cocktail historian revives 80 rare and authentic recipes from star bartenders of the past.

The Whisk(e)y Treasury
Walter Schober
Neil Wilson Publishing, 2002.
Originally published by Wolfgang Krüger Verlag, 1999.
An A-Z lexicon of brand owners, distilleries, and industry terms.

The Whiskeys of Ireland
Peter Mulryan
O'Brien, Dublin, 2002.
The most recent work on the subject.

Whisky
Aeneas Macdonald
Angel's Share, Glasgow, Reprinted 2005.
Originally published by Maclehose, Glasgow, 1930.
A classic early whiskey book.

Whisky à la Carte
Bob Minnekeer and Stefaan Van Laere
with Johan Martens (photographer)
Lannoo, Tielt, Belgium, 2004.
Published in Dutch.
Forty recipes dedicated to whiskey—specific Scottish malts, Irish whiskey, and bourbon.

The Whisky Bible
Jim Murray
Carlton Books, London, 2004.
The whole world of whiskey distilled into a dram-sized volume.

The Whisky Distilleries of the United Kingdom
Alfred Barnard.
Birlinn, Edinburgh, 1887. Reprinted 2003.
The classic account of visits to UK distilleries.

Whisky: Technology, Production and Marketing (Alcoholic Beverages Handbook)
Inge Russell (Ed.)
Academic Press, Oxford, 2003.
Richly detailed account of the whiskey process, from raw materials to the marketplace.

MAGAZINES AND WEBSITES

Celtic Malts
International news, issues and debates, among devotees. Online magazine.
www.celticmalts.com

Malt Advocate (Published in the United States)
www.maltadvocate.com

Whisky Magazine
(Published in the United Kingdom)
www.whiskymag.com

Ulf Buxrud
A Swedish computer entrepreneur and devotee of Macallan, Ulf Buxrud has created a personal website that offers an extraordinary compilation of news, sources of reference, useful addresses, titles of publications, and general information of assistance to the whiskey-lover.
www.buxrud.se/whisky.htm

Jürgen Deibel
Contributor to Michael Jackson's *Whiskey*.
www.deibel-consultants.com

Stuart Ramsay
Contributor to Michael Jackson's *Whiskey*.
www.stuartramsay.com

Distillery Addresses

SCOTLAND

Aberfeldy
Perthshire,
PH15 2EB
tel: 01882 822010
www.dewarswow.com

Aberlour
Banffshire,
AB38 9RX
tel: 01340 871285
www.aberlour.co.uk

Ardbeg
Port Ellen,
Islay, Argyll,
PA42 7EA
tel: 01496 302244
www.ardbeg.com

Ardmore
Kennethmont,
by Huntly,
Aderdeenshire,
AB54 4NH
tel: 01464 831213

Auchroisk
Mulben,
Banffshire,
AB55 6XS
tel: 01542 885000
www.malts.com

Aultmore
Keith, Banffshire,
AB55 6QY
tel: 01542 881800

Balvenie
Dufftown, Banffshire,
AB55 4BB
tel: 01340 820373
www.thebalvenie.com

Benrinnes
Aberlour, Banffshire,
AB38 9NN
tel: 01340 872500

Benromach
Invererne Road,
Forres, Moray,
IV36 3EB
tel: 01309 675968
www.benromach.com

Blair Athol
Perth Road,
Pitlochry, Perthshire,
PH16 5LY
tel: 01796 482003
www.discovering-distilleries.com

Brackla
Cawdor, Nairn,
Inverness-shire,
IV12 5QY
tel: 01667 402002

Bruichladdich
Islay, Argyll,
PA49 7UN
tel: 01496 850221
www.bruichladdich.com

Bunnahabhain
Port Askaig,
Islay, Argyll,
PA46 7RP
tel: 01496 840646
www.blackbottle.com

Caol Ila
Port Askaig, Islay,
PA46 7RL
tel: 01496 302760
www.discovering-distilleries.com

Cardhu
Aberlour, Banffshire,
AB38 7RY
tel: 01340 872555
www.discovering-distilleries.com

Clynelish
Brora, Sunderland,
KW9 6LR
tel: 01408 623003
www.discovering-distilleries.com

Cragganmore
Ballindalloch,
Banffshire,
AB37 9AB
tel: 01479 874700
www.discovering-distilleries.com

Craigellachie
Aberlour, Banffshire,
AB38 9ST
tel: 01340 872971

Dailuaine
Carron,
Aberlour,
Banffshire,
AB38 7RE
tel: 01340 872500

Dalwhinnie
Inverness-shire,
PH19 1AB
tel: 01540 672219
www.discovering-distilleries.com

Deanston
Perthshire,
FK16 6AG
tel: 01786 841422
www.burnstewartdistillers.com

Dufftown
Keith, Banffshire,
AB55 4BR
tel: 01340 822100
www.malts.com

Edradour
Pitlochry, Perthshire,
PH16 5JP
tel: 01796 472095
www.edradour.co.uk

Girvan
Ayrshire,
KA26 9PT
tel: 01465 713091

Glen Grant
Rothes, Morayshire,
AB38 7BS
tel: 01340 832118
www.maltwhiskydistilleries.com

Glen Elgin
Longmorn, Elgin,
Moray, IV30 8SL
tel: 01343 862000

Glen Moray
Bruceland Road,
Elgin, Morayshire,
IV30 1YE
tel: 01343 542577
www.glenmoray.com

Glen Ord
Muir of Ord, Ross-shire,
IV6 7UJ
tel: 01463 872004
www.discovering-distilleries.com

Glen Spey
Rothes, Aberlour,
Banffshire, AB38 7AU
tel: 01340 832000

Glenburgie
Forres, Morayshire,
IV36 0QX
tel: 01343 850258

Glencadam
Brechin, Angus,
DD9 7PA
tel: 01356 622217

Glendronach
Forgue,
Aberdeenshire,
AB5 6DB
tel: 01466 730202

Glendullan
Dufftown, Banffshire,
AB55 4DJ
tel: 01340 822100

Glenfarclas
Ballindalloch,
Banffshire,
AB37 9BD
tel: 01807 500257
www.glenfarclas.co.uk

Glenfiddich
Dufftown,
Banffshire,
AB55 4DH
tel: 01340 820373
www.glenfiddich.com

Glengoyne
Dumgoyne,
Stirlingshire,
G63 9LB
tel: 01360 550254
www.glengoyne.com

Glenkinchie
Pencaitland,
Tranent, East Lothian,
EH34 5ET
tel: 01875 342005
www.discovering-distilleries.com

Glenlivet
Ballindalloch, Banffshire,
AB37 9DB
tel: 01340 821720
www.theglenlivet.com

Glenlossie
Birnie,
By Elgin,
Moray,
IV30 8SF
tel: 01343 862000

Glenmorangie
Tain, Ross-shire,
IV19 1PZ
tel: 01862 892477
www.glenmorangie.com

Glenrothes
Burnside Street,
Rothes, Aberlour,
AB38 7AA
tel: 01343 555111
www.glenrotheswhisky.com

tel: 01542 783042

tel: 01340 810 486

www.canadianmist.com

Glentauchers
Mulben, Keith,
Banffshire,
AB5 2YL
tel: 01542 860272

Glenturret
Crieff, Perthshire,
PH7 4HA
tel: 01764 656565
www.famousgrouse.co.uk

Highland Park
Kirkwall,
Orkney,
KW15 1SU
tel: 01856 874619
www.highlandpark.co.uk

Inchgower
Buckie,
Banffshire,
AB56 5AB
tel: 01542 836700

Knockando
Aberlour, Banffshire,
AB38 7RT
tel: 01340 882000

Lagavulin
Port Ellen,
Islay, PA42 7DZ
tel: 01496 302730
www.discovering-distilleries.com

Laphroaig
Port Ellen,
Islay, Argyll,
PA42 7DY
tel: 01496 302418
www.laphroaig.com

Linkwood
Elgin, Moray,
IV30 8RD
tel: 01343 862000

Loch Lomond
Lomond Estate,
Alexandria, G83 0TL
tel: 01389 752781
www.lochlomondistillery.com

Lochnagar
Crathie, Ballater,
Aberdeenshire,
AB35 5TB
tel: 01339 742716
www.discovering-distilleries.com

Longmorn
Elgin, Morayshire,
IV30 3SJ

Macduff
Banff,
Banffshire,
AB45 3JT
tel: 01261 812612

Mannochmore
Birvie, By Elgin,
Moray, IV30 8SF
tel: 01343 862000
www.malts.com

Miltonduff
Elgin, Moray,
IV30 3TQ
tel: 01343 547433

Mortlach
Dufftown, Banffshire,
AB55 4AQ
tel: 01340 822100
www.malts.com

Oban
Argyll, PA34 5NH
tel: 01631 572004
www.discovering-distilleries.com

Scapa
St Ola, Kirkwall, Orkney,
KW15 1SE
tel: 01856 872071

Springbank
Campbeltown, Argyll,
PA28 6ET
tel: 01586 552085
www.springbankwhisky.com

Strathisla
Seafield Avenue, Keith, Banffshire,
AB55 3BS
tel: 01542 783044
www.maltwhiskydistilleries.com

Strathmill
Keith, Banffshire,
AB55 5DQ
tel: 01542 885000
www.malts.com

Talisker
Carbost, Skye,
IV47 8SR
tel: 01478 614308
www.discovering-distilleries.com

Tamdhu
Knockando, Aberlour,
Banffshire,
AB38 7RP

Teaninich
Alness, Ross-shire,
IV17 0XB
tel: 01349 885001

Tobermory
Mull, PA75 6NR
tel: 01688 302645
www.burnstewartdistillers.com

Tomintoul
Ballindalloch, Banffshire,
AB37 9AQ
tel: 01807 590 274

Tormore
Advie by Grantown-on-Spey,
Morayshire PH26 3LR
tel: 01807 510244

IRELAND

Cooley
Dundalk, County Louth,
Ireland
tel: 0353 42 937 6102
www.cooleywhiskey.com

Midleton
County Cork,
Ireland
tel: 0353 21 463 1821
www.jameson.ie

Old Bushmills
County Antrim,
BT57 8XH
tel: 028 2073 1521
www.bushmills.com

CANADA

Alberta
Calgary, Alberta
tel: (403) 265-2541
www.albertadistillers.com

Black Velvet
Lethbridge, Alberta
tel: (403) 317-2100
www.bartonbrands.com

Canadian Club
Walkerville, Windsor, Ontario
tel: (519) 254-5171
www.canadianclubwhisky.com

Canadian Mist
Collingwood, Ontario
tel: (705) 445-4690

Gimli
Gimli, Manitoba
tel: (204) 642-5123
www.diageo.com

Glenora
Glenville, Inverness County,
Nova Scotia
tel: (902) 258-2662

Highwood
High River, Alberta
tel: (403) 652-3202
www.highwood-distillers.com

Kittling Ridge Estate Wines & Spirits
Grimsby, Ontario
tel: (905) 954-9225
www.kittlingridge.com

Maple Leaf
Winnipeg, Manitoba
tel: (204) 940-7000
www.mapleleafdistillers.com

Potter's (Cascadia)
Kelowna,British Columbia
tel: (250) 762-3332
www.centuryreserve.ca

Unibroue
Des Carrieres, Chambly, Quebec
tel: (450) 658-7658
www.unibroue.com

Valleyfield
Salaberry-De-Valleyfield, Quebec
tel: (450) 373-3230
www.bartonbrands.com

UNITED STATES

Barton
Bardstown, KY
tel: (502) 348-3991
www.bartonbrands.com

Bernheim
West Breckenridge,
Louisville, KY
tel: (502) 585-9186
www.heaven-hill.com

Boulevard
Lawrenceburg, KY
tel: (502) 839-4544
www.wildturkeybourbon.com

Brown-Forman

Louisville, KY
tel: (502) 774-2960

Buffalo Trace
Franklin County, KY
tel: (502) 223-7641
www.buffalotrace.com

Clear Creek
Portland, OR
tel: (503) 248-9470
www.clearcreekdistillery.com

Four Roses
Lawrenceburg, KY
tel: (502) 839-3436
www.FourRosesbourbon.com

George A. Dickel & Co.
Tullahoma, TN
tel: (931) 857-3124
www.GeorgeDickel.com

Heaven Hill
Bardstown, KY
tel: (502) 348-3921
www.heaven-hill.com

Jack Daniel's
Lynchburg, TN
tel: (931) 759-6183
www.jackdaniels.com

Jim Beam
Clermont, KY
tel: (502) 543-2221
www.jimbeam.com

Maker's Mark
Loretto, KY
tel: (270) 865-2881
www.makersmark.com

Stranahan's Colorado Whiskey
Denver, CO
tel: (303) 296-7440
www.stranahanscoloradowhiskey.com

Triple Eight
Nantucket, MA
tel: (508) 325-5929
www.tripleeight.com

Woodford
Versailles, KY
tel: (859) 879-1812

Woodstone Creek
Cincinnati, OH
tel: (513) 569-0300
www.woodstonecreek.com

US MICRODISTILLERIES
Anchor
San Francisco, CA
tel: (415) 863-8350
www.anchorbrewing.com

Charbay
St. Helena, Napa Valley, CA
tel: (800) 634-7845
www.charbay.com

Edgefield
Troutdale, OR
tel: (503) 669-8610
www.mcmenamins.com

Essential Spirits Alambic
Mountain View, CA
tel: (650) 962-0546

Isaiah Morgan
Summersville, WV
tel: (304) 872-7332

St. George Spirits
Alameda, CA
tel: (510) 769-1601
www.stgeorgespirits.com

Saint James Spirits
Irwindale, CA
tel: (626) 856-6930
www.saintjamesspirits.com

West Virginia Distilling Co.
Morgantown, WV
tel: (304) 599-0960
www.mountainmoonshine.com

JAPAN

Hakushu
Kita-Koma-gun,
Yamanashi 408-0316
tel: 551 35 0316
www.suntory.co.jp

Fuji-Gotemba
Shizuokaken Gotemba
Shibanuta 970
tel: 550 89 3131
www.kirin.co.jp

Miyagikyo
Miyagiken Sendaishi,
Aoba, Nikka 1
tel: 22 395 2111
www.nikka.com

Yamazaki
Shimamoto-cho,
Mishima-gun,
Osaka 618-0001
tel: 75 961 1234
www.suntory.co.jp

Yoichi
Yoichigun, Yoichimachi,
Kurokawacho 7-6
tel: 135 23 3131
www.nikka.com

EUROPE

WALES
Gwalia
Penderyn,
CF44 OSX
tel: 01685 813300
www.welsh-whisky.co.uk

GERMANY
A Racke GmbH
Gaustr. 20,
55411 Bingen
tel: 06721 188 0

Privatbrenneri Sonnenschein
Alter Fahrweg 7-9,
58456 Witten-Heven
tel: 02302 56006
www.sonnenschein-brenneri.de

Robert Fleischmann
Bamberger Strasse 2, 91330
Eggolsheim-Neuses
tel: 09545 7461
www.fleischmann-whisky.de

AUSTRIA
Brennerei Weidenauer
Leopolds 6, 3623 Kottes
tel: 02873 72 76
www.weidenauer.at

Reisetbauer
Axberg 15, A-4062 Thening
tel: 07221 63 690 0
www.reisetbauer.at

FRANCE
Claeyssens
59118 Wambrechies
tel: 03-20-14-91-91
www.wambrechies.com

Guillon
Hameau de Vertuelle,
51 150 Louvois
tel: 03-26-51-87-50

Menhirs
Pont Menhir,
29700 Plomelin
tel: 02-98-94-23-68
www.distillerie.fr

Warenghem
Route de Guingamp,
22300 Lannion
tel: 02-96-37-00-08
www.distillerie-warenghem.com

POLAND
Lubuska Wytwornia Wodek Gatunkowych
65-018 Zielona Gora,
Ul. Jednosci 59
tel: 068 3254 841
www.polmos.zgora.pl

CZECH REPUBLIC
Kojetin
Olomouc 772 48,
Hodolanska 32, PSC 772 48
tel: 064 1753 111
www.lihovar.com

Kuba MBC
Lubika 14/83,
772 D0, Olomouc

ASIA AND AUSTRALIA

PAKISTAN
Murree
Hattar
tel: 0995 617013

INDIA
Amrut
Bangalore, S60 027
tel: 0 80 227 6995

AUSTRALIA
Bakery Hill
Balwyn North,
Victoria 3104
www.bakeryhilldistillery.com.au

Lark
Hobart, Tasmania 7000
tel: 03 6231 9088
www.larkdistillery.com.au

Tasmania
Cambridge, Tasmania 7170
tel: 03 6248 5399
www.tasdistillery.com.au

Whisky Tasmania
Burnie, Tasmania 7320
tel: 03 6433 0439

Acknowledgments

AUTHOR'S ACKNOWLEDGMENTS

The author and contributors would like to thank the following for their help in providing information for this book:
Waqar Ahmed, Russell Anderson, Elaine Bailey, Liselle Barnsley, Micheal Barton, Bill Bergius, Jim Beveridge, David Boyd, Neil Boyd, James Brosnan, Derek Brown, Lew Bryson, Stephen Camisa, Alec Carnie, Catherine O'Grady, Neil Clapperton, Paula Cormack, Isabel Coughlin, Simon Coughlin, Bill Crilly, Katherine Crisp, Barry Crockett, Jim Cryle, Bob Dalgarno, Ed O'Daniel, Douglas Davidson, Jonathan Driver, Gavin J. P. Durnin, Duncan Elphick, Kate Ennis, Campbell Evans, Harold Fergusson, Robert Fleming, Gary M. Gillman, John Glaser, Alan Gordon, Lesley Gracie, Alan S. Gray, Natalie Guerin, John Hall, Tish Harcus, The Heather Society, Ian Henderson, Stuart Hendry, Robert Hicks, Sandy Hislop, David Hume, Bill Jaffrey, Neelakanta Rao R. Jagdale, Brigid James, Larry Kass, Shawn Kelly, Eily Kilgannon, Mark Kinsman, Malcolm E. Leask, Christine Logan, Jim Long, Bill Lumsden, Lauchie MacLean, Iseabail Mactaggart, Luc Madore, Fritz Maytag, Jim McEwan, Frank McHardy, Sharon Mclaughlin, Claire Meikle, Marcin Miller, Euan Mitchell, Matthew Mitchell, Shuna Mitchell, Mike Miyamoto, Brendan Monks, Nicholas Morgan, Chris Morris, Malcolm Mullin, Nuala Naughton, Margaret Nicol, B. A. Nimmo, Richard Paterson, Lucy Pritchard, Annie Pugh, John Ramsay, Stuart Ramsay, Kirsty Reid, Mark Reynier, Rebecca Richardson, Dave Robertson, Geraldine Roche, Dominic Roskrow, Colin Ross, Colin Scott, Jacqui Seargeant, Catherine Service, Raj Singh, Sukhinder Singh, David Stewart, David Stirk, Andrew Symington, Rachel Barrie, Jens Tholstrup, Graeme Thomson, Margaret Mary Timpson, Hide Tokuda, The Urquhart Family, Alistair Walker, Barry Walsh, Jan Westcott, Amy Westlake, David Williamson, Graeme Wilson, Alan Winchester, Julian van Winkle, Gordon Wright, Kate Wright, Vanessa Wright.

PUBLISHER'S ACKNOWLEDGMENTS

The publisher would like to thank the following for their kind permission to reproduce their photographs: (Abbreviations key : (a) = above, (b) = below, (t) = top, (b) = bottom, (tl) = top left), (bl) = bottom left, (cr) = center right, (tr) = top right, (br) = bottom right, (bc) = bottom center, (cla) = center left above, (clb) = center left below).

10: Karsten Davideit (Jürgen Deibel); 11: Nick Osborne (Willie Simpson), Finlandia Vodka (Ian Wisniewski); 14: akg-images (t); 16: Corbis/Hulton-Deutsch Collection (b), Courtesy of the Trustees of the V&A (t); 20: Corbis/Bettmann (b), Hulton Archive/Getty Images (t); 21: Corbis/Hulton-Deutsch Collection (b), Courtesy of The National Library of Ireland (tr), Ronald Grant Archive/United Artists (tl); 22-23: Getty Images/Andrew Sacks; 28: Corbis/Raymond Gehman (br); 29: Corbis/Kevin R.Morris (l); 30: Getty Images/Foodpix (t); 35: courtesy of Nova Scotia Tourism, Culture and Heritage (l); 36-37 Corbis/Bob Rowan (b); 36: The Art Archive/Dagli Orti (t); 39: www.agripicture.com (cr), Doug Houghton Photography (br), Holt Studios International (tr), 40-41: Corbis/Niall Benvie (bl); 42: Corbis/Fritz Polking/Frank Lane Picture Agency (tl), Corbis/Niall Benvie (cla), Corbis/Yogi Inc. (clb), Garden and Wildlife Matters (bl), Corbis/Niall Benvie (br) 50: Simpson's Malt (t); 58: The Art Archive/Archaeological Museum, Florence/Dagli Orti (t); 80: Whisky Magazine (b); 81: Whisky Magazine (t); 82: Corbis/Macduff Everton (br); 90: Corbis/Sandro Vannini (t); 128: Corbis/Adam Woolfitt (b); 129: Glyn Satterley Photography (l); 130-131: Scottish Viewpoint (b); 131: Corbis/Lawson Wood (tl); 138: Scottish Viewpoint (bl); 180: Corbis/Patrick Ward (b); 186: Robert Harding Picture Library/Medio Images (b); 202: Corbis/Paul A.Souders; 203: Anthony Blake Photo Library/Bear Images; 206: courtesy of Nova Scotia Tourism, Culture and Heritage (b); 207: Alamy Images/Jenny Andre (t); 246: Corbis; 263: Corbis/Macduff Everton; 268-269: Alamy Images/Ferruccio; 270: Anthony Blake Photo Library/Rob Lawson (cr); 274: Anthony Blake Photo Library/Joff Lee (t); 277: Anthony Blake Photo Library/Sian Irvine (t).

The publishers would also like to thank the following for their assistance with images :
Allied Domecq, Burn Stewart Distillers Ltd, Chivas, Clear Creek Distillery, Diageo, The Easy Drinking Whisky Company, Edgefield Distillery, The Edrington Group, Four Roses Distillery, The Essential Spirits Alambic Distillery, Glenora Distillery, George Dickel Distillery, Glenmorangie plc, Heaven Hill Distilleries, Highland Park, John Dewar and Sons Ltd, Lark Distillery, Morrison Bowmore, Reisetbauer Distillery, Slyrs, Suntory, London, Tobermory Distillery, Buffalo Trace, Van Winkle Distillery, Richard Paterson/Whyte and Mackay, William Grant and Sons.

Dorling Kindersley would also like to thank Becky Alexander for copy-editing, Chris Bernstein for compiling the index, Sarah Barlow for proof reading, Jane Laing, Caroline Reed, and Carla Masson for editorial assistance, and Ruth Hope for design assistance. Thanks also to Olaf Henricson-Bell and Katharine Tuite for additional help.

INDEX

D

E